THE PARTISAN

ALSO BY
JOHN A. JENKINS

The Litigators: Inside the Powerful World of America's High-Stakes Trial Lawyers

Ladies' Man: The Life and Trials of Marvin Mitchelson

THE PARTISAN

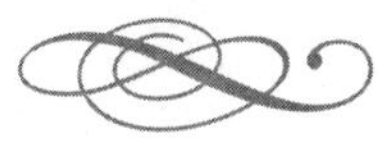

The Life of William Rehnquist

JOHN A. JENKINS

PublicAffairs
New York

Published in the United States by PublicAffairs™,
a Member of the Perseus Books Group

Printed in the United States of America.

PublicAffairs books are available at special discounts for bulk purchases in the U.S. by corporations, institutions, and other organizations. For more information, please contact the Special Markets Department at the Perseus Books Group, 2300 Chestnut Street, Suite 200, Philadelphia, PA 19103, call (800) 810-4145, ext. 5000, or e-mail special.markets@perseusbooks.com.

Book design by Pauline Brown

Library of Congress Cataloging-in-Publication Data

Jenkins, John A.
The partisan : the life of William Rehnquist / John A. Jenkins.
p. cm.
Includes bibliographical references and index.
ISBN 978-1-58648-887-1 (hardback)—ISBN 978-1-58648-888-8 (e-book) 1. Rehnquist, William H., 1924–2005. 2. Judges—United States—Biography. 3. United States. Supreme Court—Officials and employees—Biography. 4. United States. Supreme Court—History. I. Title.
KF8745.R44J46 2012
347.73'2634092—dc23
[B]

2012021002

First Edition

10 9 8 7 6 5 4 3 2 1

To Daryl Alexander, Michael VerMeulen,
and Alex Ward:
You believed.

CONTENTS

RESEARCHERS

WASHINGTON, DC

Chelsey D. Goff

Alyssa Hellman

Amanda Rogers

PALO ALTO, CALIFORNIA

Malia Wollan

INTRODUCTION

IT WAS FRIDAY EVENING, December 10, 1971, and President Nixon was calling.

Congratulations were in order. William Rehnquist had survived a messy confirmation battle and soon would take his chair as the newest justice on the Supreme Court. The good wishes were coming from all over, of course, but none was as important as this first and only talk that Rehnquist would ever have with the president. The White House operator already had Rehnquist on the line when Nixon came on. The president was ebullient.

"Well, you must feel like Chief Justice Hughes," Nixon began. "He had 26 voting against him, too."

Rehnquist was at a loss for a rejoinder, still getting his feet under him. "Is that the exact number?"

Of course it was. "I just got it in front of me. So, like Hughes, you can go out and say, 'I had 26 against me.'"

Neither man was much for small talk. Rehnquist listened as the president went on, kidding about an endorsement of Rehnquist's nomination by the liberal newspaper columnist Joseph Kraft. Treasury Secretary John Connally, a shrewd Texas politico, had shown Kraft's column to Nixon, "and I said 'I've made a mistake!'"

"Listen," Rehnquist broke in, "I can't tell you how much I appreciate your giving me this opportunity."

"Well, this is a great thing, to be such a young man, to go on the Court." Nixon exulted when he thought about the young reactionary who now was on the Court. Rehnquist was only forty-seven years old, ten years the junior of any other justice.

"You'll make a great record, and, you know, the very fact that—." Nixon halted, then started again. "I'll give you one last bit of advice because you're going to be independent, naturally. And that is, don't let the fact that you were under heat change any of your views."

"I'll remember that, Mr. President."

"I told Warren Burger* that, and he didn't get much heat, but I told him, 'Just don't come down here'—the way I put it to him—'and let the Washington social set change you.' So just be as mean and rough as they said you were. OK?"

"Thanks, Mr. President."

"Good luck. Bye."

ONLY SEVENTEEN MEN HAVE PRESIDED over the Supreme Court, shaping our lives and our destiny as much as any president or leader of Congress. John Marshall gave voice to the judiciary's authority in *Marbury v. Madison.* Roger Taney set the nation on the path to civil war in *Dred Scott.* William Howard Taft modernized the judiciary. Charles Evans Hughes led a divided Court through the upheaval of the Great Depression. Earl Warren used the Bill of Rights to craft vital new protections for individual liberties and helped to steer the nation peacefully through the civil rights revolution.

William Rehnquist's life story is profoundly significant yet largely unknown, which is how he wanted it. Rehnquist's place on the Court was at once an accident of history and an inevitable result of it—something that Rehnquist had secretly coveted since law school and yet could never have connived to obtain. His nomination in 1971 was one of the modern political era's most unlikely appointments: a spur-of-the-moment selection, of a candidate bereft of judicial credentials. He is the last of a breed.

Rehnquist was a brilliant loner who used the Court to advance his right-wing agenda. But to call Rehnquist simply a conservative would be to miss the essence of what defined him. Rehnquist's judicial philosophy was nihilistic at its core, disrespectful of precedent and dismissive of social, economic, and political institutions that did not comport with his black-and-white view of the world. Rehnquist instinctively knew whose side he was on when it came to criminals and law abiders, minorities and the white majority, the poor and the rich, the powerless and the powerful. He set his plan accordingly. Infatuated with his own genius, he spoke his mind, cast his votes, and damned his critics.

*Burger was the chief justice whom Nixon appointed in 1969.

Early on, Rehnquist's iconoclasm made him a darling of the political right. He was perfectly cast as the brash, articulate outsider. But as chief justice, Rehnquist did not—indeed, could not—evolve. Dogma trumped leadership. Thus, despite his intellectual gifts, Rehnquist left no body of law or opinions that define his tenure as chief justice or even seem likely to endure. Instead, Rehnquist bestowed a different legacy, and the story of how it came to be is important in the political canon. Rehnquist made it respectable to be an expedient conservative on the Court.

The Supreme Court now is as deeply divided politically as the executive and legislative branches of our government, and for this Rehnquist must receive the credit or the blame. He provided the clear voice for instinctual decision making that pushed the Court markedly rightward. His successor as chief justice, John Roberts, is his natural heir.

The Rehnquist Court (1986–2005) thus was molded in his image, and the change endures. In thirty-three years on the Supreme Court (nineteen as chief justice), from 1972 until his death at age eighty in 2005, Rehnquist was at the center of the Court's dramatic political transformation. He was on a partisan's mission, waging a quiet, constant battle to imbue the Court with a deep conservatism favoring government power over individual rights.

Disciples like Roberts carry on.* Under Roberts, who clerked for Rehnquist, the Court remains unrecognizable as an agent of social balance even after its 5–4 decision upholding the Affordable Care Act. Gone are the majorities that rejuvenated the Bill of Rights, enfranchised black citizens, dismantled southern segregation, protected people from police abuse, removed religion from public schools, forced a president from office, and safeguarded a woman's right to abortion.

The story of how and why Rehnquist rose to power is as compelling as it is improbable. Rehnquist left behind no memoir,** and the fact that there has never been a serious biography of him is understandable: Rehnquist was an uncooperative subject, and during his lifetime he made an effort to ensure that journalists would have scant material to work with.

---

*"John Roberts is proving to be an absolutely first-rate law clerk, and I hope that if you have any more like him you will not hesitate to let me know if they have an interest in clerking for me," Rehnquist wrote in 1981 to US Court of Appeals Judge Henry J. Friendly, for whom Roberts previously clerked.

**In 2001, he offered this explanation: "[For a memoir] to be interesting, you know, you have to say that 'This is a good person,' 'That's a bad person,' 'That's a medium person,' 'He really let me down here.' And I just don't want to do that."

When, in December 1984, then–Associate Justice Rehnquist sat for two hour-long interviews with me in his chambers,* his answers revealed much about his personality and philosophy, but they were also reflective of a cagey lawyer's literalism and shrewdness. Replies were confined to the specific question; information was seldom volunteered. Sometimes he feinted with a plea that he simply didn't understand the question. The justice was particularly reticent about matters he considered personal—names of the judges he played poker with, details about his family. "I'm not going to write your story for you," he said.

His participation was "under duress," he asserted at the time. More than a decade later he hadn't changed his mind. He wrote to the editors at the *New York Times Magazine:* "You are correct that I did give an interview to John Jenkins for the article which appeared in your magazine; it may have been in part the impression that article made on me that led me to decide not to grant any such interviews in the future."

To be William Rehnquist was to consider one's self misunderstood—and with good reason. Rehnquist often appeared to be living in a private world of his own invention, and probing strangers were not welcome. Nixon, though, knew what he was getting. Right after his surprise announcement of Rehnquist's nomination,** on the night of Thursday, October 21, 1971, Nixon telephoned his attorney general and gleefully spoke about the "four good men"† he had named to the Court so early in his administration. "And Rehnquist is the smartest of the whole goddamn bunch! And he's on our side, isn't he?"

"I think you did a great thing for the Court," John Mitchell replied.

"I really built them up," Nixon went on. "You know, and I talked about respect [for] the law, whether you agree and obey the law, and all

---

*These were Rehnquist's first and, for most of his tenure, only on-the-record interviews about his role on the High Court. Toward the end of his career, as he authored historical works about the Court, Rehnquist gave an occasional interview. Invariably, the subject matter focused on his books, the interviewer was friendly, and the format was forgiving.

**Rehnquist's was one of two nominations Nixon made that day. Also nominated was Lewis F. Powell, Jr., a Richmond lawyer and former president of the American Bar Association. Powell, sixty-four at the time, succeeded to what was considered the "southern seat" left vacant by the retirement (and death a week later) of Hugh Black. Rehnquist took the seat vacated by John M. Harlan.

†Nixon had previously named Chief Justice Warren E. Burger, in 1969, and Associate Justice Harry A. Blackmun in 1970.

that. And they oughta appreciate it, the bastards! . . . Be sure to emphasize to all the southerners that Rehnquist is a reactionary bastard, which I hope to Christ he is."

Even as a young man in the 1950s, Rehnquist boldly preached an uncompromising brand of conservatism, and he espoused—and acted on—views that were racist even by the standards of that era. Confronted later in the Senate, he took a disingenuous approach with his critics, lying his way out of trouble. Having taken his knocks in two brutal confirmation hearings, he deeply mistrusted the press, and he did his best to frustrate coverage or, failing that, to keep the stories about him one-dimensional.

Rehnquist privately grumbled about the liberal media—"they have a particular point of view. If they want to be a house organ for the ACLU, that's their privilege." He muttered about all of the other usual liberal suspects. Upon his death, he made sure his papers would be far from Washington, at the conservative Hoover Institution at Stanford University, and he put significant restrictions on their availability.

Yet, oddly for someone so attuned to public criticism, Rehnquist also professed not to care what others thought. "If you're bothered by what the press says about you," he told me, "you're not cut out for this job." Rehnquist endured the liberals' rebukes in the service of a higher mission.

Rehnquist presents a fascinating study in political character. To a casual observer he appeared diffident, almost invisible, yet he possessed huge reservoirs of intellect and self-confidence. He had an outsized ego, yet none of the egoist's outward swagger. He was authoritarian yet rebellious. He was an inveterate gambler, yet he almost never took a chance.

Rehnquist was driven by an outsized desire to *win.* Winning is an end in itself for the average politician, but for Rehnquist it was different. For him, winning provided affirmation: of his skill, intelligence, viewpoint, principles, superiority. He wanted to be right, and he wanted that acknowledged. The subject did not particularly matter—it could be a constitutional crisis or the most trivial of arguments. Nor, interestingly, did the stakes. In fact, small stakes were obligatory in his wagers, because although Rehnquist was a gambler he was not a risk taker. The ego-validation Rehnquist received from winning (and from standing by his principles in defeat) really mattered to him, and it defined his life on and off the Court.

In the academic discipline of political psychology, Rehnquist serves as a unique case study: flash frozen from the day he arrived. Rehnquist's views never changed, and that remained true even after he made the move from associate justice to chief justice. "Justices fall into three types," said Dr. Margaret Hermann, a psychologist and Syracuse University professor who has studied the behavior of Supreme Court justices. "With the first two types, either *law* ('the Constitution says . . .') or *ideology* controls." When a case comes in, it's usually easy to predict which way those justices will vote; it's preordained. But the third type is much different. "Prior life experience interacts with the cases, and the justice just deals with each case almost as a cost-benefit equation: 'This is my experience; this is how I see it, let's move on.'" In that world, results and efficiency are what matter. "And that's Rehnquist."

Rehnquist, the son of a paper salesman, grew up in a Republican household where the dominant figure was his well-educated mother. She was a University of Wisconsin English literature major who spoke five languages.* The family's hometown of Shorewood, Wisconsin, near Milwaukee, was a homogeneous idyll of lakefront mansions and well-tended bungalows, but in the midst of the Depression the Rehnquist family's fortunes soured. In 1939, his parents defaulted on their mortgage, and the sheriff sold the only home Bill Rehnquist had ever known in a foreclosure sale for the outstanding debt, $7,000. A succession of humiliating rentals followed. The Rehnquists' old-fashioned verities had taken a serious hit. And although young Bill Rehnquist clung to those values, he was determined not to end up like his father. When it came to money he would obsess over even the smallest amounts, to the point of pettiness.

On August 23, 1947, Rehnquist began making entries in the first of several journals that together constitute a highly selective account of his years as a student at Stanford University. Here he scrawled his poker partners' names and winnings, his records of bets, what he earned (mowing lawns) and what he spent (down to the penny), and sums of money that others owed him. The notebooks document the miscellany of a young man's life, but the writings are also fascinating for the picture they paint of a twenty-three-year-old who already had his mind set.

"Finished *Supreme Court and the National Will,* by Dean Alfange," Rehnquist wrote in his first entry. Alfange, a liberal legal commentator of

*French, German, Italian, Portuguese, and Italian.

the day, advocated judicial activism, which Rehnquist curtly dismissed. "Not overly impressed. Mostly a rehash of what I already knew."

Two pages later, Rehnquist was brooding about money due him from someone named Herman: "He wants me to go back to work for him. Tomorrow I will deliver him an ultimatum." The debt gnawed at Rehnquist for days: "Went over to Herman's but no one was there. I'm getting quite discouraged about the whole thing. I would hate to think I was just 'out' that money. It will weigh on my mind until I finally collect it. I should be happy now that my days of manual labor are finally over, but that is always in the back of my mind." Finally, Herman paid him $10. "Things look a little brighter for collecting the remainder."

Rehnquist was proud of his principled tenacity, and he acknowledged its origins. On September 24, 1986, he wrote to his mother two days before he was to be sworn in as chief justice:

> Next week I will be 62 years old, and as I look back I have had a remarkably fortunate life. I am sure that much of the success I have had is due to the fine bringing up that you and Dad gave me. I still remember some of the long discussions that you and I had about many different things, and I also think that one of the things that both you and Dad taught me was to stand up for what I believed. I will be thinking of you this next Friday.* Love, Bill.

Like many public figures, Rehnquist presented a face to the public that often was at odds with the private man. My purpose here is to unmask that private face, using wherever possible Rehnquist's own words and the trove of materials deposited at Stanford, and in so doing to set the record straight about one of the most ambitious, brilliant, and partisan jurists ever to occupy the chief justice's chair.

Because any investigative biography is necessarily selective, it is important that readers understand what this book is, and what it is not. This book spans the arc of Rehnquist's life and seeks to separate man from myth. I am particularly interested in the origins of Rehnquist's conservatism and how that motivated him on the Court. Anyone looking for a comprehensive

*Friday, September 26, 1986, the day of his swearing in.

survey of Rehnquist's jurisprudence, however, will not find it here. Although I shall not stint in offering my own opinion of things, I also acknowledge that there are scores of other books and law review articles that seek to explain or make sense of Rehnquist's judicial philosophy, many listed in the bibliography.

Toward the end of his career, Rehnquist played a part in two historic events, presiding at the Senate impeachment trial of President Bill Clinton in 1999 and voting with the Court's 5–4 majority to end the Florida presidential-election recount—and thus give George W. Bush the victory—in the cliffhanger election of 2000. Both events have been the subject of extensive exposés in their own right and I don't intend to exhaustively retrace that terrain.* Likewise, readers will not find paeans here from Rehnquist's friends and relations. Although I do not doubt that family was important to Rehnquist, those relationships are best explained by Rehnquist's extensive and revealing correspondence with the people close to him, and that documentary evidence is what I have relied upon in this work.

On the mid-December day of Rehnquist's Senate confirmation in 1971, Harry Blackmun picked up a pen and wrote to the young justice who was soon to be seated beside him.

> I have refrained from writing heretofore because I did not wish to embarrass you or upset the delicate balance of these days that have been so critical for you. But now that the ordeal—of having one's entire life bared by those who, it seems, seek to destroy more than they seek to be informed—is behind you, I extend my congratulations and warm welcome.
>
> You will have many years here, and successful ones, and your influence on the Court as an institution will be great and enduring.

Blackmun's encouraging welcome was probably more a politeness than a serious attempt at prediction. He was right about Rehnquist's durability,

---

*In any event, although both the Clinton impeachment and the Court's decision in *Bush v. Gore* were of epic national importance, Rehnquist's role in each was relatively minor. As the constitutionally prescribed presiding officer in the impeachment proceeding, Rehnquist mostly was an observer. Coining a phrase from Gilbert and Sullivan's *Iolanthe,* he later said: "I did nothing in particular, and I did it very well." Rehnquist voted with the majority in *Bush v. Gore,* but the opinion was unsigned. Author Jeffrey Toobin, in his book *The Nine,* attributes authorship of the majority opinion to Justice Anthony Kennedy.

but he could not have guessed at the kind of Court that Rehnquist would inhabit or the iconoclasm that would be his hallmark long after his patrons Richard Nixon and Ronald Reagan vanished. Assessing his own significance, Rehnquist quixotically would compare himself not to Antonin Scalia, Lewis Powell, Warren Burger, or other Court conservatives but to an ideological opposite, one who shared his essentially solitary temperament, a fellow loner.

Change would come to the Court, not to Rehnquist. When he reflected on his judicial philosophy many years later, he declared: “I can remember arguments we would get into as law clerks in the early ’50s. And I don’t know that my views have changed much from that time.”

Asked to assess his own growth as a justice, he was genuinely taken aback: “You equate *change* with *growth*?” Rehnquist didn’t.

It did not matter whether, or how far, he and his Court of reliable conservatives fell out of step with the times. There was a certain natural order to Rehnquist’s world, and it had been established a long time ago.

John A. Jenkins
Washington, DC

ONE

Shorewood

WILLIAM REHNQUIST WAS BORN in Milwaukee on October 1, 1924. Baby Billy was the first child of thirty-year-old William Benjamin Rehnquist, a sturdy first-generation Swedish-American who was born in Milwaukee and never left, and Margery Peck Rehnquist, twenty-seven years old and also a native of Wisconsin, from nearby Berlin. The two were a devoted if somewhat enigmatic couple: Bill Senior the stolid, quiet Republican, a wholesale paper salesman lacking a college education;* Margery the active, well-educated social secretary of the family, proudly working as a freelance translator for local companies.**

Milwaukee was the city people commuted to, but the smart money lived eastward, on Lake Michigan. The Rehnquists settled in Shorewood, a mile-square North Shore enclave with mansions fronting the lake and tidy bungalows neatly laid out elsewhere on a rectilinear grid. They bought a newly built tan stucco house at 4132 North Prospect Avenue right after they were married, and it was there that Bill and his younger sister, Jean, grew up. "It was a village full of Republicans," the *Washington Post* would later report, "even in the midst of the Depression. . . . Race relations were no problem in Shorewood in those days. There were no blacks living there."

---

*He ran the local sales office of Chicago-based Bradner Smith & Company.

**"I feel sad to get no more translations," Margery Rehnquist wrote to her son in 1986, "but after more than 50 years of it I guess it isn't surprising."

"Everybody we knew was pretty much Republican," one of Rehnquist's closest childhood friends, Jerry Oberembt, recalled. "We learned early on how bad Roosevelt was. Our parents would listen to FDR on the radio, gnash their teeth and then turn the dial to Father Coughlin."*

Shorewood ran its own schools, and they were among the best anywhere. Billy Rehnquist walked to afternoon kindergarten at the Atwater grade school, "carrying a small mat so we could take a nap after we got there." He made lifelong friends and recalled memorable experiences for his grandson in a 2003 letter:

> My [fifth-grade] homeroom teacher was named Miss Wild—she had black hair and was quite tall. She had a reputation for being a hard grader, and so we said about her that she was "Wild and wooly and full of fleas, and hard to carry above the D's."
>
> She taught English, and made each of us memorize a poem during the year. I chose "Horatius at the Bridge," which I came to regret because it was so long. But I think memorization is a good exercise, and I can still remember the end of that exciting poem. . . . We learned long division in that grade. I don't think we had homework in any subject for any grade.

He showed a competitive streak early on, racing other elementary-school kids on his bicycle in the springtime after dinner, and playing the new Depression game of Monopoly for hours on end in the winter.

Rehnquist entered high school in 1936. Shorewood High was dynamic, "one of the ten best in the country," and it produced its share of local and national politicians; Shorewood alumni included a congressman and a state senator. It was there that teachers and classmates began taking notice of this young man some called "Rennie," and who nicknamed himself "Bugs." He had a puckish sense of humor, superior cartooning skills, and considerable intellect. Shorewood High was a cluster of tan brick structures in a campus setting. It regularly sent its graduates to the Ivy League. Rehnquist didn't work particularly hard, but good grades came to him easily.

Charlotte Wollaeger, who taught English and speech to Rehnquist when he was a fourteen-year-old freshman, remembered him as someone

---

*Coughlin, a "radio priest" and third-party candidate of the 1930s, was bitterly opposed to the policies of President Franklin Roosevelt.

who came to class with his mind made up. "He was a big boy, tall, nice looking, laughed easily, had a good sense of humor. He was an interesting boy, rather determined in his point of view. There was not much give. He always felt he had answers to the question, and people respected him for that. He was a leader. He took leadership positions well. He had confidence in himself and was more mature than most. At Shorewood High School, the kids were aware of politics. It was an educated community. They took part in things."

Wollaeger recalled Rehnquist's mother as "motivated, energetic," and someone who "instilled respect for education," but she never met his father. Wollaeger was surprised to learn years later, during his confirmation hearings, about Rehnquist's deep conservatism; she didn't recall sensing that at the time. "I just wonder if it was something that came from the home."

Roy Genskow came up two years behind Rehnquist at Shorewood and later became a science teacher there. "His mother was the dominant force, had strong views" Genskow said. "More than his father; his father wasn't home most of the time." It was Rehnquist's mother who grounded him when he failed to do his homework. Genskow recalled Rehnquist as "studious, active in clubs, not a highly social fellow, with an intellectual bent."

"The community at that time was a conservative one," Genskow went on. "The North Shore has long been considered a conservative stronghold. Many of the conservatives were America Firsters.* That was the intellectual level he was at, even then."

Shorewood High reflected its all-white community. The year Rehnquist graduated, the spring prom featured a Harlem theme and the school newspaper advertised the event using black dialect. Prom-goers were greeted by a "black-faced doorman" and passed through a doorway with "unique decorations in the form of Negro heads" overhead. Other than as a curiosity, explained Genskow, "blacks weren't a factor in his life at all."

The school had a conservative consciousness and drummed it in. When legendary FBI head J. Edgar Hoover came to Milwaukee in 1940 to address the International Association of Chiefs of Police, the school paper sent a student reporter to interview the director in his hotel room.

---

*The America First Committee was an isolationist group that opposed entry into World War II. It drew its 800,000 members mainly from the Midwest, but support quickly evaporated after the Japanese attack on Pearl Harbor. Yale student and future justice Potter Stewart was one of its founders.

Rehnquist's sister, Jean, was three years younger than Bill. "I can remember the dining room table, the usual arguing and give and take. It was a time when we got to know each other. Both my mother and father were strong personalities. One didn't dominate the other. But we did have an atypical mother. My father was more stoical; he probably didn't communicate as much as mother did. She was a vice president of the American Association of University Women. She instilled a sense of honesty and morality. Certain things were expected—we had to respect mother and dad—but we felt free to air our views."

Politics permeated the household. On election night in 1932, the Rehnquists threw a party at their home to celebrate their candidate, the Republican incumbent Herbert Hoover. But Hoover took the blame for the Great Depression and lost to Franklin Delano Roosevelt in a landslide. In 1936, Jean Rehnquist wasn't yet ten years old when the Republicans launched their "stop Roosevelt" campaign. The GOP standard-bearers were Kansas governor Alf Landon and Chicago publisher Frank Knox, and she recalled how the Rehnquists embraced their slogan: "Get off the Rocks with Landon and Knox." In 1940, the Rehnquists brought their children to campaign events for Wendell Willkie and Robert Taft as both men vied for the Republican nomination, still to no avail. The Rehnquists were anti–New Dealers, "staunch Republicans," highly frustrated by four successive losses in presidential elections to Roosevelt alone.

In his senior year, Rehnquist became co–feature editor of the high school newspaper, the *Ripples.* The paper's news editor was his classmate and neighbor from across the street, Guy Scrivner: "Our parents' expectations were high. The school was a point of pride in the village. The kids were all just highly motivated. We were just a plain, wholesome suburban community."

Rehnquist wrote the *Ripples* humor column, revealing a whimsical side that would stay with him throughout life. He dubbed himself a "boreign" correspondent, lampooned teachers and the administration, and got into hot water with his April Fool's issue. But his family's combination of angry conservatism and driving ambition also pushed Rehnquist to early activism. He took to his soap box about politics, chastising the "self-styled news 'interpreters' [who] have been doing a little too much spouting of their own. There is no fault to be found with straight news broadcasts; they perform a valuable public service. But thorns to the 'commentators,' the overly dramatic Gabriel Heatter, the pompous H. V. Kaltenborn, and Walter Winchell with his corps of tattlers." Rehnquist went out for the cross-country team, was a homeroom representative to the student council, and served as a hall monitor—one of 77 out of 1,232 students. "Hall monitors, supervised by Miss Linda Barry, have really made this year a memorable one," the school yearbook wrote. It listed "cartooning" as Rehnquist's favorite pastime, "in and out of school."

Japan bombed Pearl Harbor during Rehnquist's senior year at Shorewood High. The attack was seared into Rehnquist's memory. Sixty-one years later, he returned to his high school: "I can still remember all of us being herded into the auditorium on December 8 to hear President Franklin Roosevelt's message to Congress, in which he referred to December 7 as a date which would live in infamy, and asked Congress to declare war on Japan. As we got up from our seats to leave afterwards, I think almost every one of us knew that the plans we had made for the future were going to be radically changed."

America First isolationists disappeared almost overnight, and a patriotic wave came over the village. Rehnquist helped organized a school assembly called "Wake Up, America" and became active in a patriotic group called the United States of Young Americans, which reenacted the founding of the country. Rehnquist played a teenage secretary of state in the Federalist cabinet.

Shorewood's Civil Defense Council started mobilizing, and within a month it had 176 high-school volunteers. The students devised a messenger service capable of contacting every home in Shorewood within an hour, and appointed 15 block captains, including Rehnquist. Besides helping with the messenger service, it was the job of Rehnquist and the other block captains to report draft dodgers and look for "any subversive activities which might lead to the sabotaging of our national unity, [or] any crimes whatsoever, perpetrated during the national emergency." Rehnquist and his buddies had made college plans, but they also knew that the wartime draft awaited them. They quit their summer jobs a week early and rented a couple of cottages on Silver Lake, a few hours from Milwaukee, for one final celebration.

Bill Rehnquist was all of seventeen.

TWO

A Change of Name and Place

THE SHOREWOOD *Ripples* of April 24, 1942, carried news of Bill Rehnquist's full scholarship to Kenyon College in Gambier, Ohio. He would receive $450 a year for four years, the paper said, "on the basis of his character, promise, and high scholastic standing." His intended major: political science.

Rehnquist would not last long.

The bucolic atmosphere at the small, liberal-arts school did not suit him. Kenyon had a 1,000-acre campus and a 380-acre nature preserve, but that was not what Rehnquist was looking for. Whatever that was, it wasn't to be found at Kenyon. On his own for the first time, Rehnquist pushed limits.

Barely on campus a month, he set out in October of that year to spend a Saturday night with a hometown friend who was at Kent State, 105 miles away. Rehnquist was broke, so he hitchhiked. When he got to Kent, the friend was nowhere to be found—and Rehnquist had no place to sleep and no money for a room. What was he to do? Rather than staying at Kent, Rehnquist inexplicably decided to hitch 6 miles up the road to the county seat and spend the night on the courthouse lawn at Ravenna.

But there was a problem. The village of Ravenna had a vagrancy ordinance, and the police were enforcing it. An officer came along and told Rehnquist that he would arrange for him to sleep in jail. One thing led to another, and soon the newly minted eighteen-year-old was under arrest* and spending his Saturday night in jail. When, years later, he would have to explain the arrest to the hard-liners of the Nixon administration, he said simply: "I was released the next morning, and I do not believe any further action was ever taken."

Back at Kenyon, Rehnquist was having a hard time seeing the point of staying in school. With America at war, eighteen-year-olds were beginning to be drafted; Congress had lowered the draft age, from twenty-one, symbolically on Armistice Day, November 11, 1942. By the time he arrived at Kenyon, Rehnquist recalled, the college advisers were urging young Kenyon men to make the most of their time on campus by signing up for "some sort of military program." The military courses, it was hoped, might keep them on campus longer. Rehnquist signed up for a pre-meteorology program that emphasized math and physics, hardly the strong suit of a political science major.

Rehnquist didn't last beyond the first semester at Kenyon, and he hardly ever spoke of his very short time there. Kenyon reciprocated, never claiming him as its own. Years later, after his death, there would be a debate at Kenyon about whether even to acknowledge that Rehnquist attended the liberal bastion—even though, as one alum put it, he was "the most important Kenyon matriculate since Rutherford B. Hayes."

"We felt," the Kenyon administration explained, "that it would be presumptuous, misleading and ultimately disrespectful to 'claim' the chief justice as Kenyon's own, given that he spent less than three months at the college and that, in discussing his education and intellectual background, most authorities—including Rehnquist himself—have little or nothing to

*The ordinance Rehnquist was arrested for violating was as quaint as it was comprehensive, making it a crime punishable by up to ninety days in jail (thirty days for the first offense) to be "a vagrant, common street beggar, common prostitute, habitual disturber of the peace, known pickpocket, gambler, burglar, thief, watch stuffer, ball game player, or [anyone] who practices any trick, game or device with intent to swindle, or any person who cannot give a reasonable account of himself." Rehnquist disclosed the arrest on his security-clearance application when he joined the Nixon administration in 1969, but his criminal record was not following him around; the sheriff's office routinely destroyed arrest records after ten years for anything except the most dangerous crimes like murder, rape, and arson. The FBI's massive national criminal database wasn't created until 1967, so Rehnquist's arrest never showed up in the national computer database, either. His record would not have been so easily erased had Rehnquist been arrested today.

say about Kenyon. Our decision may or may not have been a wise one. But it did not arise from political ideology."

Instead of returning to Kenyon for his second freshman semester, Rehnquist appears to have just hung around for a month and a half. His whereabouts during that time are unclear, but it's likely that he stayed close by Kenyon, because on March 4, 1943, he enlisted at Ft. Hayes, the nearest Army base in Columbus, Ohio, 56 miles away.

Being on his own in Ohio gave Rehnquist an opportunity to redefine himself, to leave any part of his old life behind if he chose to. Filling out his enlistment papers, the young man decided a change was in order. Rehnquist would give himself a new middle name.

Exactly why Rehnquist did this isn't clear, although there is speculation: Chief Justice Roberts, who served as Rehnquist's clerk and presumably heard the reason, said it was Rehnquist's mother, strong willed and superstitious, who got him to do it: "The Chief was originally named William Donald Rehnquist. He changed his middle name to Hubbs, a family name, when his mother was told by a numerologist that he would have a successful career if his middle initial were 'H.'"

Rehnquist bought into the superstition and found an ancestor for whom he could rename himself: his maternal grandmother, Alice Hubbs. Common law allowed the change as long as it wasn't done for a fraudulent purpose, so Rehnquist reaffirmed his motherly bond and signed "Hubbs" to his three-year enlistment papers. He started using the new name. The "Donald" his parents gave him was left behind.*

Now he was an enlisted man, and a full-fledged participant in the Army's pre-meteorology program. As Rehnquist later related it, he was assigned to Denison University to continue his meteorological studies, double-bunking in the basement of what had been a freshman dorm.** "I had a good academic record in high school, but had never gone beyond plane geometry and had no physics. . . . I was hanging on by the skin of my teeth." Eleven months later, Rehnquist was still at Denison when "someone

*Rehnquist was definitive about the timing of the name change—"at time of entry into the Army"—on his sworn affidavit for a government security clearance in 1969. He recollected differently, however, in a 1993 handwritten bench note to Harry Blackmun, found in Blackmun's papers. Rehnquist told Blackmun that he changed his middle name "while in high school."

**Denison has no record of this.

high up in the Air [Corps] brass realized that somewhere the people setting up the pre-meteorology programs had mistakenly added a zero to the number of weather forecasters that would be needed." The program closed down, at which point Rehnquist and the others could make a choice: go to officer candidate school, or remain enlisted men and be sent to air bases. An iconoclast even then, Rehnquist thumbed his nose at becoming an officer. "I had had enough spit and polish for awhile and opted for the air bases."

It was just another example of Rehnquist going his own way, said Roberts. "One of his many unconventional choices."

It was still a time of racial segregation—the US military would not integrate its ranks until 1948. White soldiers received what were seen as preferential assignments. Rehnquist was sent to Will Rogers Field in Oklahoma City, where he got on-the-job training as a military "weather observer," making hourly teletype reports and sending weather balloons aloft. After three months, he was ordered to Carlsbad, New Mexico. "What godforsaken country!" Rehnquist thought when he got there. "But after three months there, I had come to like it, and determined that, if possible, someday I would come back and live in the southwest." After three more months, he was off to Hondo, Texas, and after a few more months he was on his way to Chanute Field in Illinois, about 130 miles south of Chicago, and then on to Fort Monmouth, New Jersey. "The program was designed to teach the maintenance and repair of weather instruments, but so far as I know none of us who successfully completed the program ever repaired a single instrument." The war was all but over. Finally, in the summer of 1945, Rehnquist, now almost twenty-one years old, was ordered to North Africa: Cairo, Tripoli, Tunis, Casablanca.

The memories of each remained vivid. Tripoli, he recalled many years later, was "breathtakingly beautiful . . . like something out of the Arabian Nights." The Mediterranean was an intense blue, the buildings whitewashed stucco. "Every morning we had to look in our shoes to make sure there were no scorpions." The Bay of Tunis, on the other hand, "was a giant cesspool with a perfectly terrible odor coming from it." And Casablanca? "Too good to be true." He made excursions to Rabat and Marrakesh, the latter "one of the truly spectacular settings of any setting in the world—you are sitting in the desert under palm trees, but as you look up you see the Atlas Mountains 10,000 or 11,000 feet above you, snowcapped. No wonder Winston Churchill liked to go there to paint!"

It was March 1946 by the time Rehnquist returned to the States on a Lykes freighter converted to a troop ship, eleven days at sea, sleeping in the hold with "hammocks five deep going all the way up to the ceiling. I was unlucky enough to get the top hammock, which was no fun when you are seasick." Even though he'd seen no action, he still considered himself to be a modest contributor to the Allied victory: "I, and millions like me, learned to obey orders, do what we were told."

THREE

"Hate Black"

IN THE LATE WINTER OF 1946, the military obligingly discharged Sergeant Rehnquist at Ft. Sheridan, Illinois, a couple of hours by bus from the family home in Shorewood.

As someone who claimed to have learned to obey orders and do as told, Bill Rehnquist was playing seriously against type. He wasn't ready to return home, and he certainly wasn't ready to shovel the snow of a hard Milwaukee winter. After all, he'd just been to Casablanca and "realized that if you lived in the right climate, you didn't have to shovel snow for four or five months a year."

Rehnquist promptly stuck out his thumb and hitchhiked with an Army buddy to the West Coast. From Chicago they went out to Portland, then down to Los Angeles and back to Milwaukee. He returned on Memorial Day only to find his hometown still covered with several inches of snow from what the locals called a late-season blizzard. "Then and there," Rehnquist "decided to seek a more equable climate." No more frigid winters. "I wanted to find someplace like North Africa to go to school."

There were palm trees on the Stanford University campus in Palo Alto, and so by the fall of 1946 was Rehnquist. He cobbled his finances together, relying on G.I. Bill benefits along with some scholarship funds and money earned by, among other things, running the breakfast shift at Encina Commons, the campus dining hall. "I had so many other part-time jobs, I can't remember them all." Rehnquist once again declared a major in political science, carrying his one semester's worth of credits from Kenyon. But there was a snafu in the registrar's office. Instead of coming in as a second-semester freshman, Rehnquist was a second-semester *junior;* he had just three semesters to go. "I think they gave me credit for all sorts of very non-academic stuff," he later recalled.

AS A SOLDIER IN NORTH AFRICA, Rehnquist had read *The Road to Serfdom,* the 1944 antisocialist manifesto written by Austrian free-market economist Friedrich A. Hayek. Hayek's book was a libertarian broadside, forcefully arguing against central economic planning. With the world at war and debates taking place about the origins of fascism, Hayek made the case that fascism as well as socialism had common roots in governmental control: the loss of economic freedom inevitably led to the loss of individualism and inexorably to the state's control over an individual's right to property, prosperity, and political freedom.

Hayek's book had an impact on Rehnquist, so much so that more than a half-century later he was still marveling at how Hayek "and a couple of his intellectual cohorts probably did more to counter the socialist brand of liberalism than any other writers of their time."

Rehnquist's strict libertarian outlook, molded by his parents and now deeply ingrained by the time he arrived at Stanford, soon would receive its first rigorous intellectual testing. The legendary Stanford professor Charles Fairman taught an undergraduate course in constitutional law, and Rehnquist was enrolled. Fairman was "a brilliant and imposing figure," the Stanford alumni magazine reported, "a demanding teacher and exacting scholar of constitutional law and court history."

The magazine quoted another of Fairman's students during that time: he was "quite austere, but as you came to know him, the more you'd like him. He had a dry sense of humor. . . . He tended to teach in a very descriptive manner, trying to communicate to you how each justice had grown up, and what made him tick."

Fairman became Rehnquist's mentor and role model. Rehnquist recalled, with a grin, one of the first books that Fairman assigned. It was Fairman's own, written just a few years earlier, a biography of Supreme Court Justice Samuel Miller. It was the first book Rehnquist ever read about the Constitution.

Fairman's choice of Miller as a subject was not mere coincidence. The justice, appointed by Abraham Lincoln, played an important role in limiting the Supreme Court's interpretation of the three constitutional amendments collectively known as the Civil War amendments.* Fairman had a particular interest in the 14th Amendment, and in whether that amendment applied the Bill of Rights to the states. Fairman was certain that the historical record—the intent of the "founders"—proved it did not. The Stanford professor became a darling of the political right at a time of great racial upheaval in postwar America.

The debate about individual rights was as intense as it was timely, coming at the end of a world war waged against Hitler's Germany, an explicitly racist totalitarian state. Americans were being forced to confront their own racial views, and racial segregation in the United States was under attack in the courts. By the time Rehnquist arrived at Stanford in 1946, Thurgood Marshall, director of the NAACP Legal Defense and Education Fund, was already mounting what would be the first successful challenge to segregationist educational policies in Texas; his unanimous victory in *Sweatt v. Painter,*** in an opinion written by Chief Justice Fred M. Vinson, made clear that the separate-but-equal standard of the past was doomed.

The 14th Amendment spoke bluntly: "No State shall make or enforce any law which shall abridge the privileges or immunities of citizens of the United States; nor shall any State deprive any person of life, liberty, or property without due process of law; nor deny to any person within its jurisdiction the equal protection of the laws."

As Fairman taught it, however, the debate was far from settled. In Rehnquist's new world, Hayek's doctrinaire views about individual rights now converged with Fairman's. Both commentators saw inherent danger from an infringing central government. Fairman taught that the "privileges and immunities" referred to in the amendment were few, and he wrote a *Stanford Law Review* article on the subject in 1949 that is viewed as a classic and still is widely cited. Fairman's narrow interpretation came through vividly in lectures to undergraduates such as Rehnquist. "He clearly taught that the

---

*The 13th Amendment, added in 1865, outlawed slavery; the 14th Amendment, adopted in 1868, protected individual rights; and the 15th, added in 1870, prohibited voting discrimination on the basis of race "or previous condition of servitude."

**339 U.S. 629 (1950)

14th Amendment did not apply the Bill of Rights to the states," a student of that era recalled.

And the lesson stuck; Fairman's conservative views stayed with Rehnquist for the rest of his life, even when Fairman, perhaps, no longer saw their merit.* Rehnquist's 1973 dissent in *Roe v. Wade,*** legalizing abortion, was squarely based on Fairman's teachings: Rehnquist wrote that it was the founders' intent to leave such matters to the states. And almost thirty years later, in a 5–4 decision† holding that Congress lacked authority to enact the Violence Against Women Act, Rehnquist based his opinion on the "good law" of cases that the Supreme Court had decided in 1883, because they were decided by those "who had intimate knowledge and familiarity with the events surrounding the adoption of the 14th Amendment." Rehnquist dedicated his final book, *Centennial Crisis,* written barely a year before his death, to Fairman, the professor "who first introduced me to the Supreme Court." Fairman's shadow seemed always to lurk as Rehnquist soldiered ahead.

In his time, Fairman lashed out at justices who didn't read the historical record as he did, but he was at his most vitriolic in going after liberal Justice Hugo Black. Soon, Fairman's obsession became Rehnquist's.

Arriving at Stanford Law School a few years after taking Fairman's course, Rehnquist would twice make the following journal notation about Fairman's nemesis, now his by adoption, in bold capital letters:

"HATE BLACK"

Rehnquist made that statement, the first time with an exclamation point (!), in margin notations alongside his notes about Black's opinions. The comment seems well considered, not an emotional outburst: it was

---

*Charles Lane, writing in *Stanford Magazine* in 2005: "Fairman, who died in 1988, probably would not have approved of some of the ways in which his views were applied. In the '50s, he publicly supported the Court's decision in *Brown.* He felt 'there was no way to defend separate but equal.' . . . Fairman [also] donated money to the Democratic presidential candidates in 1984 and 1988. If Fairman had had his way, Walter Mondale would have become president in 1985, and Ronald Reagan would not have been around to appoint Fairman's former student as chief justice in 1986."

**410 U.S. 113 (1973)

†*United States v. Morrison,* 529 U.S. 598 (2000)

written carefully and then repeated a few pages later. It might also be misconstrued except for the obvious fact that Rehnquist's note taking was about Black and Black's fellow travelers on the Court whom Rehnquist called "the Black group."

The first time he penned the words "Hate Black," Rehnquist drew above it a finely rendered sketch of a human eye, all-seeing and wide open. Rehnquist was a detailed note taker and, unlike in later years (when his handwriting deteriorated to little more than a scrawl), he wrote in a fine cursive style. He also filled his journals with random jottings and sketches that revealed a sardonic wit. One cartoon featured a foolish-looking "Sir Basil Pimpwell"; another showed a grim-faced tax collector wearing a Fu Manchu moustache and a police badge in the shape of a five-pointed star, with "US" in the center. Rehnquist was entertaining himself. But he was also exhibiting an early interest in the personalities of the Supreme Court.

On a Court filled with outsized figures, none was more formidable than Felix Frankfurter—Black's opponent on and off the bench. When Rehnquist wrote approvingly about a justice's opinion in those student days, more often than not the respected justice would be Frankfurter, whom Fairman also favored. As much as Rehnquist's disfavor of Black was a marker for a lifelong sentiment, so, too, was the approbation of Frankfurter that he first picked up from Fairman. Rehnquist would soon come to know Frankfurter, but he held the justice in high regard even before they met. Like his loathing for Black, Rehnquist's admiration for Frankfurter endured to the end. As a justice on the Court, Rehnquist would adopt Frankfurter's first name—"Felix"—and sign himself as such in letters to close family members.

In all, Rehnquist kept six journals while a student at Stanford and its law school. The private writings reveal a young man who already considered himself the cerebral peer of great legal minds. He had a vaulting ambition to engage in intellectual battle with them. Indeed, in debates taking place in his own mind, and on the pages of his journals, he already was doing so.

Possessed of an artist's vivid imagination, Rehnquist tried to envision his future. Frankfurter, Rehnquist later claimed, told Rehnquist the clerk that "the one thing you absolutely should never do was to try to plan to be a member of this Court, because there was no way you could go about it." But even before he got to the Court as a clerk, Rehnquist knew it was what he wanted. He already could see it, or at least thought he could. On one of the last pages of his sixth and final Stanford journal, young Mr. Rehnquist, not more than twenty-seven years old, addressed a question to himself in the margin. In it he awarded himself an honorific, and there's little doubt that he had in mind the fact that it was the standard form of address not just for judges in general but for justices of the Supreme Court:

"What now, Hon. W. H. Rehnquist?"

FOUR

Basic Moral Rights

REHNQUIST SPENT HIS FIRST YEAR at Stanford in a nondescript dorm, called the Village, which was filled with business students. But he had a change of venue the following fall. In September 1947, with just one undergraduate semester remaining—thanks to the registrar's clerical error—Rehnquist showed up at Encina Hall.

"Dorm" was decidedly a misnomer for Rehnquist's new quarters. Stanford's founder actually had modeled Encina Hall on a grand Swiss resort he'd visited in 1888. Drawings were rushed back to Stanford's architect, Charles Allerton Coolidge. Within three years Stanford had its first building, "the grandest dormitory in the country," Stanford's magazine reported a century later, "an imposing four-story sandstone edifice with a stately lobby, huge dining hall and the luxury of electricity and hot running water."

The place housed four hundred men, and from day one it developed a different reputation on campus: the Madhouse. "Student high jinks ran from annoying pranks to outright vandalism and violence. . . . Encina's long, wide halls and cavernous stairwells encouraged student rambunctiousness. Throwing things into the lobby, from trays full of dishes to heavy furniture, became a favorite game." The 1948 Stanford yearbook called it "Encina Asylum" and ran an accompanying picture of Rehnquist acting as dealer in a nine-man card game.

There were other signs that Rehnquist wasn't letting academic rigors take much of a toll. In April 1948, he wrote a letter to the *Stanford Daily,* taking the editors to task after they "implicitly" took sides in an editorial about the campus elections. Dripping with sarcasm, the letter was an early showcase of Rehnquist's ability to craft an artful argument in furtherance of a principled stand, no matter how petty the issue:

> To the Editor:
>
> I would like to express my strong objection to the editorial in Friday's *Daily.*
>
> 1. It seems to me to be a course of doubtful validity for *The Daily* to implicitly take sides in a student body election. Though there probably is no by-law to prohibit it, I believe that a majority of the student body would agree with me when I say that *The Daily* should be operated not as the private property of the editorial board but as a trust for the entire student body.
>
> 2. The piece implies (a) that student government is a matter of vital concern, only to be mentioned in reverent whispers, and (b) that student government, such as it is, requires another George Washington or Abraham Lincoln for student body president.
>
> Both of these assumptions are erroneous. The importance of student government certainly cannot stem from the vast powers which it possesses. Whether Hustle House or Alpha Cholera is chosen to have a dance Saturday is a matter of undoubted interest, but hardly of commanding importance.
>
> Isn't student government important because it is practice [*sic*] in democracy? No. Those who make this claim confuse their means with ends. Men do not institute government in order that they run it democratically; rather they see that since the subjects for legislation demand that broad powers be invested in the national and state governments, democracy is the best means for controlling these powers. When, as in the case of Stanford student government, the subject matter on which the government operates is so microscopic as to be of little or no importance to anyone, democracy as a means or as a form loses its meaning.
>
> Likewise, the office of student body president need not be approached with quite the humble respect which *The Daily* implies. From my observations, the prime requisite of the ASSU* president is a genial manner

*Associated Students of Stanford University

> and a habit of saying "hello" on Quad. I would like to vote for a man who has not forgotten how to laugh at himself rather than one who is completely overawed by his own mouthing of meaningless phrases and impossible promises which pass under the name of campaign oratory.
>
> I suggest that the editor relax or soon he will be eligible for Students Concerned.* What our political campaign needs is fewer platforms and more free beer.

By the end of that academic year Rehnquist had collected not one but two degrees from Stanford, and soon would be on his way to begin a third, at Harvard. His shortened Stanford undergraduate stint—just three semesters—brought an undergrad degree in January 1948, along with admission to Phi Beta Kappa. Harvard had already admitted him to its PhD program in political science, but his studies there wouldn't begin until September 1948. So, there was the matter of what to do with the idle semester that presented itself in the spring of 1948. Rehnquist decided to make the most of the government program to which he was entitled. "The idea of going out and going to work between then and September never really occurred to me when I had the G.I. Bill of Rights," Rehnquist recalled, with a sheepish laugh, almost four decades later. "So I just arranged to get a Master's degree in the time that was left, before I'd have to go to Harvard."

Rehnquist titled his 100-page thesis "Contemporary Theories of Rights," hitting the requisite length on the nose through a style that combined the worst elements of prolixity, turgidity, and pomposity—scores of words where just a few would suffice: "When we compare the emotional dynamism of the vast written literature on the subjects of philosophy and politics with that of the great tragedies in the field of drama, with the masterworks of art, and with the finest efforts of the great musical composers, we may well have misgivings as to whether the logical treatise method which has characterized almost all of philosophy since its inception can ever sufficiently grasp the human reality which is the nexus of the problems which it seeks to solve." As a show pony for Rehnquist's knowledge of political philosophy and his ability to deeply mine *Roget's,* it was a *tour de force.* But the writing was as pretentious as it was lifeless. The twenty-three-year-old gave his

*A small group of Stanford students, concerned about the possibility of a third world war, formed Students Concerned during the 1947–1948 academic year. It soon disbanded.

work plenty of ostentatious academic polish but none of the zing of the letter he'd written to the *Stanford Daily* a few months earlier. Still, Rehnquist's opus, read alongside the opinions he later produced at the Court, revealed that his philosophy was already set at Stanford.* Here was Rehnquist's judicial nihilism as it first burst forth. A fully formed judicial canon could be seen in his theory that the most basic moral rights were, in essence, *negative.* In other words, the state had an inherent moral duty to refrain from certain injurious actions rather than an affirmative obligation to provide for certain needs.

As Rehnquist wrote it, freedom from *coercion* was the most fundamental moral right, but there were also a few others that he put into the same anti-coercive realm: freedom of speech, freedom of religion, and the right to due process. All the other freedoms were *political*—this would include civil rights, gender rights, privacy, and all manner of other freedoms that Rehnquist did not see as moral imperatives. He called these *positive* liberties, and they were not guaranteed. Because political liberties had no moral basis, they would have to await legislative adoption. The majority—or, certainly, their elected representatives—would decide the scope of those freedoms. And if the majority didn't see fit to act? Well, then those other freedoms just would not exist.

Rehnquist was unyielding on this point throughout his life. To illustrate the post-Stanford stasis of Rehnquist's views on moral rights, and how crisply Rehnquist drew the line between negative and positive liberties, consider the majority opinion that Rehnquist wrote in 1989, *DeShaney v. Winnebago County Department of Social Services.*** The case raised the issue of what duty a government has to protect citizens who are not in the custody of the government against the violence of other private persons. Rehnquist's answer: None.

"Nothing in the language of the Due Process Clause itself requires the State to protect the life, liberty, and property of its citizens against invasion by private actors," Rehnquist wrote in *DeShaney.* "The Clause is phrased as a limitation on the State's power to act, not as a guarantee of certain mini-

---

*I have relied on Douglas W. Kmiec's excellent and comprehensible translation of Rehnquist's thesis, "Young Mr. Rehnquist's Theory of Moral Rights—Mostly Observed." Kmiec is a professor of law at Pepperdine University.

**489 U.S. 189 (1989)

mal levels of safety and security." *DeShaney* involved an abusive father who beat his young son so severely over a period of years that the boy suffered irreversible brain damage. Wisconsin social service officials knew of the abuse but did nothing. Rehnquist wrote for the 6–3 majority that the 14th Amendment's Due Process Clause was a protection against unwanted government interference, and not an entitlement to government aid. He said the restrained actions of the Wisconsin authorities were correct, because being too quick to intervene would have its own price: a state actively intruding into parent-child relationships.

Rehnquist's self assurance reflected the majoritarian homogeneity of Shorewood and the simplicity of an earlier time when white men ruled. With Rehnquist's credo one didn't have to connect many dots. It was a simple politico-judicial philosophy. Political majorities were free, but not compelled, to act upon their impulses. If you were not in the majority you could not expect protection against the majority's views, except in the few narrow, negative areas.

ON AUGUST 14, 1948, REHNQUIST LEFT Stanford and began the drive back to Wisconsin, his new MA degree in hand. There would be some important stops along the way as Rehnquist continued his self-education. He began a journal of the trip and, in a military manner, carefully noted times of departure ("0630") and other significant occurrences ("flat tire just outside of Baker"). He meticulously drew maps to record each leg of the journey and, in his narrative, highlighted the major stops (Las Vegas: "Flamingo Club"; Grand Canyon: "magnificent spectacle"; Phantom Ranch: "wonderful food, swimming pool"; Zion: "gas 33 cents a gallon"; Salt Lake City: "got me interested in Mormons"). Undeterred by his vagrancy arrest a few years earlier, Rehnquist was still camping overnight in places he considered fair game for squatters, and his diary recounts that he pitched at least one such camp on the courthouse lawn—"at 2100"—in the Old West town of Vernal, Utah. He was proudly carrying his Stanford master's thesis with him, although he really didn't expect anyone to have any great interest in it when he arrived home in Shorewood.

But he was wrong. Rehnquist's Aunt Mamie expressed a willingness to have a look, "so I gratefully took it down to her house. She was the head of the Reference Room at the Milwaukee Public Library, and her only interest in it was to see whether I had arranged the bibliography in accordance with the Dewey Decimal System!" So much for that. Rehnquist's next stop was Harvard, where the twenty-three-year-old intended to begin working on a PhD in political theory.

Rehnquist's solitary year at Harvard stands out for several reasons, not least for the disdain in which he soon held its liberal faculty. He kept no journal of his Harvard experience, but he apparently took a passionate, and quick, dislike for almost everything about Harvard and started looking almost immediately for a way to get back to Stanford. The sole exception to his overall phobic reaction was his delight in a course about the History of England between 1815 and 1914. Rehnquist simply admired the professor for bringing the characters to life.

When he arrived at Harvard, Rehnquist was on an academic's trajectory. His goal certainly was to become a professor. Hayek's writing was still on his mind and World War II still fresh in his memory. He wanted to pursue his own theories about the events that led to Nazism. Rehnquist was cynical about the Germans, believing they allowed themselves to be conned into a devil's bargain, trading their freedom for a false sense of well-being. As Rehnquist saw it, the Germans enabled Hitler's rise by giving up any real opportunity for upward mobility and economic freedom in exchange for "a firm assurance that their station in life would be maintained." Harvard would prepare him, Rehnquist thought, to be a political philosopher, addressing issues—such as this one—that he considered "fascinating and necessarily at the heart of any discussion about what is the 'good society.'" In short, Harvard would put his views to the test.

But his time at Harvard quickly led to disappointment and despair. He was disenchanted; his grades were poor; he disliked many of his professors. "I had a feeling there was more preciousness about the academic life than I would care for." Rehnquist, not prone to show much emotion, even admitted that he was depressed. One of his law clerks later put it bluntly: Rehnquist saw academics generally as "liberal blatherers."

"I did not very much cotton to most of my professors," Rehnquist later confessed, and he certainly didn't like the Ivy League. A Shorewood classmate recalled bumping into Rehnquist on the Harvard campus. "He said he just couldn't take Harvard liberalism," the classmate recalled. "It was just too much for him."

Anxious to return to Stanford, Rehnquist converted his first year's coursework at Harvard into another MA degree, which was finally conferred in March 1950. The year at Harvard was a walk-through. If Rehnquist ever wrote anything significant in the way of a thesis while he was there, the university has long ago lost track of it and Rehnquist never mentioned it.*

Looking for a way out of Harvard, Rehnquist "took some vocational tests which Uncle Sam paid for under the G.I. Bill of Rights. These showed that I seemed to have the greatest aptitude for being a lawyer, so I decided to go to law school." That Rehnquist would so cavalierly make this decision based upon a vocational test strains credulity, particularly given his earlier enthusiasm at Stanford for Fairman's course in constitutional law. Yet that was always his story, and as time went on it became lore.

In later years, Rehnquist would write that his deep disappointment at Harvard was "a blessing in disguise." Returning to the Stanford campus to begin law school in the fall of 1949, he made lifelong friends that included Sandra Day and her future husband John O'Connor, met his future wife, ** and generally found a law school that suited his need for orderliness and intellectual discipline. There were no "blathering" professors, just lectures that hewed closely to the casebooks.

William Baxter, a law school classmate who later became a Stanford professor, recalled Rehnquist as "a complete standout. When the professors got through abusing everybody and wanted the right answer, they would call on Bill." The Stanford law school experience of Rehnquist's day put a sharp focus on the nuts and bolts of torts, contracts, and property and an emphasis on memorization. Constitutional law was comparatively mundane; the Warren Court, with its soaring ambition, was not yet in session.

Rehnquist took scrupulous notes and seemed to absorb everything. Despite his earlier collection of degrees, law school, he later wrote, was his "intellectual awakening":

> It was the one time in my life that I can remember being utterly absorbed both in my classes and in talking with my classmates about the subject

---

*Harvard couldn't find a record of Rehnquist's having written a thesis.

**Natalie "Nan" Cornell was five years younger than Bill Rehnquist; he met her during the summer of 1951, after his second year of law school.

> matter of the classes. There is more than one law school dean or law review board member who will tell you that one of the biggest factors that goes into the making of a good law school is a good student body. You don't really get any great intellectual stimulus from a teacher, however brilliant, if you don't have some people to whom you can talk after class about the subject of his lecture that day. You don't have to develop the frenzy of the study groups and "paper chase" to become deeply interested in the subject matter and still keep a balanced perspective on your life as a whole.

As usual, Rehnquist didn't just excel but stood out—"outlandishly conservative and outlandishly bright" is how Charles Lane of the *Washington Post* described him in *Stanford Magazine.* "Articulate and abrupt" was Baxter's characterization. Brash and ambitious, Rehnquist became editor in chief of the *Law Review* and graduated a semester early, in December 1951. He had the top grades in his class, according to Stanford, but not the number-one ranking that he might otherwise have earned: contrary to a legend that Rehnquist never tried to debunk, that accolade was unattainable because Stanford did not rank its law school classes at the time.

FIVE

On to Washington

BY THE LATE SUMMER OF 1951, Bill Rehnquist was looking ahead: he was a semester away from graduating law school, and he was in the job market. There were nibbles from California law firms. His girlfriend and future wife, Nan, had just graduated from Stanford and could come along. But Rehnquist had his eyes on a different prize. He wanted to move to Washington, to become a clerk at the Supreme Court.

The law school graduates who went to the Supreme Court were the brightest of their class, and they worked long hours in slavish loyalty to their bosses, the justices. It was the clerks who read through the slush pile of petitions for *certiorari**—each year there were thousands of appeals to the High Court—and culled those that might be worthy of the justices' consideration. Likewise, the drafting of each justice's opinions was typically handled by clerks.

The justices of the Supreme Court in 1951 contained a high proportion of judicial legends—among them William O. Douglas, Tom Clark, Felix

*A writ of *certiorari* is the primary means by which a case comes to the Supreme Court. Litigants who seek review by the Court file a petition for the writ. The justices vote on each petition. If at least four of the nine justices agree, the writ is granted and the Court hears the case. More than eight thousand petitions are filed annually; only about 1 percent are taken up by the Court.

Frankfurter, Hugo Black, and Robert Jackson. Douglas was a rugged outdoorsman and individualist who helped clean up Depression-era Wall Street as chairman of the Securities and Exchange Commission. He had been on the Court since age forty and now was a vigorous fifty-two with a roving eye. Clark, fifty-one, was President Harry Truman's attorney general and political confidant. Vienna-born Frankfurter, small and wiry at age sixty-eight, had been a Harvard law professor and was the Court's resident intellectual. The liberal Black, sixty-five, was a politician who served two terms as a US senator from Alabama. He recanted his Ku Klux Klan past after becoming Franklin D. Roosevelt's first appointee to the Court. Jackson, fifty-nine and another of FDR's appointees, had been America's chief prosecutor of Nazi war criminals at Nuremberg.

Then, as now, the justices pulled many of their clerks from the Ivy League. Rehnquist was anything *but* that, of course, but he had an "in" with Jackson that he intended to use as leverage.

Rehnquist's connection to Jackson was a law professor named Phil C. Neal, who, though not much older than Rehnquist, already had quite a résumé: Harvard College, Harvard Law, a member of the brain trust that organized the United Nations, and—this was key—a two-term clerk to Justice Jackson during the Supreme Court's war terms of 1943 and 1944. The two men kept in touch.

Neal, who taught administrative law, was also a protégé of Fairman's. And, like Fairman, he thought he discerned something special in Rehnquist. Stanford law graduates had not been very successful in getting Supreme Court clerkships, but Fairman thought Rehnquist had a shot. "He was a very strong student, a pretty mature fellow."

Jackson was making his annual pilgrimage to the Bohemian Grove, the two-week summer encampment in Monte Rio, California, where two thousand rich and powerful men—and only men—gathered for drinking, cigar smoking, and what they considered to be boyish, old-fashioned fun. On the trip, Jackson stopped off at Stanford; he was to dedicate the new law school building, and he also intended to drop by and see his former clerk Neal.

Neal told Rehnquist about Jackson's planned visit and then abruptly asked Rehnquist whether he would be interested in clerking for the justice. "The suggestion came out of the clear blue sky, but of course I said yes." An interview was arranged.

By Rehnquist's own account, in his 1987 history of the Court,* their meeting on the Stanford campus in August 1951 seemingly was a disaster. Jackson did most of the talking, opening with a question about Rehnquist's Swedish genealogy and then reminiscing about some of the Swedish clients he had represented while practicing law in upstate New York. It was hardly an interview. After courteous thanks from Jackson to Rehnquist for having come by, "I walked out of the room convinced that he had written me off as a total loss in the first minutes of our visit."

Rehnquist followed up with Jackson the next month, expressing his "gratitude for the privilege of talking to a justice of the Supreme Court" and politely inquiring about the clerkship: "I shall certainly be honored by whatever attention you are able to give my request for a clerkship."

At first, Jackson didn't offer much encouragement. "I shall probably not come to a decision until next spring, but I will advise you as early as I can."

It was not the answer that Rehnquist wanted to hear or that he was ready to accept. Flouting conventional politeness, he wrote a respectful—but unmistakably tenacious—reply that put Jackson on the spot:

> At the risk of presuming, I write to ask you if there is any possibility that you will make your clerkship appointment at a date earlier than you led me to believe in our conversation last August. At that time you suggested February as a possible time for decision.
>
> My position as one graduating from law school this December leads me to make this request. I have in the past several weeks received offers of jobs with various firms in California. There is no doubt in my mind that my first choice would be the clerkship with you, but I trust you can see my point of view when I say that I am hesitant to decline an attractive vested interest on the chance of a mere expectancy materializing. Or, in non-legal terminology, a bird in the hand is worth two in the bush.
>
> I realize that you must have numerous applicants for the position with you, and that considerations far more weighty than those set forth above must of necessity determine the time for selection. I trouble you with this inquiry as to the date of selection solely in order to help me with my own planning.

---

*William Rehnquist, *The Supreme Court* (New York: William Morrow & Co., 1987).

Rehnquist did not have to wait very long for his answer. By early December 1951, Jackson was feeling the burden of the Supreme Court's workload. He didn't think that his sole clerk, a young lawyer named George Niebank, would be able to keep up: "The work will become too heavy for one man sometime in the spring." Rehnquist's early law school graduation would fit Jackson's plans perfectly—in short, because Rehnquist was qualified and available. "I will need an additional clerk by the first of March and could, perhaps, arrange to take one somewhat earlier. I felt at our talk at Stanford that you and I would get along pretty well together and, if we can make proper arrangements, I will be glad to take you on." It was the first of what would turn out to be an improbable series of right-place-at-the-right-time twists in Rehnquist's fortunes at the Supreme Court.

Rehnquist was pleased, and he responded at once. "I am available as of January 1." He was willing and anxious to get there. "The opportunity represents the culmination of a desire nurtured thru [*sic*] three years of law school."

But Jackson urged him to take the California bar exam first. It would be "unwise," the justice counseled, "to pass up the first opportunity to try for the bar." He reiterated the admonition a week later, urging Rehnquist to sit for the California bar while his studies were still fresh in mind. "The sharpest blade will soon get rusty from disuse."

Jackson's insistence that Rehnquist take the California bar forced Rehnquist's hand. He had to admit that the promised jobs in California—his leverage for pressuring Jackson about the clerkship—were ephemera. Rehnquist wrote back to explain "exactly why I propose to act against your advice[.] I take the risk of burdening you with my introspection."

> I have decided under the circumstances not to take the California bar. I have never been sold on California as a place to either live or practice, though I have thoroughly enjoyed my schooling here at Stanford. Before I knew of my job with you, I had contacted several firms in New Mexico and Arizona, since the southwest has always been my first love as a part of the country in which to live. I received encouraging responses from some of them, and since notifying them of my tenure with you they have said that I should get in touch with them at the end of my term. I therefore feel reasonably confident that I will be able to get some sort of job in either Albuquerque or Phoenix, which would necessitate taking either

> the New Mexico or Arizona bar. The California bar would do me no good in either of these states. . . . Realizing full well the import of your remark that even the sharpest blade becomes rusty from disuse (and assuming that it is applicable to my case at all), I cannot but feel that the sensible choice is to wait. . . .

Jackson dropped the debate and told Rehnquist to just get to Washington. The Supreme Court clerkship was an almost unbelievable stroke of luck. Young Bill Rehnquist—brilliant, grasping (but for what, he knew not), restless, with a chip on his shoulder and something to prove—went home to Wisconsin and packed his '41 Studebaker Champion for the drive east. The little car had no heater.

SIX

An "Unhumanitarian Position," and Other Memos

REHNQUIST'S CLERKSHIP WITH JACKSON ran from February 1952 to June 1953—a term and a half. When Rehnquist hit Washington in the middle of a snowstorm, a hospitable great-aunt gave him a bedroom in Washington's Northwest section until he could rent his own apartment nearby, on Wisconsin Avenue. By then Nan had also come to Washington. Bill and Nan became engaged during his clerkship, and they were married in August 1953. But in the meantime, Nan found a short-term job at the new, and still very clandestine, Central Intelligence Agency. Keeping secrets would have suited her perfectly, for throughout her life she fiercely protected her (and later also her children's) privacy. She not only shunned the limelight but also managed the considerably more difficult feat of avoiding almost any mention in Rehnquist's letters and papers—a biographer's frustration that would have delighted husband and wife.

Bill Rehnquist was awed by just about everything about the Court—its magnificent building across the street from the US Capitol; its Corinthian columns; the quietude of the Great Hall; the pomp and ceremony inside the courtroom. He soaked up the atmospherics. At the same time, his observations brought a quick and enduring judgment about what he saw as the unseemly power of Supreme Court clerks to skew the Court's decisions. Rehnquist stewed—as he had at Harvard—about the influence of a liberal elite.

What is interesting about Rehnquist's time as a clerk is the ease with which he mixed in with the liberal crowd whose politics he obviously detested. Rehnquist disguised his condescension behind the role he adopted for himself among the clerks: the role of charming rogue. To Rehnquist's young mind, the clerks as a group harbored "extreme solicitude for the claims of communists and other criminal defendants." At a Court that already leaned to the left, Rehnquist saw the other clerks as a liberal cabal, even more so than their bosses. They were biased toward federal power at the expense of the states and had a predisposition against private enterprise. Indeed, his fellow clerks had "great sympathy toward any government regulation of business." Rehnquist disdained them.

Even so, Rehnquist developed an easy-going, fun-loving persona that seemed genuine. Jackson's archives yield a trove of photographs of a playful Rehnquist cavorting at one of the Court's fountains or kicking back with his feet propped on the desk and a cigarette in his hand. In 1953, Rehnquist went so far as to spoof the Court with irreverent lyrics to Pish-Tush's solo in Act I of Gilbert and Sullivan's *Mikado:* The justices "Bill and Hugo . . . Felix too" were "verbose and mum, and smart and dumb." Thinking his thirty-eight lyrical lines to be very clever work, Rehnquist tucked them into an envelope and proudly mailed them to Jackson, who didn't seem that impressed. The justice scribbled "No Ans" on the back and never replied.

This duality—the public mask of jollity, the brooding private man—remained the same throughout his life. As in later years when he returned to the Court as a justice, Rehnquist didn't find it difficult to ingratiate himself with his colleagues. He had a chameleon-like knack for that, so much so that, in a 1996 profile in the *New York Times Magazine,* author David J. Garrow recounted how delighted all seven of Rehnquist's colleagues were when they were interviewed by the American Bar Association in 1986 about Rehnquist's becoming chief justice.* The ABA reported that even "lowly paid" people at the Court were enthusiastic. "There was almost a unanimous feeling of joy."**

---

*Warren Burger, who was stepping down as chief justice, was not interviewed.

**In spite of their joy, there is also little doubt that every justice at some point or another was on the lash end of Rehnquist's whip as he ran the business of the Court. He could be a ferocious critic.

THE ISSUES BEFORE THE COURT themselves offered little joy. The justices were grappling with racial matters that had divided the country almost from its inception. African-Americans still faced blatant discrimination in the South and insidious discrimination everywhere. The Supreme Court had enabled this by its post–Civil War decision in *Plessy v. Ferguson,** which held that state-imposed racial segregation in public facilities was not "unreasonable."

At issue in *Plessy* was a Louisiana law requiring railroads to maintain "equal but separate accommodations for the white and colored races" and barring persons from occupying rail cars other than those to which their race had been assigned. A broad alliance of black and Creole citizens—along with the railroad officials, who objected to the additional costs of separate cars—challenged the law. But when the case came before the Court, the justices decided 7–1 that the separate-but-equal state law violated neither the 13th Amendment (abolishing slavery) nor the Equal Protection Clause of the 14th Amendment. Only Justice John Marshall Harlan raised a voice against racism, declaring that the "Constitution is color blind, and neither knows nor tolerates classes among its citizens." The decision in *Plessy* presaged an epic racial struggle that would last for generations.

By the time of Rehnquist's arrival at the Court in early 1952, the National Association for the Advancement of Colored People and its legal arm, the Legal Defense and Education Fund, had already won significant legal victories in its quest to end state-imposed racial segregation in public accommodations and education. The NAACP's effort was led by Thurgood Marshall, the great-grandson of a slave and the son of a dining-car waiter and schoolteacher. The NAACP's strategy was to build legal momentum against "Jim Crow" laws by winning victories first at the state level. Marshall's team had been at it since the mid-1930s, tearing down the segregationist laws at first brick by brick and then confronting broader challenges that took the issues into federal court.

In 1948, the federal government took Marshall's side for the first time, in an *amicus curiae* brief in *Shelley v. Kraemer.*** Marshall won that case,

*163 U.S. 537 (1896)
**334 U.S. 1 (1948)

with the Supreme Court unanimously invalidating state judicial enforcement of covenants barring people from owning or occupying property on racial grounds. Then, in 1950, two more Supreme Court decisions—*Sweatt v. Painter** and *McLaurin v. Oklahoma State Board of Regents***—invalidated the state-imposed "Jim Crow" laws as they pertained to segregated law schools (*Sweatt*) and graduate schools (*McLaurin*).

As Thurgood Marshall and the NAACP continued their campaign, pressure mounted on the Supreme Court to act. Case by case, the idea was taking hold that the NAACP's efforts could lead to substantive improvements in public education for African-Americans. But *Plessy* still endured as the law of the land. Privately, many of the justices had already concluded that *Plessy* would fall.

Into this maelstrom rode Rehnquist. He had been in Jackson's chambers for five months when the justices announced they would take the case of *Brown v. Board of Education.*†

Brown had its origins in the segregated facilities for schoolchildren in Topeka, Kansas. In *Brown,* the NAACP was laying the groundwork for a broad constitutional breakthrough against local school segregation. This was the logical next step in its strategy, since the NAACP would be building on its previous wins at the Supreme Court in *Sweatt* and *McLaurin,* the two earlier cases that struck down separate-but-equal education in public law schools and graduate schools.

Although *Brown* was already wending its way through the judicial system when the Supreme Court ruled for the NAACP in *Sweatt* and *McLaurin,* the lower-court decision in *Brown* went the other way, making *Brown* the right case to take to the High Court. A three-judge federal district panel in Kansas ruled in *Brown* that "no willful, intentional or substantial discrimination" existed in Topeka's schools. Relying on *Plessy,* the judges also found that the physical facilities in white and black schools were comparable and that the lower court's decisions in *Sweatt* and *McLaurin* applied only to graduate education. The future of *Plessy*—and of continued racial injustice in America—now was squarely on the Supreme Court's doorstep. The justices would have to decide this case.

---

*339 U.S. 629 (1950)
**339 U.S. 637 (1950)
†347 U.S. 483 (1954)

Rehnquist was opinionated about *Brown;* he had an absolute certitude about the limited scope of the Equal Protection Clause of the 14th Amendment. The reason traced back to his early days at Stanford: Fairman's long shadow was still with Rehnquist, reminding him that the amendment wasn't a free pass to apply the Bill of Rights to the states. Nothing that Rehnquist had seen or read since his early days at Stanford had caused him to doubt Fairman's understanding.

With America roiling as the country tried to come to grips with past racial injustice, other discrimination cases came in. *Brown* was not the only such case that the justices agreed to decide during their October 1952 term. Another case, *Terry v. Adams,** challenged an appeals-court ruling that effectively denied blacks the right to vote in a Texas Democratic club election that had determined every countywide race since 1889. Registered white voters were automatically members of the Jaybird Democratic Association, which held an unofficial primary to select candidates for county offices, but blacks couldn't join the club. The issue was whether the club was purposefully designed to exclude blacks from voting, in violation of the 15th Amendment.

Taken together, *Brown* and *Terry* brought into play all three of the so-called Civil War Amendments that were enacted to protect the rights of blacks. Rehnquist already staunchly believed that those amendments should be interpreted very narrowly—he thought the "founders" wanted it that way—and he was peevish about liberals such as Hugo Black who thought otherwise. Now, as a clerk who might have some influence, Rehnquist was front and center with his own opinions about *Brown* and *Terry v. Adams,* which he clambered to offer to Jackson. In a personal, conversational style, Rehnquist wrote three highly revealing, intensely opinionated memos that Jackson disregarded, but which history did not.

Rehnquist's 1952 memos put him squarely on record as an ardent segregationist. They would also later threaten his nomination to be an associate justice, and cloud his nomination to be the chief justice, until Rehnquist deflected the criticism by blaming the writing on Jackson. But that excuse—that the segregationist views were Jackson's, not Rehnquist's—carried its own obloquy for Rehnquist among the many who knew and revered Jackson. In the view of author Richard Kluger, Jackson was "a staunch libertarian

---

*345 U.S. 461 (1953)

and humanist," admired as much for his work at Nuremberg as for his principled stand *against* segregation in *Brown.* It was unthinkable that Rehnquist's writing represented the justice's views. Rehnquist's memos, and what most saw as his outright lies about them, would dog Rehnquist for the rest of his life. Those troublesome communiqués also would seal Rehnquist's lifelong antipathy toward the press—he avoided questions as long as he didn't grant interviews—and earn him at least one bitter enemy in the Senate. Rehnquist became Ted Kennedy's conservative foil.

To put his views on record about *Brown,* Rehnquist crafted a memorandum that he titled "A Random Thought on the Segregation Cases." It was a two-pager, undated but clearly written in 1952, probably between the day on which the justices heard oral arguments for the first time in the case—Tuesday, December 9—and the end of that week when the justices first met in conference to discuss it. Rehnquist divided the memo. It read like a lecture, and the first page was especially pedantic. Kluger, writing in *Simple Justice,* his epic tome about *Brown,* described the first page of Rehnquist's memo as "a gratuitous thumbnail sketch [by Rehnquist] of the Court's earlier tendency to read its own economic views into the Constitution." In Rehnquist's view, the Court's past economic interventions had failed. Now, in *Brown,* Rehnquist warned that the Court was once again mistakenly injecting itself into what were purely private matters. He spoke approvingly about the NAACP's legal foe. As Kluger put it, young Rehnquist "bemoaned the possibility of the Court's reading its own social views in the Constitution by now voting to outlaw segregation." Rehnquist wrote to Jackson:

> In these cases now before the Court, the Court is, as Davis* suggested, being asked to read its own sociological views into the Constitution. Urging a view palpably at variance with precedent and probably with legislative history, appellants seek to convince the Court of the moral wrongness of the treatment they are receiving. I would suggest that this is a question that the Court need never reach; for regardless of the Justice's individual

*John William Davis, an eminent Wall Street lawyer of his day, represented the pro-segregation side in *Brown.* Davis was the founding partner of the law firm Davis, Polk, Wardwell, Sunderland & Kiendl; he had been a congressman, solicitor general, and ambassador to Great Britain and argued more cases before the Supreme Court than any attorney up to that time.

> views on the merits of segregation, it quite clearly is not one of those extreme cases which commands intervention from one of any conviction. If this Court, because its members individually are "liberal" and dislike segregation, now chooses to strike it down, it differs from the McReynolds* court only in the kinds of litigants it favors and the kinds of special claims it protects. To those who would argue that "personal" rights are more sacrosanct than "property" rights, the short answer is that the Constitution makes no such distinction. To the argument made by Thurgood, not John, Marshall** that a majority may not deprive a minority of its constitutional right, the answer must be made that while this is sound in theory, in the long run it is the majority who will determine what the constitutional rights of the minority are. One hundred and fifty years of attempts on the part of this Court to protect minority rights of any kind—whether those of business, slaveholders, or Jehovah's Witnesses—have been sloughed off, and crept silently to rest. If the present Court is unable to profit by this example it must be prepared to see its work fade in time, too, as embodying only the sentiments of a transient majority of nine men. I realize that it is an unpopular and unhumanitarian position, for which I have been excoriated by "liberal" colleagues, but I think *Plessy v. Ferguson* was right and should be re-affirmed. . . .

Illustrative though it was of his own segregationist views, Rehnquist's memo was not a factor in the Court's consideration of *Brown.* The justices were at loggerheads, but their division was over how and when to order

---

*Rehnquist would have been quite familiar with the philosophy of James Clark McReynolds, an associate justice on the Supreme Court from 1914 to 1941. McReynolds opposed the growing social and regulatory power of government, and for a time was successful at bringing a majority to his view. He was a staunch conservative who was also rude, impatient, intolerant of women, and so anti-Semitic that he could not be civil to his Jewish brethren Louis Brandeis and Benjamin Cardozo. McReynolds led the majority that initially blocked the New Deal initiatives of Franklin D. Roosevelt, but suddenly lost his anti–New Deal majority in 1937 when Chief Justice Charles Evans Hughes switched sides and joined the liberals on the Court. Rehnquist's reference to the "McReynolds court" thus is as much a slam against Hughes as it is an acknowledgment of McReynolds's conservative sway. McReynolds kept up his opposition to the New Deal, dissenting from a decision upholding the Social Security Act by saying he could find no authority in the Constitution for the federal government to be a "public charity."

** The comparison to the great Chief Justice John Marshall, author of *Marbury v. Madison,* was an intended slam by Rehnquist against Thurgood Marshall.

relief, not whether to do so. Jackson had his own concerns. The justice wanted to end segregation, but he also had a concern about fair play: he didn't want to accuse the South of behaving unconstitutionally for all those years.

The justices went back and forth, but by the time of Rehnquist's departure in June 1953 they still hadn't decided what to do. *Brown* would have to be set over for reargument. The justices called a second round of arguments for the following October.

As the justices mulled *Brown,* Rehnquist began to sink his teeth into *Terry v. Adams,* the other important civil rights case that also was in front of the justices. Rehnquist wrote two revealing memos about *Terry* that further showed his disdain for the civil rights movement. In the first, he offered his views about whether Jackson should vote to grant *certiorari.* Rehnquist was unsympathetic to the black plaintiffs who had been excluded from voting:

> I have a hard time being detached about this case, because several of the Rodell* school of thought among the clerks began screaming as soon as they saw this that "Now we can show those damn southerners," etc. I take a dim view of this pathological search for discrimination, a la Walter White,** Black, Douglas, Rodell, etc., and as a result I now have something of a mental block against the case. For that reason, in spite of doubts as to its transcending importance in the absence of a conflict among circuits, and notwithstanding my feeling that the decision is probably right to a lawyer, rather than a crusader, I shall over-compensate and recommend a grant.

The justices did, in fact, vote to grant *certiorari,* thus enabling the Court to hear the case of the black plaintiffs. Soon, drafts of opinions in *Terry* began circulating from some of the other justices; it became clear that a majority of the justices would vote to invalidate the so-called white primary. Despite having recommended that the justices hear the case, Rehnquist now was up in arms. The young clerk certainly didn't deny that there was private discrimination in the actions of the Jaybirds, but he saw no evidence that the state was behind it. That was fatal to the case, because the majority,

---

*Fred Rodell was a Yale Law School professor and a protégé of William O. Douglas.

**Walter White headed the NAACP from 1929 to 1955 and was the moving force behind the NAACP's civil rights lawsuits.

after all, had the right to act as it wished unless the law (not the Court) said otherwise. Rehnquist thus wanted to shut the door on the black plaintiffs. His principled reaction recalled the judicial nihilism of his master's thesis at Stanford: minorities had no inherent moral (or constitutional) right to be free from discrimination.

Rehnquist fell back instinctively on his ideology. He criticized the two justices whom he saw as the leaders of the liberal majority, Black and (despite previous adulation) Frankfurter. Black, already a nemesis in Rehnquist's mind, refused to see the plain fact that there was no state-sponsored racial discrimination. He "simply assumes the whole point in issue." Frankfurter, Rehnquist continued, had marshaled "skimpy support" for any finding of discrimination. Rehnquist wrapped up his argument with a recommendation that Jackson file a dissent:

> The Constitution does not prevent the majority from banding together, nor does it attaint success in the effort.* It is about time the Court faced the fact that the white people in the South don't like the colored people; the Constitution restrains them from effecting this dislike through state action, but it most assuredly did not appoint the Court as a sociological watchdog to rear up every time private discrimination raises its admittedly ugly head. To the extent that this decision advances the frontier of state action and "social gain," it pushes back the frontier of freedom of association and majority rule. Liberals should be the first to realize, after the past 20 years, that it does not do to push blindly through towards one constitutional goal without paying attention to other equally desirable values that are being trampled on in the process.

Justice Jackson rejected Rehnquist's argument in *Terry* and in May 1953 was one of eight justices finding that blacks had been unconstitutionally denied voting rights.** Although *Brown* still awaited reargument, Jackson eschewed Rehnquist's efforts to bring him around in that case as well.

---

*"Nor does it attaint success in the effort": Used in this context, "attaint" implies dishonor or disgrace. Rehnquist saw neither in the actions of the all-white democratic club. He believed it was the majority's right to get together and decide to act in a certain way, however exclusionary that might be.

**Justice Sherman Minton was the sole dissenter.

While the Court was on summer recess and gearing up for a reprise of *Brown,* Chief Justice Fred Vinson died suddenly of a heart attack on September 8, 1953.* Vinson's replacement, Earl Warren, would be the one to lead the Court to its unanimous decision in *Brown* in 1954.

Rehnquist's memo about *Brown* did not surface until just before the 68–26 Senate vote on his nomination to the Court, in 1971. With his confirmation hearings already closed, Rehnquist was able to let the clock run out by maintaining that the segregationist views were Jackson's and then waiting to see if anyone came forward to conclusively prove otherwise. Jackson certainly wasn't going to be heard from; the justice had died suddenly in October 1954, less than five months after *Brown* came down.

But in 1984, new evidence discovered by Jackson's biographer, Professor Dennis J. Hutchinson of the University of Chicago Law School, contradicted Rehnquist's explanation. Interviewed for my *Times Magazine* profile of Rehnquist, Hutchinson told me that after inspecting all of the justice's papers from the Court—"every box, every detail"—he found no other instance during Justice Jackson's thirteen years on the Court when, as Rehnquist the Court nominee insisted happened, Jackson asked a law clerk to prepare a memo for conference discussion summarizing the justice's views. "An absurd explanation," Hutchinson concluded. Taken together, the *Brown* memo and the two *Terry* memos were conclusive proof of Rehnquist's views. They also confirmed that Rehnquist misled the Senate with his earlier explanation that the views in the *Brown* memo were Jackson's.

Adding to the weight of the evidence was a letter that Rehnquist wrote to Felix Frankfurter in 1955, the year following Jackson's death. Rehnquist offered Frankfurter a biting assessment of his former boss. Rehnquist's surprisingly harsh critique found fault with Jackson's opinions and questioned the justice's impact on the Court. The fact that Jackson had shunned Rehnquist's advice in *Brown* seemed to dismay him. But Rehnquist also recognized that he might have damaged his standing with Jackson; he never felt that he had become the justice's personal friend. Liberated by Jackson's death, Rehnquist expressed antipathy toward his old boss that scholars read as Rehnquist's disappointment with *Brown* and the Warren Court. The tone of the letter, one of sharing a confidence, was also an indication of just how charmed Rehnquist had been by Frankfurter.

---

*Vinson had written the Court's 9–0 opinions in *Sweatt* and *McLaurin.*

When I asked Rehnquist whether his views on *Brown* had changed since his days as a law clerk to Jackson, he replied warily. *Brown,* he said, now was the law of the land. "When you say that black people have to go to one school and white people the other, it is a denial of equal protection."

Had he always felt that way, though?

"You mean, from my infancy?" It was a dodge. When pressed, Rehnquist replied, "Well, I think before, there was a perfectly reasonable argument the other way."

For the first and only time in his public life, he owned up to the segregationist stance he'd taken while a law clerk.

A few weeks after the *Times Magazine* profile, I met with Justice John Paul Stevens in his chambers. Stevens was fond enough of Rehnquist on a personal level, but he had little use for his conservative judicial philosophy. He chuckled at the furor over Rehnquist's comments.

"I don't think Bill liked that article very much," Stevens said with a grin. "You sort of roughed him up a bit."

The accompanying cover photograph showed Rehnquist looking like an avenging angel, his face screwed into a frown, his black-robed arms spread like wings. A "rather grim visage of me on the front cover," he wrote his sister Jean.

SEVEN

"Like a Bunch of Old Women"

COLD WAR HYSTERIA WAS AT its height during Rehnquist's time as a clerk in the early 1950s. America was caught up in the communist-baiting hearings of Senator Joseph McCarthy, who was from Rehnquist's home state of Wisconsin. Rehnquist took the communist threat seriously. The country awaited the execution of Julius and Ethel Rosenberg, the married couple sentenced to death for smuggling atomic secrets to the Soviet Union. The Rosenbergs were arrested in 1950 by the FBI for spying. Their trial was one of the most controversial of the century. In April 1951, they were convicted in federal court and sentenced to die in the electric chair. Their last hope for mercy was the Supreme Court. But in October 1952, with Rehnquist still clerking for Jackson, the Court ruled against granting *certiorari.* The justices did not want the politically charged case.

The Rosenbergs remained on a path to execution. But Rehnquist grew impatient as the Rosenbergs' case wound its way through a seven-months-long process of further appeals that ultimately led right back to the Supreme Court. The fuse on the Rosenbergs' case actually was quite short by the standards of today's death-penalty cases. But as four execution dates came and went, Rehnquist couldn't see the point of delaying.

By the time the Court was due to adjourn on June 15, 1953, Rehnquist had packed his car and would be on his way west.* A law practice awaited in Phoenix, as did a wedding to Nan in San Diego.**

As a result he missed the dramatic development that took place on the last Friday of the Court's term: with the Rosenbergs' execution imminent, an application for a stay of execution was presented to the Court by the couple's lawyers. Jackson was the circuit justice in charge, and when the Supreme Court clerk presented it to Jackson he referred the petition to the full Court with the recommendation that an oral argument be heard. With all eyes now on the Court, a drama was rapidly unfolding.

The justices gathered at the Court on the following Monday, June 15, the last official day of the Court's term. But a majority of the justices, still anxious to avoid a case that was more ideological than legal, opposed hearing the petition, and so it appeared once again that the Rosenbergs were out of time, and out of luck.

The next day, Justice Douglas, the liberal firebrand who was known to follow his own iconoclastic instincts, suddenly jumped into the fray. Douglas, who along with Black and Frankfurter opposed executing the Rosenbergs, issued a stay of their death sentence based upon an obscure procedural technicality. Whether the majority liked it or not, the justices would have to entertain the doubts that Douglas now raised. The justices held a special session two days later, Thursday, June 18, hearing several hours of arguments from the lawyers for both sides and then huddling in their private conference. But Douglas could not muster the votes to prevent their execution, and the justices vacated the stay on June 19. In the heat of the moment, Douglas created for posterity a picture of himself as the solitary crusader, standing up for the Rosenbergs "in an atmosphere in which the barbarity of capital punishment coalesced with the hysteria of anti-Communism." The Rosenbergs were executed that evening at Sing Sing Prison in Ossining, New York†—before Friday sundown, so as not to offend their Jewish heritage.

---

*The fact that Rehnquist had already departed the Court is inferred from a subsequent letter he wrote to Jackson. The undated letter, written soon after the Rosenbergs were executed, makes it clear that he was not present when the end-of-term fireworks over the Rosenberg case erupted at the Court.

**Bill Rehnquist and Nan Cornell were married in San Diego on Saturday, August 29, 1953.

†The federal Bureau of Prisons did not have an electric chair, so the one at Sing Sing state prison was used.

Thus did Douglas force the Court to go on record about the Rosenbergs' case. Soon after the execution, the justices did what the majority had been trying to avoid and finally issued a short opinion that put them on record about the case.* Chief Justice Vinson read it from the bench, and individual justices who wanted to be heard also filed their own concurring and dissenting opinions. Jackson's concurrence focused on procedural issues and the inappropriateness of the Court's hearing the last-minute appeal rather than on "the wisdom or appropriateness to this case of a death sentence." Jackson dodged the whole emotional issue by simply noting that, in the case of these two convicted spies, the death sentence was "permitted by law and, as was previously pointed out, is therefore not within this Court's power of revision."

Word of the justices' opinion, and of the Rosenberg's execution on the same day that the stay was vacated, reached Rehnquist as he was on his way to set up his law practice in Phoenix. Rehnquist was elated—not just because of the quick end for the Rosenbergs but also because Jackson focused his opinion on the procedural elements of the case rather than dwelling on the execution. When Rehnquist arrived in Phoenix, he wrote back to Jackson:

> I wanted to write as soon as I could, and tell you how much I admired the opinion that you wrote on that occasion. The point you stressed was one—perhaps *the* one—that was bothering every lawyer in the country, and yet it really took some guts to write an opinion on this lawyer's point, and subject yourself to the inevitable maudlin outcry about "technicalities" when "human life is involved." I think it was fitting that your opinion should have been written by the one whom many lawyers to whom I have talked consider to be the only lawyer on the Court.

**Rosenberg v. United States,* 346 U.S. 273 (1953). Even though the Rosenbergs' death sentence had already been carried out, Vinson's opinion "recited the history of this unusual case at length because we think a full recitation is necessary to a proper understanding of the decision rendered." The opinion discussed "two questions of power": whether Douglas had the power to issue the stay (the answer was yes), and whether—and why—the Court had the power to quickly dispose of the procedural question that was Douglas's basis for the stay, instead of sending it back to the lower courts. "The Court has the responsibility to supervise the administration of criminal justice by the federal judiciary. This includes the duty to see that the laws are not only enforced by fair proceedings, but also that the punishments prescribed by the laws are enforced with a reasonable degree of promptness and certainty. The stay which had been issued promised many more months of litigation in a case which had otherwise run its full course."

> In my opinion, the Rosenberg case had dragged on too long as it did, and only by ending the way it did was the Court's position saved from a sharp drop in the public eye. Sometimes one has to get away from Washington to know what average Americans think; I must have talked about the case with more than fifty people in the Midwest and on my way here, and of these only one did not wholeheartedly approve of what the court did. Capital punishment is essentially a legislative decision, and certainly there are good arguments against it. But once the decision is made, the courts must accept it the same way they do other legislative decisions. Every condemned man deserves the right to a careful hearing and review through the orthodox channels, but this does not mean that the highest court of the nation must behave like a bunch of old women every time they encounter the death penalty. I think there is no doubt but what the average state court does a better job with a run of the mill capital case than the federal judiciary, particularly the Supreme Ct [*sic*], did with the Rosenbergs. This is because they regard the death penalty as differing, if at all, only in degree, from other important legislative decisions which they are bound to enforce.

Rehnquist told Jackson that he was thinking about writing an article for the *Stanford Law Review* about the Rosenberg case. Rehnquist would focus on the procedural tactics used by the lawyers to delay the execution. He wondered what Jackson thought about that idea. Jackson told him to go right ahead, but "I cannot guarantee against criticism as a result of it." Rehnquist changed his mind. Instead of writing about the contemporary death-penalty case that absorbed America, he found a new subject that captivated him.

EIGHT

Hanging Judge

ALTHOUGH TWENTY-EIGHT-YEAR-OLD Bill Rehnquist was anxious to get to Phoenix, along the way he made time for a week-long detour to Ft. Smith, Arkansas, a frontier town on the border with Oklahoma. Rehnquist had an idea for a book, and he stopped off to do some research. The object of his fancy—and admiration—was Judge Isaac Parker, the infamous "hanging judge" who had carried out more death sentences, more quickly, than anyone else in American history. Rehnquist stumbled upon Parker's record while researching an opinion for Jackson. Rehnquist learned that Parker was a respected lawyer from St. Joseph, Missouri, who had served with distinction as a city attorney, county prosecutor, and state judge. Parker had even been elected to two terms in Congress—all this by the age of thirty-seven, whereupon in May of that year President Grant named Parker to be the US District Judge for the Western District of Arkansas.

In the thrall of what Rehnquist called this "fascinating minutiae," he decided to do some freelance research. Rehnquist wanted evidence that the swifter a sentence was carried out, the greater was its deterrent value. And Parker's hangings were swift indeed.

Parker meted out 172 death sentences as a federal judge in the Western District of Arkansas from 1875 until 1896. For fifteen of those years, until an act of Congress in 1891, no right of appeal was authorized. The absence of appeal rights was a legal fluke that had to do with the unique geography of Parker's district. His jurisdiction included the vast Indian Territory that comprised almost all of what would later become the state of Oklahoma; with no court available to try most criminal cases, the job fell by default to Parker. And when Congress established Parker's jurisdiction, it failed to provide an appeal process until fifteen years after Parker arrived in the territory. Until 1891, not even the Supreme Court could hear an appeal from one of Parker's sentences. Parker was judge, jury, and the final appeal in a lawless territory that, according to Rehnquist, was peopled following the Civil War by "fugitives, desperadoes and ne'er-do-wells." After Supreme Court review was instituted, Parker complained that many of his sentences were overturned on technicalities—an opinion with which Rehnquist agreed.

In all, Judge Parker sent 88 men to their deaths on the gallows—including a group of 6 killers who were hanged on the same September day four months after he took up his gavel. (Parker originally intended an 8-man hanging, but one man was killed while trying to escape and another had his sentence commuted because of his youth.) Among the 172 whom he condemned, some avoided the noose by dying in jail, or being killed while trying to escape. Others received a presidential reprieve—their last and only option given the absence of judicial review.

When it came to Parker, Rehnquist could only marvel at the speed and certainty with which he carried out his sentences. How had Parker done it? What lessons could the "bunch of old women" on the Court, slowed by liberal clerks and their own posturing, take away? Phoenix could wait. Holed up in Ft. Smith in the early summer, Rehnquist aimed to get some answers. He pawed through newspaper morgues to look at old clippings, and went through what court records he could find.

Rehnquist found one Ft. Smith newspaper editorial, praising the hanging judge's first year in office, that captured Rehnquist's own views: "The certainty of punishment is the only sure preventive of crime."

Rehnquist never got around to writing the book—too many knockoffs soon were flooding the market, he later said, with lurid titles like *Hell on the Border: He Hanged 88 Men, Hanging Judge,* and *He Hanged Them High: An Authentic Account of the Fanatical Judge Who Hanged 88 Men.* But Rehnquist never lost his admiration of Parker. Years later he still was a believer: "Judge Parker's trials were swift, and there was no appeal, but the fundamentals of due process were undoubtedly present."

Rehnquist returned to Parker's hanging grounds, and to the topic of his research, in 1983 during a speech at the University of Arkansas. He chose this subject and this venue because he still had some things he wanted to say about the weight of the evidence when it came to Parker's hangings. For those who might still be skeptical about the deterrent value of Parker's swift sentences, Rehnquist delved further into the historical record, sharing some interesting reports about vigilante justice during the San Francisco gold rush. Rehnquist spoke in defense of vigilance committees, although any historian of Rehnquist's repute surely also would have known of their considerable abuse in the South, promoting racial hatred and injustice.

"I think it important to recall the history of vigilante justice in our own country," Rehnquist said. "Vigilante," he reminded his audience, came from the Spanish word for watchman or guard. Vigilante groups weren't "mere lynch mobs"; rather, they often were the only law around, and so they constituted "improvised courts" that maintained law and order in the mining camps. "The trials were always swift and informal. Because there were no jails, penalties were usually limited to banishment, whipping, or hanging." After the San Francisco vigilance committee's creation, "many criminals left the city. Others were banished on threat of hanging." Vigilantism was working.

But when the committee went out of existence a few years after the Gold Rush began, unrest came surging back. Crime and corruption were again rampant. "When one machine politician murdered a U.S. marshal and then 'fixed' the ensuing legal proceedings, and another murdered a newspaper publisher, the committee rebounded with a double hanging. It remained in action for three months, during which there were only two murders in San Francisco, as compared with more than one hundred during the six months before the committee was formed. Desperadoes were hanged or deported until a semblance of order was restored. . . .

"The Gold Rush experience was by no means unique. 'Prairie necktie parties' were common throughout the western territories, where a horse thief was considered as bad as, if not worse than, a murderer and where formal justice was ineffective if not nonexistent. The work of these vigilantes made orderly settlement possible and paved the way for effective courts and enforcement agencies."

The speech was raw Rehnquist—bitter, biting. It would have been hard to imagine hearing such trenchant comments from the more statesmanlike, and in some ways diminished, persona that Rehnquist showed to the public after he became chief justice in 1986. Indeed, the speech cannot be found in Rehnquist's papers at Stanford, nor is it available from the Supreme Court's online archive.

It was evidence that in 1983, when Rehnquist was at the top of his elocutionary game, he showed little if any evolution in his views since Stanford. It also illustrated the formative—and *negative*—effect of his Supreme Court clerkship.

The blunt remarks harkened back to the young Rehnquist, who was frustrated by process and what seemed to be the red tape of *habeas corpus** petitions. What some called procedural fairness during the Rosenberg trial, Rehnquist saw as an unjustified "collateral attack" by the couple's lawyers. Taking his place on the Supreme Court less than two decades after coming to his epiphany about the hanging judge, Rehnquist still chafed about what he saw as excessive appeals in criminal cases. To Rehnquist, the swift, sure justice of the old-fashioned vigilance committees raised a question for the contemporary criminal justice system: "At what point should there be finality?" Rehnquist was resolute that offenders should be punished without unreasonable delays, and in his speech about the hanging judge he spoke out about a recent Supreme Court case to give his argument a human face.

The case involved a man named Jimmy Lee Gray, who was an unredeemed murderer by every account. The Supreme Court had denied Gray's last-minute appeal by a 6–3 vote, whereupon he was executed by the state of Mississippi in its gas chamber exactly three weeks before Rehnquist's speech in Ft. Smith. The execution had gone badly—so much so that the warden expelled all the witnesses midway through it. But Rehnquist was not concerned about that. He was, instead, appalled at the procedural safeguards that had allowed the case to drag on to that point. Gray had, after all, "abducted a three-year-old girl, carried her to a remote area, and after sexually molesting her, suffocated her in a muddy ditch and threw her body

*The writ of *habeas corpus*—literally, Latin for "you have the body"— has its origins in the Magna Carta as a remedy against the Crown. The writ allows a judge to inquire into the legality of any form of loss of personal liberty. There is no statute of limitations on the writ and, historically, no limit on the number of times it may be sought (although this was changed as to federal courts in 1996). In essence, the writ orders the person who is responsible for the detention—for example, the warden or jailer—to produce the petitioner (i.e., the *body*) quickly, in court, so that a judge may decide the lawfulness of the detention.

into a stream." That was seven years earlier. Since then Gray had been found guilty by a jury, sentenced to death, granted a new trial, found guilty, and sentenced to death again.

"One might think the case would end there. But, Rehnquist fumed, "as anyone familiar with modern *habeas* procedures will know, there followed a series of collateral attacks on both the conviction and sentence that lasted over three years." Rehnquist counted up eighty-two separate judicial reviews for Gray, by twenty-six different state and federal judges. "And in none of those proceedings was the guilt of Jimmy Lee Gray ever called into question."

Rehnquist decried "interminable delays in the criminal justice process, or final decisions, issued many years after the initial trial that set free a criminal defendant for reasons other than doubt about his established guilt. Such spectacles are equally unpalatable to many members of society. . . . The view that our system of criminal justice exists merely to safeguard the rights of the defendant, whatever the cost in delaying or frustrating justice, is equally one-sided and ultimately, I think, equally dangerous. . . . A breakdown in the criminal justice system leads eventually to a state of anarchy, and no society will long tolerate anarchy."

Rehnquist's full-throated oratory about the hanging judge and the road to anarchy went to an extreme, but his intolerant views on procedural delays in criminal cases and his desire to grease the skids for imposing swift punishment were constant almost from the instant he arrived at the Court. Whether it was opinion writing, running the Court, or operating the machinery of death, Rehnquist was all about efficiency: getting on with things, not wasting time.

As an associate justice, Rehnquist was a quick worker who shunned the customary long bench memos from his clerks in favor of short, brisk walks where cases could be discussed and issues pinpointed, and he demanded the same measure of alacrity from his clerks: first drafts of opinions had to be completed in ten days. "He likes to get his work done and get home," explained a former clerk, Ronald L. Blunt. A penny-pincher, Rehnquist for a long time drove a blue Volkswagen Rabbit to the Court from his Virginia home, arriving by 9 A.M. and leaving most days by 3 P.M.*

---

*In 1986 he traded in the Rabbit but not his work schedule. Rehnquist bought a new crimson-colored VW Jetta that, he said, had a lot more "pep." Wife Nan thought "it is turning me into a hot-rodder, but I will try to restrain myself."

Once he became the chief, Rehnquist imposed his pace on the others. He wrote a memo to his colleagues in 1989 reminding them that "the principal rule I have followed in assigning opinions is to give everyone approximately the same number of assignments of opinions for the Court during any one term." But, as David Garrow described things in the *New York Times Magazine* in 1996, Rehnquist warned that he would look less favorably on any justice who failed to circulate a first draft of a majority opinion within four weeks or who failed to circulate the first draft of an anticipated dissent within four weeks of the majority opinion. There were other nitpicking caveats as well. "It only makes sense," Rehnquist asserted in his memo, "to give some preference to those who are 'current' with respect to past work." When Justice Stevens complained about the rigid deadlines, Rehnquist responded by chiding those justices who continued to run late. "I suggest we make a genuine effort to get these cases down 'with all deliberate speed.'"

And how far back could one trace Rehnquist's definition of "deliberate speed"? Among Jackson's papers, wrote author Garrow, was another Rehnquist memo, in *another* Brown case, this one called *Brown v. Allen.** The Court's decision in that case marked the beginning of an expansive view of federal *habeas corpus* jurisdiction—but even in his clerkship days Rehnquist was arguing *against* expansion. Rehnquist the clerk wanted to keep state criminal defendants out of the federal courts altogether unless they were denied the right to counsel. He thought the line had to be drawn somewhere.

Rehnquist reiterated his views two decades later, chastising the majority and leading the four new Nixon appointees in dissent when the Court in 1972 invalidated the death penalty in *Furman v. Georgia.*** Rehnquist was shocked that the majority would strike down "a penalty that our nation's legislators have thought necessary since our country was founded" and that covered crimes as diverse as "murder, piracy, mutiny, hijacking, and desertion in the face of the enemy." The laws of forty state legislatures were "consign[ed] to the limbo of unconstitutionality. . . . How can government by the elected representatives of the people coexist with the power of the federal judiciary, whose members are constitutionally insulated from respon-

*344 U.S. 443 (1953)
**408 U.S. 238 (1972)

siveness to the popular will? . . ." A further four years later, with two justices switching sides, Rehnquist found himself in the majority when the Court reinstated the death penalty in *Gregg v. Georgia.*[*] In 1987, with Rehnquist now the new chief justice, the Court closed off yet another line of attack on the death penalty when it ruled, 5–4, in *McCleskey v. Kemp*[**] that even solid statistical evidence of a pervasive racial bias in capital cases did not violate the Constitution. In *McCleskey,* the Court came within a vote of making a fundamental change in the capital justice system. It would get no closer.[†]

But death-row prisoners still could file petition after petition for *habeas corpus* review, thus delaying their execution for years. So Rehnquist focused on shutting down that avenue. And finally, as a seventy-two-year-old chief justice, Rehnquist got most of what he wanted.

In 1996, Congress enacted a law called the Antiterrorism and Effective Death Penalty Act, and President Bill Clinton signed it. The law was clear, and it was also simple in its intended effect. Henceforth, *habeas* petitions would be one and done, in order to speed up executions. Criminals could have one free bite of the apple, but *only* one. There was no right to a second *habeas* hearing.

When the first test of the new law came, the case was once again from Georgia. Time was finally running out for a criminal named Ellis Wayne Felker. Felker had already done time for aggravated sodomy and had been on death row for thirteen years for the brutal rape and murder of a cocktail waitress in 1981; he was a master at using *habeas* writs but now faced imminent execution because the new law ended his *habeas* appeals. Felker's lawyers challenged the constitutionality of the aptly named Effective Death Penalty Act, and less than twenty-four hours later the Supreme Court took

---

*428 U.S. 153 (1976)

**481 U.S. 279 (1987)

† In *McCleskey,* another *habeas* case from Georgia, the Court accepted the validity of a study prepared by David C. Baldus of the University of Iowa Law School and two colleagues, Charles Pulaski and George Woodworth. Their study of two thousand murder cases in Georgia controlled for 230 variables and proved that people accused of killing white victims—as was Warren McCleskey—were four times as likely to be sentenced to death as those accused of killing black victims. Justice Lewis Powell wrote the hair-splitting majority opinion that said the Baldus study "offered no evidence specific to [McCleskey's] own case" and was therefore irrelevant, regardless of its validity. In 1991, after he retired, Powell was asked by his biographer whether there was any vote he would have liked to change. "Yes," replied Powell. "*McCleskey v. Kemp.*"

the test case. The justices convened a rare special session at the end of their term. It was the first such session since the Pentagon Papers case* a quarter-century earlier, a clear indication of the important message the justices wanted to send. And send it they did. Rehnquist quickly produced a unanimous opinion in *Felker v. Turpin*** that affirmed the constitutionality of the law and spelled the end of Felker's appeals. "Not long after Ellis Wayne Felker finally goes to the electric chair," author Garrow predicted, "the entire pace of death-row executions all across America will pick up speed as one *habeas* petition after another is quickly cast aside by the courts. Rehnquist's victory may not yet be 100 percent complete; his triumph nonetheless is remarkably impressive and still growing."

Felker went to Georgia's electric chair less than five months later. And the number of executions did, indeed, jump as predicted. By Rehnquist's reckoning, things were looking up. Execution rates in the ten years following Rehnquist's opinion in *Felker* never fell back to pre-1996 rates; in some years there were twice as many executions as before *Felker.*

Examining the continuum of his tenure at the Court, one would find it all too easy to see Rehnquist's continuing admiration of Hanging Judge Parker. Rehnquist undoubtedly saw himself in the same mold, getting the job done to keep order among the lawless. Swift imposition of the death penalty was what Rehnquist wanted, but there was more to Rehnquist's philosophy than mere blood lust. Rehnquist had a philosophical problem with the inefficiency of the entire legal process, and he used the intent of the founders as his excuse to add giddy-up to the system. This wasn't just about life or death; it was really about cutting red tape in all its forms. Hastening judgment day.

While he was on the Court, Rehnquist didn't keep a diary, seldom gave interviews, and didn't feel any compunction to explain himself, so it was hard to know whether his restiveness bespoke some perverse commitment to principle or just a profound lack of empathy. But his harsh pronouncements led some to wonder. During Rehnquist's confirmation battle for chief justice, Nat Hentoff, the celebrated writer for the *Village Voice,* was bewildered that Rehnquist could be warmly regarded by friends and family,

---

**New York Times Co. v. U.S.,* 403 U.S. 713 (1971)

**518 U.S. 651 (1996)

yet "often appeared to be remarkably mean spirited, more so perhaps than any member of the modern court. It is as if those he cannot see—in places remote from the majesty of the Court—are not fully human." Rehnquist wanted "corpses . . . to pile up at an ever more spirited rate." Hentoff doubted that Rehnquist's views were fundamentally about ideology. After all, not every staunch conservative thought like Rehnquist. Rather, Hentoff reasoned, Rehnquist was just wired that way, with a cold heart. "This has less to do with ideology than with the very nature of the nominee."

I wondered about that, too. During interviews with Rehnquist, I made a point to ask whether there was *any* punishment that he considered to be cruel and unusual.

Rehnquist said nothing for a full fourteen seconds. He professed to be searching his memory for some "decided cases" that predated his time on the Court. "I'm simply not going to get into a dialogue about different kinds of punishments and whether I think, shooting from the hip, they are or are not cruel and unusual." Finally he came up with an unexpected example—from a 1910 case.* The punishment Rehnquist considered cruel and unusual, "and rightly so": hard labor while in chains.

I asked him whether death, in itself, wasn't cruel and unusual. Was it just the manner in which it was being done?

"Yeah."

Whatever the reason, throughout his career Rehnquist remained true to his beliefs and transparent in his intentions when it came to hastening the verdict and speeding the executioner. He put his impatience on display and proffered solutions that ranged from prosaic to extreme. Rehnquist had high praise for the British practice of allowing few appeals from trial-court judgments in criminal cases, and of punishing those whose appeals are later deemed frivolous. Due process was important, he said, but society's "moral judgments of its members" must also be vindicated. He made the bold suggestion that the automatic right of appeal be ended in federal civil cases.

Rehnquist liked to reminisce about his early days practicing law in Phoenix. Times were different then. The only federal judge was an FDR appointee named Dave Ling. Rehnquist recalled that Ling closed his courtroom between late June and Labor Day, which meant "Phoenix functioned

---

* *Weems v. U.S.*, 217 U.S. 349 (1910)

without a federal judge during the summer months, and somehow got along very well." In Ling's twenty-five years on the bench, Rehnquist didn't think the man ever wrote an opinion or had a law clerk. "I screwed up my courage one day and asked him why he never wrote any opinions. His response was, 'If you want an opinion in your case, you take it to the Ninth Circuit.* That's what they're there for.'"

*This is the federal appeals court whose jurisdiction includes Arizona.

NINE

Rugged Libertarianism

THERE WERE FOUR HUNDRED LAWYERS in all of Maricopa County, Arizona, when Rehnquist arrived there in July 1953. Phoenix was still a sweltering cow town—literally. Cattle grazed thirty blocks from the city center; on summer days the temperature soared well above 100 degrees. More than half the streets were unpaved. Rehnquist had no friends and knew exactly one person in town, a law school classmate named Fred Steiner.

Rehnquist delighted in telling the story of his improbable decision to move there. Rehnquist had one version. His onetime clerk and future chief justice, John Roberts, told a slightly different one. Reporters rewrote and further embellished the saga. The story evolved, but basically it went like this in the simplest telling by Rehnquist: He hated the Milwaukee winters and early on found his preferred climate first in Casablanca and later at Stanford; Phoenix was a logical choice.

Roberts added some grace notes to the legend, claiming that Rehnquist used his clout as Jackson's clerk to order an analysis from the Library of Congress as to which cities received the most sun over the course of a year. Tampa was first, but too humid. Albuquerque was second, but had too much old money; it would be hard to break into the legal ranks there.

Phoenix came in third, and bingo.* Stories like that, whether true or not, were a way to soften Rehnquist's serious mien and give weight to his reputation as the impish rogue.

The *New York Times* gave the story yet another hoary spin, writing in 1971 that Rehnquist had actually flipped a coin to make his decision. Rehnquist obviously got a kick out of describing, and hearing others recount, how he arrived in Phoenix seemingly out of the vapor. But despite the constant telling, nobody got the missing link that the very private Rehnquist kept for himself: his future wife Nan grew up in Phoenix. Rehnquist's choice might have seemed "nonconventional," as Roberts put it—after all, there were not many Supreme Court clerks gravitating to Phoenix—but in fact it was utterly normal: he went to live in his in-laws' hometown.

The law firm that Rehnquist joined was also predictable. The firm of Evans, Kitchel & Jenckes was one of Phoenix's biggest—with nine lawyers, counting Rehnquist, on the eighth floor of the Title & Trust Building that also housed most of the city's other firms. The name partner was Denison Kitchel, a forty-five-year-old Harvard Law School grad with a connection to Felix Frankfurter; the justice had been one of Kitchel's professors at Harvard.

Rehnquist added a coda to his story about moving to Phoenix, and it had to do with Frankfurter. According to Rehnquist, the elder justice, seventy years old at the time, had come to Rehnquist's engagement reception in Washington, DC, learned of his plans to move to Phoenix, and urged him to get into politics there. Rehnquist was surprised when Frankfurter told him he was familiar with Kitchel's law firm. In time, Frankfurter's counseling Rehnquist that conservatives as well as liberals ought to be active on the political scene became another part of the legend.

Superficially, at least, Kitchel, sixteen years his elder, seemed to be of like mind with Rehnquist. When Herman Obermayer, Rehnquist's close friend in later years, wrote a memoir about his late pal, Obermayer described the affinity between Rehnquist and Kitchel: both men gravitated to the nascent conservative movement being formed around Barry Goldwater in Phoenix—but for very different reasons. Kitchel relished being the backroom power broker, while Rehnquist was the ideological purist. Each used the other to advance his respective ends.

---

*In a letter to Jackson even before his clerkship began, Rehnquist listed Phoenix and Albuquerque as his top choices, so Roberts's story may be apocryphal.

In retrospect, it made sense that Rehnquist and Kitchel found each other. "Bill's appearance on the national scene can be traced directly to an obscure political machine in the Sun Belt city of Phoenix, Arizona," wrote Obermayer. "For one brief shining moment, Barry Goldwater made Phoenix an important gathering place for politically conservative intellectuals. Luck put Bill in the right place at the right time." Kitchel's connections "gave Bill political access he had never dreamed of," added Obermayer. "Barry Goldwater was his philosophical soul mate."

Kitchel was fresh from running the conservative upstart Goldwater's successful US Senate campaign in 1952, the year Republican Dwight Eisenhower gained the White House. Goldwater was a department store executive and a freshman member of the Phoenix City Council, totally unknown outside of his hometown. But with Kitchel guiding his campaign on Eisenhower's coattails, Goldwater won a squeaker and became Arizona's first Republican senator in a generation. Kitchel became Goldwater's confidant, lawyer, and political mentor, shrewdly pushing the right-of-center Goldwater onto the national scene. Soon he was a conservative icon.

Kitchel had all of the connections and polish that Bill Rehnquist lacked: he was educated at St. Paul's, Yale, and Harvard Law; son of a prestigious Wall Street lawyer; and married to a glamorous heiress. Kitchel sensed Goldwater's charisma and began grooming him to craft a new path for conservatives, one that was far to the right of the party's mainstream.

Over the course of a decade, Kitchel and Goldwater leveraged their brand of rugged libertarianism to gain control of the Republican Party but then quickly lost it with Goldwater's landslide defeat for president in 1964 by Lyndon Johnson. Goldwater's loss pushed the GOP away from the Arizona machine's conservative dogmatism and back into the hands of the mainstream, led by the opportunist Richard Nixon who had been Eisenhower's vice president. But in 1953, Rehnquist's timing couldn't have been better. Getting close to Kitchel was just a stroke of luck; he opened the door to a new world of right-wing fellow travelers.

Rehnquist and his bride moved into a small tract home at 2628 East Earll Drive. The young lawyer earned $300 a month with Kitchel, half of what he would have made if he'd taken a job in a big firm in Washington or New York. It was a rough summer. Rehnquist tried and failed to get Kitchel to raise his salary by $50 a month (the clerkship didn't carry much weight in Phoenix), he wasn't yet admitted to the bar, he didn't have clients, and during those first months he didn't have much to do. When the work finally did start coming, it wasn't exactly the kind that Rehnquist desired. He wanted to get into the courtroom. That would come, but first there were some gun-slinging Republicans to get to know better.

In Obermayer's telling, Rehnquist played the conservative purist to Kitchel's pragmatist. Both men had strong personalities and used the nascent conservative movement, and each other, to build clout. But the big egos clashed. "Bill was much too ambitious and independent to remain the protégé of a domineering intellectual for long." The two men had a falling out and Rehnquist resigned to work for a competitor. There was a bitter, and lasting, estrangement. Even though both men carried on with the Arizona Republicans, the two barely spoke for the remaining forty-plus years. Rehnquist wrote Kitchel out of his life and didn't talk about him.

Rehnquist bounced from one firm to another, always in the Title & Trust Building, until in 1960 he moved in with a liberal Democrat, James Powers, to form the two-man firm of Powers & Rehnquist. They were an odd couple. Powers was another of the Harvard Law crowd, typically not Rehnquist's cup of tea. But Powers also displayed a bit of the dilettante, including an affectation for writing fiction, and Rehnquist obviously took to his opposite. The two often lunched together, and Powers noticed something: Rehnquist made right-wing views sound so reasonable that others like Powers could be lulled into agreement. "It was a revelation to talk to someone [conservative] who had thought out positions, knew history and political science," Powers recalled. "It was the first time it had occurred to me that [conservative ideas] make some sense." Rehnquist hit on a winning formula, and the partnership prospered in part because of his liberal counterpart. Instead of being repelled by Rehnquist's extremism, clients were attracted by the bipartisanship. Bill and Nan Rehnquist settled into an agreeable life in Ozzie and Harrietville. There were three babies in the space of four years—James in 1955, Janet in 1957, and Nancy in 1959. The family moved up the economic ladder and into a spacious home at 1617 Palmcroft Drive, in one of Phoenix's best neighborhoods.* Nan joined the

*Before moving to the Palmcroft home in 1961, the Rehnquists in 1954 built a small tract home at 1635 East Rovey Ave. Rehnquist wrote Justice Jackson on April 26, 1954, that "we have also gotten a forest service summer home lot in a drawing recently held; it is up in the high country about one hundred miles from here. I am getting to feel quite settled and domestic. If you ever decide to join your friend William O. in an Arizona winter vacation, be sure and stop and see us in Phoenix."

Phoenix Junior League, engaging in social service with the white-glove set. Arizona was booming and Rehnquist rode the wave. By 1969, Rehnquist's Arizona investments included a ranch and building lots in Yavapai County, land in Apache County, and commercial property in Maricopa County; a farm in Delta County, Colorado; and a diversified portfolio of stocks.

But what was unusual about Rehnquist was how he compartmentalized his different lives—family, professional, political. At home Rehnquist played the proud (if sometimes stern) patriarch and provider, bestowing fond nicknames on his wife and kids. (Son Jim was "Weakfish." Daughters Janet and Nancy were "Foozy" and "Bombna." Sister Jean was "Feebelia.") But he could be harsh and unyielding in his public persona. Those very different public and private faces, limned so clearly by the time Rehnquist reached the Supreme Court, first became evident in Phoenix.

TEN

"What the Court Really Needs Is a Chief Justice"

REHNQUIST WAS STILL SETTLING into Kitchel's law firm in the spring of 1954 when Justice Jackson, for whom he clerked the previous year, suffered a heart attack. Jackson had just turned sixty-two years old. The justice's infirmity—he would be hospitalized for two months—was only the latest in a succession of events that shook the Court in the midst of its ongoing debate about *Brown.* The previous September, after the death of Chief Justice Vinson, also suddenly of a heart attack, newly elected President Eisenhower gave the chief justiceship to Earl Warren, the California governor (and, before that, the state's attorney general) who had run unsuccessfully for vice president in 1948 on the Republican ticket. Warren's claim to the center chair was tenuous at first because he had only a recess appointment from Eisenhower; Congress didn't confirm Warren until

March 1 of the following year. So it fell to Warren to unite the Court on *Brown,* even though his leadership hadn't been legitimized by Congress.* To young Rehnquist, now almost thirty years old and still with Kitchel, Warren seemed a political hack whose claim to the job was suspect—and he didn't mind saying so.

On April 26, 1954, the ex-clerk wrote what would be his last letter to his former boss Jackson, now laid up in the hospital. The letter** carried news about Rehnquist's passing the bar in March 1954 and his nascent career of writing briefs and motions and some "suggested amendments to Taft-Hartley."† But as usual the missive was more interesting for the opinions Rehnquist expressed, in a breezy style of faux familiarity that didn't evoke a reply from Jackson. Rehnquist touched the usual bases—giving kudos to his former boss for some *habeas* dissents (as if Jackson would be surprised!) and for a dissent in an obscure maritime law case called *Pope &*

---

*Professor Mark Tushnet of Georgetown University provides a cogent explanation of the leadership role that Warren actually played: "There's some controversy among historians about what was actually going on inside the Court [leading up to the *Brown* decision]. Some people think, based on their reading of the documents, that in the first go-round [1953] the Court was very closely divided. At the time, the Chief Justice was Fred Vinson, who was from Kentucky. He was not an ardent integrationist by any means. Stanley Reed, who was also from Kentucky, was actually a segregationist. Felix Frankfurter was ambivalent about whether the Constitution could be interpreted to outlaw segregation. Robert Jackson had similar views. I think that if they'd been forced to take a vote the first time around there would have been a majority to overrule *Plessy* and to strike segregation down, but no one was forcing them to take a vote. Vinson, who was the leader of the Court, was not going to do it. So they had this discussion and it was inconclusive. Frankfurter couldn't figure out how to do what he wanted to do, so he proposed that the cases be reargued. Over the summer, between the first argument and the re-argument, Vinson died. Eisenhower had promised to appoint [California Governor Earl Warren] to the first vacancy that opened on the Supreme Court. Eisenhower didn't expect the first vacancy to be the Chief Justice and he tried to sort of say to Warren, 'Well, I didn't really promise this to you,' but Warren held him to the promise, and became Chief Justice. Warren was vigorously in favor of overruling *Plessy,* or at least finding school segregation unconstitutional, and when he got to the Court that sort of tipped the balance decisively. Once you had a majority in favor of it, the people who had been reluctant lost their ambivalence and signed on: Frankfurter rather easily. . . . Jackson played around with writing separate opinions and couldn't write one that he found satisfactory, so he eventually signed on. At the very end, Earl Warren went to Stanley Reed and said to him, 'Stanley, look, eight of us are going to find segregation unconstitutional. It would be a terrible thing for this country for there to be a dissent on this question, so if you're a true patriot you will join us in [supporting the decision].' And Reed agreed, and so the decision was unanimous."

**A notation indicates it was hand-delivered, probably via the US attorney's office in Phoenix.

†Taft-Hartley is a federal law governing the activities and power of labor unions.

*Talbot v. Hawn.** The young lawyer wondered aloud about a relatively benign labor decision that Jackson had authored, *Garner v. Teamsters.*** But those comments were just a prelude to expressing what he really had on his mind. Rehnquist had fixed his opinion about the new chief justice, and he was characteristically outspoken in his intolerance of what he viewed as an inferior intellect. He also thought "most everyone" agreed with him. The fact that Rehnquist so cavalierly dismissed Warren after he had authored a mere four opinions† betokened, in the extreme, both naiveté and arrogance. Rehnquist's letter revealed a young man whose worldview was firmly set and whose ego didn't allow for self-doubt. It presaged a period of intense activism in Phoenix by a man so sure of himself that there could be no tolerance of a different view:

> Dear Mr. Justice,
>
> I was disturbed by the intelligence which recently penetrated the wilds of Arizona that you had gone to the hospital with a mild heart attack. Assuming that this was not just an ingenious device on your part to get a rest during the regular term of court, I send every wish for a speedy and complete recovery.
>
> I know that you are anxiously awaiting my critique of the year's work of the Court to date; I am, in short, surprised to find out how thoroughly I agree with most everything you have done, and how well you seem to get along, without me. Particularly good, I thought, were your dissents in the *habeas corpus* matters and in *Hawn v. Pope & Talbot,* and your state tax opinions. The one opinion which has opened up much speculation, as you might imagine, is the Garner decision; not so much for the holding, which one cannot but agree with, but for some of the dicta to the effect that what Congress has not proscribed the states must also keep hands off. Since our firm represents Phelps-Dodge, we are anxiously awaiting the next chapter, either judicial or Congressional, in this drama of (to put it as I am sure Felix would) "the delicate balance between the orbits of federal and state jurisdiction."

---

*346 U.S. 406 (1953)

**346 U.S. 485 (1953)

†Three were unanimous, reflecting the usual mix of mostly routine business that the justices could clear out early in the term, before grappling with big decisions like *Brown.*

> Most everyone here was quite disappointed by the nomination of Warren to the Chief Justiceship; perhaps this is less than fair to the man, since there certainly is no affirmative blot on the record. But I cannot help choking every time I hear the line pedaled by, among others, *Time* magazine, to the effect that "what the court really needs is not so much a lawyer as an administrator and conciliator." What the court really needs is a Chief Justice; an ability to handle the administrative side and to compromise dissidence would be an asset to an able, experienced lawyer in the job, but they certainly are no substitute for some experience in the forums whose actions he is called on to review, nor for the ability to think and write about law. I think the few opinions of Warren's I have seen have not been very good, but I don't suppose one should hold that against him; maybe writing opinions is an art for which the knack is acquired. . . .
>
> I have occasionally reflected on the experience which I got while working for you; I think there is a tendency when one first leaves a job like that, and turns to the details of a general law practice, to feel, "Why, hell, that didn't teach me anything about practicing law." In a sense it didn't, and in that regard I am sure you would be the first to agree that there is no substitute for actually practicing. But I can't help feel that, in the addition [*sic*] to the enjoyment from the personal contacts, one does pick up from a clerkship some sort of intuition about the nature of the judicial process. It is so intangible I will not attempt to describe it further, but I think it is valuable especially in appellate brief writing.

On May 17, 1954, Jackson left the hospital and went directly to the Supreme Court so that he could be present when Chief Justice Warren announced the Court's unanimous decision in *Brown.* Soon, against doctors' orders, Jackson returned to his usual rigorous work schedule. On October 12, 1954, he suffered another heart attack that killed him.

Warren soon established himself not only as an esteemed leader for turbulent times but also as an intellectual lion of the Court. But Rehnquist remained unimpressed, and he began voicing that opinion with increasing frequency, seeking out platforms to express his views. Rehnquist's first major political speech was on September 20, 1957, before the Maricopa Young Republican League at the Phoenix YMCA building. Warren, Douglas, and Black were all "left wing," he told the group. Warren was a "fine

California politician" but not much of a lawyer. "He was a vote getter who held one political job after another, but he was 58th out of 65 in his law school class."

Rehnquist joined a slew of clubs and civic organizations as a way to make not only business contacts but also a name for himself in Republican circles. He signed up for the Maricopa Toastmasters' Club and won the award in 1956 as the club's best speaker. He was a member of the Phoenix Quarterback Club, which devoted itself to postgame discussions and analysis. But as he spoke up about matters less innocuous, he gained a reputation as someone whose florid rhetoric often outshouted the occasion. Rehnquist's orations sounded more and more like stump speeches, if not outright tirades. When the Phoenix City Council in 1964 was considering what many deemed a modest public accommodations ordinance,* Rehnquist showed up to testify against it—one of only three out of thirty-three speakers to voice opposition: "You are talking about a man's private property," he intoned. Rehnquist was up in arms, in full pomp in defense of individual property rights:

> I am a lawyer without a client tonight. I am speaking for myself. I would like to speak in opposition to the proposed ordinance because I believe the values it sacrifices are greater than the values it gives. . . . I venture to say there has never been this sort of an assault on the institution [of private property] where you are told, not what you can build on your property, but who can come on your property. . . . What has brought people to Phoenix and to Arizona? My guess is no better than anyone else's, but I would say it's the idea of the lost frontier here in America. Free enterprise, and by that I mean not just free enterprise in the sense of the right to make a buck but the right to manage your own affairs as free as possible from the interference of government.

When the city council passed the ordinance anyway, Rehnquist wasn't content to let it sit. He wrote a preaching, didactic letter to the *Arizona Republic* that harkened back to his student days and prefigured his stance on

---

*Requiring lunch counters, restaurants, shops, and other public places to serve everyone regardless of race.

the Court. With its tortured allusions to "the founders," Lincoln, and the definition of "freedom"—as well as slams against "the command of the government" and "the drastic restriction on the property owner"—Rehnquist's letter to the editor read as much like one of his Stanford term papers as it did one of his future lone dissents:

> The ordinance, of course, does not and cannot remove the basic indignity to the Negro which results from refusing to serve him; that indignity stems from the state of mind of the proprietor who refuses to treat each potential customer on his own merits. . . . Unable to correct the source of the indignity to the Negro, [the ordinance] redresses the situation by placing a separate indignity on the proprietor. It is as barren of accomplishment in what it gives to the Negro as in what it takes from the proprietor. The unwanted customer and the disliked proprietor are left glowering at one another across the lunch counter. It is, I believe, impossible to justify the sacrifice of even a portion of historic individual freedom for a purpose such as this.

Rehnquist took up the cudgels repeatedly in Arizona when *Brown* and similar laws of the land were being locally debated. His strident views may have seemed intolerant or even segregationist, but when he testified or spoke out he gave himself some protective cover by speaking up for freedom and free enterprise and thus wrapping his views in the flag. A full thirteen years after *Brown,* he went on record against an integration plan for the Phoenix schools, saying that the school superintendent ought to mind his own business and leave the segregated neighborhood schools as they were. "We are no more dedicated to an 'integrated' society than we are to a 'segregated' society," Rehnquist said. "We are instead dedicated to a free society, in which each man is equal before the law, but in which each man is accorded a maximum amount of freedom of choice in his individual activities."

Rehnquist was scorned by the local NAACP, but he kept up his activism, seemingly undaunted. He was in charge of "ballot security" for the Arizona Republican machine in the biennial elections from 1958 through 1964, challenging the literacy of black and Hispanic voters.* When the *New*

*Literacy tests as a qualification for voting were legal, until outlawed by the Voting Rights Act of 1965.

York Times went looking for critics at the time of his Supreme Court nomination in 1971, the newspaper didn't have trouble finding them. Local NAACP leaders called him a racist, "the only major person of stature in the state who opposed the Arizona civil rights bill." A judge called him "basically a humorless man, somewhat prissy in his attitudes." Another unnamed lawyer—only Rehnquist's NAACP critics went on the record—observed that "unlike a lot of Arizona politicians who tried to follow the public thought, Rehnquist really is a deep philosophical conservative. He apparently just sat down and thought it out and decided intellectually that he is against anything liberal." Various ex-law partners came forward to deny that Rehnquist was a racist, saying his opposition to civil rights reform was based on his view that the proposals were unconstitutional.

So what were Rehnquist's views on race?

Rehnquist certainly espoused views and exhibited behavior in Phoenix that was racist even by the norms of that place and time. It would be nearly impossible to argue otherwise. Yet the man lived in and moved in such a self-isolating bubble that he may not even have appreciated how out of touch and offensive his views were. Seen up close at the time by a childhood friend of his son's, Rehnquist exhibited a strange mixture of small-town virtues and what might simply have been mindless discrimination. He seemed almost not to know any better. And while that didn't excuse his behavior, at least it might have explained it.

"I was Jim Rehnquist's best friend in elementary school," the childhood friend explained, "right up through eighth grade when the Rehnquists moved to Washington. I spent many nights and vacations with them; knew [Rehnquist's other children] Jan and Nancy. Their household was a 'Father Knows Best/Leave It to Beaver' household. They were very into their religion. I'm Jewish, but Mrs. Rehnquist always wanted me to go to church, which I refused. I remember Bill Rehnquist playing a wooden recorder as we sang songs around a Christmas tree. . . . They had a cabin up north. I'd go up there with them and at night they played a card game called 'Authors.' You had to match the titles with the authors. We were only in elementary school and we were already learning about Nathaniel Hawthorne."

The friend spoke with childlike reverence as he recalled how touched—and amused—he was when the Rehnquists came to his Bar Mitzvah ceremony. "They were the only non-Jewish family I invited, and they came. It was a conservative congregation, and the way this congregation worked, the

Saturday service started at 9 o'clock but that was for the older, Eastern European crowd. Most people didn't start coming in 'til 10:30 or so. So when I got there around 10:15, thinking I'm early, I saw two rows of the older men up front nodding and praying in Hebrew, and the Rehnquists all the way in back. They had been there since 9, with all the kids, and they were just trying to figure out what was going on! . . . I have fond memories of what a family guy Mr. Rehnquist was. I never saw impatience. And Mrs. Rehnquist was very stereotypical. They had a guest house in back. Not huge. Mrs. Rehnquist had sewing equipment in the guest house. They didn't flaunt wealth. Weren't ostentatious.

"Bill Rehnquist was always laughing, very fun loving. He had an affluent white family. It was the 1960s. And I definitely saw the racist side."

The friend recalled attending football games with Bill and Jim Rehnquist at nearby Arizona State University. "And I specifically remember Bill Rehnquist saying more than once: 'Look at that jungle bunny run!' referring to a black player."

"I remember that phrase: 'Jungle bunnies.' The negative stuff that came out later; it all rang true. The election in '64; I have a very specific recollection when Goldwater lost. Bill Rehnquist said, 'The Democrats stuffed the ballot box.' I remember that phrase. He was passionate. An earlier memory: I do recall that he worked at the polling places to make people pass literacy tests. It's very possible there were racial slurs then, too. That was in character." Rehnquist's activism gained him favor with one group that mattered very much to him: the Goldwater Republicans. Despite his falling-out with Kitchel years earlier, Rehnquist insinuated himself into the Arizona mafia that surrounded Goldwater. According to Obermayer, Rehnquist was the "house intellectual" and played a key role as a strategist in Goldwater's 1964 presidential run. If that is true, the forty-year-old Rehnquist helped to lead Goldwater's campaign right over the cliff.

Goldwater looked to be a shoo-in for the GOP's nomination after New York governor Nelson Rockefeller dropped out of the race following Goldwater's upset win in the California primary on June 2. In essence, all Goldwater had to do was show up for the Republican convention at the Cow Palace in San Francisco the following month; a unified party would be behind him and the nomination would be his.

Three weeks before the convention was to begin, the Senate ended eighty-three days of debate on the Civil Rights Act of 1964 and brought up the epic bill for a final vote. Passage was certain after a filibuster by Southern Democrats was broken nine days earlier, so all eyes turned to Goldwater, who had announced the previous day that he would vote *against* the bill as a matter of principle. Goldwater insisted the bill was unconstitutional. His stance was puzzling because it was at odds not only with his previous Senate votes in favor of civil rights legislation and abolition of the poll tax but also with his personal history. Goldwater ended racial segregation in his family department stores and was instrumental in ending it in Phoenix schools and restaurants and in the Arizona National Guard.

The hand of Rehnquist had struck again. With his usual certitude, Rehnquist had persuaded Goldwater that the Act, the most important equal-rights law since Reconstruction, offended the Constitution. When the erratic Goldwater started speaking out on the issue, his comments were almost a word-for-word replay of Rehnquist's jihad years earlier against the forced integration of lunch counters. "Unconstitutional," Goldwater now soberly intoned. It violates "our most sacred right," that of property.

Goldwater's campaign slogan was "In your heart you know he's right." But even that catchphrase, which sought to rationalize so much about the mercurial senator, could not explain such a quixotic casting of his vote on such an important bill. It was political suicide, branding the senator not only as an extremist but as a bigot. Passage of the Civil Rights Act was already assured, with or without Goldwater and the five other Republican "nays" that he dragged along with him. (All five supported Goldwater's nomination and probably secretly hoped to be selected as his running mate.)

Goldwater's handlers started an effort to get rid of Goldwater's campaign manager, who was none other than Denison Kitchel. But Goldwater trusted him. Kitchel held on, and so, somehow, did Rehnquist. And that was a good thing for Goldwater, because after his Rehnquist-induced act of political *seppuku* the candidate did not have a lot of supporters beyond the true believers. The Goldwater campaign fell into shambles almost as soon as he got the nomination. Even if they weren't speaking to each other, Kitchel and Rehnquist both spent the rest of the campaign backpedaling, trying to explain that Goldwater wasn't really a racist. Money got so tight at the end that Rehnquist joined the campaign full-time as a volunteer and became a Goldwater speechwriter in the last month of the campaign. And when Lyndon Johnson trounced Goldwater that November—the Arizonan carried just six states and received 36 percent of the popular vote—Rehnquist wrote Goldwater's unapologetic concession remarks.*

It was a short and tame concession for such a rabble-rouser, but Goldwater nonetheless marked the moment. His candidacy was just the beginning of "a philosophy that I represent, a Republican philosophy that I believe the Republican Party must cling to and strengthen in the years ahead." Goldwater was prescient. Sixteen years later, with Ronald Reagan,** the party would, indeed, muster what Goldwater that day referred to as "the army that we need."

But this much was clear in the immediate aftermath of the election of November 3, 1964: Goldwater was unemployed and Kitchel was permanently sidelined. Rehnquist needed a map to the new power players in Arizona.

He found that in Richard Kleindienst.

---

*Goldwater's main speechwriter was Karl Hess, who later became an anarchist. Hess wrote the most memorable line of Goldwater's campaign, delivered by the candidate in accepting the Republican nomination: "Extremism in the pursuit of liberty is no vice; moderation in the pursuit of justice is no virtue."

**Reagan, then a Hollywood actor, burst onto the Republican scene as a keynoter at the 1964 convention that nominated Goldwater.

ELEVEN

Cowboys in Washington

RICHARD KLEINDIENST'S ORIGINS were as blue collar as Bill Rehnquist's, and probably as conservative. Kleindienst, just a year older than Rehnquist, was the son of a brakeman for the Santa Fe railroad, and he'd grown up in the dusty railroad crossroads of Winslow, Arizona. He knew his way around the state, but he also knew the value of a Harvard education and of having friends in high places. He told a cloying story of his young mother's last words to him, on her deathbed in 1937: "Hitch your wagon to a star, Dickie, and if possible, someday try to go to Harvard." The high school freshman ended up doing both, going to Harvard on the G.I. Bill and then moving on to Harvard Law. When Kleindienst came back to practice law in Phoenix in 1950, he linked up with Kitchel—and, thus, with Goldwater.

In 1952, as the Goldwater-for-Senate campaign was cranking up, Kitchel and Goldwater hatched a plan to blanket the state with forty young Republican candidates for the Arizona House of Representatives. They became Goldwater's grassroots operatives, walking door-to-door to turn out the vote, and Kleindienst was one of thirty-five Republican newcomers who rode into the Arizona legislature on Goldwater's coattails.

When Rehnquist arrived in Phoenix the following summer, there was an immediate connection. Kleindienst and Rehnquist were close in age and had the common experience of having served in the Army Air Corps from

1943 to 1946. The two men shared the same conservative outlook and resentment toward the Eastern elite. With their wives they shared the same social circle.

By 1960, the thirty-seven-year-old Kleindienst had parlayed his connections into something much bigger. He was Goldwater's surrogate to the Nixon presidential campaign, sent by the Arizona senator to Nixon's Chicago hotel suite at midnight on the night of Nixon's nomination for president in 1960. Said Nixon: "I want your advice and help in the selection of a vice presidential running mate."

Kleindienst recalled having only one thought: "How in hell did I wind up here?"

With Kitchel out of the GOP's picture after Goldwater's drubbing in the 1964 presidential campaign, that question was easier to answer four years later. Stalwarts like Kleindienst would have to pick up the pieces of what was left of the GOP organization in Arizona. By 1967, Kleindienst was the GOP's Arizona state chairman. He asked Rehnquist to be the party's general counsel. And when, in 1968, the resurgent Richard Nixon won the presidential election, the president-elect remembered the young Goldwater organizer he'd first met in that smoke-filled hotel room in 1960. Kleindienst got the number-two job in the Department of Justice, working as the deputy attorney general for John N. Mitchell. Mitchell was one of Nixon's closest friends and confidants, and had been Nixon's campaign manager. Mitchell's influence as attorney general in the Nixon administration would be broad, and he was going to need someone to make things run smoothly at Justice. Kleindienst would be Mitchell's traffic cop.

The Nixon transition team operated out of the Pierre Hotel on Fifth Avenue in New York City. With Kleindienst in place, attention now turned to the other political jobs to be filled at Justice. One of the plum political jobs was that of assistant attorney general in charge of the Office of Legal Counsel. In essence, the AAG heading up that office served as the lawyer for the attorney general and, by extension, for the president. The job also was a stepping stone: not too many years before, the person in that chair had been Nicholas deB. Katzenbach, who moved up to become the deputy AG under Robert Kennedy, and then attorney general when Kennedy became a senator from New York. Kleindienst certainly wanted someone he could trust. "Whenever Mitchell asked me for my recommendation to fill that vital post, I came back with the same name—Rehnquist," Kleindienst said.

But Mitchell wasn't buying, at least not at first. "Damn it," Nixon's consigliore shot back, "there has to be at least one other person smart enough for the job. It's bad enough that the deputy attorney general will be a cowboy from Arizona. Two cowboys at one time would be ridiculous."

"Listen to me," Kleindienst replied. "You are going to need the best person you can get. Why don't you get off your New York City high horse and at least talk to him?"

Soon, Rehnquist was making a trip to the Pierre—after first, according to John Roberts, having gone to the Phoenix public library to determine what the Office of Legal Counsel actually did. Kleindienst introduced Rehnquist to Mitchell and then left the two of them alone. An hour later, Rehnquist walked into Kleindienst's office and told him he was taking the job. He submitted his paperwork to Egil Krogh and John Ehrlichman, two Nixon loyalists who would end up, along with Mitchell and Kleindienst, among the disgraced Watergate henchmen.

Kleindienst later succeeded Mitchell as attorney general and a few years after that ended up pleading guilty to perjury amid the Watergate scandal. Although Rehnquist and Kleindienst undoubtedly worked closely together during Rehnquist's three years at Justice, there is little on the public record indicating that they were close.* Kleindienst was squishy where Mitchell was iron, and iron was what Rehnquist admired. Cool and tough to the end, Mitchell fought, went to prison, lost everything, but never ratted out Nixon. It was Mitchell whom Rehnquist looked up to. Along with Nixon's, it was Mitchell's photograph Rehnquist kept on view in his chambers at the Supreme Court.

On January 28, 1969, forty-four-year-old Rehnquist came back to Washington and moved into a tiny studio apartment near the Justice Department. He would be able to walk to work until Nan and the kids joined him—they later moved into a home on a half-acre lot in suburban Virginia. The rent suited the frugal Rehnquist: $178 a month, plus $20 for parking.

---

*Rehnquist is referred to only a few times in Kleindienst's 247-page autobiography, *Justice,* and those scant mentions are mostly for Kleindienst to take credit for Rehnquist's nomination to the Court. In 1981, when Kleindienst was again facing perjury charges, this time related to an insurance swindle, Rehnquist wrote to a mutual friend that he hoped Kleindienst would be acquitted; he was. Other than that, Kleindienst, who moved back to Arizona and died in 2000, was out of the picture once Rehnquist moved up.

The next morning, he showed up on Capitol Hill for his confirmation hearing accompanied by none other than Barry Goldwater.

It was an oddball homecoming for them both. Here was Rehnquist, the outsider's outsider who eschewed Washington, rolling in with Goldwater, a freshman senator all over again, having just won back the Senate seat that he gave up for his failed presidential run four years earlier. It was a Senate tradition for the home-state senator to accompany a presidential nominee. If there were hard feelings, or any feelings, between the two they weren't visible that morning. Rehnquist and Goldwater made quick work of the proceedings. When Mississippi Senator James Eastland called on one after another of the four other senators who were present that morning, all but one replied with a terse "no questions." Only Senator Philip Hart, the venerable liberal from Michigan, had anything to ask. Hart wanted to know, maybe just as a throwaway or maybe because he actually had prior knowledge of an objection the NAACP had raised but not pursued, whether Rehnquist would uphold Supreme Court decisions that he disagreed with.

Rehnquist was blunt in reply. It was the obligation of every lawyer "to call it as he sees it. You give them the interpretation of the law that you honestly place on the thing." To anyone familiar with Rehnquist's rants against *Brown* and lunch-counter integration, the nominee's pledge to call things as he saw them amounted to an unmistakable promise to shake up the liberals.

And Hart was one of the Senate's most passionate liberals. Was Hart listening? Hard to tell. It was lunch time. Hart simply replied, "All the information that comes to me is that you have a very gifted legal mind. I am glad to support you." That was it.

Rehnquist thanked Hart. Goldwater thanked Eastland. Eastland thanked his fellow senators. And then the gavel fell. Rehnquist's first star turn on the Hill was over in less than two minutes. Without realizing it, the senators were anointing the Nixon administration's new conservative in chief. No future confirmation hearing would be so easy for Rehnquist.

FOLLOWING GOLDWATER'S PRESIDENTIAL defeat Rehnquist began once again to keep a journal. Politics was definitely on his mind. He would thumb to a blank page in one of his old Stanford notebooks and fill it with a passage he'd just read or some bit of historical ephemera he'd just discovered. Sometimes it would just be a clever musing of his own. The entries were sporadic—a year or more might go by without anything being added. Then Rehnquist would rediscover the notebook and subject it to more furious jottings. There was a definite pattern to the things that Rehnquist wanted to get down. He did not want to forget just how cynical politicians could be.

His first entry in 1965 was about John Quincy Adams: "Principal mistake was said to have been that he left all of his enemies in office upon assuming the presidency."

He noted a senator's comment about Roger Taney, the chief justice from 1836 to 1864 who became anathema for authoring in 1857 the infamous *Dred Scott* decision: "No man ever prayed as I did that Taney might outlive James Buchanan's term, and now I am afraid I have overdone it."*

Something resonated about this quote from Eugene Gerhart's biography of Justice Robert Jackson, so it also went into the journal: "Conservatives are those who worship dead radicals."

On Christmas Day 1965, Rehnquist penned a warning about political opportunists: "Possible serious flaw in popular government is use to which it may be put by ambitious demagogues. Not only are there those leaders who will on occasion defy popular sentiment if they believe it wrong, and those who will merely follow what they believe it to be, but yet a third kind—who will actually attempt to create a public demand for something, not because they believe it right or desirable, but because it will enable them to be elected."

Rehnquist hadn't made any entries for quite some time when, on the eve of the 1968 election that soon would greatly alter his own life, he inscribed a few sentences from Michael Holroyd's biography of the troubled and gifted British writer of the early twentieth century, Lytton Strachey. Strachey's biographies veered into the psychological. What Rehnquist copied into his journal perfectly encapsulated the private fears of a public man: "The world of his youthful ideals had turned sour and neurotic. . . . The obverse of his exaggerated, schoolboy wish that everyone should love

*Quoting Senator Benjamin Wade.

him was a curiously inverted form of vanity—the uneasy suspicion that people were planning his downfall." Did Rehnquist seek acceptance yet absorb the private pain of criticism? The words captured the feelings of a man whose public face feigned stony indifference but whose behavior shouted out for acknowledgment and acceptance. To someone who felt misunderstood if not downright vilified, the passage would have been meaningful—indeed, revelatory.

Rehnquist cut quite a figure upon his return to the Nation's Capital. Popular fashion had taken a quirky turn in this flower-child era of peace and love, and among Nixon's Brooks Brothers disciples the comparatively youthful Rehnquist was easy to spot with his Buddy Holly eyeglasses, straggly modish hair, long sideburns, and an array of outrageous suits and clashing ties that exclaimed "Look at me!" When Rehnquist laughed, his blue eyes brightened and he flashed a smile that revealed imposing dental work. He was a rangy, gawky man, six feet two inches tall, slightly stooped. Loping around in Hush Puppies, grin on his face, head bobbing as if following some imaginary tune, Rehnquist ignored all the sartorial norms. He got the attention he sought.

But he did not, apparently, like Washington any more the second time around. In letters to his family, he expressed his distaste for the snow—"I did not think moving to Washington would be like moving to Boston"—and the politics—"This is in truth a 'one industry' town and the newspapers and television shows would virtually have to shut up if they couldn't write and telecast about things such as this." But being in the company town also had its advantages, and soon enough Rehnquist was back to his conservative jeremiads, this time launched with much greater fanfare from his bully pulpit at the Justice Department.

Within three months of arriving at Justice, Rehnquist put together a nineteen-page memorandum for John Dean, another young Justice Department newcomer who had been brought in by Kleindienst. Dean, who would later become Nixon's White House counsel, was advising Mitchell on crime-and drug-control legislation, and Rehnquist thought the department needed some radical new thinking. Rehnquist's April 1, 1969, memorandum was classified, and it never traveled beyond Dean's briefcase (he took it with him to the White House), but Dean thought of it as a potential smoking gun—"actually, it was more like a smoking cannon left out on the testing range." Rehnquist proposed *rewriting the Constitution* to drastically limit the rights of criminal defendants, and repealing the protections of Bill of Rights when it came to actions by states and localities.*

Rehnquist's memo "was, in fact, a brutal critique of how the Supreme Court had gone astray in the field of criminal law," Dean later wrote, "and it clearly signaled Rehnquist's reactionary thinking on a wide range of controversial Supreme Court cases." The memo recited his familiar litany of complaints about decisions he thought favored the interests of criminal defendants and impeded prosecutors. *Habeas corpus* petitions got the usual treatment, as did the Warren Court in general for its failure "to hold true the balance between the right of society to convict the guilty and the obligation of society to safeguard the accused." Dean called the memo a map of Rehnquist's thinking on the Supreme Court's role in criminal justice and marveled that it never surfaced in either of his confirmation hearings. "Written at a time when Rehnquist had no inkling he would devote three decades of his life to the matters he had set forth, it is his candid assessment of a significant field of constitutional jurisprudence he believed needed to be radically changed. Reading it today, I realize that had anyone wanted to know what Rehnquist might do as a Supreme Court justice, he had explained it in 1969. Here was a relatively young, right-wing [soon-to-be Supreme Court] nominee summarizing dozens of Warren Court decisions, including such sacred cows as *Gideon v. Wainwright*** (guaranteeing a lawyer to all defendants) and the *Miranda*† decision, and concluding that 'there is indeed substantial doubt as to whether these decisions reach desirable results.'"

Rehnquist believed that the most effective way to achieve his ends would be to appoint a panel of eminent right-wing thinkers to do the dirty work of redrafting. When Dean ran it past Mitchell, the attorney general thought the idea was an awful one; he worried that Rehnquist's "eminent thinkers" would be hard to control and that the whole effort might blow up in Nixon's face. So that was that; Rehnquist's memo was DOA. But Rehnquist didn't intend to let that be the last word.

---

*The 14th Amendment extended the Bill of Rights to cover state actions. Rehnquist's memo proposed taking away that constitutional safeguard.

**372 U.S. 335 (1963)

†384 U.S. 436 (1966)

Just as had been the case during Rehnquist's prior time in Washington in 1952 and 1953, the country was once again embroiled in national debate and restive about its future. This time, the issue was not just race relations—wounds were still fresh from the assassinations of Martin Luther King and Robert Kennedy the year before—but also the increasingly unpopular war in Vietnam. Demonstrators were taking to the streets and engaging in violence to proclaim their views. The year that Rehnquist took up his Justice Department post, hundreds of radical Weathermen protesters armed with clubs, lead pipes, chains, and brass knuckles rampaged through Chicago to protest the Vietnam War. The rioters called it the Days of Rage; ringleaders were captured by the FBI and went to prison.*

Five weeks after the 1969 Chicago riot, the largest antiwar protest in America's history took place in Washington, with a crowd of 500,000 protesters. Forty thousand people marched past the White House, each carrying the name of a soldier who had died in Vietnam. Trying to keep the marchers away, Nixon ordered a solid row of DC Transit buses to be parked along the curb between the marchers and the White House. It was a sorry sight as well as a sign of the times.

Rehnquist saw these as grievous threats. He became an advocate for harsh actions to be taken by the government in response. His rhetoric was over the top. No venue was too tiny or obscure to be undeserving of Rehnquist's loquacity. Soon after arriving at Justice, he made a speech before the Kiwanis club in Newark, Delaware—not your typical news-making forum—that landed smack on the front page of the *New York Times.* "Disobedience cannot be tolerated," he intoned, "whether it be violent or nonviolent disobedience. If force is required to enforce the law, we must not shirk from its employment." The country underestimated the risk from "new barbarians," Rehnquist said in the same speech. "I suggest to you that this attack of the new barbarians constitutes a threat to the notion of a government of law which is every bit as serious as the 'crime wave' in our cities. . . . The barbarians of the new left have taken full advantage of their minority right to urge and advocate their views as to what substantive changes should be made in the law and policies of this country." He added: "The original barbarians—the invaders of the Roman Empire—did not

*In 1971, the Weathermen went even further, placing a bomb at the US Capitol and blowing up part of the historic building's ground floor.

seem to pose a threat to the empire when they first appeared on the banks of the Danube. . . . We must be prepared, if necessary, to devote whatever energies are necessary, at whatever sacrifice to private gain or pleasure, to see that these essential values of our system are maintained."

He was apparently well received enough in Delaware that the next year he went before another Kiwanis club, this time in Houston, with a similar message: "Law and order will be pursued at whatever cost in individual liberties and rights."

Such comments were widely picked up, and a few years later they became grist for the angry debate over his qualifications for the Court. In 1975, he was still brooding about the lashing he'd taken. The more Rehnquist thought about it, the more he honestly didn't believe he'd even made those extreme comments about law and order. So he had his secretary find the original speech, and there it plainly was: Rehnquist had, indeed, uttered the words precisely as attributed. But, Rehnquist plaintively averred in a letter to his son who was away at college, the quote was out of context. "I was offering this as a dire prediction of what might happen, rather than as an expression of my own view of the desired state of affairs."

Rehnquist still hadn't tuned in to how his own message was being received. He thought that his flower-power ties somehow trumped antediluvian ideology. In 1970, massive May Day protests were taking place on campuses, and six students were dead as a result: four killed and nine wounded in a shooting by the Ohio National Guard at Kent State University, and two killed and twelve wounded by the Mississippi authorities at Jackson State University. In the wake of Kent State and Jackson State, Rehnquist decided that he was the right person in the Nixon administration to open a dialogue with students on campus. He made plans to visit fifty college campuses, "trying to get live human beings on the other side of the discussion table." The plan bombed. On one campus, 1,200 students turned out but the front rows were filled with defiant marijuana puffers; it was more like a sit-in. At Arizona State University, almost no one showed up. Questioners wanted to know why the taxpayers were footing the bill. Good question, Rehnquist replied. "Cost versus value is something that will have to be evaluated."

Rehnquist seemed to relish being the "lawyer's lawyer" at the Justice Department. He was not expected to make policy, but rather to find whatever justification he could for the policies that Nixon wanted. The Constitution was like the bible; with a close reading, you could find support for almost anything. Rehnquist searched its crevices. With his flypaper memory for historical trivia and his by now well-worn theories of individual liberty, Rehnquist styled himself as the administration's resident constitutional theorist. He roamed the political landscape in support of the Nixon administrations' law-and-order policies. Only after Nixon's downfall would it become apparent that there was a cynical, almost cartoonish side to how the administration used Rehnquist as a front man and lightning rod, pandering to the ultra-right. Although he probably didn't know it at the time, Rehnquist was even being used by the Nixonites to exact their own paranoid revenge against the Kennedys. That would come out only years later with the full release of the White House tapes. But Nixon's underlying motives, whatever they might have been, didn't seem to matter to Rehnquist in the moment. Rehnquist relished being the tough-talking gadfly: mild manners, bold views. He was a modern Judge Parker in pink pinstripes, with a psychedelic tie.

Part of Rehnquist's job was screening candidates for appointment to the Supreme Court. When the *Washington Post* editorialized against G. Harrold Carswell, one of Nixon's underqualified—and unsuccessful—Supreme Court nominees, off went a nasty letter to the paper from Rehnquist containing this single, verbose sentence: "In fairness you ought to state all the consequences that your position logically brings to train; not merely further expansion of constitutional recognition of civil rights, but further expansion of the constitutional rights of criminal defendants, of pornographers and of demonstrators." Translated, the *Washington Post* was a house organ for the ACLU.

Rehnquist was a veritable one-sentence wonder. He lectured government whistleblowers in the *Civil Service Journal:* "If Justice Holmes mistakenly failed to recognize that dismissal of a government employee because of his public statements was a form of restraint on his free speech, it is equally a mistake to fail to recognize that potential dismissal from government employment is by no means a complete negation of one's free speech." Translated, Rehnquist supported firing whistleblowers.

In 1970, Congress was considering an amendment to the Constitution to confer equal rights upon women. Rehnquist prepared a memo for Leonard Garment, a White House lawyer who was part of Nixon's inner circle. As was typical, Rehnquist wrote nine pages of dense prose about existing constitutional protections and the scope of the 14th Amendment—its protections for women were already sufficient, of course—and then gratuitously threw in a quote that he liked, from Oliver Wendell Holmes, about the differences between men and women. Finally he got to his point. "The overall implication of the equal rights amendment," Rehnquist advised the White House, "is nothing less than the sharp reduction in importance of the family unit, with the eventual elimination of that unit by no means improbable. It may be that the country is heading in this direction anyway, and that there is very little that the administration can do to stop it. But this surely does not mean that the administration ought to support a change which will in fact hasten the dissolution of the family."

Nixon had campaigned against Washington as a crime capital, and it was up to Rehnquist to be the spokesman in front of Congress for bills that would allow the police to break down doors to catch crooks red-handed (the euphemism was "no-knock searches") and then to put them behind bars without the possibility of bail ("preventive detention"). He defended government wiretapping and the Army's surveillance of private citizens and accused the critics of government surveillance of something that, to Rehnquist, was a cardinal sin: inconsistency.

The Army's surveillance program touched a nerve among liberals and the media. What the Army compiled and maintained amounted to a giant police database about people who had engaged in perfectly lawful political activity. The military's domestic data gathering actually had begun under Nixon's predecessor, Lyndon Johnson, following urban riots in 1967 and 1968 that reached a crescendo after the assassination of Martin Luther King. The idea was that if soldiers were going to be called in to function as a domestic police force to restore order, the Army needed to have a data bank of reports about possible troublemakers, to head off violence before it could be incited. The Army had a thousand undercover agents in the field; they went to meetings in civilian clothes, took notes about the usual suspects, and filed reports.

That made sense to Rehnquist. He argued for keeping closer tabs on subversives and implied that domestic surveillance could have prevented JFK's assassination. Kennedy's 1963 killing and the 1968 assassinations of the president's brother Robert and the civil rights leader Martin Luther King were still fresh in the public's collective mind. "The critics blasted the Secret Service because they didn't stop Oswald from planning and committing President Kennedy's murder. They wanted to know why it wasn't prevented. When the Army [pursued] this line of thinking and began preventive investigation, it came under attack." It seemed an easy equation for Rehnquist.

Of course, Rehnquist also went to Capitol Hill asking for his all-time favorites: repeal of *habeas corpus* and an end to the exclusionary rule.* Any system that "permits a convicted defendant to spend the next ten or twenty years litigating the validity of the procedures used in his trial is a contradiction in terms." As usual, the bills attracted huge controversy but went nowhere.

On May 1, 1971, the Nation's Capital was girding for more antiwar demonstrations on the anniversary of the Jackson and Kent State killings. The planned protests were designed as a kind of street theater by a group of pranksters who called themselves "Yippies"—the name a comic riff on "hippies." Nixon had already announced that the United States would be pulling out of Vietnam, but with the withdrawal proceeding slowly the Yippies declared that they would shut down the government. Their slogan was audacious: "If the government won't stop the war, we'll stop the government." In the largest civil-disobedience action in US history, 35,000 protesters camped out near the Washington Monument, ready to disrupt the Monday-morning rush hour using hit-and-run tactics to block commuter routes and the bridges across the Potomac with old cars, trash cans, and their own bodies.

But the Nixon administration was ready with extreme measures of its own. Determined to keep the city open, the president refused to give federal employees the day off (traffic was snarled all over) and airlifted in 10,000 soldiers from East Coast bases plus 4,000 paratroopers from the 82nd Airborne Division to back up 5,200 DC cops and 2,000 National Guardsmen. They swept in using tear gas, clubs, and whatever force was necessary to arrest the protesters. Thus, before most of the May Day tribe could even take to the streets, they were handcuffed and taken into custody—a new meaning for "preventive detention." It was yet another first for the Nixonites: the largest mass arrest in US history.

Civil liberties be damned, Nixon intended to teach the protesters a lesson. Twelve thousand were arrested. But in the aftermath of the police

*In criminal law, the exclusionary rule is the legal principle that evidence obtained by the government in violation of a defendant's constitutional right may not be used.

sweeps, there was a huge problem: the DC jail was already at capacity and there was nowhere those arrested could be held. A makeshift outdoor jail was quickly set up by authorities who erected an eight-foot-high chain-link fence around a Washington Redskins football practice field at RFK stadium. No food, water, or sanitary facilities were made available; sympathetic citizens brought supplies and passed them through and over the fence.

The administration's actions were an egregious violation of constitutional rights. Charges against most of the protesters were dropped and the government eventually paid millions of dollars in damages. But Nixon and Attorney General Mitchell were pleased.

Rehnquist had the task of defending the government's action, which he did with his usual gusto. The protesters, according to Rehnquist, had "Communist-oriented or related backgrounds." Suspending ordinary civil rights, Rehnquist asserted, was justified because there was a civil emergency. "The doctrine which there obtains is customarily referred to as 'qualified martial law.' In that situation, the authority of the nation, state or city . . . to protect itself and its citizens against actual violence or a real threat of violence is held to outweigh the normal right of any individual" to insist on normal constitutional rights when arrested.

Rehnquist's diatribes against the Vietnam protesters, and his advocacy of the Army's surveillance of ordinary US citizens, would dog him for years after he reached the Supreme Court. When victims of the clandestine Army surveillance program filed a class action against the Defense Department, they came within one vote of winning—until Rehnquist cast the tie-breaking vote against them.* There was a howl of outrage—beginning with Bill Douglas—when the case came down on the last Monday of Rehnquist's first term on the Court.

Critics claimed Rehnquist shouldn't have participated because of his direct involvement with the White House in defending the Army program. In dissent, Douglas called the Army's spying "a cancer on our body politic. . . . When an intelligence officer looks over every nonconformist's shoulder in the library, or walks invisibly by his side in a picket line, or infiltrates his club, the America once extolled as the voice of liberty heard around the world no longer is cast in the image which Jefferson and Madison designed, but more in the Russian image."

**Laird v. Tatum*, 408 U.S. 1 (1972)

The outcry so stung Rehnquist that over the summer he wrote letters to three of his fellow justices, seeking advice on whether to respond to his "snide" critics. "The *New York Times* and the *Washington Post* tend to feature the matter at every opportunity," he complained in a letter to Potter Stewart. The chief justice already had advised Rehnquist that any further explanation would be futile, if not counterproductive. Byron White, on the other hand, endorsed Rehnquist's explaining himself. So that left Stewart, the only one of the three who had dissented in the case, as the tie breaker. Stewart told him to go ahead and issue a statement. But, Stewart added, "I am sure you are not so sanguine as to think that the memo will satisfy the N.Y. Times, Washington Post or other critics. It will probably just further irritate them, and they do have the last word." Rehnquist did, indeed, issue a lengthy if lame justification at the start of the Court's term the following October, claiming that he felt an obligation to participate in order to prevent a stalemate in the case.* (A 4–4 tie would have let stand a DC appeals-court decision in favor of the surveillance victims.) The complaining never fully stopped.**

**Laird v. Tatum,* 409 U.S. 824 (1972)

**In 1973, new Justice Rehnquist was in hot water again over his Nixon-era loyalties, and once again he was defiant. With the war still not over and Nixon damaged by Watergate, Congress voted in June of that year to cut off all funding for bombing in Cambodia. The liberal Congresswoman Elizabeth Holtzman filed an ACLU lawsuit seeking to enforce the congressional ban. As assistant attorney general in 1970, Rehnquist had given a spirited defense of the legality of the bombing, so, as expected, Holtzman filed a motion to recuse Rehnquist from participating in the case. Once again, Rehnquist refused to recuse himself, voting the next day with the 8–1 majority to let the bombing continue—with the redoubtable Bill Douglas going his own way as usual. The hullaballoo about Rehnquist's failure to recuse himself in *Laird v. Tatum* started up all over again after his 1986 nomination to become chief justice.

TWELVE

Changes on the Court

WHEN RICHARD NIXON TOOK OFFICE on January 20, 1969, it was already clear that he would have one important vacancy to fill on the Supreme Court. The prior June, at the end of the Court's term, Chief Justice Earl Warren had gone to the White House to tell President Lyndon Johnson of his intention to retire. His departure date was open; Warren agreed to stay on until a successor was in place.

Warren was seventy-seven years old, and in a letter to Johnson he said his departure was "solely because of age." It was time "to give way to someone who will have more years ahead of him to cope with the problems which will come before the Court." But there was another motive for the timing of his resignation. The politically savvy Warren believed that Nixon would win the coming election, and Nixon had made it clear that he would appoint judges who would reverse the precedents of the Warren Court. Warren wanted to give Johnson a chance to reshuffle the lineup at the Court, before it was too late.

Warren's timing was off. The Vietnam War raged on and demonstrations against it were escalating. Johnson was already a lame duck, having announced on March 31 that he would not run for reelection. The beleaguered president had little political clout left, but he nonetheless decided to move forward with a controversial choice to succeed Warren. Johnson nominated his friend and confidant Associate Justice Abe Fortas, whom he'd named to the Court in 1965, to be the next chief. Fortas was a reliable vote for Warren and would carry on in his stead. To replace Fortas, Johnson nominated another crony, Homer Thornberry, a Texan who had taken over Johnson's seat in the House of Representatives before being nominated to the US Court of Appeals. Naming Thornberry was intended to mollify southern Democrats who were skeptical about Fortas.* It was a craven political move by Johnson, and it backfired.

The Republicans smelled blood as the November elections neared, and there was no way that they were going to give Johnson either of those appointments without a fight. Senators used Fortas's confirmation hearings that autumn as a forum to attack the Warren Court's decisions, such as *Gideon* and *Miranda,* claiming they aided criminals and damaged the state. There were also claims that Fortas's closeness to Johnson violated the principle of separation of powers. Fortas became the first sitting justice to testify at his own confirmation hearing for chief justice. But Fortas didn't help himself, reinforcing with his own testimony his reputation as an inscrutable opportunist, LBJ's alter ego, and all-around fixer. Even one of Fortas's own clerks later said, "It wouldn't surprise me if he was robbing banks on the side or writing novels under another name."

Fortas's nomination was doomed when it was revealed that Paul Porter, one of his old law partners, had raised $30,000 on Fortas's behalf from Fortas's friends and former clients, and that half of the money (40 percent of a justice's salary at the time) had been paid to Fortas for teaching a summer course at the American University Law School. When the Fortas nomination finally came to the floor, Republicans and southern Democrats launched a historic filibuster—the first ever against a Supreme Court nominee. A cloture motion to stop the filibuster failed. Johnson had overestimated his Senate support and didn't have enough clout left to help his old friend. Nixon stayed above the fray but sent word through backchannels that he sup-

---

*Johnson was under the same political pressure as Richard Nixon later would be to rebalance the Court whose decisions had tilted decidedly leftward under Warren, and he particularly felt the heat from the South. Johnson cynically tried to palm off Fortas as a southerner. Calling the press into the Oval Office to announce Fortas's nomination, Johnson referred to his man as "Justice Abe Fortas, of the state of Tennessee," but the ploy was transparent and Johnson should have known better. Fortas had, indeed, been born in Memphis, but he lived in an ornate mansion in Georgetown and his roots as an insider's insider were beneath Johnson's feet.

ported the alliance against Fortas. His reputation in tatters and his confirmation prospects hopeless, Fortas asked Johnson to withdraw the nomination on October 1, 1968. Warren would open the Court's new term a week later.

Into this maelstrom walked Rehnquist, less than four months after that.

In yet another twist of fate, Rehnquist came on as a bit player and ended up with a leading role. The stage was set as soon as Nixon won the election—at which point he began shrewdly calculating how and when he could pick off some of the members of the Court's liberal bloc. Hugo Black was eighty-two years old. Douglas was seventy. Replacing the chief was already a given, so Nixon could actually take his time with that; Nixon arranged for Warren to remain until the end of the Court's full term, in June 1969. Having bought himself some time on the chief justiceship, Nixon set about creating one more vacancy. He intended to drive the weakened Fortas off of the Court entirely. Rehnquist would help.

White House counsel John Ehrlichman (Rehnquist's Stanford Law School classmate, class of '51) orchestrated the plan against Fortas, with the help of the Justice Department. Justice officials had learned about a $20,000 retainer that Fortas, while a sitting justice, had accepted from the family foundation of Louis Wolfson, who was under investigation by the Securities and Exchange Commission.* The information was passed to a Nixon-friendly *Life* magazine reporter named William Lambert. Lambert was a tough investigator and a Pulitzer Prize winner, but he also was a reliable, trusted conduit when the White House wanted to get a story out without leaving fingerprints. *Life* had Lambert's exposé about Fortas ready for its edition that would hit newsstands on Sunday afternoon, May 4, 1969. Whether true or not, the revelation would be incendiary, far worse for Fortas than the prior year's revelation about the law school payments.

Ehrlichman already had an advance proof of the *Life* story, and he saw an opening for the White House to use the new revelations as leverage to quickly force Fortas off the bench—under the threat of a grand jury investigation. But this was a delicate matter, because there was no precedent for the Justice Department going after a sitting Supreme Court justice. Only

*Fortas kept the money for eleven months but returned it after Wolfson was indicted on federal stock fraud charges.

Congress had the power to remove a sitting justice, through impeachment. The White House needed protective cover for its threatened investigation.

On May 1, three days before publication by *Life,* Rehnquist sent Attorney General Mitchell a memorandum providing a precedent for the Department of Justice to investigate the Fortas-Wolfson relationship. Rehnquist said that Mitchell instructed him "to assume the most damaging set of inferences about the case were true" and to "determine what action the Justice Department could take." In essence, Mitchell had instructed Rehnquist to ignore the facts. This Rehnquist did, providing the scenario that became the Nixon game plan to drive Fortas from the bench.

Rehnquist connected the dots inferentially, as instructed. He began by assuming that the *worst* inference to be drawn was that Fortas, while sitting on the Court, had intervened in the government's prosecution of Wolfson. (In fact, Fortas had not.) In essence, the worst-case scenario was that Fortas had taken bribes. Next, Rehnquist searched the federal criminal code and found an obscure statute that made it a crime under certain circumstances for an officer of the judicial branch to be paid for services on behalf of a third party. Having found this possibly relevant federal statute, Rehnquist had to determine whether the Justice Department could prosecute Fortas while he was a sitting justice. In pursuit of that, Rehnquist, who had little time for legal precedent generally, unearthed a 1790 law, along with an attorney general's opinion from 1796, which he thought supported prosecution.* And so on May 1, Rehnquist sent Mitchell the memorandum advising that if the department had the evidence, it could prosecute Fortas even though he was a sitting member of the Supreme Court.

Rehnquist's memo gave Mitchell what he needed to move the game forward. The exultant Mitchell sent a US marshal to fetch an early *Life* copy off the newsstand in New York, and Justice's public-relations team started phoning reporters who covered the department to tell them about the story. The *Life* story was front-page news, and Mitchell boasted at a White House staff meeting that there would be more revelations. The *Washington Post* was already calling for Fortas's resignation. Members on both sides of the aisle were asking whether the administration was involved in the leak.

---

*In fact, it did not. What Rehnquist apparently did *not* tell Mitchell was that the 1790 bribery law was not necessarily designed to prosecute a sitting judge; rather it provided a remedy after the judge had been removed by impeachment.

When Dean asked Kleindienst, the latter simply replied, "Junior, there are some things it is better you do not know," then proceeded to all but take credit for the leak himself. Then Mitchell made his move.

On Wednesday, May 7, Mitchell went to the Supreme Court for a secret meeting with Earl Warren. The attorney general asked the chief justice for his help in getting Fortas to resign, and he hinted that the Justice Department would go forward with its criminal investigation—the Rehnquist memo vouchsafed that—if Fortas demurred.

To ratchet up the pressure even more, Mitchell had his department reopen an old investigation that focused on Fortas's wife, Carolyn Agger, a highly paid tax law specialist, and Fortas's former law partner Porter. A grand jury was convened, even though a previous investigation found nothing improper.

On the morning of May 14, Dean was called into a meeting with Mitchell and Will Wilson, the head of the department's Criminal Division. The discussion centered on the difficulty of building a criminal case against Fortas. Mitchell said that if Fortas didn't resign, the department might formally submit a report to the House of Representatives calling for his impeachment. But by the afternoon the whole thing was over. "Mitchell's bluff had succeeded beyond his wildest expectations." Fortas submitted his resignation; it would be announced in the morning.

"At the Justice Department there was a small celebration in the attorney general's office," Dean related. "Mitchell summoned Will Wilson and his deputy Henry Petersen to congratulate the team that had been running the smoke machine. When Deputy Attorney General Dick Kleindienst stepped off the back elevator and into Mitchell's office, he was elated by the news. Kleindienst said the occasion called for a drink, so they opened the bar, pouring heartily to toast their success. The celebration was capped with a call from the president, congratulating them on a job well done."

Exactly a week later, Nixon announced that Warren Burger would be replacing Earl Warren as chief justice. Burger was recommended to Nixon by two other men whom he'd asked about taking the job: Herbert Brownell, Eisenhower's first attorney general, and William P. Rogers, Eisenhower's second (and Nixon's first secretary of state). Neither man wanted it—the backstory was that J. Edgar Hoover, who had worked for both, didn't want *them.* In any event, both touted Burger, Burger wanted the job, and Nixon liked him. When Mitchell and Kleindienst snuck in a meeting with Burger during the fracas over Fortas, both were struck by what a perfect fit Burger was. With his wavy white hair, resonant baritone, courtly demeanor, and conservative views, he was right out of central casting. To make the surprise announcement, Nixon smuggled Burger and his wife into the White House through an underground tunnel in the adjacent Treasury Department building. Two weeks later, Burger was confirmed in the Senate by a vote of 74–3. Now Nixon could turn to filling Fortas's seat.

THIRTEEN

Southern Strategy

THE PROCESS FOR CHOOSING Fortas's replacement would turn out to be neither quick nor painless. Despite the relative ease with which Nixon had placed Burger in the chief justice's chair, Congress was still stirred by partisan passions over Fortas's failed approval as chief justice the year before. Further inflaming the judicial confirmation process on Capitol Hill were the efforts of Nixon's loyalists, led by House minority leader Gerald R. Ford, to start an impeachment action against the liberal Justice Douglas. Nixon's *bona fides* as a straight shooter on judicial nominations were being questioned.

Nixon had put down a marker during the campaign that he would find a southerner for the Court, not knowing, of course, that his first vacancy would be for what had euphemistically become known as the "Jewish seat." The chronology of succession for Fortas's seat went directly from Benjamin Cardozo (1932–1938) to Felix Frankfurter (1939–1962) to Arthur Goldberg (1962–1965) to Fortas. So there was the added complication of Nixon's having a campaign pledge to fulfill that was directly at odds with tradition.

Nixon set up a tight circle to vet prospective nominees who could fulfill his "southern strategy." Nixon passed names to Mitchell. New Chief Justice Burger did likewise. Rehnquist, meanwhile, did his own litmus testing and also sent names to Mitchell. John Ehrlichman tried to keep a watchful eye on the process. But it was Rehnquist who functioned as the *de facto* personnel director for future justices. If a candidate was seriously considered, Rehnquist met with him to size him up in person.

Nixon's attempt to transform the "Jewish seat" into a new "southern seat" soon turned into a fiasco. How and why the White House bungled the process—bad choices, badly managed—is a story that has been told and retold in terms of only its most obvious elements. The essence of the story is that the members of Nixon's team were so new to Washington that they failed to make the necessary political calculations. What was less well known, until the publication of Dean's *The Rehnquist Choice* in 2001, is the role that Rehnquist, operating behind the scenes, played in this theater of the absurd. Nixon's chief of staff, H. R. Haldeman, later wrote in his diary that the judicial-selection events that played out in the early days of the Nixon administration were a learning experience, helping the White House to sharpen its teeth for battles to come. Rehnquist certainly was one of those who learned from the failures. Even more to the point, he also benefited from the hard political lessons that the Nixonites learned.

Nixon's first choice for the vacant Fortas seat was Clement Haynsworth, a federal judge from Greenville, South Carolina. Rehnquist, quarterbacking the vetting process, did not take long to give the green light. He reviewed twelve years of the judge's decisions and affirmed, in a memorandum for Mitchell, that Haynsworth was indeed a "strict constructionist" who "will not be favorably inclined toward claims of either criminal defendants or civil rights plaintiffs." In other words, Rehnquist liked Haynsworth because he was tough on criminals and was a segregationist. That was what he assumed Nixon wanted. A quick FBI investigation revealed a conflict-of-interest accusation against Haynsworth a few years earlier by the textile workers union: Haynsworth held stock in a company whose case he decided. But that 1963 matter was deemed trivial by Rehnquist and the White House. After all, the chief judge of the US Court of Appeals for the Fourth Circuit had found no impropriety. Neither had Robert Kennedy, the attorney general at the time. Besides, J. Edgar Hoover gave Haynsworth two thumbs up as a law-and-order conservative.

So Nixon sent Haynsworth's nomination to the Senate on August 18, 1969, without calculating that the Senate was in deep payback mode for the filibuster and, later, the ouster that Nixon masterminded against Fortas.

Haynsworth was a wealthy man, a southerner, and had a segregationist past—all strikes against him by the lights of the northern Democrats who held sway on the Senate Judiciary Committee. Opposition quickly mounted. Haynsworth protested that the 1950s were a different time, "when none of us was thinking or writing as we are today." And Haynsworth had a point; he could point to more recent decisions that he authored, striking down "white only" membership restrictions and supporting black militant H. Rap Brown. Haynsworth even pleaded that he had authored a pro-*habeas* opinion. The NAACP was unpersuaded and took a stand against him.

But when it came to Haynsworth's alleged conflicts of interest, the senators couldn't forget the recent Fortas history. The whole debate about financial impropriety was rekindled, but this time it was Haynsworth who was thrown into the fire. Birch Bayh, Democrat of Indiana, led the fight. He reopened the conflict-of-interest issue that Rehnquist thought had been put to rest by Robert Kennedy in 1963. Bayh said it wasn't Haynsworth's integrity that he was questioning but, rather, Haynsworth's judgment for not stepping aside and recusing himself in a case to which he had an obvious connection.

Now it was time for Rehnquist to patch up his earlier bad vetting work. A week and a half before Haynsworth's confirmation hearings were to begin, Rehnquist burst in, right on cue, with a legal opinion stating that Haynsworth had acted appropriately. But there was more. Rehnquist gilded the lily by asserting that Haynsworth *had a duty* to take part in the disputed case, and that Haynsworth had done nothing wrong "as a matter of common sense, as well as of law."

By the time Haynsworth's confirmation hearings began on September 17, his nomination was doomed, but Nixon held on tight and urged Haynsworth to do likewise. The Arizona mafia enlisted one of their own to help out: John P. Frank, a distinguished Phoenix constitutional lawyer who had defended Ernesto Miranda before the Supreme Court, backed up Rehnquist and told the Senate Judiciary Committee that Haynsworth had no choice but to do what he did. The White House tried to muscle recalcitrant senators. But in the end Nixon suffered his first major congressional defeat when, on November 21, he could get only 45 votes for Haynsworth, with 55 voting against. It was the first time since 1930 that the Senate had voted down outright a Supreme Court nominee, and only the second time in the twentieth century. Adding to the sting, all three of the top Republican leaders in the Senate voted against confirmation: Minority Leader Hugh Scott (Pennsylvania), Assistant Minority Leader Robert P. Griffin (Michigan) and Margaret Chase Smith (Maine), chair of the Republican Conference.

"So we learned something," H. R. Haldeman wrote in his diary, "and politically probably came out ahead."

The vote only stiffened Nixon's determination. The president immediately issued a statement:

> An outstanding jurist, who would have brought great credit to the Supreme Court of the United States, has been rejected by the United States Senate. I deeply regret this action. I believe a majority of people in the nation regret it.
>
> Especially I deplore the nature of the attacks that have been made upon this distinguished man. His integrity is unimpeachable, his ability unquestioned. The Supreme Court needs men of his legal philosophy to restore the proper balance to that great institution.
>
> The nation is fortunate that Clement Haynsworth's ability and judgment will remain available to the judiciary through his continuance as Chief Judge of one of the largest and busiest appellate courts in the nation.
>
> When the Congress returns for its second session in January I will nominate another associate justice. The criteria I shall apply for this selection, as was the case with my nomination of Judge Haynsworth, will be consistent with my commitments to the American people before my election as President a year ago.

There was no doubting what Nixon meant. Rehnquist would be vetting another southerner.

NIXON'S NEXT CHOICE, on January 19, 1970, was a Florida judge, G. Harrold Carswell, who seemed superficially to have the right credentials but who, in fact, turned into a far greater embarrassment for the White House than Haynsworth. "A colossal mistake," John Dean said of the nomination. "A complete screw-up by Nixon's advisers."

Dean disputed the conventional wisdom of the day, which was that Nixon nominated the unqualified Carswell out of pique at the Senate. "The Carswell nomination was the result of poor staff work," Dean flatly stated. "Nixon did not pick Carswell because he was angry with the Senate. It was afterward that he would be truly angry."

It was new Chief Justice Burger who pointed Nixon toward Carswell, but it was Rehnquist who pronounced him judicially fit for the job. To be sure, the nominee had surface appeal. At age fifty, Carswell had already climbed high, serving five years as a federal prosecutor in Florida before moving to the federal court, where he'd been for eleven years. Nixon had elevated him to the federal appeals court a mere seven months earlier. Rehnquist vetted Carswell's decisions and affirmed him to be a strict constructionist. Moreover, Carswell passed another important litmus test: he'd already been confirmed *three times* by the Senate; already investigated *three times* by the FBI. Surely any skeletons in the closet had come out by now. Mitchell called the choice too good to be true.

But despite Burger's confidence in the nominee, Rehnquist's vetting of his opinions, and the FBI's vast investigative resources, it took only days for the news media to sniff out evidence that Rehnquist and his Justice Department team missed.

While he was a federal prosecutor, Carswell had helped to convert a public golf course into a private club in order to avoid integrating it. He had signed the incorporation papers for a "white only" booster club at Florida State University. When he ran unsuccessfully for the Georgia state legislature in 1948, he told an American Legion group: "I am a Southerner by ancestry, birth, training, inclination, belief, and practice. I believe that segregation of the races is proper and the only practical and correct way of life in our states. I have always so believed and I shall always so act. . . . I yield to no man as a fellow candidate, as a fellow citizen, in the firm, vigorous belief in the principles of white supremacy, and I shall always be so governed." To Carswell's Senate foes, the campaign speech was a smoking gun. But even those who might have dismissed such comments as being of a different era could not escape the truth. Carswell had told a racist joke to the Georgia Bar Association a mere two months before his nomination to the Supreme Court.

Rehnquist and those he relied on had failed to uncover any of that. Six years later, it would be revealed that Carswell, although married with four children, also was a homosexual.* Observed Dean: "While Richard Nixon was always looking for historical firsts, nominating a homosexual to the High Court would not have been on his list."

The Senate opposition to Carswell came to a slower boil than with Haynsworth, in part because the Senate was wearying of the battles with Nixon. But as the evidence against Carswell mounted, Bayh once again took the lead against the nominee. Mitchell and Kleindienst had kept mostly to the sidelines during the Haynsworth battle, but now they, too, joined Rehnquist in defending Carswell. Mitchell put out a statement decrying the "false and misleading" statements of Carswell's opponents. Kleindienst made the rounds of the Sunday-morning talk shows and predicted that Carswell would be confirmed. After some civil rights attorneys said they had been treated discourteously by Carswell when they appeared before the judge, Rehnquist drafted a letter disputing the allegation and had it signed by an attorney for the Equal Employment Opportunity Commission.

Carswell's nomination was being managed on the floor by the ranking Republican on the Senate Judiciary Committee, Roman L. Hruska of Nebraska. A master of malapropism, Hruska did his nominee no favors when he walked outside of the Senate chamber to speak to reporters as debate began. Someone asked Hruska to respond to the charge that Carswell was a mediocre judge. Well, Hruska replied in a comment that became legendary, "even if he was mediocre, there are a lot of mediocre judges and people and lawyers. They are entitled to a little representation, aren't they, and a little chance? We can't have all Brandeises and Cardozos and Frankfurters and stuff like that there." If there were any undecided senators remaining, Nixon lost them right there. Carswell went down to defeat, garnering—as had Haynsworth—only 45 votes. It was April 8, 1970, and the Court had been sitting with only eight justices for almost a year.

Nixon took what he could from the defeat. He reminded his southern base about how hard he had worked to put one of its own on the Court,

---

*Carswell was arrested in 1976 after meeting an undercover officer in a men's room at a Tallahassee shopping center and then going with him to a wooded area. He was indicted by a grand jury but pleaded no contest to a charge of battery and paid a $100 fine. In 1979, Carswell was attacked and severely beaten by a male stranger he had invited to his Atlanta hotel room. William Sullivan, the FBI's assistant director at the time, later cited the failure to ferret out Carswell's homosexuality as evidence of just how sloppy the bureau's investigation had been.

and then declared that he was putting his strategy on ice. He had concluded that the Senate as "presently constituted" would not confirm a nominee to the Supreme Court "from the South who believes as I do in the strict construction of the Constitution." Haynsworth and Carswell, the president said, "have endured with admirable dignity vicious assaults on their intelligence, their honesty and their character. As long as the Senate is constituted the way it is today, I will not nominate another Southerner and let him be subjected to the kind of malicious character assassination accorded both Judges Haynsworth and Carswell. I understand the bitter feeling of millions of Americans who live in the South about the act of regional discrimination that took place in the Senate yesterday. They have my assurance that the day will come when men like Judges Carswell and Haynsworth can and will sit on the High Court."

Haldeman talked to Nixon after the vote and then wrote in his diary that Nixon thought the "main fault was Justice. He called Carswell, good brief chat. No substance except urged him to stay on court. He will." Twelve days later, Carswell resigned and ran unsuccessfully for a seat in the Senate from Florida.

Burger, meanwhile, passed another name on to Nixon and the president wasted no time in acting on it. This time his nominee was Burger's boyhood friend from Minnesota (and the best man at Burger's wedding), Harry Blackmun, a sixty-one-year-old federal appeals court judge. Burger and Blackmun were jocularly called the Minnesota Twins, and the fact that the latter would vote like Burger was taken for granted. Nixon was sailing into a safe harbor to the north, and he wasn't going to waste any time getting there.

The president announced the Blackmun nomination on April 13, 1970. After Nixon's obloquy on his team's vetting of Carswell, Rehnquist took no public role. Kleindienst preemptively got out in front of the financial conflict of interest issue, revealing in a letter to the Senate Judiciary Committee chairman that Blackmun had ruled in three cases despite owning stock in one of the litigants. That didn't matter now. Blackmun was a northerner and the Senate had tired of the jousting. The senators confirmed him by a vote of 94–0 on May 12. By the time Blackmun took the oath, the Court had been shorthanded for 391 days. Not since the Civil War had there been such a long stretch without a full Court.

Blackmun had been billed by Nixon as a "strict constructionist," but the Minnesotan would be anything but that as he matured on the Court.

Blackmun later recalled in an interview: "I was rather cross-examined by two members of the Department of Justice, one of whom was no less than William H. Rehnquist. He was assistant A.G. in charge of the Office of Legal Counsel. He and I have kidded about that ever since, because whenever I depart from his position, I say, 'Bill, you never should have recommended me,' and so forth. He's easy to kid with, he always kids back."

FOURTEEN

Two More Vacancies

IN SEPTEMBER 1971, a little more than a year after finally getting Blackmun in place, the Nixon administration found itself with two more vacancies on the Court.

First, on September 17, came the resignation of Hugo Black—the *Hated* Black of Rehnquist's Stanford notebook. Black, eighty-five years old and the first of FDR's nine Supreme Court appointees, was one of the Court's liberal mainstays—and he had been hanging on through Nixon's first term. But Black also had a resignation letter in his desk drawer, waiting for a date. During the Court's summer recess, Black checked himself in to Bethesda Naval Hospital, and he was still there in mid-September as the new term loomed. Black knew he could not last and told Burger of his intention to retire. Burger immediately telephoned Mitchell, Nixon's attorney general, with the news. Mitchell told Haldeman, and Haldeman told Nixon. The news of Black's resignation was immediately released to the press. Two days after that, Black suffered a stroke, and he died on September 25.

But there was more. When Burger telephoned Nixon on the afternoon of September 17 to discuss Black's rapidly declining health and resultant resignation, Burger revealed something else that Mitchell had already given the president a heads-up about: Justice John Harlan was also gravely ill and would soon resign. Harlan was an Eisenhower appointee, a conservative, and one of Nixon's favorites. Getting rid of the liberal Black was one thing. But Nixon had already blurted out to Mitchell earlier that afternoon that he didn't want Harlan's resignation. In spite of Harlan's declining health, Nixon wanted him to stay. "We've never needed a stronger, more vigorous man."

Harlan had long been in ill health and his near-blindness was well known, but now Burger told Nixon that "something much more serious"—spinal cancer—was crippling Harlan. Harlan had been hospitalized for five weeks, also at Bethesda Naval. In frustration, Harlan had transferred to get what he thought would be better care at George Washington University Hospital. Burger planned to visit him there at 4:30 P.M. The chief justice thought Nixon would be getting two simultaneous vacancies. Indeed, Harlan did resign on September 23, and he died three months later.

The timing of all this could not have been much worse. It was now September 1971, and jockeying for the Democratic nomination to oppose Nixon in the 1972 presidential election was getting under way. The waning year of a presidential term was not a propitious time for the White House to be sending a nomination to the Senate, as LBJ had earlier found out. The fact that Democrats controlled the Senate only further complicated this already infelicitous opportunity. But Nixon relished a chance to get his third and fourth justices on the Court (only Washington, Lincoln, and Taft had named more in a first term), and he and his inner circle began to plan privately to see how they could achieve their ends. Nixon started thinking out loud about the vested interests he had to pander to: maybe he would appoint a conservative southerner, or maybe consideration should be given to a Jewish nominee, "if we want to play to the Jews." There would be much plotting. Only with the later release of the White House tapes did the full extent of their scheming become clear.

The planning for how to fill these two Supreme Court vacancies went on for a month and remained a tightly held secret throughout that time. Rehnquist was not brought in. Instead, he was given another important chore that summer and fall—the first task that provided Nixon with an up-close view of him—and he struggled with it.

ON SUNDAY, JUNE 13, 1971, the *New York Times* began publishing excerpts from a vast, secret document that came to be known as the Pentagon Papers. It was an encyclopedic history of the Vietnam War written by analysts at the Department of Defense, comprising forty-seven volumes and running seven thousand pages in length. However dry and turgid the document, the mere existence of this "secret history," with its candid assessments of the futility of the Vietnam conflict, cast fresh attention on the war that Nixon had made a campaign promise to end.

Nixon, always at odds with the press, could not abide that the *Times* had decided to publish classified documents that further undermined what little public support remained for the war. Nixon was apoplectic, and the whole administration was whipped into a lather. In a situation like this, Rehnquist would immediately have been designated as the in-house attack dog against the media. But this time he was absent, recuperating from the first of what would be many operations on his spine.

Mitchell ordered Rehnquist back into the office and told him to get his team together because Nixon wanted to stop further publication. Some sort of plausible legal justification was needed for such an unprecedented action, and Rehnquist would have to provide it. There was, of course, the irritating obstacle of the 1st Amendment and its restriction of prior restraint of the press. The Supreme Court had never been hospitable to government interference with a newspaper's right to publish. The controlling case was *Near v. Minnesota** and there wasn't a lot of wiggle room for the government. But Rehnquist knew what he needed to do. He gave Mitchell the desired legal opinion: there was "a reasonable possibility that the government would succeed in the action." The Justice Department filed for an injunction against the *Times.*

But there was no stopping Daniel Ellsberg, the Pentagon Papers coauthor who had given the secret document to the *Times.* Soon the papers were in the hands of sixteen other newspapers as well. There were not enough fingers to plug every hole in the dike, but Nixon was obsessed with the *Washington Post,* one of those that had picked up where the *Times* left off. Nixon wanted to go after the *Post* as well, and he had the liberal newspaper added as a defendant in the case, which was rapidly making its way

*283 U.S. 697 (1931).

to the Supreme Court. Meanwhile, Rehnquist made a call to Ben Bradlee, the *Post*'s executive editor, and told him to stop the presses. Rehnquist must have recognized the futility of that. Bradlee told Rehnquist to buzz off, and the *Post* ran a story about Rehnquist's call the next morning. By then, Rehnquist could see he had a losing case. He packed up his family and took off for a scheduled vacation. The Nixon administration carried its case against both newspapers all the way to the Supreme Court, which quickly ruled 6–3 against the government.* Rehnquist wasn't there to witness the oral argument or Nixon's defeat. He was still at the beach.

But now that Nixon had lost the case, the White House inner circle began to see a possible silver lining. The Pentagon Papers raised a legitimate issue: whether the government was needlessly keeping secret materials that should have been released long ago. Nixon saw that the Pentagon Papers could be used as justification for an all-encompassing review of the whole concept of the government's system of classifying documents. In one of those *Aha!* moments, Nixon realized that by championing declassification in the name of good government, he might be able to finally get revenge against the hated Kennedys without leaving fingerprints.

Rehnquist, now back from his vacation, was put in charge of this project that took on vast personal importance to Nixon: the declassification of secret materials from past administrations. Rehnquist headed an interdepartmental task force that included the departments of Defense and State, the Atomic Energy Commission, the National Security Council, and the Central Intelligence Agency. An argument could be made that sunlight was the best of disinfectants and thus the declassification project was simply being undertaken in the public interest. That was the walk and talk, and it had the added benefit of literal truth. There were tons of documents dating from World War II onward that had no national-security justification for remaining secret. But some of those documents carried a heavy embarrassment factor. There were long-buried classified papers relating to various rogue operations of the CIA, including the disastrous Bay of Pigs invasion of Cuba and the assassination of South Vietnamese president Ngo Dinh Diem. Both had occurred during the Kennedy administration. When the

---

***New York Times Co. v. United States*, 403 U.S. 713 (1971). The vote was 6–3, with Burger, Blackmun, and Harlan dissenting.

expected flood of declassified documents came pouring out, Nixon wanted to make sure those were shunted to his office so that they could be leaked by Nixon's White House operatives. Nixon had a score to settle with the Kennedys. Whether Rehnquist knew it or not, his bureaucratic assignment to get those classified documents out into the open had a very personal importance to Richard Nixon.

On Wednesday, June 30, 1971, the Pentagon Papers defeat came down against Nixon. Nixon brooded about it that night, but by the next morning—July 1—he was in full shout, a bundle of excitement, as he sought the advice of J. Edgar Hoover,* Haldeman, and Charles Colson. Colson had the title of special counsel, but in reality he was Nixon's link to the ex-CIA operatives who carried out dirty tricks and black-bag jobs for the White House. Colson was devious—as Nixon put it to Haldeman that morning, "Colson, of course, sees an opportunity in everything"—and he had persuaded Nixon that there was potential gold in the Pentagon Papers defeat: it paved the way for public disparagement of the man whom Nixon always considered had stolen the 1960 election from him. Nixon could paint the war in Vietnam as Kennedy's responsibility. "Kennedy decided to go forward and got us involved," the president explained, "and it shows that Kennedy was the one who got us in the damn war. We got the Kennedys in this thing now." Hoover fed Nixon's paranoia when he told the president that Byron White's vote against Nixon the day before was to be expected, given that White was a friend of JFK's: "Of course. Whizzer White is of the old Kennedy crowd."

Indeed, as if on cue, the *New York Times* had restarted its Pentagon Papers coverage that very morning with a story disclosing that JFK knew about and approved plans for the military coup d'état that overthrew Diem and led to his assassination. Diem's killing ended what little vestige of democracy remained in Vietnam, and it started the country's downward spiral. "This is a conspiracy," Nixon told Haldeman. "It does involve these people [the Kennedys], and they are not on very good ground in many cases. Also, we now have the opportunity really to leak out all these nasty stories that will kill these bastards! I don't know whether you noticed this

*In his telephone conversation with Hoover, Nixon called the Pentagon Papers decision "unbelievable" and "stinking," and he vowed "to change that court." He said of the six justices who voted against him: "You know those clowns we got on there. I'll tell you, I hope I outlive the bastards."

morning, but even the *Times,* to my great surprise, gave a hell of a wallop to the Kennedy thing—Kennedy and Diem. Agreed?"

"Yup," Haldeman replied. "So did the *Post.*"

Nixon was stoked. Later that day, he walked over to his office in the Executive Office Building next door to the White House and gave a pep talk to the various representatives of the defense and intelligence agencies who were supposed to be declassifying the materials from World War II, the Korean War, and the Bay of Pigs invasion. He told them he wanted action. The president wanted everyone to work faster. No more foot-dragging. Rehnquist was running the meeting, but the reality of the situation was that no one was in control; the national-security bureaucracy was self-perpetuating. Each of the intelligence agencies was a power unto itself and none of them was about to cough up dark secrets. Rehnquist was powerless.

Nixon was frustrated at how the meeting went. This was the first time he had seen Rehnquist up close, and he was not impressed. Nixon had asked his White House counsel John Dean to accompany him, and he turned to Dean as he walked out.

"John, who the hell is that clown?"

"I beg your pardon?"

"The guy dressed like a clown, who's running the meeting?" Nixon repeated.

"Oh, you mean Bill Rehnquist."

"What's his name?" Nixon asked again.

"Rehnquist," Dean answered.

Nixon repeated the name. He asked Dean to spell it. Then he asked, "Is he Jewish? He looks it."

"I don't think so," Dean replied. "I think he's of Scandinavian background."

"Thanks," Nixon replied as he turned to walk away. "That's a hell of a costume he's wearing, just like a clown." Rehnquist had on a pink shirt that clashed with a psychedelic necktie, and Hush Puppies, which were seldom seen in the corridors of the White House. He sported bushy muttonchop sideburns and wore heavy black eyeglasses. Dean didn't know what to make of Nixon's comment. He couldn't tell if the president was amused or appalled.

Rehnquist's declassification project never went anywhere, despite Nixon's continued fulminations and all manner of dirty-trick plotting by Ehrlichman and Colson. But try they did.

Three and a half weeks after that first meeting with Rehnquist's group, Nixon was again complaining about the slow pace. It was July 24, 1971. Nixon talked to John Ehrlichman and Egil Krogh, the two Nixon loyalists who'd been among the first of the palace guard that Rehnquist met when he joined the administration. By now, both men were deeply involved in all sorts of White House intrigue, and eventually they would both serve prison time for it. "Nobody follows up on a God damn thing!" Nixon said of Rehnquist's project. "We've got to follow up on this thing. However, we, uh, we, uh, we had that meeting. You remember the meeting we had when I told that group of clowns we had around there? Rehnchburg and that group?"

Nixon recalled Rehnquist's mode of dress more vividly than his name.

"Renchquist," Ehrlichman corrected the president, but getting the name wrong himself.

"Yeah, Rehnquist," Nixon answered. The president remembered now.

"Yeah," said Ehrlichman.

Nixon couldn't understand what was going on. After all, he'd read them the riot act, told them what he wanted.

"They're going to come back at you with a whole new classi—"

"Good."

"—fication scheme."

"Right."

There was nothing in Nixon's tone to indicate that he saw Rehnquist as anything other than a dull cog in a process that wasn't progressing anywhere near as fast as he had hoped.

In frustration, Nixon started working on an end-around. A new plan was hatched to pressure Senate Democrats into holding hearings about JFK's connections to the CIA plots. Cables implicating JFK in the assassination would be fabricated by a White House operative named E. Howard Hunt.

Ehrlichman suggested Colson as a mastermind of the operation: "Suppose we get all the Diem stuff and supposing there's something we can really hang Teddy [Kennedy] or the Kennedy clan with. I'm going to want to put that in Colson's hands."

"Yep," Nixon replied.

"And we're really going to run with it," Ehrlichman continued.

Colson sent an Eyes Only memo to the president, proposing that they begin what Colson called another "*Life* operation" like the one the White

House had so deftly used to get rid of Fortas. As with Fortas, the recipient of the leak (presumably to include the forged cables) once again would be *Life* reporter William Lambert, who would write what Colson rather cynically called "the true story behind the Diem coup." Colson reminded Nixon that they had used Lambert and *Life* the year before to plant another false story that led to the election defeat of Senator Joseph Tydings (D-MD).

It would be hard to imagine that Rehnquist didn't feel the pressure. "We should very soon release declassified documents relating to the Lebanon crisis, the Cuban missile crisis and perhaps one or two others," Colson exhorted in his Eyes Only memo to Nixon. "Releasing of declassified documents will keep press interest alive in the whole issue. We should start doing it soon to avoid the charge of election year politicking. The Ellsberg operation can continue independently.* It may or may not prove fruitful, but we do have certain pay dirt in the coup story."

*A secret White House group called "the Plumbers" (so named because it investigated and stopped leaks) was assigned to burglarize the office of Daniel Ellsberg's Los Angeles psychiatrist in an effort to uncover evidence to discredit Ellsberg, who had leaked the Pentagon Papers.

FIFTEEN

"You Might Consider Bill Rehnquist"

THE PRESIDENT KNEW ALMOST IMMEDIATELY who his top choice to fill Black's seat was going to be: Congressman Richard H. Poff, a Republican from a small town in southwest Virginia. Nixon was still trying to fulfill his southern strategy, and he had already been eyeing Poff as a possible option during the Haynsworth and Carswell debacles. Nixon listed off his criteria. Hugo Black was from Alabama and so his seat almost certainly had to go to a southerner as far as Nixon was concerned. The president also thought Poff, the ranking Republican on the House Judiciary Committee, might get a smoother confirmation ride since he was already a Capitol Hill insider. Poff was forty-seven years old, young enough to help a Nixon Court make its mark decades into the future. Plus, Poff was available and he wanted the nomination, having made a low-key but persistent personal campaign for it since Nixon was elected in 1968.

"All right," the president told Haldeman as soon as he heard about the impending vacancies. "I want Poff." Poff would get Black's seat.

Dean knew Poff very well, and liked him; Dean had once served as the chief counsel for the Republicans on the House Judiciary Committee, where Poff was the senior Republican. He also knew Poff to be a constitutional expert; the congressman had actually drafted the 25th Amendment relating to presidential disability, making him what amounted to a rare living "framer." When Dean moved over to Justice and began handling congressional relations, his good relationship with Poff continued. All this was just further affirmation that Poff should be at the top of Nixon's short list. Poff was still the man.

But vacancies were coming too fast for Rehnquist to keep up. On the day that Harlan's resignation landed at the White House, Rehnquist was still preoccupied with trying to fill Black's seat; he phoned Dean to see what the White House counsel knew about Poff. Mitchell, in turn, was badgering Rehnquist, conferring with him in person or by phone on four different occasions throughout that day, all the meetings having to do with trying to speed up the vetting of Poff. Everybody was getting into the act because they feared another foul-up. When Dean spoke to Rehnquist, Dean made it clear that the White House—in actuality, Dean himself—also intended to play an active role in the vetting. As Nixon's man in charge, Dean took it as his responsibility to avoid a repeat of the Haynsworth and Carswell fiascos.

"Rehnquist's earlier passivity about Carswell in particular had struck me as surprising," Dean later wrote. "I had no idea why he had not reacted after studying [Carswell's] opinions. How he let Mitchell and the president go forward with that nomination, without a warning, remained a mystery."

In any event, Rehnquist and Dean agreed to split the vetting responsibilities when it came to Poff. Dean and David Young, another White House assistant on Ehrlichman's team, visited Poff at his House office that weekend, when it was quiet. They spent three and a half hours together, the two cross-examining Poff about every possible aspect of his life and career. Considering that he was both a Nixon appointee and a southerner, the knives would inevitably be out for him. Indeed, as soon as the speculation began about Poff's probable nomination, the NAACP voiced its opposition. It was already clear from this immediate blowback that Poff was going to be in for it.

Despite his years of quiet campaigning for a seat on the Court, it took Poff exactly one week to decide that this confirmation battle was not for him. He had an 800-pound gorilla in his living room and skeletons in the closet.

The obvious problem for Poff was his civil rights history. As a young congressman, Poff had signed the Southern Manifesto, a document condemning *Brown* (and all racial integration) that 101 southerners in the House and Senate put their names to in 1956. He had also voted against every landmark civil rights bill of the 1960s. The manifesto decried the "unwarranted exercise of power" by the Supreme Court, which, "contrary to the Constitution, is creating chaos and confusion in the states principally affected. It is destroying the amicable relations between the white and Negro races that have been created through 90 years of patient effort by the good people of both races. It has planted hatred and suspicion where there has been heretofore friendship and understanding."

Signing the document was something that Poff thought he had to do at the time, but fifteen years later he was one of many politicians who wished they could erase their name from it. As part of his quiet campaign for a Supreme Court vacancy, Poff had tried to renounce the manifesto, giving an interview to the Norfolk *Virginian-Pilot* in which he admitted to a craven political fear that he might lose his rural Virginia seat if he didn't sign. Now, with a confirmation battle looming, the interview transcript soon was circulating in Washington, and Poff began looking like one more cynical politician. Poff was a practiced vote-counter on the Hill. It was going to be close, and his nomination might not survive a filibuster.

Then there was the skeleton in the closet, a secret that Poff unaccountably had been keeping. Poff feared that a messy confirmation process would somehow uncover the fact that his twelve-year-old son, Tom, was adopted. It seemed hard to imagine why the existence of an adoption should be secret, or why keeping that secret was worth giving up his Supreme Court dream—particularly since some reporter was bound to find it out and reveal it anyway, as Jack Anderson did in his Washington Merry-Go-Round column less than two months later. But that was how Poff saw it, and in the end the White House didn't try to dissuade him.

Poff put out a statement blaming his withdrawal on the likelihood of a long Senate battle. "From press reports, it is clear that the confirmation process would be protracted and controversial. I have been called a racist. I am not. I have never been. I will never be. With respect to the Southern Manifesto, my voting record and whatever I have written or said, I can only ask that all remember the temper of the times. . . ."

An obviously frustrated Nixon thought a good man had been brought down even before the fight began. He fretted about yet another setback to his southern strategy and devilishly threatened, as Haldeman wrote that day in his diary, "to go for a real right-winger now. . . . He wants to get someone worse than Poff and really stick it to the opposition now." Maybe Senator Robert Byrd of West Virginia, "because he was a former KKKer."

Nixon had been privately threatening since the early days of the Haynsworth battle to send up Senate Majority Whip Robert Byrd's name as payback. Byrd was a powerful Democrat and a master both of pork-barrel politics and the Senate's arcane parliamentary rules, but he was also a petty man with a second-rate intellect. Nixon's nominating Byrd would paint the Democratic Senate leadership into a corner. The Senate would be forced to confirm him, because no senator would want to vote against Byrd and risk his wrath if he didn't get on the Court. Nixon saw it as a way to rub the Senate's nose in the mess he thought the Democratic leadership had created.

In the end, Nixon decided to short-list Byrd, and some other southerners, for one of the two slots.

A process that had been followed, with a few exceptions, from the days of the Eisenhower administration was for a committee of the American Bar Association* to review the short list of prospective Supreme Court nominees and offer an opinion as to whether each was well qualified for the High Court. All manner of law school deans, professors, and lawyers conducted interviews and pored over a candidate's writings. The ABA's vetting was supposed to be unbiased and confidential, but in practice it was neither, allowing an obviously unqualified candidate like Carswell to easily slip through. If anything, the ABA actually added to the intensity and politicization of the debate, because its evaluation process leaked like a sieve. There was no way that a president could seek the ABA's discreet counsel. Instead of lending gravitas and authority to the selection of an eventual nominee, the ABA incited a public free-for-all.

With Nixon's earlier Supreme Court nominations, the ABA screeners had done their work after the nominations were announced. But in the

---

*The ABA group was called the Standing Committee on the Federal Judiciary. Every president from Eisenhower through Clinton consulted in advance with the committee to rank nominees to federal judgeships, although the consultation process often was neither smooth nor satisfactory as far as the White House was concerned. George W. Bush finally stopped the practice of seeking the ABA's advice, although the ABA committee continued to conduct its own appraisals of federal judicial nominees after their names were sent to the Senate for confirmation. Barack Obama resumed the practice of consulting ahead of time with the ABA committee. The committee consisted of fifteen members: two members from the Ninth Circuit, one member from each of the other federal judicial circuits, and the chair of the committee. The president of the ABA appointed members for staggered three-year terms, and no member could serve more than two terms. Interestingly, the Poff nomination was the first of Nixon's presidency in which he gave the ABA a list to screen in advance. His earlier Supreme Court nominations were sprung as surprises.

aftermath of the Poff nomination's quick demise Nixon saw a way to use the ABA for political inoculation. For the first time in his presidency, Nixon—acting through Mitchell—gave the ABA his list of prospective Supreme Court nominees to evaluate in advance. Nixon and Mitchell correctly calculated that if the list leaked, as it soon did, it would be red meat for the media. Only Mitchell and a few others knew that Nixon also had some other favored candidates in mind. The president held their names back out of a fear that premature disclosure would destroy their chances.

The ABA list that Mitchell sent on October 13, 1971, was either a White House trial balloon or the political equivalent of an advance guard marching through the minefield. Either way, Nixon would wait and see what dangers lay ahead. There were two women (there had never before been a female nominee) and four southerners among the six names:

- Mildred L. Lillie, fifty-six years old, a judge on the California Court of Appeals
- Herschel H. Friday, forty-nine, a municipal bond lawyer (and school board attorney) from Little Rock, Arkansas
- Sylvia Bacon, forty, a judge on the District of Columbia Superior Court
- Charles C. Clark, forty-six, of Mississippi, a judge on the US Court of Appeals for the Fifth Circuit
- Paul H. Roney, fifty, of Florida, also a judge on the US Court of Appeals for the Fifth Circuit
- Robert Byrd, fifty-three, of West Virginia, the Senate majority whip and a member of the Senate Judiciary Committee

Rehnquist was not on the list because he wasn't yet on Mitchell's or Nixon's radar as a viable candidate. He was still mired in the declassification project. But also not on the list was a man whom Nixon appeared already to have settled on: Lewis F. Powell, sixty-three years old, a former president of the ABA from Richmond. Powell was a wealthy Virginia gentleman who was, quite literally, to the manor born—the first Powell, one of the original Jamestown colonists, had arrived on Virginia soil in 1607. Older than the others, Powell had previously resisted Nixon's entreaties to join the Court, but now Powell signaled he was ready. Nixon and Mitchell kept his name secret, and Powell had not yet given a definitive "yes" to the direct question of joining the Court. But when the time came for Nixon to make his move, the president had already made up his mind that Powell was the man for Black's southern seat, if he could get him.

There remained the matter of Harlan's successor, and Nixon was actively engaged in the search. The short list delivered to the ABA on October 13 was supposed to help Nixon decide, but instead it had the opposite effect. Surely anyone as media-savvy as Nixon would have known that such a list would not stay secret for long, but Nixon seemed genuinely surprised when the names were revealed by the Dow Jones newswire that evening and landed on the front page of the *New York Times* the following morning. Nixon was angry about the leak, but to an even greater extent he had trepidation about the looming cannibalization—Nixon's term—of the people on the list.

Mitchell blamed "Democrats" on the ABA committee for the leak. As was so often the case, Nixon began intriguing for a way to turn the bad news into good—to find the proverbial silver lining. Nixon was his own best friend when it came to conjuring the dark side of politics, and he quickly came up with an ingenious, if diabolical, plan. He would confound the ABA's process by flooding the bar committee with even more names, all red herrings. "Send up a half dozen more names," Nixon demanded in a 9 A.M. phone call to Mitchell. "Would you do that? Just to keep it confused. Could you just, send up, you know, like send down the dean of that law school.* I don't want to limit this, send down one of those Jewish—send [Edward] Levi's [president of the University of Chicago] name in, too. Would you do that please? Get that done right away, OK?"

"Now—," Mitchell tried to break in.

"I've got to do it because I just can't leave this hanging here, hanging here for a week now without—"

"Which type of names?" Mitchell was still trying to get a handle on Nixon's thinking.

"Oh, God! I don't give a damn who they are. Some Jews and liberals and so forth. Like Levi of Chicago; he'd be all right as a name."

---

*Nixon may have been referring to William H. Mulligan, who had been dean of the Fordham University Law School until a few months earlier, when the president named him to the federal court of appeals in New York. The president was getting pressure to appoint a Catholic to the Court and, because Mitchell was a Fordham Law graduate, might have surmised his AG would know Mulligan.

"Well, if you do that, of course, then it's gone to the public, and—"

"Well, send Johnson of, of that other one down there."

"Frank Johnson?" Mitchell knew Johnson as an eminent federal appeals court judge from Alabama and the author of landmark civil rights decisions.

"Yes, Johnson. But that [*sic*] you've already sent [Charles] Clark, you could send the fellow from the law school, down there. From Texas?"

"Right."

"Just pick, if you can, John. Send out any kind of names that are conservative enough. Powell. I don't know. . . . Any you can think of, just to confuse it some. Because they're going to tear these to pieces. They will. I mean, they'll always seize on what you've got as mediocrities and so forth and so on. That's what I'm concerned about. . . . I've become convinced the bar has broken its pick with me, come to the point where, with the bar—the next time we have an appointment they aren't going to have a chance to look at it, John.* Good God, I have more judgment and you have more judgment on who the hell oughta be, is qualified for the Court. What the hell does the bar know about it? Good God, I can take a bar examination better than any of those assholes."

"I agree," Mitchell replied, now clearly getting Nixon's drift. "The bar is not doing this [again]. This is what we would expect with anybody we send up."

"That's why we're not going to give 'em a chance again," Nixon continued. "They've broken their pick. . . . I think our strategy was right the other time, just not to ask the bar. They squeal, but that's—I'm really sick of the bastards anyway. They're such a bunch of sanctimonious assholes. But I've told Ehrlichman to get off his ass and get me whatever little check he's gotta make. I really think we've gotta get it done, now. I mean, I don't—they're really going to tear this, they're going to jump up and down on this now."

Nixon now wanted to move much faster to get both vacancies filled. Still, Nixon reckoned that he couldn't pull the list back from the bar at this point; he would have to hold his nose and let that process play out, even as he sent out more smokescreens: "When we get it from the bar, we're

*Nixon made good on this threat. Mitchell announced that henceforth the White House would no longer seek the ABA committee's recommendation on prospective Court nominees.

just going to have to go with it, [even though] I don't want to. You see, the mistake we made with Poff is we let him get up there—and let them cannibalize him. I just don't want [the nominees] to get killed before we do with this. I want the positive stuff first."

Nixon returned to the *Times* story. He brooded not so much about the story but about the page-one headline, which was dismissive of the lawyers on the short list:

MOST NOT WELL KNOWN; POTENTIAL CHOICES
DO NOT INCLUDE LEADING JUDICIAL FIGURES

"I'm going to deny this story, by the way," Nixon advised. He told Mitchell to do likewise when the attorney general met the press for a scheduled news conference later that day. "Tell them we have several other names we're considering. Let the bar lie all they want."

"That's perfectly all right," Mitchell replied.

"Tell them it's just among many we're considering. It's premature, routine checks on a position." Nixon had it all figured out.

"We can cover that," Mitchell agreed.

"Get 'em off on a red herring."

It was Thursday. The ABA would take the weekend to come back with its opinion on Herschel Friday and Mildred Lillie—the two that Mitchell had, as part of the smokescreen, falsely told the ABA were Nixon's top choices. But Nixon surmised that the leaked list would set off furious speculation in the ensuing days, and that pressure against him would keep mounting unless he ended it by making an announcement quickly. "There'll be editorials over the weekend," he told Mitchell, correctly predicting the spate of negative commentary that was about to come. "I just want to beat the bastards on this. I just don't want to create an impression that we're looking for a bunch of nonentities, a bunch of southerners and women, you see. And goddamnit—"

"Well, as long as they have [that as] your philosophy, they're going to attack them," Mitchell interjected. It was pointless to do anything but agree with Nixon at this point.

Nixon ignored Mitchell's comment and just barreled ahead. "My plan is, if we get out first, as soon as we get it, I'm going to do this on television. Then we get the goddamn story out first, and then we're way ahead of them." In the space of that one phone call with Mitchell, Nixon had come to a decision. He would give Mitchell and Ehrlichman a week, no more, to get the background checks done and find him another nominee to go along with his presumptive choice of Powell. Nixon saw it as imperative that he move fast to head off the opposition that was sure to build and solidify the longer he waited. Come hell or high water, Nixon was going to announce two names in a week.

Meanwhile, just as Nixon had predicted, Senators Kennedy and Bayh immediately called Nixon's list "an insult to the Court." Nixon began getting hammered by commentators in the influential newspapers, news magazines, and television networks. *Time* magazine headlined its story "Nixon's Not So Supreme Court."

Among the many who weighed in that weekend was Alan Dershowitz, a young Harvard law professor who was starting to make a name for himself as a biting liberal commentator and a defender of the underdog. Dershowitz was the youngest full professor of law in the school's history and already had become something of a notorious gadfly on the Harvard Law faculty.

Dershowitz was also full of holy wrath in much the same way that Rehnquist was, except that Dershowitz leaned way to the left. In the fall of 1971, the thirty-three-year-old had just begun a year-long fellowship at Stanford's Center for Advanced Study in the Behavioral Sciences. In his spare time he was also writing opinion pieces for the "Week in Review" section of the *New York Times.* As soon as the short list of Supreme Court candidates (Lillie, Friday et al.) hit the newspapers he dashed off a piece for that coming Sunday's *Times,* exhorting the Senate to maintain its principled stand against Nixon's conservative nominations. The Supreme Court, Dershowitz insisted, was being wrongly treated by the Senate as an extension of Nixon's cabinet. Instead, it needed to demand independent thinkers who weren't just rubber stamps for Nixon's policies; there was an obligation to maintain the Court's "uniqueness" as an independent third branch. Based on the short list and Nixon's other rejected nominees, Dershowitz could see what was coming: a nominee who lacked sympathy with the values reflected in the Bill of Rights—justice, liberty, and equality—and who instead favored "order, security, and efficiency." The following Sunday, Dershowitz had another piece in the *Times,* urging the Senate Judiciary Committee to take a close look at the hard-liners who'd been nominated. Both were polished efforts by the young professor, reasoned and logical rather than full of fire and brimstone. If Dershowitz wondered whether anyone was paying attention, he was soon going to find out.

In the meantime, over the next few days Nixon's thinking about the second seat continued to evolve. Both nominees would have to be eminent and unassailable. Powell certainly fit the bill and was a southerner to boot, but he was also an older man and Nixon didn't expect him to serve more than ten years.* That made it important that his other choice be significantly younger, someone who could serve thirty years or more and might someday move up to chief justice. Nixon had begun to lean in the direction of Howard Baker, forty-five years old and an up-and-coming Republican Senator from Tennessee. Nixon thought the Senate would not be too hard on one of its own. It did not hurt that Baker was the son-in-law of the late, legendary Senate Republican leader from Illinois, Everett McKinley Dirksen.**

But Baker certainly hadn't been petitioning for the job and didn't know the offer was going to be coming. Nixon instructed Mitchell to hit him with it, cold turkey. When Mitchell put the arm on him, Baker didn't exactly jump at the opportunity. That was a red flag for Nixon and his White House circle, and they started discreetly looking for a backup in case Baker folded.

By Tuesday, October 19, the end game was under way with a self-imposed urgency from Nixon. The president had decided to reveal his two choices in a five-minute live television address from the White House two days later, at 7:30 P.M. on Thursday, October 21. That would be one week to the day after the page-one story in the *Times* that disparaged his trial-balloon list of nominees. Nixon's press secretary, Ron Ziegler, would wait until Thursday morning to ask for the television time. In the meantime, Mitchell and Nixon had two days to get their two nominees signed up. They started working on Powell and Baker.

Powell was the easier of the two. Mitchell had already softened up Powell when Nixon finally reached him that Tuesday evening. Powell had some concerns—his eyesight was failing him, and he wanted to be straight with Nixon that he might not be a long-termer on the Court. Nixon assured Powell that this didn't matter: "What happens in the next five years is ter-

---

*Nixon told Mitchell when they were ruminating about Powell's selection: "I'd say that two years of Powell is worth of somebody else, and that's the damn truth."

** Dirksen had died in office two years earlier, at age seventy-three.

ribly important without going beyond that even." Powell also fretted that he might be attacked by black leaders "who will think that I was not aggressive enough in aiding integration." Again, Nixon told him not to worry. Powell wanted to talk to his two law partners, and to his wife. He would think things over and give a definite answer the next day. Fine, Nixon said. Mitchell would await his call.

Attention turned to Baker. "We sort of knocked Howard off his feet with surprise," Mitchell reported to Nixon soon after meeting with Baker. The young senator was worried about making ends meet on a justice's salary. Nixon counseled Mitchell to stress the insurance and retirement benefits, and the ability of justices to supplement their income through speeches and outside writing. "I just want you to press him, John," Nixon said. "The more I think about it . . . they are just not going to crucify another senator up there." The president pointed out that Baker had a good relationship with Senator Edward Brooke of Massachusetts, who had led the fight against Carswell. Brooke was an anomaly if ever there was one: the Senate's only African-American, and a Republican.

"Well, now, that isn't going to hurt. I have a feeling that this guy [Baker] is intelligent and [has] a strong mind. I must say—not as sure as he could be, but you know that on most stuff he is going to be good. You just can't expect him to be 100 percent."

Mitchell quickly got into selling mode, trying to allay any nagging doubts that Nixon might have about Baker. "The way he was talking about your philosophy—"

"Did he sound all right?"

"Oh, completely."

Baker just needed to make up his mind. And, with the clock ticking, Mitchell was still concerned about having a backup plan in case Baker didn't come through. The president had kept the selection process so secret that only a few of his staff members knew anything. Even Dean was completely out of the loop; he was still vetting the red herrings and knew nothing about Baker. Since Dean thought he was supposed to be the White House's point man on the search, that meant that his counterpart at Justice, Rehnquist, probably also had no idea about the new tangent that the search had taken—and would next take.

Two weeks earlier, after Poff's withdrawal and before the firestorm over the list of six, Dean had been brainstorming possible candidates with

Richard A. Moore, another of Nixon's advisers. Moore was an old Nixon loyalist, a white-haired sage, and held the title of special counsel to the president. Dean urged Moore to consider Rehnquist. "If the president really wanted a strict constructionist," Dean recalled later, "I had his man." It was certainly an intriguing idea, but as the search evolved with Dean (and Rehnquist) out of the inner loop, there it lay.

Moore was a lawyer and an ex-broadcasting executive from California, and Nixon trusted him as an image-maker. Although Moore initially was cold to the idea—he saw no political upside for Nixon—in the days that followed the idea of Rehnquist as a possible fall-back began to take hold in his mind. It was a wild hare, but Moore thought it just might work.

A week later, Dean had a chance to share his brainstorm with Mitchell in a telephone call. They spoke the day after the dustup about Nixon's short list. Mitchell's initial reaction was the same as Moore's had been. Politically, it was just too risky.

But when Baker still hadn't made his intentions known with only two days remaining before Nixon's televised address, Mitchell was worried enough to start trying out some other names on Nixon. It was 5:38 P.M. on Tuesday. The speech was Thursday. Nixon had no second man. Mitchell was clearly concerned.

"I still haven't heard back from Howard Baker yet either, although he said he'd call me back before 5. I guess he's searching his soul."

"Sure," Nixon replied absent-mindedly.

Mitchell plowed ahead. "Another thought's occurred to me, Mr. President. If we can't get Baker and Powell doesn't pan out, you might consider this Bill Rehnquist over here that everybody is so high on."

"Mmm, hmm," Nixon murmured as he mulled this surprising suggestion from Mitchell. "Well, let me ask you—what are his qualifications?"

"Well, first of all—"

"He's an assistant attorney general," Nixon correctly recalled.

"Yeah, in charge of the Office of Legal Counsel. In fact, Walsh* has stated on a number of occasions, why in the hell don't you put up somebody like Rehnquist?"

"Yeah." Nixon replied distractedly, offering nothing to keep Mitchell's conversational gambit alive.

---

*Lawrence Walsh was the chairman of the ABA's Standing Committee on the Judiciary, the group to which Nixon had sent his short list for prescreening.

"So I think that would clear," Mitchell continued anyway. The attorney general meant that the ABA panel most likely would rate Rehnquist as being qualified for the Court.

"Right." Nixon was still offering Mitchell no encouragement to continue. It didn't matter; Mitchell was determined to get the story out.

"He is, as I say, an arch-conservative. He was a great student. And a pretty tough guy."

Nixon said he understood all that, but he pushed back and wanted to know more. What were Rehnquist's qualifications? How old was he? How long had he practiced law? Where was he from? Had he ever actually handled an appellate case? Ever worked in a big law firm in a big city "and all that jazz, you know." Nixon was worried that Rehnquist was just too small-townish, not distinguished enough. The president still wanted Baker. "Howard damn well oughta do this. Tell him we just won't take no for an answer."

By the next afternoon, with just one day to go before his announcement, Nixon got what he called "great" news: the ABA committee had done its work, and its members rejected both of Nixon's red herrings, Mildred Lillie and Herschel Friday, as unqualified. The political implications of this were clear: Nixon had inadvertently hit political paydirt. He was off the hook when it came to naming Lillie and Friday and could blame the ABA for stymieing his original plan;* he could take full credit for trying to nominate a woman (Lillie, whom he actually never intended to nominate) and a man from the Deep South (Friday, ditto); and he could run with the men (Powell and Baker) who'd been his first choices all along.

Except that Mitchell still hadn't heard from Baker. The senator had, in essence, disappeared; he was off the grid at a time when Nixon had already begun drafting the nationally televised address he planned for the following evening. Baker, it turned out, had already secretly visited Potter Stewart at the Court to find out firsthand what the life of a justice was like. The senator was still agonizing over the decision.

Meanwhile, Nixon told the White House operators to find Mitchell and get him on the line. While the president was waiting, he called his old friend Dick Moore into his office. It was 4:20 P.M., late Wednesday afternoon. Nixon's announcement was scheduled for Thursday at 7:30 P.M.

---

*"Get that out," Nixon told Mitchell when he learned of the ABA committee's vote. "We've got to do it before we make the damn announcement [of Nixon's nominations for the two vacancies]. . . . And the stacked jury thing [the idea that no southerner or woman, no matter how qualified, would get the ABA's support] is going to really kill them."

Moore had been out of the loop, along with the rest of Nixon's White House staff, but now Nixon brought him in. The president was thinking aloud about how the various scenarios might play out the following evening. There was not a lot of time left, and Nixon half-apologized for not revealing more sooner, but "I've taken this judge thing out of the hands of our staff, for reasons you're well aware of. They're all leaking too much." Nixon tried out his scenario on Moore: The ABA would get the blame for rejecting Lillie and Friday. Then Nixon would be free to nominate Powell (to Nixon's surprise, Moore had never heard of him) and Baker. "Of the two of them, [Baker] is probably the weakest." But a man of Powell's age and obvious distinction would "buy" Nixon the necessary political support for the younger Baker. "You've then got a guy who's there 30 years. And who, also, if a Republican is around, is a potential candidate for chief justice."

Then Nixon spun out some alternative scenarios. The president said he still thought Baker eventually would come over—Nixon was waiting for Mitchell to call back—but what if Baker folded? Nixon quickly listed a few other names as possibilities; he had some ideas. But in fact there wasn't anyone seriously on Nixon's radar besides Baker. Nixon's discussion with Moore showed that the president was worried and needed a backup plan.

Moore decided that since he was sitting there with Nixon he might as well reintroduce Rehnquist's name. Moore knew that Nixon had all but dismissed Rehnquist the day before, during Nixon's phone call with Mitchell, but Moore figured there was no harm in trying again.

Nixon quickly turned Moore aside. "They're just going to say he's not qualified. I mean, they're just going to say, what the hell, he's a nice fellow—"

Moore persisted. "He's the most conservative, so—"

"I know he's conservative, I know all that. He'd be a fine member of the Court, but how the hell could you just put a guy who's an assistant attorney general on the Court?"

But when Moore reminded Nixon that Rehnquist had clerked for Justice Jackson and graduated at the top of his Stanford class, Nixon seemed to warm up. The president began quizzing Moore just as he had Mitchell the day before, peppering him with all manner of questions. "Be a hell of a judge," Nixon finally agreed. Then he telephoned Mitchell.

Baker was still incommunicado, dodging Mitchell. "I have not been able to get a hold of our little senator friend," Mitchell told Nixon. "I don't know whether—"

Nixon stopped him. "Let me ask you this. I just got Dick in here, Dick Moore, a minute ago." (Moore was actually still sitting in Nixon's office.)

"Yeah."

"And I may reevaluate. He comes down very hard [positively] on your man Rehnquist. He just thinks that, you know, second in his class at Stanford, was clerk to Robert Jackson, uh, and then from your account, apparently conservative."

"Absolutely."

"And would make a brilliant justice. Would you agree?"

"Yes, sir."

"What would the country say about him?" Nixon asked. "He sure is qualified, isn't he?"

"I would believe so. I don't think there's any question about it."

Nixon asked again about Powell and pondered for a moment whether to make an announcement about him right then. Not a good idea, Mitchell advised, because they hadn't heard officially from the ABA committee. "We want to program that committee," Mitchell counseled, "so we can blame the woman* on that."

"Yeah, all right, call me back when you get it," Nixon replied. "But remember, let's figure on the Rehnquist thing, the political mileage basically is the same. . . . The idea being that we are appointing a highly qualified man. That's really what it gets down to. . . . Incidentally, what is Rehnquist? I suppose he's a damn Protestant?"

"I'm sure of that," Mitchell responded. "He's just as WASPish as WASPish can be." Mitchell had that right.

"Yeah," Nixon continued, "well, that's too damn bad. Tell him to change his religion."

"All right, I'll get him baptized this afternoon."

"Well, get him baptized and castrated. No, they don't do that. I mean they circumcise. No, that's the Jews. Well, anyway, whatever he is, get him changed."

Dick Moore had been sitting across from Nixon, listening to the president's end of the conversation. Now he got up and headed directly to

---

*"The woman" was Mildred Lillie, one of Nixon's red-herring candidates who had been judged unqualified by the ABA committee. Nixon and Mitchell planned to blame the ABA for derailing what would have been the first woman nominated to the Court.

Mitchell's office at the Justice Department, halfway between the White House and the Capitol. When Moore got there he found Rehnquist slumped in a chair, looking dazed. Mitchell had just told Rehnquist he was under consideration. Rehnquist soon was recovered enough to banter with a reporter for the *Washington Star* who asked Rehnquist whether Nixon might pick him for the Court. "Why should he?" Rehnquist quipped. "I'm not a woman, black, or mediocre."

Later that night, the other finalist for the job finally showed up. Baker, no longer AWOL, materialized in Mitchell's office at the Justice Department, and the two men talked deep into the evening. Nixon had already instructed Mitchell not to strong-arm Baker; the president didn't want him for the Court if the senator had any misgivings at all. Mitchell's meeting with Baker went late. Nixon tried to get Mitchell on the phone that night to find out what happened. The president and his attorney general finally spoke at 11:27 P.M., for twelve minutes. Baker, Mitchell said, still needed more time. The senator would make his decision in the morning—the morning of Nixon's address to the nation.

MITCHELL TELEPHONED NIXON again the following morning with his update. It was Thursday, October 21, the day Nixon had chosen to make the announcement. The president was already working on notes that would be turned into a final draft by his speechwriter, William Safire.

Mitchell informed Nixon that Baker had decided that he wanted the job but wouldn't be unhappy if he wasn't the president's choice. It had been a tough few days for the senator. He'd been struggling, and Nixon's taking it out of his hands would be a relief. Baker's unexplained absence the day before had actually turned out to be a hasty trip back to Tennessee to seek advice from kith and kin.*

Good, Nixon responded, because "I really think I'm going to not—I'm going to close the [Baker] option and go the other way. I have a feeling

*"Baker surprised me," an exasperated Mitchell told Nixon the night before. "He is apparently on an airplane coming back from Knoxville, and has left no word about why he went or anything about it. He'll be in here at—." Nixon cut Mitchell off: "Maybe we leave him off the list."

I'm going to go the other way. That's just my gut reaction. What do you think? . . . You've got a man [Rehnquist] who's unknown. But with a hell of a record. The 'unknown' thing with Rehnquist is going to really not wash good, [but] if he was high in his class—." Nixon was fixated on class rank as a sign of native intelligence and intellectual prowess. The president was still stung by the Carswell debacle. He was probing for Rehnquist's law school ranking. "Was he first or second or something like that?"

"He was first in his class." (Not true because Stanford didn't rank its law graduates then.)

"You think he was first?"

"He was first. Yes, sir."

"Yeah. Mmm, hmm. Well, that's a hell of a club."

"Phi Beta Kappa, of course." Mitchell was piling it on.

"Phi Beta Kappa, first in his class, law clerk to one of the great judges of this century, and practiced law as a lawyer's lawyer and so forth." Nixon waxed with grandiloquence. He was talking himself into choosing Rehnquist. "Damn it, I really think we ought to go that way."

"All right," Mitchell agreed. "Well, I'll turn Baker off."

Nixon gave Mitchell some pointers on what to say to let Baker down easily. But he had made his decision: "Okay, take him off."

It was an astonishing late turn of events. In less than ten hours, Nixon was going to spring a surprise on the press and the country by announcing two Supreme Court nominees whom he'd seemingly plucked out of the blue. The president had never talked to Rehnquist about the nomination, and had not a scintilla of personal knowledge about him other than the bad impression gleaned from their one brief encounter and the anecdotes he'd heard from Mitchell. (By contrast, Nixon had spoken briefly by telephone with Powell.) It was a right-place-at-the-right-time replay of how Rehnquist had fortuitously gotten his clerkship with Jackson—a clerkship that the president was using as a proxy for Rehnquist's fitness to be a justice. Rehnquist was *qualified and available.* As an indication of how few people actually knew what was about to happen, even Haldeman was unaware of the Rehnquist choice; Haldeman was running to Dick Moore, asking what Moore knew. Rehnquist, the darkest of dark horses, had not been vetted by the FBI or anyone else, nor did *he* even know for sure that he was Nixon's choice.

"And the reason Rehnquist had never been on anybody's radar before," John Dean later explained, "was because Rehnquist was *running* the radar machine over at Justice, looking for these justices. And he was sort of shocked to find out that he was even being considered and didn't find out until the morning that Nixon would announce him. I'm not quite sure what would have happened had Rehnquist said No."

Mitchell hastily summoned Rehnquist to his office to give him the news. Kleindienst was there, too, as was Moore who had returned to bask in the good fortune. The three of them told Rehnquist that his nomination would be announced that evening. Kleindienst, who actually had nothing at all to do with the closely held decision, later would take credit, "because of my part in bringing Rehnquist to Washington," and in a way you could see his point. Rehnquist had been a bobbing cork in the backwater of Arizona politics until Kleindienst pulled him out and placed him into the big pond. Right place. Right time. Luck. Pluck. Fate. All the elements had unimaginably turned Rehnquist's way.

Nixon was immensely satisfied with his short televised address that evening. The gist of the message was wholly his, and he had worked hard on it, writing the first draft in longhand on a yellow lined pad before turning it over to the speechwriters for some polishing. The result was long on platitudes and short on substance, but that was probably smart; why give ammunition to his opponents? Nixon worked the "first in his class" reference into his address, of course. He also described Rehnquist as "the President's lawyer's lawyer" possessing "one of the finest legal minds in this whole nation today." No points and authorities for that, it was just a matter of fact. "He has discharged his responsibility as the President's lawyer's lawyer with such great distinction that, among the thousands of able lawyers who serve in the federal government, he rates at the very top as a constitutional lawyer and as a legal scholar."

It was actually a lot simpler than even that. The fact was, with Rehnquist and Powell, Nixon was getting exactly what he wanted, a conservative and a southerner, and he had outfoxed not only the press but his own staff. Nixon picked up the phone and got Mitchell on the line. "We really threw a bombshell at these bastards tonight, didn't we?" Nixon pretty much used the term "bastards" generically and offhandedly to describe any and all who weren't otherwise with him in the room or on the phone, but he was salting it in even more than usual that night.

"We really did," Mitchell replied. There was no denying that Nixon had thrown everyone quite a curve ball.

"What do you think? I haven't watched the TV. I never look at these things. How's it coming across?"

"Well, let me tell you. They were just so flabbergasted they didn't know what to say." Mitchell was referring to the news reporters who anchored the networks' coverage. He knew Nixon's distaste for them. "The more important thing is the phone calls that have been coming in here from all over. From all segments."

Nixon was curious. "Are they—"

"And it's just great," Mitchell confirmed.

"About both, even about Rehnquist?" Nixon thought that if either of the nominees was going to be vulnerable, it would be Rehnquist.

"Oh, yeah," Mitchell went on.

"Of course. That 'first in his class' is what these goddamn snobs—that's what impresses them.* And law clerk to Jackson, that impressed [George] Meany,** they tell me."

Mitchell laughed. "It could be. I think the important thing is 'the lawyer to the president.'"

Nixon liked that. "This means, John, that we will have appointed four good men. Everybody recognizes that Burger is a good man. Blackmun is a good man. Powell, of course, everyone will recognize it. And Rehnquist is the smartest of the whole goddamn bunch. And he's on our side, isn't he?"

Mitchell didn't even bother to answer that. He was still amazed at how he and Nixon had managed to pull two rabbits out of the hat. "The reception over this is just unbelievable. Before I left the office, I talked to some reporters—"

"Yeah?" Nixon wanted the gossip.

"And the commentary was that they were completely flabbergasted."

"After the speech? They were out of their minds!"

"And I think I have the bar behind us." When Mitchell went on to explain that Lawrence Walsh, the head of the ABA's judicial-selection committee, was "very enthusiastic," Nixon was dismissive. "He's just impressed

---

*Stanford Law School actually did not rank its class, although as editor in chief of the *Stanford Law Review* Rehnquist would have earned the distinction. Powell was also said to be first in his undergraduate class ('29) at Washington and Lee University in Lexington, Virginia.

**Meany, a labor leader and sometime Nixon antagonist, was president of the AFL-CIO.

because [Rehnquist] was first in his law class. I'm not a goddamned bit. I'm more interested in the man."

"I think you did a great thing for the Court." Mitchell tried to wind it down, but all Nixon could talk about was the high jinks they'd just gotten away with.

"I really built them up, you know!" the president exclaimed. "And I talked about respecting the law, whether you agree and obey the law and all that. And they ought to appreciate it, the bastards!"

"Well they should," Mitchell agreed. "And you said it in a very mild-mannered way. You got across to the American public."

But now Nixon was anything but mild-mannered as he made his final point to Mitchell: "Be sure to emphasize to all the southerners that Rehnquist is a reactionary bastard, which I hope to Christ he is. . . . In a pure sense, it's like China. . . . The bastards were completely taken by surprise. They didn't know what the hell was gonna hit 'em! Ha! Doesn't that amuse you? We kept it quiet!"

Nixon was, quite simply, exuberant.

Now the confirmation games would begin anew.

SIXTEEN

"What Now, Hon. W. H. Rehnquist?"

MITCHELL HAD READ THE SITUATION CORRECTLY. There was no immediate negative backlash among senators that evening; reaction was either favorable or guarded. Even Birch Bayh, the Indiana Democrat who had led the successful fights against Haynsworth and Carswell, agreed that Rehnquist and Powell "appear to be significantly better qualified than some of the other names leaked to the public." That didn't mean Bayh would support them. Ted Kennedy, another Democratic bellwether, also said he was "tremendously relieved," but he, too, wasn't prepared that night to declare for Nixon's pair.

It didn't take long for positions to harden. But the element of surprise gave Nixon an edge, and he cunningly took advantage of it by pressing for confirmation hearings to begin almost immediately. The interregnum was a scant two weeks, hardly enough time for the NAACP and others to get organized for another fight.

It soon was obvious that Powell was going to sail through the confirmation process—to almost every senator, he was a *tabula rasa* and thus a safe Yes vote. But Rehnquist presented an entirely different target. He was far too visible and well known as the Nixon administration's law-and-order henchman to avoid close scrutiny. And his early anti–civil rights activism in Phoenix was coming back to haunt him. The NAACP was once again up in arms, sending out angry press releases and firing off urgent telegrams to senators, even though Rehnquist testified—at length—that he had changed his mind about a lot of things. He denied that he was ever a member of the John Birch Society. He said he had never harassed voters. He now realized "the strong concern of minorities for the recognition of these rights." And so on.

Not everyone was convinced by Rehnquist's apparent change of heart. Dershowitz, the young Harvard professor who had authored the negative *New York Times* commentary about Nixon and Rehnquist, certainly wasn't. But his mistrust was instinctual, not grounded in proof. Soon, however, Dershowitz was approached by someone with a story to tell. His source was a woman who claimed to have known Rehnquist when the soon-to-be justice was an undergrad at Stanford. The woman now worked at the Center for Advanced Study in the Behavioral Sciences at Stanford, where Dershowitz was a research fellow. She had seen Dershowitz's widely circulated opinion pieces lashing out at Nixon and Rehnquist. She wanted to use Dershowitz as a conduit for revealing that Rehnquist the student was anti-Semitic.

"She came to me as a good citizen, because of my writing for the Week in Review section," Dershowitz recalled. "Her allegation was that there was a group called 'Bill Rehnquist's Brown Shirts,' at Encina Hall, and they marched to martial music and made 'Heil Hitler' salutes. She had a direct eyewitness view of it." Encina was the original Madhouse. Dershowitz's source told him that Rehnquist's friends had harshly admonished him, "You've gotta stop this stuff." If true, it was a damning allegation. But Dershowitz was on treacherous shoals; he needed to find corroborating eyewitnesses.

Dershowitz decided to conduct his own investigation. Of particular note were two people who helped him. One was Dershowitz's twenty-five-year-old research assistant, Joel Klein. Klein had just graduated from Harvard Law School. He would go on, in turn, to become a clerk to Lewis Powell, the head of the Justice Department's Antitrust Division, New York City schools chancellor, and the right-hand man to press mogul Rupert Murdoch. The other person Dershowitz dragged in was Derek Bok, who in 1971 was the newly appointed president of Harvard University and, immediately before that, Dershowitz's dean at Harvard Law School. Bok was Stanford '51, the same year Rehnquist and Ehrlichman had gotten their Stanford law degrees. But even more important to Dershowitz, Bok had been an ardent, and vocal, opponent of the Carswell nomination.

Dershowitz said he instructed Klein to track down "Jewish Stanford graduates" who had lived in Encina Hall, to see if any of them would confirm the story. There weren't many, because Stanford wasn't a welcoming place to Jews back then. (In 1997, Stanford's commencement speaker, Justice Stephen Breyer, noted: "When my father was at Stanford, he could not join any of the social organizations because he was Jewish, and those organizations, at that time, did not accept Jews.") That was just a shot in the dark, and it went nowhere. Next came Bok. The Harvard president knew nothing about it. Dershowitz even pleaded for help from Ted Kennedy's staff, but they didn't want to touch the rumor unless someone was willing to come forward. In the end, Dershowitz held off and didn't recount the details until after Rehnquist's death. As much as anything, this was an indication of the futility with which all but the die-hards—the NAACP, the National Organization for Women, the AFL-CIO, and some others—viewed opposition to Rehnquist.

Nevertheless, soon Bayh was once again fighting the good fight in opposition. The usual Democratic liberals such as Ted Kennedy and Michigan's Philip Hart were doing their utmost to make Rehnquist sound a lot like the hanging judge that the young nominee so admired. With Rehnquist's prior record, that was hardly difficult. All Powell could do was just wait around with a "Where am I?" look, biding his time until the debate was done. Powell was the elder statesman, there was no doubting that. And he was also Rehnquist's insurance policy.

The two nominees were marching toward confirmation in lockstep, which meant that if the Senate didn't move ahead on Rehnquist, they were not going to get Powell. By putting the two men forward at the same time, Nixon had indeed made a shrewd and effective calculation. Rehnquist and Powell were being presented to the Senate as a twofer, and the Republican leadership made that clear when another Democratic liberal, John Tunney of California, tried to use a parliamentary maneuver to delay the Rehnquist vote by placing a temporary hold on Rehnquist's nomination. Out of senatorial courtesy, the hold had to be honored for at least a week; it couldn't even be debated. So Tunney's maneuver looked clever, at least superficially. Ordinarily it would have meant that Powell's nomination would proceed quickly to a floor vote, while Rehnquist's languished. But as soon as the Democratic hold was placed on Rehnquist's nomination, the *Republicans* put a similar hold on Powell—not because any Republican (or, for that matter, any Democrat) was against Powell, but because they wanted to make it clear that his nomination was linked to Rehnquist's. Bayh was furious—the Republicans were "tying these men together like a Christmas package." But he was powerless to do anything other than let the two nominations remain linked, and it appeared that Rehnquist was on his way to a comfortable confirmation vote.

Then came a bombshell from *Newsweek.* The magazine had a copy of the 1952 memo from law clerk Rehnquist, rejecting *Brown* and supporting the separate-but-equal doctrine of *Plessy.* The hearings on Rehnquist and Powell had been over for weeks, and the Senate was due to start debate on Powell's nomination the following day, with Rehnquist's right after. But the memo was an obvious problem for the White House. If genuine, it confirmed everything the NAACP and others had been saying all along about the racist views of Rehnquist. Bayh went to the Senate floor and declared that *Newsweek* had come up with "new and disturbing information concerning Mr. William Rehnquist's commitment to equal justice in this country."

The vote on Powell went ahead as planned, 89–1, and not one senator uttered a negative word about him. Only Democrat Fred Harris of Oklahoma voted against Powell, on the ground that he was an elitist without compassion for "the little people." Senator Paul Fannin, a Republican of Arizona who was one of Rehnquist's handlers, marveled at the love fest. "Debate is not very exciting when—as in this case—there is nothing to debate. After the first round of wonderful praise for Mr. Powell, all else is repetition."

But Rehnquist was not going to get off so easily. As the debate got under way on December 6, 1971, Bayh was again pointing to *Newsweek*'s revelation as evidence of Rehnquist's "inability to realize and implement the great promises" of the Constitution. Edward Brooke, the only black man in the Senate, criticized Rehnquist's "narrow view of the rights of man."

The White House still thought it had the votes to get Rehnquist approved, but the racist memo was a wild card. The White House needed to reassure Rehnquist's Senate supporters that he wouldn't embarrass them. Although Rehnquist privately protested to Mitchell that he couldn't even recall writing the memo, he soon delivered a letter disavowing it to the Senate Judiciary Committee Chairman, James O. Eastland of Mississippi, a man with his own checkered past when it came to civil rights and the Southern Manifesto.

Rehnquist's story, in his letter to Eastland, was that the memo was a reflection of Jackson's views, not his own. Rehnquist got support via a telegram from Jackson's other law clerk that year, Donald Cronson, who was by then an executive with Mobil Oil in the company's London office. Jackson's longtime secretary, Elsie Douglas, forcefully went the other way. She blamed Rehnquist for "smear[ing] the reputation of a great justice" and said that Rehnquist's rationalization was totally false, "incredible on its face."

But it was getting late in the year and the senators wanted to go home for the holidays. Most of them had already made up their minds and were not anxious to start a whole new tussle with the White House. Besides, the whole affair came down to whom the senators believed. Great civil libertarians of the era had marched into the hearing room making such slurs against Rehnquist that even Ted Kennedy felt an obligation to rebuke them.* Rehnquist had given sworn testimony before very incredulous senators, and he had dodged every one of them as they took their best shot. The books were closed on all that testimony. It was all over. But the last-minute letter to Eastland was not written under oath; even if Rehnquist was lying—as was almost certainly the case—what recourse did the senators have?** The smoking-gun memo had materialized too late to have any effect.

Bayh wanted the Senate to reopen its confirmation hearings and delay a vote until the middle of January. But the Republican leadership was having none of that, and made a preemptive move to invoke cloture even before the Democrats could get a filibuster started. To ensure that every senator was present for the vote, the leadership ordered a group picture of the entire Senate to be taken at the instant of the vote. Rehnquist loved the

---

*Joseph Rauh, a legendary civil liberties lawyer from Washington, said he was dissatisfied with Rehnquist's affidavit denying membership in the John Birch Society. It was, said Rauh, "the weakest denial I've ever heard. What about all the possible relationships short of membership?" Kennedy shot back: "Your suggestion is completely unwarranted and uncalled for. You've left an atmosphere that I think is rather poisonous. I am completely satisfied [with Rehnquist's disclaimer]."

**In *The Rehnquist Choice,* John Dean recalled his reaction at the time to Rehnquist's letter: "To be blunt, I thought he had lied. . . . If he did not remember writing the memo, which would not be surprising since it happened 19 years earlier, he should have said so. If it did reflect his position in 1952—which I suspected to be the case for it was consistent with what I knew about him—why not admit it and say he had changed his views? Frankly, I thought his letter was inviting trouble. While it was not perjury to send a letter with a bogus explanation to Chairman Eastland, it was wrong, it was a false representation, and stupid."

irony of that and kept the photo in his Supreme Court office. He threw his head back in laughter when he talked about it: "The only way they were sure they could get enough people there to invoke some cloture motion was to say that the *National Geographic* would take a picture!" Even then, the ploy didn't work—the motion to cut off debate fell 11 votes short of the required two-thirds majority.

A clearer indication of the Senate's fatigue came when Bayh immediately thereafter made his motion to postpone the vote on Rehnquist until January 18, 1972, so as to allow for more hearings and sworn testimony to find out who was telling the truth about the racist memo. Bayh's proposal was crushed, 70–22. The vote indicated that the Republicans had a sufficient margin to stop a Democratic filibuster if one really did begin.

So there would be no reopener on the Rehnquist nomination. And thus there was no reason for Bayh and the Democrats to delay the inevitable. The next vote was straight up-or-down on Rehnquist, and the margin comfortable enough if well short of a ringing endorsement: 68–26. It was Friday afternoon, December 10, 1971. Dick Moore started calling around, gathering the gang for a toast to the new justice by Mitchell and Kleindienst.

"What now, Hon. W. H. Rehnquist?" The question that Rehnquist had idly penned, as a law student two decades earlier, was unimaginably prescient.

What now, indeed?

SEVENTEEN

Roe v. Wade

REHNQUIST AND POWELL were not going to be sworn in until the New Year, so that meant they were going to miss, on the Monday following Rehnquist's confirmation, one of the Court's most important oral arguments in a generation. *Roe v. Wade* was before the Court along with a closely related case, *Doe v. Bolton,** and it would define the constitutionality of abortion. Even though *Roe* was far from being decided, the case was already causing a serious rift among the justices on a Court that had been limping along for more than a year without its full complement of members. The fact that two more Nixon appointees would be bringing the Court back to full strength was cold comfort to liberal justices like Brennan, Marshall, and Douglas.

Roe had actually reached the Court in 1970 and had been awaiting action since then. But with Harlan and Black gone, the Court was down to seven members—Blackmun called it a "bobtailed Court"—and Burger was proceeding cautiously. He wanted the justices to avoid hearing any case that might end up being decided by a vote of 4–3. Particularly in a case as controversial as *Roe,* it would not serve the Court or the country well if four justices—a potential *minority* among a full complement of nine—exerted their will as a majority.

---

*410 U.S. 179 (1973)

The chief justice, still new to his job, gave Potter Stewart responsibility for figuring out which cases could be adequately heard by seven justices. Stewart told the chief that the abortion cases really presented just a simple question of federalism: the extent to which federal courts could intervene in state court proceedings. The Court, with its constantly changing cast in the early Nixon years, had been struggling with that question, too, in a case called *Younger v. Harris.** But after hearing arguments twice during its October 1970 term and then a third time once Blackmun came aboard, the Court had finally settled *Younger* by an 8–1 vote that seemed to make clear just how limited the federal courts' powers were when it came to intervening in state prosecutions. Stewart told the chief that *Younger* paved the way for the Court to quickly dispose of the abortion cases. Burger concurred. Arguments would be held before the bobtailed, seven-man Court.

But as Blackmun saw it, Stewart had muffed his assignment:

> I was on that little committee. We did not do a good job. Potter pressed for *Roe v. Wade* and *Doe v. Bolton* to be heard and did so in the misapprehension that they involved nothing more than an application of *Younger v. Harris.* How wrong we were. I was disturbed, too, even though I was the junior on the Court at that time, about 4–3 decisions. A few cases during that period came out exactly that way, but no one raised a fuss about it, even though the four-member majority was less than a majority of a full Court.

Thus, on the Monday following Rehnquist's confirmation, the seven justices heard arguments in *Roe* and *Doe.* But it now was clear that, with the two new Nixon appointees in the wings, the stakes were much higher than Stewart and Blackmun had reckoned. Within days, the justices were clashing over who would be assigned to write the abortion opinions. On the assignment sheet that he circulated the following Friday, December 17, Burger put Blackmun's name alongside *Roe* and *Doe.*

Douglas was enraged. He was certain that the alignment in the justices' conference earlier that week had been Burger, White, and Blackmun voting to uphold the state abortion statutes and Douglas, Brennan, Marshall, and

---

*401 U.S. 37 (1971)

Stewart voting to strike them down. That meant Douglas, as the senior associate justice in the majority, should be assigning the opinions in *Roe* and *Doe,* not Burger. What was more, Douglas believed the conventional wisdom of the time that Blackmun was nothing more than the Minnesota Twin of his boyhood friend Burger and would therefore follow the chief justice in his vote. Blackmun's getting the assignment was equivalent to Burger doing the drafting himself. Douglas fired off an angry memo the next day, a Saturday, to the other justices. Burger replied the following Monday with his own memo disputing Douglas's vote-counting: "There were, literally, not enough columns [in the conference's tally sheet] to mark up an accurate reflection of the voting in either" case. The assignment to Blackmun would stand. And there the matter sat as the justices left the Court for the holidays. Instead of nine scorpions in a bottle, there were only seven.

SOON AFTER POWELL AND REHNQUIST joined the Court in January 1972, Burger called a meeting of all nine justices to discuss which cases should be scheduled for reargument. He was still concerned about the possibility of 4–3 decisions—and he included the abortion cases as likely 4–3 outcomes. Douglas objected to reargument, as did three others—Brennan, Marshall, and Stewart—who were all but certain to vote to overturn the state abortion restrictions. The Court had important work to get on with, including deciding the constitutionality of the death penalty, Douglas intoned. The justices needed to stop dithering, issue the abortion decisions, and move on.

But Burger insisted on taking a vote of the justices as to which cases should be held over. Any case moved to the next term would be argued anew, before a full complement of the nine that now included Powell and Rehnquist. And since those two new justices had a stake in the outcome, Burger thought that they should participate in the vote.

Again, Douglas objected. And this time the new arrivals undermined Burger's position. Powell told the conference that as a rank novice he wasn't in a position to second-guess his more experienced colleagues. Powell didn't intend to have anything to do with the abortion cases—and that included voting about reargument. "From a purely personal viewpoint I would be more than happy to leave this one to others." Rehnquist backed him up. The issue of rearguing *Roe* was dead for the time being.

But the squabble over reargument arose again as Blackmun struggled to get out a draft of the *Roe* and *Doe* opinions before the end of the Court's term in June. *Roe* involved a traditional, severely restrictive abortion law from Texas; the Georgia law in *Doe* was more modern, allowing abortions under certain circumstances, to avoid danger to a woman's health. Taken together, the two cases teed up the issue perfectly. Doing his drafting alone, Blackmun tinkered with various legal theories for striking down the state abortion laws, finally settling on vagueness as the basis. Blackmun circulated his draft on May 18. He defended his logic. But it was a cop-out that didn't settle the abortion issue head-on, and as such the Blackmun approach was problematic. Still, there was a fragile majority for overturning the state abortion laws, and who knew what would happen if there were a reargument with the two new Nixon justices participating.

In an orchestrated move, Douglas, Brennan, and Marshall decided it was best to take the win and move on. They would accept Blackmun's *Roe* opinion as it was. All three said so in short, adulatory notes to Blackmun on May 25 that were copied to all the other justices:

> MARSHALL: "I have several ideas which I will suggest to you when I get them into more concrete form, but with or without any suggestions I might make I wholeheartedly join your opinion."
>
> BRENNAN: "I've just finished reading your very fine opinion in the above. I am going to be happy to join it. I'll take the liberty of sending you a few suggestions for your consideration."
>
> DOUGLAS: "I now think it is best to hand it down as you have written it."

Then Stewart also came around a few days later: "I am in basic agreement." Now Blackmun had what Douglas called "a firm 5" for overturning the state abortion restrictions. The opinions were "creditable jobs of craftsmanship and will, I think, stand the test of time. . . . The firm 5 will be behind you in these two opinions until they come down."

But behind the scenes, Burger had been gathering support for reargument. He had turned around Blackmun, who circulated a memorandum to the justices telling them that he now favored pushing the abortion cases into the next term, with reargument as early as possible in October. Blackmun started out by acknowledging the pressure he was under. "Nearly all of you, other than Lewis Powell and Bill Rehnquist, have been in touch with me about these cases." Then he told them: "I believe, on an issue so sensitive and so emotional as this one, the country deserves the conclusion of a nine-man, not a seven-man, court, whatever the ultimate decision may be."

The chief had also pulled Powell into his camp. Powell's coming around was significant—he was officially neutral on the abortion cases, having already made it clear to the others that he had read absolutely nothing that had been circulated in the case. Rehnquist might be a lost cause for the pro-abortion side, but Powell was an ostensible fifth or sixth vote for the majority. It would be hard not to go along with a reargument.

Powell sent a carefully worded memo to the conference on June 1. "The question is whether the abortion cases should be reargued," he began. Powell then recounted the January decision that he and Rehnquist had made, staying out of the fray:

> The present question arises in a different context. I have been on the Court for more than half a term. It may be that I now have a duty to participate in this decision. . . . In any event, I have concluded that it is appropriate for me to participate in the pending question. I have read the memoranda circulated, and am persuaded to favor reargument primarily by the fact that Harry Blackmun, the author of the opinions, thinks the cases should be carried over and reargued next fall. His position, based on months of study, suggests enough doubt on an issue of large national importance to justify the few months delay which is the principal price of reargument.

When Powell's secretary took the memo out of her typewriter, she gave Powell a carbon-paper copy, upon which the justice scribbled an urgent note to his compatriot Rehnquist: "Bill—Please call me. Lewis." Soon, Rehnquist was writing to the conference as well, telling them he agreed with Powell. The Court should push *Roe* over to the next term.

Douglas was livid. Powell and Rehnquist hadn't participated in *Roe* and thus had no legitimacy to vote on whether it should be reargued. He wrote in a note to Burger—copying the others—that "if the vote of the conference is to reargue, then I will file a statement telling what is happening to us and the tragedy it entails."

The next day Douglas did just that, penning and circulating a blistering lone dissent to the Court's forthcoming order for reargument, reciting all over again his objections from the prior December to Burger's attempts to control the assigning of the opinions even though the chief was in the minority. Douglas crowed that even though Burger had tried "to keep control of the merits, he was unsuccessful. Opinions in these two cases have been circulated and each commands the votes of five members of the Court. Those votes are firm, the justices having spent many, many hours since last October mulling over every detail of the cases. The cases should therefore be announced."

Douglas ultimately decided not to publish his diatribe. But soon enough the scorching memo found its way into the *Washington Post.* The elder justice was by then at his summer home in Goose Prairie, Washington. Douglas protested, in a letter back to Burger, that he was "upset and appalled" and had nothing to do with the leak. But after the justices had scattered for the summer, Burger sent him a four-page single-spaced rebuke, "to keep the record straight, and to allow any future scholar who may peruse the current press accounts or papers of justices to have the 'due process' benefit of all of the facts in context."

Blackmun announced in a memo to the justices on June 3 that he was withdrawing his draft opinion. He asked that all copies of his "Spring Edition" of *Roe* be returned. Blackmun would get his reargument, but privately he gave his assurance that he hadn't switched sides and would draft a better, more robust "Fall Edition" of *Roe.* Blackmun quickly turned around a new draft after the reargument that took place during the second week of the new term. When Rehnquist saw the result, even he seemed to agree that Blackmun had delivered on his promise. Two months before *Roe* was handed down, Rehnquist wrote to Blackmun:

> Dear Harry,
>
> I have read your "fall" editions in the above-entitled cases, and although I am still in significant disagreement with parts of them, I have to take my hat off to you for marshalling as well as I think could be done the

> arguments on your side. I think I will probably still file a dissent, although more limited than I had contemplated after the Conference discussion. . . .

Rehnquist nonetheless reminded Blackmun that day that he was hearing from "a potentially adverse party, rather than from an ally." When the case came down, only Rehnquist and White dissented, each for his own predictable reasons. For White, the issue was the sanctity of human life and the Court's giving mothers and doctors "the constitutionally protected right to exterminate it." For Rehnquist, it was the absence of a woman's right to bring such a case in the first place; *Roe* had dragged on for so long that the plaintiff couldn't possibly still be pregnant, and therefore the whole case was moot as far as he was concerned. But, Rehnquist continued, if there were a viable plaintiff, *Roe* would turn on the 14th Amendment and how very restrictively it should be applied in extending the Bill of Rights to the states. He had absorbed the teachings of Fairman from thirty years before, at Stanford, and his opinion was unchanged. The historical record was frozen in place as far as Rehnquist was concerned; the founders intended to leave regulating abortion to the states.

ROE TURNED OUT TO BE the most controversial opinion of the Supreme Court in the twentieth century, and relentless public debate about it continues. When the Rehnquist Court upheld *Roe* nearly twenty years later in a 5–4 decision (with Rehnquist dissenting) in *Planned Parenthood v. Casey,** three of the five justices appointed by President Ronald Reagan and his successor George H.W. Bush, both Republicans, turned out to have the controlling votes that preserved the constitutional right to abortion. By then, the last of the liberal lions who unsuccessfully pushed for the quick result in *Roe* were gone, replaced in every case by a more conservative justice. Yet in upholding *Roe* those new justices spoke passionately about the importance of *stare decisis.* Linda Greenhouse of the *New York Times* wrote:

*505 U.S. 833 (1992)

> The core of the majority's 60-page opinion was a 16-page section on the reasons why adhering to *Roe v. Wade* as precedent was necessary, even for Justices who might well not have signed the original opinion in 1973 and who still had some doubts about it. This section, signed by all three but principally written by Justice [David] Souter, conveyed a remarkable sense of personal passion and urgency. Without a footnote, and with a minimum of legal jargon, the opinion included such phrases as "The promise of constancy, once given, binds its maker" and "Like the character of an individual, the legitimacy of the Court must be earned over time." The message of the opinion was equally straightforward: the pressure to overturn *Roe v. Wade* has brought the Court to a moment of great institutional danger. The Court's claim to legitimacy, always fragile in a democratic society that has bestowed on life-tenured judges the extraordinary power to thwart the majority's will, is nonetheless the only currency the Court really has.

Powell was long gone from the Court by then, but his legacy in *Roe* turned out to be his principled stand in 1972 that, despite being newcomers, he and Rehnquist had a *duty*—that was the word Powell used—to participate in the reargument. Had Powell not made his voice quietly heard, and brought Rehnquist along with him, the bobtailed seven-man result that Douglas and the others originally sought surely couldn't have withstood the onslaught of opposition that ensued, and certainly would not have embodied the concept of *stare decisis* as something to be cherished decades later by a Court of radically different composition. Because it was decided by the full nine, *Roe* had enduring legitimacy.

The interplay between Powell and Rehnquist in rearguing *Roe,* and in Rehnquist's later extending of the olive branch to Blackmun, made for an interesting backstory, too. It demonstrated how, at least in this case, the younger Rehnquist was watching and learning from his elder counterpart Powell, and following in his wake. Rehnquist frequently adopted the role of shrill, dogmatic dissenter as a newcomer. Powell was showing him early on that sometimes the most important thing was to move stealthily behind the scenes.

Because of the way the two men had come to the Court, they continued to share a special bond. Anniversaries of their swearing in were celebrated between the men and their wives. If Rehnquist or Powell missed a conference for some reason, the other would follow up with a long, gossipy note about whatever dust-up happened that day between the justices. And Powell was Rehnquist's cheerful victim for bumming the low-tar Merit cigarettes that both were hooked on. Rehnquist never quit smoking, but it must have seemed to Powell that he quit buying.

Powell also tried to be a mentor to Rehnquist—a relationship that did not come easily to either the courtly, shy Powell or the obstreperous, headstrong Rehnquist who in his early years on the Court was often alone in dissent. In 1981, Rehnquist wrote and circulated to the other justices a planned dissent to what would otherwise have been a routine denial of *certiorari* in a death-penalty case.* Rehnquist claimed he wanted the Court to hear that case, and every other one like it—there had been ninety similar cases in the prior ten months—and he mocked the other justices for sending the capital-punishment cases away instead of boldly confronting the slow pace of executions. Rehnquist wanted to crank up the electric chair, and he contended that the way to do that was for the Court to accept *every* death-penalty case until the backlogs on death row were cleared.

Rehnquist's dissent was like a live hand grenade being rolled into the middle of the conference table. His rhetoric was explosive. He even quoted Judge Parker, the hanging judge, in a footnote. Normally it was the liberals who argued for granting *certiorari* in death-penalty cases, as a way of *slowing* the pace of executions (indeed, Marshall and Brennan were also dissenters in this case). So Rehnquist's dissent—arguing that the Court could *speed up* the pace by hearing every such case—was taken for the slap at the other justices that it was intended to be. John Paul Stevens took such umbrage that he drafted an opinion of his own, calling out Rehnquist by name and chastising him for what Stevens characterized, in so many words, as stupidity. (For Stevens, indignation about the episode ran so deep that thirty years later he was still complaining about it in his memoir.)

Powell also had misgivings about Rehnquist's intended public rebuke of his brethren. But instead of going public with his concerns, the elder justice decided to try to reason with Rehnquist. Three weeks before the decision came down, he wrote a long memorandum to Rehnquist.

"I personally favor capital punishment as a legitimate, and with respect to some crimes, a necessary form of punishment," Powell began. He went

---

**Coleman v. Balkcom*, 451 U.S. 949 (1981)

on to talk about how the Court had wrestled with the discriminatory aspects of the death penalty, first by striking down capital punishment in *Furman* and then by reinstating it in *Gregg*—a "compromise" decision that was imperfect but necessary for getting a majority of the justices to vote for it. There were more safeguards in place now, Powell continued, and he acknowledged that this gave defendants more of an opportunity to exploit "our generous system of direct and collateral review."

But Powell did not support the idea—about to be propounded by Rehnquist in his lone dissent—that the justices were to blame. He offered Rehnquist what seemed like irrefutable evidence. Powell had tallied all the death-penalty petitions that had come to the Court since capital punishment had been reinstated by *Gregg.* There simply hadn't been many repetitive petitions. As far as Powell was concerned, that meant the problem lay elsewhere, with state governors and clemency boards. Powell had also been a member of a prestigious presidential commission on crime that was appointed amid the assassinations and riots of the 1960s, and he harkened back to that experience in trying to show Rehnquist that the problem wasn't amenable to a quick fix:

> We did express the view that I urged on the Commission, and still hold: capital punishment either should be enforced or abolished. The situation in the 1960s was that hundreds of prisoners were on "death row," but executions had substantially ceased. There was a perception that the public simply would not tolerate what would appear to be an excessive number of executions. We again are in that situation. In theory there is a substantial majority sentiment for capital punishment. In practice there simply is no stomach for it. . . . Forgive me for writing at such length. Although we share common objectives to a large extent, our views as to causes and solutions are not entirely congruent.

Rehnquist ignored Powell's counsel and went ahead with his invidious dissent. But he obviously was impressed by Powell's thoughtful approach, because seven years later Rehnquist, by now the new chief justice, asked the newly retired Powell to chair a committee of judges whose mandate was to speed up death-penalty litigation. The average death-penalty case took eight years to wend its way through the courts. The assignment was a political hornet's nest for Powell but he approached it methodically, in the end fashioning a compromise proposal that would give the accused better access to lawyers in exchange for taking away some of the *habeas* protections that delayed executions. Rehnquist liked the ideas and did his best to maneuver them into law. But with vehement opposition from liberals in Congress and the bar, the proposals didn't have a chance, and in the end the Powell Commission's recommendations went nowhere.*

*The political climate was much different in 1996. In the aftermath of the World Trade Center and Oklahoma City bombings, Congress overwhelmingly approved the Antiterrorism and Effective Death Penalty Act.

EIGHTEEN

"The Better Point of View"

Rehnquist was always comfortable being the solitary dissenter on the Court. He actually felt less burdened by his weighty office than most of his brethren. Among the other justices there was reverence for something called *stare decisis,* a Latinism denoting the sanctity of precedent. But Rehnquist felt no obligation to it. He voted as he wished in cases, and he made it plain whenever he thought prior decisions were wrong and should be overturned. So frequently was he the *only* dissenter among the nine justices that his law clerks in 1974 presented him with a small Lone Ranger doll that he put proudly on the mantel above his office fireplace. He knew the clerks referred to him as "the Lone Dissenter," which made him chuckle.

Rehnquist professed not to take the Court too seriously, describing its influence as only a "little stream of history that flows by this Court. I don't think it's a main channel at all." Although he did not discount the importance of the Court's role, he found "many other things that have a greater influence on people's daily lives than what this Court decides."

Such insouciance as to his own significance allowed Rehnquist to keep old-school banker's hours, 9 to 3 most workdays, and made time for things that interested him more: reading, writing, stamp collecting, getting out "into the hinterlands."

He was able to find time for his hobbies because he was utterly unaffected by self-doubt. There was to be no late-night agonizing for Associate Justice W. H. Rehnquist. Not that the cases weren't sometimes challenging—as Rehnquist put it breezily, "most cases that come here have two sides to 'em, and they wouldn't be here if they weren't difficult." But the fact of their difficulty, that clearly there were legal opinions stacked on both sides, made the process of resolution strangely straightforward for Rehnquist. He effectively decided that his judgments need not be made on the basis of law—there had been enough of that already by the time the cases reached the Court and there would inevitably be "a lot to what the other side says." If he voted a certain way, it was not because "the people on the other side are idiots, or that their point of view is not well taken." Instead he determined his opinions on the basis of "what seems to be the better point of view."

It was a telling admission. Rehnquist's "better point of view" was not legally derived. What he was claiming was greater moral or political authority, on which he rested his judgment. He made his mind up on the basis of how he saw the world. Precedent and legal argument interested him barely at all. It was an extraordinary mindset to bring to the nation's highest legal authority—a sort of inspired legal nihilism, led more by political instinct than anything else.

But it allowed Rehnquist to be very efficient. He no more reviewed his own decisions in hindsight than he set much store by anyone else's from the past. Instead he was all about the next case: "You've got to decide them, and decide one case and go on to the next one. And, you know, there's literally no time for thinking about past decisions: Was I right or was I wrong? You'd simply go nuts if you did that."

His conscience was untroubled by even the most difficult death-penalty cases. He never looked back. "Absolutely not! Absolutely not! I just have no inclination to. It isn't a conscious decision that I would *like* to play them back but I tell myself, 'No! No! That way lies madness!' It's just that I'm very much a liver in the present."

Rehnquist was the kind of justice he called a thoroughbred—pure in his limited and highly idiosyncratic ideology and swift to impose it. Of course, by this definition there were liberal thoroughbreds, too; in fact, the Court had been packed with them when he arrived in 1972. But Rehnquist truly believed his view of things to be clearer, more principled, than that of his colleagues on the left. They bent the law to fit their ideology; he would not.

Rehnquist set his conservative course and stuck to it, regardless of what others said or thought about him.

However there was one member of the Court who was as independent in temperament as Rehnquist. While Lewis Powell was a solid conservative, from whom Rehnquist could learn the ways of the Court and tactics for handling the other justices and the clerks, he most enjoyed and sought to emulate the defiant iconoclasm of one of the Court's genuine liberals.

Ideologically, William O. Douglas was Rehnquist's polar opposite but they were both radicals in spirit. Each in his own way exemplified the Western ethic of rugged individualism, and there was a personal bond during their time together on the Court—from Rehnquist's swearing in on January 7, 1972, until Douglas's retirement on November 12, 1975, five years before the older man's death. "Over and above anything, you have to be able to stand on your own two feet. I think it was Cicero* who said about someone, 'He saw life clearly and he saw it whole.' And you have to have a little bit of that in you. Not being bamboozled by currents, trendy ideas, that sort of thing. . . . It just captures something. Not easily conned. Not awash in current trends of public opinion." Rehnquist could think of only one other man he could respect for that: "Bill Douglas, with whom I very, very rarely agreed on Court decisions."

The admiration was mutual, however hard to believe. When Douglas looked at the younger Rehnquist, he found something to admire, someone who reminded him of himself: a loner going his own way. Douglas was forty years old when President Roosevelt appointed him in 1939; Rehnquist was just seven years older than that when he came to the Court.

Whether for reasons of altruism or opportunism, Douglas went out of his way to make the newcomer his protégé, to cultivate and actually encourage the fierce independence that he sensed in Rehnquist. He did not waste time reaching out. On the same day as the Senate vote to confirm Rehnquist, December 10, 1971, Douglas had dispatched a note: "Welcome, and congratulations. Word reached us as we were about to close our Conference today. It will be nice having you here.

---

*Actually, this was poet Matthew Arnold's description of Sophocles: "He saw life steadily and he saw it whole." Rehnquist would use the quote again in 2002, upon the death of former Justice Byron R. White, this time with the correct attribution.

"I realize that you were here before as a member of the so-called Junior Supreme Court. But I do not believe that we met while you were in Justice Jackson's service.*

"It will be very nice, I assure you, to have you here on a permanent basis."

Douglas had reason to be wary; Rehnquist had, after all, vilified Douglas when Rehnquist was a thirty-two-year-old lawyer in Phoenix. Douglas, Rehnquist told the Maricopa Young Republican League, was a left-winger among liberal justices who were "making the Constitution say what they wanted it to say." Rehnquist's comments had been circulated at the confirmation hearings, for all including Douglas to hear.

Even so, within months the seventy-three-year-old Douglas was entreating Rehnquist and his wife, Nan, to join Douglas and his fourth wife, twenty-eight-year-old Cathleen, for a visit to Douglas's summer cabin in Goose Prairie. It looked like an odd match-up, and the Rehnquists seemed to view the trip with trepidation: as the date neared for the intended visit to Prairie House, Rehnquist suggested a rain check, but Douglas would not hear of it—and so Bill and Nan Rehnquist made the trip. "Happily for you. . . . No kids!" Rehnquist wrote ahead. They were leaving "three teenagers at home by themselves, and so the length of our absence is necessarily limited."

The two couples took a mountain hike and snapped photos of each other in the shadow of Mt. Rainier. (Rehnquist promised copies but then misplaced the negatives.) Cathy Douglas and Nan Rehnquist looked for anemones. The visit went so well that Bill Douglas invited Nan and her sister to come back when he heard they would be nearby the following year.

"Bill mentioned to me that when he looked at Rehnquist he saw himself," Cathy Douglas recalled. "It certainly wasn't ideological; it was personal. [Rehnquist] was just slightly older than Bill [Douglas] had been when he came to the Court. Bill felt very sympathetic to Rehnquist, encouraged him to take up hobbies, and spent a lot of time with him, giving him the observation of Bill's own life and what it was like being a young man on the Supreme Court. When you come to the Supreme Court, the door closes. That has a different impact on a young man as opposed to, say, a man of sixty-five. The Court takes you to the end of life. Bill told me,

*Rehnquist's clerkship with Justice Robert Jackson was in 1952 and 1953.

'You can become a dry husk of a man.' Without interests beyond the law, that spark would leave you, make you less of a husband, father, justice, less of a man, really."

Douglas, his widow continued, always enjoyed the company of younger men, though seldom in his own profession. He had an innate curiosity that being with them helped to fulfill. "If you're going to survive [at the Court], you have to develop mechanisms of friendship. The institution *requires* that these friendships develop."

There was one more thing about their friendship: both men took the same approach to deciding cases, unfettered by precedent, and thus they shared an inherent ability to reach a decision quickly. Opinions flew out of their chambers. "Bill [Douglas] did his work very quickly. He thought the Court wasn't overworked—they just had to work faster and harder."* It could have been Rehnquist speaking.

Later that same summer of 1972, Eric Sevareid, the CBS correspondent, made the trip to Prairie House. On Wednesday, September 6, a special edition of "CBS Reports" featured Sevareid's interview with Douglas. The Rehnquists watched, and the following day Bill Rehnquist wrote:

> We saw your interview with Eric Sevareid on television, Bill, and I thought it came over very well. It was fun to be able to recognize the setting in which the interview took place. I was particularly impressed by your comment that if judges did not get out and mingle with people, they would become "dried husks." I have an uneasy suspicion that I am already beginning to "dry" a little bit after only nine months, but it seems to me very difficult to find appropriate channels whereby one can mingle and usefully contribute something other than the writing of judicial opinions.

Rehnquist seemed genuinely bothered, that first year, at discovering what Douglas already knew. And so he looked for outlets, signing up for night-school painting classes, prowling the local public library for books to devour,

---

*Joan Martin, Douglas's third wife, whom he married in 1963 when she was a twenty-three-year-old law student, remained in touch with Douglas after he left her in 1966 to marry Cathleen, then a twenty-two-year-old college student. Martin recalled being told by Douglas about the Rehnquists' visit to Prairie House. She bluntly asked her ex-husband just one question: *"Why?"* Replied Douglas: "I thought I could convert him." Martin said Douglas told her he'd never seen anyone on the Court who was as bright as Rehnquist.

and playing in a weekly poker game with a group of buddies including Antonin Scalia. He was a frustrated novelist with a lot of pages to show for his efforts, but no success.

> I have my own way of trying to get away from the monasticism. I'm sure my colleagues have theirs. The ways probably aren't adequate. I visit law schools and make speeches and go to classes and have question and answer sessions. I will occasionally give a speech to a bar association. I take a painting class at night school in Arlington. Where, you know, you mix with lots of people who are totally different from the kind of people you mix with regularly. I'm thinking about maybe writing a book. And there you kind of get pulled in a little different direction. You just have to keep anchors to the outside world, because a justice of this Court could do all of the work he has to do in discharge of his oath of office without ever leaving this building. The chambers are here, the courtroom is here, the library is here, the cafeteria is here. There's a gym and exercise room. And, you know, it's just a two-dimensional world if you let that happen to you.

Rehnquist grew animated when he discussed painting. He worked in acrylics and painted mostly landscapes. He once missed the president's State of the Union address before a joint session of Congress because he had paid $25 to attend a night-school painting class and wanted to get the full benefit of it, even though by his own reckoning he was "definitely one of the less talented people in the class. I'm amazed at how much a person without much talent can learn, just by doing and doing and doing. And it's just fascinating. You know, I'll bring something home. I brought something home from class last night. I wasn't really satisfied with it. But after I'd brought it home I'd go into my study every ten minutes and look at it to see, 'What does this mean?' And, you know, just to have something that absorbs you, that isn't your daily routine."

Rehnquist was an American history buff, and he liked books that delved deeply into the lives of their characters through writings and letters. He seemed to have an opinion on every one, marveling at the "theatricality" of Aaron Burr ("a flair for the spectacular"), admiring John Marshall's vision and leadership, seeing Jefferson as a good president but a "skulker," and applauding the "underrated" William Howard Taft for clearing a five-year backlog of cases as chief justice. When he borrowed, from the local public library, Volume Three of Robert Vincent Remini's trilogy about Andrew Jackson, he found it fascinating. "This just goes into great detail, from Jackson's letters and so forth. And it really kind of brings people alive. It's almost like reading someone's diary." He and Nan read aloud to each other. "And we've, oh, jeez, we've covered twenty books, probably, in the last year and a half or so. We're just finishing up William Dean Howells's *The Rise of Silas Lapham.*" The 1885 novel described a rags-to-riches mill owner who aspires to a higher social class but, in the end, loses everything—because he makes the right moral decision. "Just a tremendous appreciation. 'Cause both of us have read aloud books that one or the other of us have read separately, and commented on the fact that you just don't get very much. You just get much more from reading aloud." Rehnquist was not overwhelmed by the day job.

Many years after Douglas's death, Rehnquist still relished the comparison to his elder. "Maybe it's just my own image of myself, but I think of Justice Douglas in his last ten, perhaps fifteen years here as being very much of an iconoclast. You know, really not caring a great deal whether anybody else agreed with him or not. In fact, sometimes we used to say at conference that we thought he was disappointed if he was in the majority, because then he would have to write something that he would have to get other people's agreement with, whereas if he were all by himself he could say exactly what he wanted!"

When he made those remarks Rehnquist was sixty years old, not yet chief justice, settled in his role if not downright bored. By then he could console himself that the monastic quality of the Court "suits me better at age sixty than it did at forty-seven. At age sixty, you know, the life tenure looks good, and I know that if I were a senior partner in a law firm, with a nice corner office and views out both windows, a bunch of young people would be walking by wondering when I was going to go on semi-retired status so they could have the office. And that just doesn't happen here. So, it looks better as you get older, I think."

He was a bit heavier, his hair thinner and grayer, the eyeglasses thicker. But his smile was quick and genuine and often followed by a wry comment or clever rejoinder. He spoke slowly and with a hint of a stammer, choosing his words carefully, sometimes after pronounced pauses. Anticipating the years ahead he sounded a little disconsolate and made the prospect of the Court seem rather dull: "You know, I would love to get a new job when

I was age sixty-five and could retire. But, you know, those things just don't come along very often. So, I don't have any very good prospects except for staying here until I retire, and then probably doing a little judging, and a little teaching, or something like that."

One of the liberal senators opposing his confirmation in 1971 had muttered that "this guy is going to be around for a millennium, making bad sound good." But by 1984 Rehnquist thought he saw the finish line, and it was less than five years away. Each September, as he began to prepare for the coming term, he became downcast. It was the monotony of it; he couldn't imagine being on the Court until the turn of the century and beyond.

"As of now, I would say emphatically No! These are the kinds of questions you shouldn't answer, because, you know, I have heard colleagues say years ago that they were certainly going to think seriously about retiring when they were eligible. And, not all of them do." He stammered and hesitated, but then plunged on: "I'm gonna think very seriously about retiring when I'm eligible. October first, 1989. Attaining age sixty-five and having served more than fifteen years." That was that.

REHNQUIST'S AFFINITY WITH POWELL and his genuine affection for Douglas were in sharp contrast to his feelings for Chief Justice Burger. Their relationship was complicated. In gossipy letters to Powell, Rehnquist shared his thoughts and frustrations about the chief as he worked through what turned out, in retrospect, to be a very long apprenticeship under Burger. The comments were telling, because they presaged how Rehnquist would one day approach the difficult task of switching from the role of principled dissenter to the necessary chief justice's job of peacemaker and consensus builder. The latter was not a role that Rehnquist thought Burger played well. Privately, Rehnquist deemed Burger to be a bad mixture of pomposity, duplicity, and indecision. He would get furious if he thought the chief justice slighted him—and that did happen. When Rehnquist's own time came it was almost as if, in the words of Linda Greenhouse, he used Burger as the model of what *not* to do.

But Rehnquist's letters also indicated the quandary that Rehnquist felt. He was a detractor of Burger's, grumbling privately, particularly about how Burger failed to keep control of the Court's caseload. Rehnquist was punctilious about scheduling and deadlines, and the chief's aimless leadership on that score frustrated him no end. But Rehnquist followed Powell's lead and did not want to publicly be seen as undermining the chief. Other justices, notably Harry Blackmun, did not feel so bound; in private meetings with reporters and small gatherings with lawyers, Blackmun could be catty and almost never lost an opportunity to give the chief a dig. Eventually, frustrations about Burger's leadership simply boiled over.

Burger had been leading the Court for a decade when *The Brethren* came out toward the end of 1979. Bob Woodward's and Scott Armstrong's book about the Supreme Court was pathbreaking for its inside look at what had been, until then, mostly a secret third branch of the government. Some of the justices and their clerks had obviously been sources. By the middle of 1979, justices and journalists were well aware of the blockbuster's imminent publication. All the media attention being given to the Court brought to the surface tensions that had been simmering under Burger's unsteady leadership. *Time* and *Newsweek* were battling to get in front of the story. It was clear that Burger, already deeply insecure, was not going to fare well in any of the resultant coverage.

While Powell was recuperating from surgery at Bethesda Naval Hospital in March 1979, Rehnquist took it upon himself to keep Powell's clerks up to date about what was going on at the justices' conferences. Then he briefed Powell by letter. The deliberations about pending cases had been even more contentious than usual, Rehnquist wrote. Once again the justices were arguing over whether some cases should be held over for reargument during the next term—always a touchy subject when, as was now the case because of Powell's absence, the Court was short by one or more justices. One case that was pending, *United Steelworkers v. Weber,** was a lightning rod for liberals and conservatives alike. The case struck at the heart of affirmative-action programs: whether the Civil Rights Act of 1964 barred employers from giving preference to women and minorities in hiring. Rehnquist didn't favor helping them, and he probably sensed that he would end up on the losing end (as indeed he did) without Powell's participation. Rehnquist scribbled a note to the ailing justice, revealing that he didn't believe Burger was adequately supporting their cause:

---

*443 U.S. 193 (1979)

> I assume that the Chief briefed you on the rather strange conference discussions we had as to what cases, if any, should go over because of your illness. He was a forceful advocate (as he sometimes is not) for the proposal that at least *Weber* should go over—but there was a faction that was determined it should not, and the uneasy compromise which was reached was doubtless relayed to you by CJ[*]—if it was not, let me know if you want an account of what happened when you feel better and I will describe it to you. It was not an altogether edifying experience, at least from my point of view.

The next day, Rehnquist was sharing more gossip with Powell, this time about what he saw as more looming procedural fights with the liberals over other civil rights cases. The Court had a bunch of them on its 1979 docket as it continued to sort out issues relating to school desegregation. Twenty-five years after *Brown,* the issue wouldn't go away; attacks on *de facto* segregation in the school systems of Dallas (Texas) and Columbus and Dayton (Ohio) were pending. Rehnquist knew that he and Powell were of a like mind in opposing the Court's activism in the school desegregation cases, but he was particularly concerned about the Dallas case, *Estes v. Dallas NAACP,*[**] because without Powell's vote Rehnquist would be alone in dissent:

> The April argument calendar came out yesterday, and I was happy to see that while *Columbus*[†] and *Dayton*[††] are on, *Dallas* is not. I had heard some "sidebar" conversations in the robing room which led me to think that WJB[‡] was renewing his unsuccessful suggestion at one of the February conferences that *Dallas* be argued in April. We will surely have enough tough cases in April without *Dallas.*

Powell was concerned, too, although not necessarily from the standpoint of aggressive advocacy. Rather, Powell was worried about the effect of the coverage on the public's perception of the Court. If there were squab-

*The Chief Justice, Warren Burger

***Estes v. Metropolitan Branches, Dallas NAACP,* 444 U.S. 437 (1980)

†*Columbus Board of Education v. Penick,* 443 U.S. 449 (1979)

††*Dayton Board of Education v. Brinkman,* 443 U.S. 526 (1979)

‡Associate Justice William J. Brennan

bles among the justices, they should be settled privately, not in the media. By mid-April, after Powell had returned to the bench, he began to fret about the Court's perception in the popular press. By the time the justices took off for their customary summer recess, Powell—normally a courtly, reserved justice—decided it was time to come to Burger's aid.

What set him off was an article in *Newsweek* headlined "A Rudderless Court." The theme of the piece was that the liberal lions Brennan and Marshall had been co-opting the center, and thus in effect leading the Court, while Burger and the other three Nixon appointees had failed to define a theme. Infighting was described as common. "At times this term," the article went on, "the Burger Court has appeared on the verge of fratricide." Then there was the ongoing residue of *Brown*—a sticky problem that the Court obviously was having a hard time working out: "In each of the last two terms, the Court has struggled with the problem of quotas and affirmative action."

The fact that the magazine gave Rehnquist much higher marks lessened the overall sting for Powell a little. The sidebar about Rehnquist was titled "The Court's Mr. Right," and it praised Rehnquist for his ingenious turns of phrase—"the bench's chief rhetorician of the right . . . the champion of forces bent on stopping judicial do-goodism." It was also noteworthy for a prescient insight that would become even clearer in ensuing decades: "Not even his critics deny Rehnquist is highly intelligent—one of the brightest minds on the Court. But they charge him with an intellectual flaw: looking first to the result he wants to achieve, and only then to reading the law to achieve it."

Powell liked how his younger colleague had been treated but he otherwise fumed in a letter to Rehnquist: "The piece on 'A Rudderless Court' is sophomoric. We are criticized for deciding each case on the basis of the applicable law to its facts, rather than according to some mythical 'judicial philosophy.' Newsmen and some law professors seem disturbed, but I would hardly expect justice if I were a litigant before a court that decided cases pursuant to a 'philosophy.'"

When the justices came back from their summer break, Powell decided to enlist Rehnquist and Byron White in an off-the-record effort to rehabilitate not only the Court's image but that of Burger as well. The idea Powell came up with was to plant a story in *Time* to counter the negative impression from the *Newsweek* piece. Powell had a media-savvy clerk, David

Westin, who was already talking to two *Time* reporters, Evan Thomas and Douglas Brew.* Powell was new at this game, but his contemporaneous notes show that Westin, who almost two decades later would become the president of ABC News, was adept at setting the ground rules. Westin also told him how to play the game so that the three justices wouldn't leave any fingerprints.

Rehnquist and White went along with the plan, and the three of them scheduled a strategy session over turkey sandwiches from the Supreme Court snack bar. Powell wrote down the ground rules: there would be no taping and no attribution, but the *Time* reporters would be free to say that they had talked to "several Justices if—and only if—the article also makes clear that the justices were supportive, not critical of the Chief Justice."

The resulting article in *Time* a month later painted a much more nuanced picture of the Court and its complexities. Although Powell did not succeed in blunting criticism of Burger, he did gain some positive ink for the chief, including an acknowledgment that Burger had played an important leadership role off the bench as the head of the federal court system. Given Rehnquist's decidedly mixed feelings about Burger, the subterfuge with *Time* must have been quite a chore for him. Powell and White allowed themselves to be quoted by name in praising Burger, however faintly, but there was not one quote of support for him from Rehnquist.

Rehnquist made clear his ambivalence about Burger again in a chatty 1985 letter to Powell when the elder justice was recuperating from yet another surgery. Powell was still laid up at the Mayo Clinic in Rochester, Minnesota, after his supposedly routine surgery for prostate cancer had gone terribly awry five weeks earlier:

> We have now finished our January argument calendar, of course, and I must say I can't ever remember a less interesting or stimulating group of cases. If you had to miss one oral argument session, I don't think you could have picked a better one to miss. Even the Conference today got a little bit testy, as it does at times. Some of the Chief's discussion is quite good, when he feels very strongly about something and when he feels he has a majority with him; but some of it can be singularly uninspiring.

---

*Thomas went on to become *Newsweek*'s editor at large and a professor at Princeton. Brew became *Time*'s West Coast bureau chief.

Sometimes when he runs out of things to say, but doesn't want to give up the floor, he gives the impression of a southern senator conducting a filibuster.

I sometimes wish that neither the Chief nor Bill Brennan would write out all their remarks beforehand and deliver them verbatim from the written page. Bill is usually thorough, but as often as not he sounds like someone reading aloud a rather long and uninteresting recipe. Then of course Harry Blackmun can usually find two or three sinister aspects of every case which "disturb" him, although they have nothing to do with the merits of the question. And John Stevens, today, as always, felt very strongly about every case, and *mirabile dictu** had found just the right solution to every one. As you might imagine, my conference discussion was, as always, perfectly suited to the occasion: well researched, cogently presented, and right on target!

Burger's perceived failings would motivate Rehnquist to do things differently when his time came to assume the role of chief justice. Rehnquist put a higher value on fairness and efficiency in assigning and issuing opinions than he thought Burger did. And, unlike Burger, he didn't relish the administrative details and didn't agonize over things; he got the job done and moved on.**

*A Latinism meaning "wonderful to tell."

**Rehnquist complained about the administrative burden of his new role as chief justice. Less than a month after becoming chief, he wrote to his daughter Nancy: "My new job is definitely more demanding than my old one, with a number of administrative details to be looked after which didn't concern me at all when I was an Associate Justice. I don't know that administrative [*sic*] is necessarily my strong suit but I do find it stimulating to have to deal with new kinds of issues to which I previously paid no attention. There are also a fair number of demands for the Chief Justice to make ceremonial appearances, 'greet' various groups, and the like; some of this is probably required, but thus far I have been quite stingy with my time in this respect."

NINETEEN

Lone Dissenter

FROM THE MOMENT HE JOINED THE COURT, Rehnquist insinuated himself into the confidence of his colleagues in a way that seemed, and indeed was, quite natural for him. Rehnquist showed his public face to its full puckish effect. His opinions may have set him apart, but the new associate justice was often ready with an endearing *bon mot* or a clever practical joke. He organized betting pools—Rehnquist would wager on anything, and he kept careful track of his winnings and insisted the losers settle up with him. He peppered the chief with suggestions on how to liven things up at a place that to him seemed not only staid but dreary. It was hard not to like the man.

But behind the façade lurked a different person. Rehnquist maintained a certain formality with his law clerks; he didn't want to be called "Bill," and the clerks were uncomfortable with "Mr. Rehnquist," so finally the clerks settled on calling him "Boss." Incoming clerks were so instructed. His secretaries addressed him as "Sir."

Rehnquist also evinced a steely will to achieve the results he wanted. Rehnquist's office had the usual Washington trophy wall, on which Rehnquist had hung portraits of two of his great predecessors, John Marshall and Charles Evans Hughes, and of Justice Oliver Wendell Holmes. But a photograph amid the staid oils said much more about what Rehnquist stood for. It was of his former boss in the Nixon administration, Attorney General John N. Mitchell, a law-and-order man, Richard Nixon's hammer.

Mitchell was the only attorney general ever to serve a prison sentence—and he would die in disgrace. Other former White House aides had decided to forego the ordeal of a trial and plea-bargained with the Watergate special prosecutor, but Mitchell didn't play the game. He was indicted, stood trial, gave up nothing, and was convicted. The ultimate Nixon loyalist, he lived by his own code: no interviews, no kiss-and-tell memoir. Mitchell's austere stare was a clue to Rehnquist's intent: he would push the Court rightward; if necessary he would wait out the Warren Court's last liberals. What was important was to put his markers down, *stare decisis* be damned. And that made it easy for Rehnquist to decide what side to come down on in a case. If you were a homosexual, a racial or religious minority, a woman, an alien, an accused criminal, or someone facing the death penalty, you were not going to get Rehnquist's vote. Rehnquist saw cases in black and white and he did not struggle with the grey. The line was brightly drawn. He disdained liberals and had little sympathy for the rights of minorities. He was an uncompromising law-and-order man, anxious to limit criminal appeals and get on with executions. As Alan Dershowitz put it, "His vote could almost always be predicted based on who the parties were, not what the legal issues happened to be."

Since ideology and results were what counted, Rehnquist also didn't need to spend a lot of time crafting memorable opinions. His efforts were workmanlike and prepared swiftly. Early on he became known not for his opinion writing but rather for his spirited conservative rhetoric, his dissents against the Warren Court's last lions, and his votes that often appeared heartless. In the totality of his career, not one of Rehnquist's majority opinions stood out as distinguished. Indeed, when pressed, even Rehnquist could not name one that he was proud of: "I get asked that question fairly frequently," he said, "and honestly, I not only don't have a catalogue but I can't really think of any one. If I sat down some day, I'm sure I could go through the Reports and dig up a dozen or so that I think are good, constructive contributions. But certainly nothing stands out in my mind." It was almost as though he didn't want to be remembered as a jurist.

As a new justice, Rehnquist quickly proved himself to be a rigid conservative. He articulated a vision of broad governmental power, rather than broad constitutional protections, and his new career seemed to be an elaboration of the views about *Plessy* that he first expressed to Justice Jackson twenty years earlier. This led to the plethora of acerbic one-man dissents—

in cases where he opposed school desegregation, women's rights, civil-service jobs for aliens, and health care for the poor, among other issues. If his many critics in academia accused Rehnquist of being disingenuous in his opinion writing, well, so be it. Indeed, in more than a few instances, Rehnquist buttressed an opinion or a dissent with his own perception of the Constitution's "tacit postulates,"* or with a version of history "too well known to warrant more than a brief mention."**

Given the chance, Rehnquist said he would overturn the *Miranda* decision, which warned criminal suspects of their right to remain silent and to have a lawyer. He chafed at the delays in executions caused by what he viewed as excessive appeals, and he started an immediate push to repeal the right to *habeas corpus* appeals. It didn't matter to Rehnquist that even his own conservative colleagues found that prospect disquieting. Unable to achieve his ends judicially, he waged an unsuccessful private lobbying battle to get Congress to write a new law instead.

Commentators in law reviews struggled to parse Rehnquist's writings for evidence of what was referred to in the academic vernacular as a "consistent constitutional theory." The efforts almost always came up lacking—and readers will not find that exercise repeated here—because the only real judicial consistency lay in Rehnquist's reactionary ideology. He was a pragmatist who voted in each case, after all, to get the result that he considered "the better point of view."†

It made complete sense that even the prideful Rehnquist didn't have a mental list of his own distinguished writings. What stood out were the memorable outcomes—the notable consequences of Rehnquist's black-and-white view of the world. This was particularly true in the early years when Rehnquist wasn't leading the Court and didn't need to act as an arbiter or forge compromises. He consistently supported law enforcement in

---

**Nevada v. Hall,* 440 U.S. 410, 433 (1979)

***Trimble v. Gordon,* 430 U.S. 762, 777 (1977)

†Professor Erwin Chemerinsky of the University of Southern California Law School uses the term "ahistorical" to describe Rehnquist, as well as Scalia and Thomas. "In the area of affirmative action, these justices show no deference to majoritarian decision making; they consistently vote to strike down affirmative action even when it is approved by popularly elected legislatures. . . . Where history does not support their conclusions, the conservative justices on the Rehnquist Court ignore it. Instead, they simply impose their conservative ideology, which opposes affirmative action, to strike down acts of the democratic process."

cases that involved the rights of the accused, writing majority opinions that made it easier for police to get search warrants and harder for defendants to challenge the results. He joined majority decisions allowing life sentences for petty shoplifters* and upholding the imposition of the death penalty on minors who commit murder, and on mentally retarded murderers.**

Under Rehnquist's view of the Constitution, state officials could execute juveniles for murder, arrest gay people for homosexual acts in their homes, and prohibit women from having abortions, but they could not give a slight preference to African-American students seeking admission to a state university. Rehnquist voted against every affirmative action program that the Court ever considered. Regardless of a program's mandate from elected officials, if preferences were given to blacks, women, Latinos, or other minorities, Rehnquist did not hesitate to step in.

Commented David Savage, the Supreme Court reporter for the *Los Angeles Times:* "In the early 1950s, he did not think the segregation of black school children was unconstitutional. In the 1970s, he did not think discrimination against women violated the Constitution. Now, he insists that any discrimination against white males violates the Constitution."

---

*In *Lockyer v. Andrade,* 538 U.S. 63 (2003), and *Ewing v. California,* 538 U.S. 11 (2003), the Court upheld life sentences imposed on shoplifters pursuant to California's three-strikes law for repeat felons. Leandro Andrade had stolen $153 worth of videotapes from a K-Mart. Gary Ewing had stolen three golf clubs worth $1,197 from a Los Angeles–area golf course.

**Author Sue Davis succinctly summed up these harsh but predetermined realities in her entry about Rehnquist in the first edition of the *Oxford Companion to the Supreme Court,* written not long after Rehnquist became chief justice and before commentators—including Davis herself, in a revised entry for the second edition—felt compelled to try to rationalize a Rehnquist philosophy. His consistent support for law enforcement was exemplified by cases such as *Rakas v. Illinois* (1978) and *Rawlings v. Kentucky* (1980), in which he wrote opinions for the majority restricting a defendant's ability to challenge police searches. Rehnquist's opinion in *Illinois v. Gates* (1983) formulated a new rule that made it easier for police to obtain a warrant on the basis of an informant's tip. He wrote for the majority endorsing a "public safety" exception to the *Miranda* rules in *New York v. Quarles* (1984); endorsed diluting the exclusionary rule with an exception based on the "good faith" of the police in *United States v. Leon* (1984); and wrote the opinion for the majority upholding pretrial detention in *United States v. Salerno* (1987). He joined the majority in decisions upholding the imposition of the death penalty on minors who commit murder (*Penry v. Lynaugh,* 1989) and on mentally retarded murderers (*Stanford v. Kentucky,* 1989). Rehnquist voted with the majority in *New Jersey v. T.L.O.* (1985), holding that 4th Amendment requirements for search warrants didn't apply to searches of students by school officials. His opinion in *Wainwright v. Witt* (1985) made it easier for prosecutors to exclude from capital cases prospective jurors who opposed the death penalty. The list just went on and on.

Sometimes the result was so predictable for him—because of the parties, the issues, or both—that even Rehnquist made a joke of it. When the state of Indiana enacted a ban on nude dancing, Rehnquist wanted the Court to uphold the law and looked every which way for a rationale.* But the Court's prior 1st Amendment opinions were troublesome. In other words, Rehnquist couldn't get around the old bugaboo of *stare decisis,* the honoring of judicial precedent. After three awkward stabs at getting around the 1st Amendment problem, he finally just gave up and circulated a new fourth draft to his colleagues that told them in essence to ignore the free-speech issue—forget the precedents—and concentrate on the state's interest in morality and public order. He explained it all with a whimsical cover memorandum that poked fun at his inability to come up with anything better, and he quoted ("surely from memory," one commentator said) Johnny Mercer's 1940s hit, "Acc-Cen-Tchu-Ate the Positive": "The theme of this fourth draft is a very positive one, and it can be summed up in the following verse from a once popular song: 'Accentuate the positive/Eliminate the negative/Latch on to the affirmative/Don't mess with Mr. In Between.'"

Initially, the Court's majority, a vestige of the Warren years, was unsympathetic to Rehnquist's entreaties from the right. But Rehnquist's rhetoric stood out as much as his style of dress, and he got the attention he sought. Distinguished academics, even the admittedly liberal ones, sensed Rehnquist's potential for leadership. "He's the one with the agenda," asserted A. E. Dick Howard, a law professor at the University of Virginia, when we spoke about Rehnquist the year before the justice became the chief. "He has claim to the leadership role on the court."

Laurence Tribe, a law professor at Harvard Law School, was more speculative back then but no less struck by what he saw in Rehnquist. "As he moves closer to the center as the Court moves right, his voice could become weaker against equally strong intellects," he told me. (Tribe perceptively foresaw the looming arrival of a justice like Antonin Scalia, a firebrand who was even more conservative than Rehnquist.) "On the other hand, he could have an enormous impact, particularly if he were elevated to Chief Justice. That has happened rarely because it can cause terrible friction with the other Justices."

**Barnes v. Glen Theatre, Inc.*, 501 U.S. 560 (1991)

When Tribe expressed that view in late 1984, he couldn't possibly have known that a mere eighteen months later Burger would step down. But Tribe identified Rehnquist's distinctive voice as one of conservative leadership. The Harvard law professor correctly sensed that President Reagan someday might shrewdly play an angle that would give the president, in essence, two appointments at once.

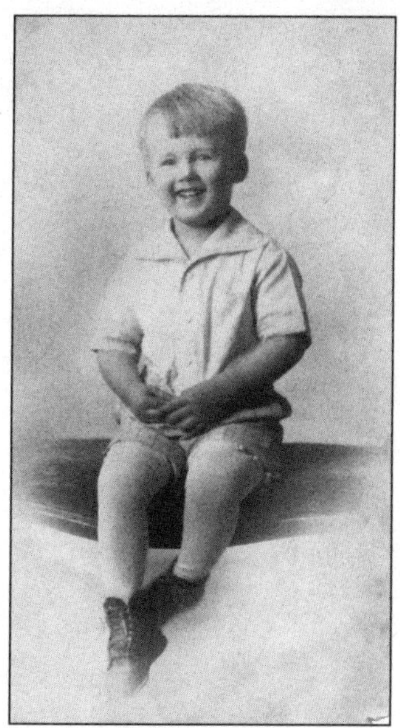

Billy Rehnquist, about four years old, c. 1927–1928. Studio photograph taken in Milwaukee, Wisconsin. *Credit:* Photographer unknown, collection of the Supreme Court of the United States.

Summer of '42. Rehnquist and his high school friends quit their jobs a week early and rented two cabins at Silver Lake, Wantoma, Wisconsin. The wartime draft awaited them. Rehnquist, age seventeen, is at far left. *Credit:* Photographer unknown, collection of the Supreme Court of the United States.

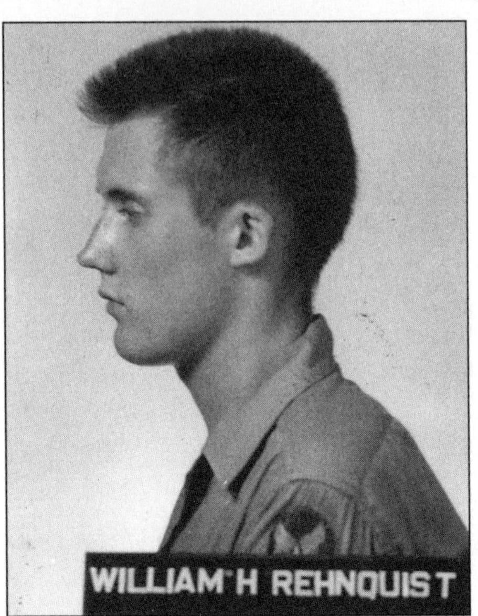

Rehnquist chose enlisted life over the "spit and polish" required of an officer. By 1944, when this identification photo was taken, he was a twenty-year-old army sergeant stationed in Hondo, Texas, in the waning days of the war. Later postings were better. Tripoli was "breathtakingly beautiful" and Casablanca was "too good to be true."

Credit: United States Army photograph, collection of the Supreme Court of the United States.

A clerk for Justice Robert Jackson: February 1952 through June 1953. During that time, Rehnquist pushed his own conservative agenda. Jackson had been relying on a lone clerk, George Niebank (far right), until Rehnquist arrived to help out midway through the term. To Rehnquist's young mind, the clerks as a group harbored "extreme solicitude for the claims of communists and other criminal defendants."

Credit: Photograph by Sam Daniels, collection of the Supreme Court of the United States.

Nan Cornell. Cornell accompanied Rehnquist to Washington for his clerkship and went to work for the CIA. The two were married in August 1953, around the time this photograph was taken. *Credit:* Photographer unknown, collection of the Supreme Court of the United States.

The Nixon years. After making a name for himself in Phoenix, Rehnquist joined the Nixon administration in 1969 as the Justice Department's tough-talking advocate for rewriting the Constitution to limit the rights of criminal defendants. His efforts didn't succeed, but Nixon's trusted attorney general, John Mitchell, took notice. *Credit:* Photographer unknown, collection of the Supreme Court of the United States.

Mitchell's men. Rehnquist is third from right, top row, in this group portrait of top Justice Department officials in the Nixon administration, c. 1969–1971. His Phoenix patron Richard Kleindienst, then deputy attorney general, is second from left, bottom row. John Mitchell is center, bottom row. *Credit:* Photographer unknown, collection of the Supreme Court of the United States.

New justices. Lewis Powell and Rehnquist, along with their families, went to the Oval Office for a December 21, 1971 photo opportunity with President Richard Nixon, eleven days after their Senate confirmation. Nixon made his improbable choice of Rehnquist without ever speaking to him about the job. Standing behind Powell are his children: Lewis, Penny, and Jo. *Credit:* White House photograph, collection of the Supreme Court of the United States.

William O. Douglas. Douglas mixed eastern urbanity with a westerner's rugged individualism, and Rehnquist found common ground with the older man. The respect was mutual. "Bill mentioned to me that when he looked at Rehnquist he saw himself," Cathy Douglas recalled. "It certainly wasn't ideological; it was personal." On November 1, 1973, Douglas made an appearance at Yale University with Jane Fonda and other celebrities. *Credit:* Copyright © Roger Ressmeyer/Corbis.

Three clerks, one natural heir. John Roberts, far right, clerked for Rehnquist during the 1980–1981 term. Left to right in this 1981 photo of Rehnquist's three clerks during that term: Dean Colson, Rehnquist, Robert Knauss, Roberts. "John Roberts is proving to be an absolutely first-rate law clerk," Rehnquist wrote. *Credit:* Photographer unknown, collection of the Supreme Court of the United States.

Rehnquist turns fifty-eight. President Ronald Reagan presided over a birthday luncheon for Rehnquist in the state dining room of the White House, October 1, 1982. From left: Chief Justice Warren Burger, Justice William Brennan, Justice Thurgood Marshall, Rehnquist, and the president. *Credit:* Copyright © Charles Tasnadi/Associated Press.

Shake hands, come out fighting. "Mainstream or too extreme?" Ted Kennedy asked as the Senate Judiciary Committee began hearings on Rehnquist's nomination to be chief justice, July 29, 1986. As soon as Ronald Reagan nominated Rehnquist, Kennedy put the family's personal private investigator on the case and told him to start digging. From left: Committee members Charles Grassley (R-IA), Kennedy (D-MA), Howard Metzenbaum (D-OH), Strom Thurmond (R-SC), and Patrick Leahy (D-VT), with Rehnquist second from right. Thurmond chaired the committee. *Credit:* Copyright © Lana Harris/Associated Press.

The confirmation hearing. Rehnquist awaited questioning by the Senate Judiciary Committee on July 30, 1986, accompanied by his wife Nan and son Jim. He gave an unflappable performance in two days of testimony that was televised live. *Credit:* Copyright © Lana Harris/Associated Press.

Chief Justice Rehnquist. Warren Burger administers the oath to his successor as Nan holds the bible and Ronald Reagan looks on. The ceremony was in the East Room of the White House on September 26, 1986. Reagan was surprised by the timing of Burger's retirement but didn't try to stop it. *Credit:* Smithsonian Institution photograph, collection of the Supreme Court of the United States.

The Bush inauguration. Despite suffering from thyroid cancer, Rehnquist was determined to swear in George W. Bush for a second term on January 20, 2005. He wore his signature robe adorned with four gold stripes on each sleeve. Rehnquist spoke and breathed through a tracheotomy. It would be two more months before he was well enough to return to the bench. *Credit:* Copyright © Wally Hines/ AP/Corbis.

Images of the gaunt chief justice were splashed all over. Photographers and television cameras were staked out in front of Rehnquist's Virginia townhouse. Desperately ill, Rehnquist was determined not to quit. He left home on July 12, 2005 as President Bush was conferring with senators about future Court nominees. Rehnquist died in office on September 3, 2005, less than a month before his eighty-first birthday. *Credit:* Copyright © J. Scott Applewhite/ Associated Press.

TWENTY

Bored at the Court

REHNQUIST WAS OFTEN BORED. The Court was like a tomb of the living compared to the frenetic, roller-coaster pace of the Nixon Justice Department. Rehnquist had become weary of the isolation seemingly from the moment he got there, hence the diversions—meteorology, stamp collecting, night-school art classes, cigar-and-poker nights with his buddies.* He pestered the chief justice with suggestions for enlivening things at the Court. A week before the Court was to start its new term in 1973, Rehnquist apologized in writing for what he was about to do and then launched a two-page, single-spaced memo onto the desk of the chief justice (with copies to all the other justices) asking him to please, please do something about all the dreariness:

> With all of the accumulated docket of cases before us, this may be a poor time to burden the Conference with basically housekeeping matters; I would guess, however, that it is probably no worse than any other time

*In addition to Scalia, regular players included DC lawyer Robert Bennett and his political-pundit brother Bill Bennett; federal judges Royce Lamberth, Thomas Hogan, and David Sentelle; Martin Feinstein, director of the Washington Opera; Walter Berns, a Georgetown University professor; and Clay T. Whitehead, Nixon's former telecommunications adviser. It was a politically conservative bunch. Berns served as the unofficial "corresponding secretary" of the games and said he had records of more than two hundred poker evenings going back to the 1980s.

during the Term. If some time could be found, certainly not necessarily at the first week's Conference, but at some Conference in the not too far distant future, to discuss these ideas at the time we take up other housekeeping matters, I would greatly appreciate it.

1. *Coffee hour after oral argument.* I think that the practice which each of us appears to follow at the close of a day of oral argument—plodding back to his own individual salt mine—is bad for morale. While I know there is work to be done, I am wondering if there would be any substantial sentiment in the Conference in favor of opening either the Justices' Dining Room, or one of the Conference Rooms, to all justices and law clerks who desire it, for a half-hour of coffee or tea at 3:00 P.M. on at least some afternoons following oral argument. It would give law clerks a chance to get acquainted with the justices for whom they don't work, and vice versa.

2. *Justices' Dining Room.* Seeing the dining facilities at your old court,* and at the Court of Claims, convinces me that ours combines, to a degree that might be thought impossible, baronial elegance with dreariness. Might there be some possibility of using the new Chippendale table for those justices who want to eat with other justices, but also placing two or three other tables in the same room, in addition to the table in the next room, so that one of us who wanted to have a couple of friends over to lunch could come up and eat in the same dining room, and still not disturb those of the Brethren who wish to eat with one another?

3. *Mini-Gridiron show.*** I would enjoy seeing what each annual crop of law clerks, together with such help from the justices that they might wish, could do in the way of a gridiron show or other parody or satire on the Court. If we passed this along to the law clerks in the fall, and told them that we would expect a performance sometime in the spring, I should think we could have a very enjoyable evening of it when it occurred.

4. Please don't get the impression that I am not working hard in preparation for the first Conference.

Warren Burger was dismissive if not aghast, and with characteristic self-righteousness the chief ticked off his objections one by one. Apropos of the

*US Court of Appeals for the District of Columbia

**The Gridiron Club of Washington was composed of journalists and was known for its annual white-tie dinner in which club members staged elaborate musical skits lampooning politicians, who were expected to respond in a similar spirit.

suggested "coffee hour," Burger doubted that he would attend, and he wasn't sure whether any others would, either. "There just isn't time." Besides, Burger continued, "because of last year's 'leaks'* I was not in the mood to see law clerks generally, and if we have any more of last year's business there will be minimal interest." As for the "dreary" Supreme Court dining room: "You should have seen it in 1969: an institutional rug; no sofas; no paintings; no anything but a table and chairs, as in a barracks—or mess hall. It looked like one of Gawler's** better 'display' rooms." Finally, there was the Gridiron show, which Burger just as tersely kissed off: "I'll try to keep an open mind. Something like this was tried at my old court. Just once!" So much for Rehnquist's new ideas.

Instead, Rehnquist looked elsewhere for his indulgences and diversions. He tried and failed to get the Supreme Court press corps to put on a satirical show for the justices. He quizzed his clerks about their college fight songs, most of which Rehnquist had memorized. When he got bored at oral arguments he idly wrote limericks; scribbled notes to his seatmate Blackmun, wagering on who would get assigned certain opinions; and translated English phrases into rough, schoolboy Latin. And he served as the choral director for the annual Christmas sing-along at the Court, as well as at judicial conferences—where his fondness for leading the Southern anthem "Dixie" earned him a tongue-lashing from African-American lawyers.

Stories were legion about the practical jokes that Rehnquist played. The most oft-told described an April Fool's spoof on Burger. During the chief's last year on the Court, Rehnquist posted a street photographer in front of the Court with a life-sized cardboard cutout of Burger. A sign said "Have your picture taken with the chief justice, $1." To make sure Burger saw it, Rehnquist asked him for a ride into the Court that day. Justices and clerks in every other chamber reacted with glee at how Rehnquist had deflated the pompous Burger. But the chief could also dish it back at Rehnquist on occasion. Burger was so unhappy with a Rehnquist-produced skit† at the

---

*Burger blamed law clerks for leaks that occurred as the Court grappled with *Roe v. Wade.*

**A Washington, DC, funeral home.

†In the choral performance that angered Burger, Rehnquist and his law clerk Craig Bradley changed the lyrics to "Angels from the Realms of Glory." The new lyrics spoofed Rehnquist's longstanding opposition to *Miranda:* "Liberals from the realms of theory/Should adorn our highest bench./Though to crooks they're always cheery/At police misdeeds they always blench./Save *Miranda*! Save *Miranda*!/Save it from the Nixon four!"

Court's 1975 Christmas party (and it was always the *Christmas* party as long as Rehnquist was around) that the following month he assigned Rehnquist only one opinion, in an Indian tax case.

For sheer chutzpah, though, nothing could top Rehnquist's 1983 trick on the rest of the Court. Rehnquist's tweaking of his brethren was played so close to the line, and was so well orchestrated, that other justices and clerks became convinced Rehnquist was personally attacking Thurgood Marshall and began quietly organizing a counteroffensive.

Rehnquist set up the hoax as the Court was considering what appeared, to most justices, to be a routine workers' compensation case.* At issue was whether the definition of "wages" under an obscure federal law included the 68 cents per hour that the employer contributed on behalf of each employee to a union trust fund. This was exactly the kind of case that most justices hated to get. It involved no profound constitutional issues, just a commercial dispute over the definition of a word. It was contractual arcana, and it was going to be disposed of quickly because eight of the nine justices saw the case the same way: there was nothing in the definition of "wages" that mentioned the 68-cents-an-hour trust-fund contribution.

The chief justice assigned himself the writing of the opinion; it would be an easy one to knock out fast. But when Marshall saw Burger's draft he decided he was going to be the solitary dissenter. Marshall had a point to make—one whose larger significance wouldn't be lost on Rehnquist. It was all about *stare decisis.*

Marshall faulted the other eight justices for not looking past the literal language of the wage contract to consider its intent. He quoted directly from a Supreme Court opinion** of Franklin Roosevelt's era: "Old laws apply to changed situations." Marshall's passionate dissent explained in painstaking (and persuasive) detail precisely how various legislative acts over the years had altered the traditional definition of "wages" to encompass fringe benefits like the trust-fund contributions. Because Congress hadn't addressed the issue directly, Marshall said, "we must interpret."

Marshall's broader point was a not-too-subtle dig at the strict constructionists, particularly Rehnquist. Marshall helpfully added an explanatory footnote in case anyone missed his point: "For example, a statute enacted

---

**Morrison-Knudsen Construction Co. v. Director, OWCP,* 461 U.S. 624 (1983)

***Browder v. United States,* 312 U.S. 335 (1941).

in 1880 before the invention of the automobile might well have applied to 'carriages.' Suppose that the statute required all 'carriages' to come to a stop before entering a crosswalk near a schoolyard. If the statutory purpose is to assure safety, a court should apply the statute to automobiles." But what if the statutory purpose were different? Marshall's footnote had more horse-and-buggy analogies to cover the various permutations. The whole dissent, footnotes included, was a *tour de force* running several times the length of Burger's opinion for the majority of eight.

Rehnquist saw Marshall's dissent for the personal rebuke that it was intended to be, and he decided to respond in kind—and have some fun at the expense of the other justices. Rehnquist devilishly crafted a rejoinder that ridiculed Marshall for suggesting that the words of a law could have anything other than one fixed meaning. It was a *reductio ad absurdum,* solely focusing on what Rehnquist called the faulty logic of Marshall's horse-and-buggy footnote. Rehnquist crossed way over the line between irreverence and disrespect.

"The Boss wrote a dissent about how the case *should* be construed narrowly," recalled Ron Blunt, who was one of Rehnquist's clerks that year. "He said most modes of transportation were, indeed, illegal for use on highways because the highways had to be preserved for horses and buggies. He spent an entire afternoon putting all of this together, and he came out and showed it to me: 'Well, whaddaya think?' It all logically followed!"

Rehnquist circulated his broadside to the other justices and announced that unless Marshall withdrew the ridiculous footnote he intended to have his criticism published in the official United States Reports, the bound volume of Court decisions.

Rehnquist now was almost touching the third rail. Marshall, seventy-four years old at the time, already had a reputation among the clerks and justices as someone who was beginning to lose his mental edge: "a disengaged justice who was overly dependent upon his clerks," in the words of David Garrow. In later years, Marshall's mental decrepitude would become even more obvious, and painful, as Marshall spent days in his chambers telling stories and watching daytime television. Joking with Marshall was one thing, but criticizing the legend from *Brown*—as Rehnquist obviously appeared to be doing—was quite another.

Marshall said nothing. He had been alerted by Rehnquist and knew that Rehnquist wasn't really going to publish his criticism. So Marshall went along, expressing displeasure but otherwise keeping mum. But when the Rehnquist memo hit the other chambers, the first reaction was puzzlement, and then anger among some clerks when Rehnquist's minions assured them "The Boss" was, indeed, serious. From the clerks of Chief Justice Burger and Justices Blackmun and Stevens came word that their superiors were discussing ways to head him off.

David Jaffe, who also was a law clerk for Rehnquist that year, thought that Rehnquist quibbling over transport was obviously "outrageous! Ron, Gary* and I just laughed and laughed!" But it said something about the way Rehnquist's lone dissents were viewed that no one thought he was kidding. "We thought it was hysterical," explained Jaffe. "A bit dry, perhaps, but hysterical nonetheless. But there was much consternation in the other chambers. They were just hypersensitive about it. Nobody recognized the joke at first."

So Rehnquist decided to keep going. "We were just astonished that anybody would take it seriously, but they did. Stevens's and Blackmun's clerks were so fearful that this would come out: 'Oh my God, what has he done? What's he doing to the Court?' We'd deadpan: 'The Boss did that himself. He was gravely concerned about that footnote.' . . .

"Some clerks worried that it was unfair to be taking such advantage of Marshall—and that it was going to be perceived as racist," Jaffe went on. "Even Marshall's clerks were upset. Marshall didn't even tell *them*! His clerks at first thought it was a joke, until we persuaded them otherwise, and then they felt they had to be upset."

Cory Streisinger, a Blackmun clerk that year, was one who didn't get the humor. "I thought it was in somewhat poor taste. As I recall, it was near the end of the term. Our senses of humor were not what they might have been."

Finally, with concern in other chambers bubbling over, Rehnquist decided the joke had gone far enough. He walked through his outer office, where his two secretaries sat, and into the adjoining office where all three of his law clerks had their desks. "I guess this has gone a little too far," he told them. "I've got to do something to tell them [the justices] this was a joke."

*Gary Born was Rehnquist's other law clerk that term.

Rehnquist decided he would send a signal to the other chambers. He circulated a "Dear Thurgood" letter. The occasion for his magnanimity in withdrawing his statement, he wrote with mock seriousness, was an obscure Swedish holiday commemorating a battle between Peter the Great and King Charles XII of Sweden that he, a Swedish-American, celebrated each year by doing a good deed.

TWENTY-ONE

An Aspiring Novelist

IN HIS LATER YEARS ON THE COURT, Rehnquist made no secret of his literary ambitions, and after becoming chief justice he adapted various lectures that he had given into four historical works about the Supreme Court. Since those histories were authored by a sitting chief justice, readers and reviewers took notice, and the books were generally well received as noteworthy contributions to the lore of the Court.*

But Rehnquist's historical works were rueful compromises for a man who saw himself as an artist worthy of much more. Long before Rehnquist settled for putting his name on books that described the Court's dusty past, he challenged himself to break out of his humdrum existence as the Court's junior justice. He wanted to become a novelist.

Having already confided to Bill Douglas his concern about becoming stale, when Rehnquist decided to try his hand at writing a novel during the summer break following the Court's 1973–1974 term, it was logical that he would turn to Douglas for mentoring—not just because Douglas had encouraged the younger justice to seek other outlets but because Douglas was already accomplished in the literary realm, and had connections.

---

* *The Supreme Court: How It Was, How It Is* (1987); *Grand Inquests: The Historic Impeachments of Justice Samuel Chase and President Andrew Johnson* (1992); *All the Laws But One: Civil Liberties in Wartime* (1998); and *Centennial Crisis: The Disputed Election of 1876* (2004).

Douglas was a prolific author—of fifty-one books and hundreds of articles—and he had done well financially from all that writing.* Douglas made it look easy as he balanced the writing with his Court work, but the reality was that Douglas's numerous divorce settlements forced him to constantly scramble for money from outside speaking and writing. He had even moonlighted as the president of the Albert Parvin Foundation, which was financed by a Las Vegas casino owner. It was a financial necessity.

In October 1974, Douglas was seventy-six years old and was starting what would be his last full term on the Court—setting the all-time record for longevity. Rehnquist, fifty years old, was beginning his second full term. Time was slipping away and Rehnquist was getting itchy to do something more interesting than the scrivening of opinions. Rehnquist knew—or at least *thought* he knew—that he was capable of something far more creative than redrafting his clerks' turgid prose. He asked Douglas to introduce him to people who could help.

Rehnquist was about to be carried into an entirely different world. It was one that not only awed him but fed his ego—and, more often in the early years, deflated it. Capitalizing on Bill Douglas's literary connections also presented Rehnquist with a real social challenge for the first time since he'd joined the Court. The New York literary salons were fresh territory to conquer. Rehnquist savored the possibilities, but he also realized that he was playing seriously against type—the gawky justice in an unfamiliar realm. Rehnquist wanted to keep his literary aspirations a complete secret from almost everyone, even the publishers.

Douglas put Rehnquist in touch with his personal attorney and literary lawyer, a New Yorker named Sidney Davis. Davis was a patrician Park Avenue barrister whose close friendship with the rough-hewn Douglas revealed another side of the older justice's personality. Douglas had been close friends with Davis since meeting him as an idealistic young justice at the Supreme Court in 1943, when Davis clerked for Hugo Black. Later that term, Davis came over and clerked for Douglas. The two had been friends ever since, and Douglas trusted Davis implicitly—so much so that when Douglas was pressured into stepping down from the Albert Parvin Foun-

*Douglas's outside income from books, and his writing for the counterculture journal *Evergreen Review,* had already drawn the attention of Attorney General Mitchell and President Nixon. "This goddamned Douglas makes money!" Nixon told Mitchell when the two of them were discussing how Howard Baker might supplement his salary if he became a Supreme Court justice.

dation, Davis took his place. It was a measure of Douglas's fondness for Rehnquist that when the younger justice asked Douglas to help him out, Douglas was happy to share this valuable connection.

Davis soon was reaching out to Rehnquist, at Douglas's behest:

> When I had lunch with Justice Douglas last Saturday, he told me that you were looking for a literary agent and asked me whether I could recommend one to you.
>
> My office does a fair amount of publishing and literary work, and at one time or another I have had dealings with most agents. It's a strange profession (someone once said that agenting is a delusion entirely surrounded by liars in sharp clothing), and a rather uneven one. If I may, I would suggest to you that you ought to avoid the large corporate ones. The best agents tend to be small offices, or individual entrepreneurs, and the one I recommend to you is Robert Lantz, of The Lantz Office.
>
> Mr. Lantz has been at it for a long time, and represents a very considerable body of the more successful authors. Despite the courtliness of his old-world manner and a deceptive mildness, he is a tough negotiator and the soul of discretion. He knows the publishing industry well, and vice versa, and he has a superior reputation for skill and integrity.

Rehnquist jumped at the opportunity. He replied to Davis that "your definition of the profession makes it sound fascinating, and I shall drop [Lantz] a line within the next couple of days."

Whether Rehnquist knew it then or not, Davis had just opened the door to an unbelievably well-connected Hollywood talent agent whose clients included some of the world's most famous people. Lantz was sixty years old and at the top of his game, representing the likes of Elizabeth Taylor, Richard Burton, Leonard Bernstein, Bette Davis, the photographer Richard Avedon, the film director Milos Forman, and the lyricist Alan Jay Lerner. Lantz was a throwback to another era, always cabling from some exotic filming locale or jetting about the world on a press junket, and never at a loss for a name to drop.*

---

*As they came to know each other better, Rehnquist seemed to get a vicarious kick from the gadabout nature of Lantz's life, marveling in a letter to him: "You go to Europe more than any other person I know." A few months earlier, Rehnquist sent a handwritten note to Bill Douglas thanking him for the introduction to Lantz: "He is delightful."

Lantz's life, and his circle of friends and clients—the way he operated, the two were intermixed—couldn't have been more sharply at odds with Rehnquist's. The agent was Berlin-born but had fled with his family to London in 1935, after Hitler came to power. His father was a writer of silent movies and as a young man Lantz had theatrical aspirations, even going so far as to produce plays as a teenager in Vienna and on Broadway between 1959 and 1961, after he came to America. But it was as a dealmaker that Lantz truly excelled. He had parlayed his reassuring manner and polished charm into a maze of connections that was about to become further enhanced by Rehnquist.

An enthusiastic Rehnquist fired off an introductory letter to Lantz on the same day that Douglas's friend provided the connection:

> I have virtually completed a draft of a short novel which I would like to have published. If a publisher were to be found, I think I would probably want to use a pen name, in order to avoid giving the impression of capitalizing on my position. Mr. Sidney Davis was good enough to recommend your name to me, and I wonder if you could either represent me yourself or suggest some other way of handling the matter.

Soon, Rehnquist and Lantz were engaged in robust correspondence. They had obviously hit it off, each seemingly enamored of the other even though they had never met. Lantz assured Rehnquist that the manuscript, at least for now, would be their secret. The agent would be the soul of discretion "with regard to the problem you raise." Rehnquist's anonymity was assured.

When Lantz finally got his hands on Rehnquist's untitled manuscript, what he found was disappointing. The justice had concocted a novel based on what he knew—the main story line was about a brash young law clerk traveling with a wizened federal judge, one of three who would sit in judgment of a young Vietnam War protester who had tossed an American flag into a bonfire in Phoenix. The novel raised a constitutional question—whether burning the American flag was "free speech"—and it actually anticipated a case that the Rehnquist Court would decide fifteen years later.*

---

* *Texas v. Johnson*, 491 U.S. 397 (1989) held that flag burning was protected free speech under the 1st Amendment. Rehnquist dissented from the 5–4 decision.

But the writing was amateurish, the plot anything but compelling. The opening chapter took place on a plane flight from San Francisco to Phoenix, and much of the scene-setting dialogue consisted of the pilot's verbatim instructions to the passengers prior to landing. The novel was unpublishable.

Still, Lantz obviously knew that a relationship of real value had just dropped into his lap. No Supreme Court justice had ever published a novel—good, bad, or otherwise. And even if Rehnquist's book never got between covers, for an operator like Lantz the potential downstream benefits of getting close to Rehnquist obviously would be considerable. So Lantz crafted his response very carefully. He wanted to break the news gently to this prized new prospect, so as not to completely turn him off.

Lantz thus tried to make the most of what Rehnquist turned in, giving him some good news with the bad. "It is in need of expert editorial advice," the agent began in a letter back to Rehnquist. "The story peters out." There could be no sugarcoating of the obvious. But Lantz reassured Rehnquist that reworking was "something that is required for every manuscript of course." The agent was full of suggestions in a long letter that he had obviously spent considerable time crafting. Lantz apologized in advance and proposed "a slight restructuring of everything" that he thought Rehnquist could do pretty quickly. "In the meantime my congratulations on a very good manuscript."

What was interesting about Rehnquist's literary ambitions was how willing the justice was to keep his own ego in check. Rehnquist was cut-and-dried when he edited the work of his clerks, and he could be didactic in the extreme. But with Lantz, this agent he had not yet met, he adopted an almost apprentice-like relationship. Soon enough, as they came to know each other better, the real Rehnquist persona would come to the surface. But as Lantz and Rehnquist were feeling each other out, the justice was the earnest pupil. "I am sure that I will benefit from your suggestions, whether you call them 'reactions' or 'criticisms,'" Rehnquist wrote back as soon as he received Lantz's initial critique. "I think I have some grasp of the substance with which I deal in the manuscript, but I am a complete neophyte when it comes to technique."

Rehnquist spent a frustrating year trying to turn his bomb into something that Lantz could peddle to a publisher. The effort went poorly because Rehnquist treated his unfinished novel like one more draft Court opinion. Workmanlike writing and quick turnarounds between drafts might have been good enough for the Court, but not for the publishers that Lantz courted. But the necessity of Rehnquist's fitting his fiction-writing time into the short breaks in the Court's calendar meant that the justice had no choice but to emphasize speed over quality. Since the manuscript was being manually typed—this was not yet the era of the personal computer, or even the word processor—even minor changes necessitated extensive reworking, which Rehnquist quickly tired of. Instead, he designated his inserts as A, B, and so on, then renumbered the pages and sent detailed "mechanical instructions" to Lantz as to how the jumble should be rearranged.

Working hard on his latest revisions the day after Christmas, Rehnquist excitedly told Lantz about his idea for a title. The justice said he was "presently somewhat taken with the idea of extracting a title from this couplet found in Pope's 'Rape of the Lock':

The hungry judges soon the sentence sign,
And wretches hang that jury-men may dine.

"Some of the new material . . . would offer some basis for entitling the work either *And Wretches Hang* or *That Jury-Men May Dine.*"

Lantz ignored the suggested titles but called the revisions a considerable improvement. Aiming high, he would shoot the manuscript off forthwith to Thomas Guinzburg, a founder of the *Paris Review* who by then was president of the Viking Press. Like Lantz, Guinzburg knew everyone who mattered in the publishing world; he had just hired Jacqueline Onassis as an editor. Lantz was "anxious to know what an experienced first-rate editor will have to say by way of comment on the whole work."

He got his answer a week later. Guinzburg hated it; the novel was going to need "a very considerable craftsman/editor to shape it into an acceptable novel for publication." Beyond that, the subject matter itself was simply dull, "even if certain problems of sheer writing would be overcome." But Lantz wasn't giving up. He intended to go to other publishers.

As the rejections began to mount, Lantz's letters to Rehnquist grew increasingly pessimistic. Lantz was ever the diplomat, gently explaining to the justice why it was important for him to understand "what the negative reaction consists of." Lantz proffered the opinions of George Brockway, the president of W.W. Norton:

> He says he has given it two readings, and he thinks, in a nutshell, that the plot and the story are very good and so are the backgrounds. Where he feels

> the book falls down is in the sheer writing skill, which prevents the individual characters from coming alive, at least to him, and from becoming separate individuals.
>
> For instance, he feels there is an excessive use of dialogue, and the dialogue, in his words, is "interchangeable." He feels that every detail has been dwelled upon too much, every handshake, every making of a bed, every announcement over loud speakers. All of this clutters up the flow of the very good narrative, and the discussions, the substance of which is of great interest, all seems [*sic*] to be on the same note and between the same people, i.e., they read as if they all talk the same way.
>
> In other words, what he said is that he thinks there is great potential in the background, the plot, the narrative, but it is handicapped by a lack of color in the writing and in the drawing of the different characters.

In other words, it was badly written. Lantz tried to explain that part of the problem was to be expected, since this was "a first novel by a man whose primary profession is not the writing of fiction." But Lantz also took pains to explain that Rehnquist had hobbled himself by insisting on writing under a pseudonym. "The book will have to be judged entirely on its own merit, without the benefit of the interest and glamour of your name on it." Lantz sent the manuscript off to his friend Betty Prashker, the associate publisher at Doubleday, and let her in on the secret about the author's identity. She still wanted to see big changes. Rehnquist settled in for what was to be an extensive rewrite.

Six months later, Lantz was vacationing in the south of France and Doubleday's Prashker was wondering why Rehnquist was late with promised revisions to the manuscript. The justice had been struggling, trying to balance his writing with the Court's customary end-of-the-term crunch. He finally finished the redraft after the term ended, and got a letter off to the man he was now calling "Robby" that described what he'd done. There was now a new "Chapter 1AA, to avoid the tedious process of renumbering." Rehnquist had also added a whole new chapter "in which two of the law clerks go out to a restaurant to get Mexican food for lunch. The hope here is to expand on their personal relationships a little bit, and also to get in a little bit about Mexican food, which is very popular in the Southwest."

But Betty Prashker was proving to be Rehnquist's nemesis. She soon replied that the revisions that "Author X" had spent the prior six months on weren't enough. The draft still needed more plotting and "the author should cut some of the rather static dialogue that seems to take place in elevators. I think what I am saying is that we are still at the beginning stage. The whole thing needs to be worked over, added to, pruned down; definitely put through the typewriter once or twice. Is the Justice prepared to do this?"

Lantz sent the letter on with a note of encouragement: "You should not give up, but rather persevere." Rehnquist attempted still another rewrite. Eight months later, in March 1976, Betty Prashker returned the manuscript with her own editorial revisions and editing marks all over it, as if to show the pupil what he needed to do. "I have been through the first three chapters," Prashker explained in a cover letter to Lantz. "I tried, in general, to add some depth to the characters, loosen up the style, and speed up the pace. I hope this will give the Justice some notion of the work that needs to be done. It will require a major effort. Cheers."

Rehnquist hit the ceiling when he saw how Prashker had torn apart his writing. But as still another Court term wound down without any appreciable progress toward getting his novel published, Rehnquist worried that he had overreacted and feared he might have burned a bridge. He wrote to Lantz on June 11, 1976:

> My unhappiness with the extent of Betty Prashker's suggested revisions in the manuscript was partly due to middle-of-the-term blues; it seemed to me back in January or February that I could simply never find time to do the sort of work she wanted done on it. We are just now in the last stages of the opinion writing process, busier than ever, but I think I will take my typewriter with me to Vermont* this summer, and it may be that I will have sufficient time and energy to at least try to do the sort of things she wants done. Meanwhile, if you have any other opportunities to place it, I urge you to do so.

Trying to become a novelist turned into a desultory pursuit for Rehnquist. By the end of that year, he was still at odds with himself over whether to push ahead with further revisions or just give up—"I fear I am kind of

*Rehnquist bought a summer home in Greensboro, Vermont, in 1974.

in dead center about the revision." But three months after that, he was writing back to Lantz with a new zest. Rehnquist had "become engrossed" in the six Palliser novels written a hundred years earlier by Anthony Trollope. "I am simply fascinated by them, and think that perhaps I have absorbed enough from them so as to be able to attempt a reworking of parts of my manuscript. That will have to await my summer in Vermont, but somehow I now feel I can breathe more life into the characters as Trollope did into his. Tell me if you think I am out of my mind."

As usual, Lantz's reply was heavy on ego stroking, name dropping, and above all encouragement. Lantz pointed out that Rehnquist wasn't alone in his love of Trollope's novels; they were having a good run as a BBC adaptation, and the series had recently crossed the Atlantic and now was also playing on PBS in the states. Lantz promised to visit Rehnquist in Washington "because I promised Liv Ullmann to take another look at the production of *Anna Christie* before it comes to New York. . . . You will be interested to hear that my client, Sir Terence Rattigan, is presently at work on a stage dramatization of one of the lesser known Trollope books. So you are very much *en vogue.*"

But Rehnquist soon lost his passion for the project once again, and he didn't regain it during the remainder of the Court's 1977–1978 term—or, apparently, any time thereafter. The justice wrote a short note to Lantz around Memorial Day of 1978, abashedly confessing that "I think you have every reason to be disappointed in me, but somehow the creative urge which moved me several summers ago to churn out the original draft has simply not returned. Maybe under your guidance it could." But the reality for Rehnquist was different; he'd finally made his own discovery that he wasn't suited for the frustrating existence of a novelist—at least not now—and the rest had taken care of itself. There would be no further redrafting of this particular epic. But there would be others, because Rehnquist still harbored a secret desire to see his name on a published work of fiction. Invariably the efforts were hush-hush, and invariably they were unsuccessful. But Rehnquist never fully abandoned the ambition to be a novelist, or at least to write about something he considered more exciting than his own lair at the Supreme Court. It just always seemed that Rehnquist would rather be almost anywhere else but there.

So in 1994 Rehnquist was ready to try again, but this time he figured a murder mystery would have more commercial appeal. *Death in the Paw*

Paw Tunnel was the title of Rehnquist's whodunit, set during a week in the first presidential term of—who else?—Richard Nixon. The main characters were, unsurprisingly, thinly disguised caricatures of power-hungry people Rehnquist had worked alongside at the Department of Justice back in 1971, plus the obligatory Soviet spies and bad guys. It certainly wasn't hard to pick out John Mitchell, Dick Kleindienst, J. Edgar Hoover, and the supporting cast of young Nixon administration strivers and blackmailers who were up to no good. Any lingering doubt about their true identities Rehnquist eliminated by placing the action in a Camp David–like setting where the main players were planning the department's 1971 counteroffensive against the Mayday demonstrators who wanted to shut down Washington—strategizing that Rehnquist, in real life, had been in charge of! It seemed that Rehnquist had been writing every word of the murder mystery based upon his own personal experience—presumably excepting details of the murder itself, committed by a closeted gay (and married) assistant attorney general against a department rival who is blackmailing him in order to spend lavishly on his Russian-secret-agent mistress.

The whole idea left Lantz scratching his head. To begin with, he couldn't understand why Rehnquist set the story in 1971. "Nothing is gained by going back to where others have been, i.e., the tense time around 1968 and thereafter, the Nixon years, the Soviet problem and blackmail attempts because of gay connotations." Lantz thought he could see Hollywood potential if Rehnquist dug deeper, tried harder. In his exhortations the agent showed himself to be more enlightened about the real ways of Washington than even Rehnquist:

> What I have in mind is what you used in the sketch of an early book, the institution of the three traveling judges, something about which the ordinary public knows nothing. What is there within today's Washington daily life that is fresh and different, that wasn't being used or explored ten years ago, that could embellish and enrich and update some of the characters and plot lines you have now?
>
> In your own first book you gave such a wonderful and evocative description of your arrival as a law clerk at the Supreme Court, your surprise at finding yourself at the desk with lots of documents on which suddenly you were asked to give opinions to the Supreme Court justice for whom you worked. There must be innumerable young men at the House, in the

> Senate, in the overall government, who arrive at their desk and are confronted not only with a taste of power but with the fact that they have become insiders and, as such, vulnerable to outside temptations and seductions. It doesn't have to be the Russians and espionage. It certainly doesn't have to be the Supreme Court. But all those younger and middle-aged "extras" in the rare foreign languages? What about the lobbyists? What about all the people who suddenly get involved in the day to day workings of this powerful and bizarre city?

Rehnquist quickly disabused Lantz of any notions that he had time for such literary conceits. Sure, Rehnquist told him, something "more current . . . would be easier to sell. If I depended upon royalties for my subsistence, I would certainly follow your advice and make the sort of substantial revisions you have in mind." But, Rehnquist added, he had "another gainful occupation, and [I] don't really want to try" a more ambitious rewrite. "I think for now I will just put *Death in the Paw Paw Tunnel* back in the bottom drawer of my desk."

But as the Court took its annual break over the Christmas holidays, Rehnquist was vying for Lantz's attention yet again, this time with an idea for a historical novel—"or movie or play"—based on Custer's Last Stand. Rehnquist wanted to write a fictionalized account of a court-martial of one of Custer's few surviving officers. He intended to bring in some Civil War greats even though they had had no role in the original court of inquiry: Generals Ulysses S. Grant, William Tecumseh Sherman, and Philip Sheridan. Lantz told him to forget it.

TWENTY-TWO

Code Pink

IN SPITE OF REHNQUIST'S LITERARY FRUSTRATIONS and setbacks, his friendship with Robby Lantz continued to thrive because their association gave so much vicarious pleasure to them both. Lantz made regular trips to the Supreme Court to chew things over with Rehnquist, and dropped him cards and letters from all over. "Dear Bill," read one postcard from Florence, "the Supreme Court of Life slows all problems here with prosciutto, wild strawberries, white truffles—very wise!" They both hung in, and their perseverance paid off when Lantz finally helped Rehnquist get his name on a book, thirteen years after the two first met. By then Rehnquist was the chief justice, and there was a certain curiosity about the enigmatic man and his work. It also helped that the work was *not* a novel.

Rehnquist's maiden effort, a thin work simply titled *The Supreme Court,* was part memoir (of his clerkship years) and part nuts-and-bolts recitation of how the Court operated, "an odd literary concoction" according to one reviewer but a success nonetheless. It was an easier project for Rehnquist since most of the book was derived from a series of lectures the chief justice annually gave at a summer seminar in Salzburg, Austria.* Lantz represented

*Rehnquist appreciated the summer lecture circuit. He wrote in a 1985 letter: "I may have an opportunity to do some teaching on the island of Rhodos [*sic*] a year from next July. Nino Scalia did it this past year and said it was a delightful place, and that the academic diet was definitely on the light side. I know you think that the summer is the wrong time for Greece, but Nino said that the weather on Rhodos was very pleasant and that the beaches were great." In a 1991 letter he

Rehnquist in the contract negotiations with publishers, of course, and got Rehnquist a $30,000 advance against royalties. *The Supreme Court* was a winner for its publisher, William Morrow & Co. True to his reputation, Lantz then leveraged Rehnquist's success into a better deal the next time around. For *Grand Inquests,* Rehnquist's second book, in 1992, Lantz negotiated an advance of $100,000. For the chief justice's third book, *All the Laws But One,* in 1998, the advance was still a respectable $90,000. And even though the third book's sales were disappointing, Knopf acquired the chief justice's fourth (and, it turned out, final) book, *Centennial Crisis,* for an advance of $150,000. *Centennial Crisis* came out in 2004, the year Rehnquist was diagnosed with cancer, and the book was a financial disappointment for its publisher.

The financial ins and outs of Rehnquist's book deals proved to be occasionally vexatious for him—just as Douglas's publishing deals had caused trouble for the elder justice so many years earlier. A month before new restrictions on the amount of outside income that a federal judge could receive went into effect in 1991, Rehnquist asked Lantz's office whether his next advance royalty check could be speeded up. "It is possible," Rehnquist worried, "that these restrictions might apply to advance royalties." A year later, still fretting about the royalties, he asked whether he could just assign all of his future royalty rights to his three children, naming his lawyer-daughter Janet as the trustee.*

described another possibility: "I think I will accept an invitation from St. Mary's Law School in San Antonio to teach for two weeks at Innsbruck, Austria, this July. They have offered to fly us first class over there and back, put us up in a suite at a very nice resort hotel, and in addition pay $10,000 for eight hours of teaching a course based on my book about the Supreme Court. I am hoping we can also manage side trips to the Italian Lake Country—we are only sixty miles from the Brenner Pass—and perhaps go from Vienna down the Danube to Budapest on a hydrofoil that the Harrisons took last summer and enjoyed. Even if we don't manage all those side trips, I think it will be an enjoyable experience."

*Janet Rehnquist later ran into ethical problems of her own. She was appointed inspector general of the Department of Health and Human Services after George W. Bush became president in 2001. At HHS she was responsible for a vast operation with 1,600 employees in 85 field offices, ferreting out fraud in the $400 billion Medicare and Medicaid programs. She lasted less than two years and resigned after a Government Accountability Office investigation found "serious lapses of judgment" by her, including keeping a pistol in her office and posing as a law-enforcement officer authorized to carry firearms and make arrests. She kept a poster of a life-size human target, like ones at a firing range, on her office wall.

In August 1998, after Rehnquist had left Morrow for the greener pastures of Knopf, he got the good news that Morrow would allow the publication rights of his first two books to revert back to him. This afforded him an easy opportunity to enlarge *The Supreme Court* and reissue it; Rehnquist could update the book with new material he already had prepared for his annual Salzburg lectures. But the chief justice didn't think there would be much demand for reissuing his second book, *Grand Inquests,* which was about impeachments—"unless the House of Representatives should actually impeach President Clinton!" Rehnquist's facetious tone indicated he didn't think there was a chance that was going to happen—and in August all the smart money would have bet the same way.

Of course, the House did impeach Clinton four months later, and Morrow rushed to get Rehnquist's book back into print. Two days before Christmas in 1998, as it became clear that Rehnquist would be presiding over a Senate trial of President Bill Clinton, reporters from the *New York Times* and the *Wall Street Journal* began hounding Morrow as well as the Supreme Court press office. They wanted to know how much money Rehnquist was going to get from the 25,000-copy paperback reprinting of the book. (The answer, a secret until Rehnquist's death, was $15,000.) Reporter James Barron of the *Times* went further, specifically asking how Rehnquist justified making a profit on the sale of a book about impeachment trials at the same time that he was likely to preside over one. The calls caused a tizzy in the small Supreme Court press office right before the holidays. Rehnquist sent back a reply to the press office via his secretary, Janet Barnes. "The chief [says] to say 'Yes,' that the book will be reprinted, put back in print, whatever you want to say. But his answer is 'No comment' to James Barron and anyone else about the money thing."

Rehnquist had an innate wariness of the press that went at least as far back as 1971, when he was stung by the leak to *Newsweek* about his segregationist memo written while a law clerk to Justice Jackson. This didn't preclude Rehnquist from socializing off-the-record with a favored or influential journalist when it suited him; he knew the importance of having cordial relations with the press. Rehnquist was friendly during the 1970s with Howard Simons, the managing editor of the *Washington Post.* After taking over as chief justice, he occasionally hosted evening get-togethers for reporters who covered the Court. And, particularly in Rehnquist's early years as a justice, he sometimes traded small items of gossip with one or another of the reporters who regularly covered the Court.

But the reality was that Rehnquist kept his distance from reporters and viewed doing so as a matter of not only self-interest but survival. Interviews were strictly verboten—expressing a view about *anything* might subject him to a recusal demand later on. (He made an occasional exception only to discuss his books, and only then with a friendly, trusted interviewer.) Once, at a luncheon with editorial writers, Rehnquist was asked whether the Court was influenced much by public opinion. No, Rehnquist replied, if that implied the justices could be swayed by public-opinion polls or marchers in front of the Court. The questioner persisted: What about an article that makes a persuasive argument for deciding a case a certain way? "We are always interested in clear, logical reasoning," Rehnquist replied, "no matter how unlikely the source." Rehnquist's antipathy toward the press was borne of being scalded one too many times, and from seeing the same thing happen to others.

Rehnquist had been on the Court a mere five months when Bill Douglas sent a memo to the eight other justices that served as an object lesson. Douglas warned them not to have anything to do with Nina Totenberg, then a reporter for the weekly *National Observer.* Totenberg had a reputation for breaking insider stories at the Court and was said to be quite friendly with Potter Stewart. "She tried to see me a week or so ago to talk to me off-the-record about the Court," Douglas told the others. "I never talk to anyone on-the-record or off-the-record about the Court. But I was particularly allergic about the *National Observer.* I had seen one of the reporters several years back who wanted to do a piece about me. I saw him and it was friendly visit. But as I suspected, it ended up with my decapitation. So I made it a point never to talk to a *National Observer* reporter about things as innocuous even as fly fishing or the weather."

Rehnquist followed Douglas's advice. When a producer from the CBS affiliate in Milwaukee tried to sell him on the idea of doing a live interview on the day of his confirmation as chief justice—a local-man-makes-good kind of thing—Rehnquist just tersely replied, "I intend to spend my time learning about my new job," not giving interviews. But once Rehnquist began publishing his books, it was impossible to ignore the media altogether. When *Grand Inquests* came out, Lantz began pushing Rehnquist to appear on some of the big morning talk shows such as *Today* and *Good*

Morning America, and to do interviews with *Time* and *Newsweek,* and other national media.

Rehnquist pushed back, telling Lantz that he was willing to do a few interviews on PBS and C-SPAN, but only if the questions were limited to his book. In terms of magazines, "I would also be willing to do a press interview with the *Smithsonian;* since I am a chancellor of the [Smithsonian] Institution, I don't think they would treat me too harshly. I have reservations about interviews with the regular news magazines and law periodicals which I have previously discussed with you." A few months later, as he got more pressure from Morrow's publicity department to read from his book and sign copies at a local bookstore, Rehnquist was aghast. He replied to Lantz that the latest abortion case was coming up for oral argument the following month,

> and the drumbeat of media publicity about this case brings fanatics on both sides of the issue out of the woodwork. The case will, in all probability, not be decided until the very end of June, and even after that there will be the usual adverse reactions from whichever side lost. I have been picketed about this issue when there was no case pending, and when I was simply giving a commencement speech; I think any announcement that I was going to be at a bookstore would probably bring out another crew of pickets.

The reticence endured for the rest of his life. In late 2004, when Justice Ruth Bader Ginsburg asked Rehnquist whether she should accept the Federal Judicial Center's invitation to moderate a discussion among appeals-court judges on the topic, "Terrorism, National Security, and Constitutional Rights," he advised her not to do it. Rehnquist penned a note back to Ginsburg in a barely legible scrawl: "Ruth, I think participating even as a moderator would be a mistake—this kind of case is always a 'hot button' for the media."

THE FRIENDSHIP WITH LANTZ brought a complication of a different sort when, in 1995, the director Milos Forman began working on a film (with Oliver Stone as co-producer) about the life of pornographer Larry Flynt.

Forman was a client of Lantz's, and Lantz began leaning on Rehnquist to do him a favor: permit Forman's crew to film inside the Supreme Court.

The request quickly became a torment for the strait-laced Rehnquist. Forman's planned movie, *The People vs. Larry Flynt,* was going to cover in full the notorious Flynt's dissolute life, making for a sordid-if-entertaining tale indeed. The movie had a first-rate director and marquee stars: Woody Harrelson as Larry Flynt, Courtney Love as Flynt's wife Althea, and Ed Norton as Flynt's idealistic young 1st Amendment lawyer, Alan Isaacman.

An important thread running through the movie described Flynt's non-stop legal battles to protect his free-speech rights. Flynt had actually fought all the way to the Supreme Court, scoring an 8–0 victory (and reversing an appeals-court decision against him) in *Hustler Magazine v. Falwell.** No matter what anyone thought of Flynt, his magazine, or his various other enterprises in the sex trade, the man had clearly established an important 1st Amendment precedent. Rehnquist had played a role, too: he was the author of the unanimous opinion in Flynt's case.

Lantz brought Forman to Washington and invited Rehnquist to have dinner with the two of them. Lantz prodded Rehnquist gently in letters and in person, and had the head of the production company—appropriately, the producers had named their company Code Pink—do likewise. Finally, Forman himself wrote to the chief justice. As Forman saw it, the Supreme Court was "the only real hero of our story. I would love our hero to be represented in its genuine, magnificent setting."

> What gives me the audacity to bother you again is the following logic: Although I disagree with some of the ways my tax moneys are being spent by the Government, I pay them fully and gladly. In all modesty, I must say that through the years they amount to millions of dollars. So, in my naiveté, it seemed to me reasonable that the one institution to which I wholeheartedly contribute my tax money might lend a hand in my endeavors. Columbia Pictures will of course reimburse the Court for any expenditures that might be incurred during the couple of days of filming. The work could be done on a weekend or when the Court is not in session.

---

*485 U.S. 46 (1988)

Rehnquist never relented. Once the movie came out, to generally favorable notices, Forman sent word through Lantz that he would set up a special screening in Washington for Rehnquist and his guests. Rehnquist asked the Court's public information office whether something like that had ever been done—a cultural *stare decisis*—and he received word back that, yes, it had. Someone recalled that Bill Douglas and his wife Cathy had hosted a reception for Henry Fonda and Jane Alexander when the two actors opened in Washington in the play *First Monday in October.* And Thurgood Marshall and some of the other justices and staff had also been the guests at a screening of a made-for-television movie about the *Brown* decision. So even though Rehnquist didn't want anything to do with a screening for *The People vs. Larry Flynt,* he was not going to be able to hide behind past practice as an excuse. He would just go with his gut and forget about citing precedent. After all, it was only the outcome that mattered. And Rehnquist was blunt, to make sure that Lantz got his point.

"I do not want to commit myself in advance to attend the showing of the film, and I do not want to be involved in any performance designed to obtain publicity for the film," Rehnquist instructed Lantz. "I do mean to rule out some sort of staged performance which would in any way suggest that the members of the Court sponsor or support the film."

Lantz evidently got the message. As the film was about to open on 1,200 screens around the country, he wrote back to Rehnquist early in 1997, recalling their dinner nearly two years earlier as the film project was just beginning to jell. "Your wonderfully fair comments to Milos at our dinner were of enormous help and encouragement to him and he is eternally grateful. So am I. And we have not misled or dishonored you or abused your trust." But *The People vs. Larry Flynt* seemed to mark a turning point in Rehnquist's friendship with Lantz. Around that time, Rehnquist decided he didn't need an agent. Rehnquist was an established author and figured he could save the 10 percent fee he was paying to Lantz.

TWENTY-THREE

A Betting Man

REHNQUIST WAS AN INVETERATE BETTOR, but he liked to say that he was *not* a gambler. There was a big difference to him between gambling and betting. A gambler put a meaningful amount of money at risk and got a thrill from seeing if he could beat the odds. The buzz came from walking the tightrope without a net. A bettor, on the other hand, laid down insignificant sums, and savored winning for its own sake.

That was Rehnquist. "He never bet more than $3 with me on anything, and I am not aware of his betting more than $5 with anybody else," wrote his friend Herman Obermayer. "For Bill the joy, of course, was in winning. He hated to lose at anything: tennis or cards or $1 bets."

To be a friend of Rehnquist's was to be constantly egged into seemingly insignificant bets that, in fact, were self-defining for Rehnquist. He bet on what he knew, or thought he knew. Most importantly, though, he bet to win—and he took the payoff seriously. To Rehnquist, winning constituted affirmation and defined his worldview. Matters of principle were of vital importance.

During his first fourteen years on the Court, the order of seniority meant that Rehnquist sat beside Blackmun when oral arguments took place. If Rehnquist became bored, he would hector Blackmun with a jotted note, challenging his seatmate to a test of wits: "Harry, from what operas are these choruses from?" or "What was the last year in which these cars were manufactured?" or "Harry, do you want to make any election bets?" Going all the way back to the time when he was a student at Stanford,

Rehnquist kept track of all his bets and point spreads in a detailed ledger. At the Supreme Court, he organized betting pools on sporting events and elections. After Rehnquist managed to get a Ping-Pong table installed for the clerks in the Court's gym, he made bets with the other justices on the games between clerks.

So extensive were Rehnquist's betting matrixes that the leading scholarly journal for political scientists, *PS,* even reproduced one—from the 1992 presidential election, found among the papers of Harry Blackmun at the Library of Congress—and published an analysis of it. As the authors put it, "Rehnquist, it turns out, was engaged in an activity familiar to most Americans but hitherto not recognized as one of the functions that a chief justice is supposed to perform: running an office pool. Mr. Dooley was literally correct: the Supreme Court does follow the election returns."

Obermayer reported that he and Rehnquist bet on at least twenty elections. Once, when Rehnquist lost a $1 bet to Obermayer and his wife, he paid them both but did his best to take the gloss off of their win: "I may be pardoned for expressing the view that although I lost out to you on the percentages, I got the percentage separating the two candidates exactly right, whereas neither of you did. Unfortunately, we didn't bet on that percentage." He hated to lose.

Famously, Obermayer and Rehnquist had a betting card going during the 2000 presidential election; Rehnquist was wagering that George W. Bush would beat Al Gore by a big electoral-vote margin. But Rehnquist was forced to cancel when it became clear that *Bush v. Gore* was headed for the Supreme Court. As a matter of principle, Rehnquist wrote to Obermayer on Supreme Court stationery asking for permission to withdraw, and stating his reason. The request was granted, of course. But had it not been, Rehnquist would have seriously lost face. He would have had to unilaterally renege, a devastating blow to his future bragging rights. Playing the game strictly by the book was, after all, of the utmost importance to him, and Rehnquist was never one to let someone else off the hook.

That became clear during an otherwise routine oral argument as the justices concluded their workday on December 1, 1982. The case was the kind that Rehnquist had no patience for, another *habeas* petition that the Court would end up rejecting 9–0.* One of the lawyers was explaining how the

**Morris v. Slappy,* 461 U.S. 1 (1983)

precedent that was established in another case, *Cuyler v. Sullivan,** should make his client a winner.

"I think it is a mixed question of fact and law, as set forth in *Cuyler* . . . ," explained the lawyer.

Rehnquist suddenly perked up. "Set forth in what?"

"In *Cuyler v. Sullivan,*" the lawyer repeated.

"Oh, Cuyler, yes," Rehnquist said knowingly. "He played center field for the Chicago Cubs in 1933." Rehnquist figured he would get a quick laugh that would lighten the Court's somber mien for a few moments. He knew full well, of course, that the Cuyler in the case under discussion wasn't one and the same as the baseball player.

Then, from the other side of the courtroom, the voice of Justice John Paul Stevens boomed out: "Right field."

Rehnquist was flummoxed. "Right field?" A pause. "Okay."

The whole courtroom erupted in laughter—at Rehnquist's expense.

Rehnquist was furious. He vividly recalled the illustrious Hall of Famer named Kiki Cuyler. Rehnquist and Stevens were both kids from the heartland who followed the Cubs in the 1930s, but Rehnquist was sure he was right and Stevens was wrong. Sure, Stevens was a Chicagoan (and a diehard Cubs fan) and Rehnquist was from Milwaukee, but Rehnquist knew he had Stevens on this one and he was not about to let him off. Rehnquist immediately turned to Blackmun—the Court's authority on all things baseball and who, luckily for Rehnquist, was seated next to him. Blackmun hastily scratched out a note in reply:

> Kiki Cuyler:
> 1. Stole most bases in National League (I think)
> 2. Batted 5th on best team Cubs ever had
> 3. Had a great throwing arm
> 4. Had a "meaningful relation" with P. K. Wrigley**

All of which were, of course, interesting trivia but entirely irrelevant to Rehnquist's predicament. Blackmun couldn't answer definitively the question about center or right field.

---

*446 U.S. 335 (1980)

**Chewing-gum executive Philip Knight Wrigley, also known as P.K., succeeded his father William as owner of the Cubs in 1932.

From his seat below the bench, Rehnquist's clerk Ron Blunt saw his boss furiously scribbling on a memo pad. Soon, a messenger brought Rehnquist's instructions down to where Blunt was sitting. Rehnquist wanted him to verify where Cuyler played. Time was short; Rehnquist wanted to correct Stevens from the bench. Blunt had five minutes.

Blunt ran out of the courtroom and burst into the office where his fellow clerks were working. When he explained what was going on, the other two clerks broke into laughter. "We were in hysterics," said David Jaffe, another of Rehnquist's clerks that term. "The poor lawyer must have been dumbfounded" by the interplay between the two justices. Blunt figured the fastest way, pre-Internet, to get his answer was to call the Library of Congress and ask someone to go through the *Chicago Tribune*.

"He wanted to correct Stevens," Jaffe recalled. "The idea was that we'd send a messenger back up before that argument ended. It took two days!" And when the word finally came back, it turned out that Stevens had been correct all along. Cuyler played right field. That was how the *Tribune* listed it, in box scores prepared by the Associated Press.

Still Rehnquist insisted that Blunt should keep checking. The Cubs, Rehnquist was certain, had been plagued by injuries that year, and Cuyler might have moved around the outfield. He didn't want to admit Stevens had gotten the best of him. Rehnquist wanted to bring fresh evidence to the justices' private conference.

Blunt did as he was told, but it was just no use; the clerk's efforts were unavailing. It was ever thus between Rehnquist and Stevens, two prideful men. When Stevens wrote his memoir, *Five Chiefs,* in 2011, he praised Rehnquist's evenhandedness in running the Court's internal deliberations. But after that the cheering stopped. Repeatedly, Stevens cited Rehnquist's opinions not for their erudition but rather for their narrow mindedness and intolerance, or for being just plain disingenuous, *Bush v. Gore* among them. Stevens professed a hope that someday all those Rehnquist opinions he loathed would be overturned.

Of course, that would have been no surprise to Rehnquist—and no doubt he would have responded in kind. Many years after the Cuyler incident, Stevens sent over to Rehnquist two copies of a lavishly illustrated coffee-table book about the Supreme Court. Christmas was coming; the books were to be gifts. "Dear Chief," Stevens wrote in an accompanying note, "May I impose on you to sign these two volumes so that they can be used as holiday gifts? Many thanks and Merry Christmas." Rehnquist often was asked to sign a book or an opinion by one of his fellow justices, and even by ordinary members of the public. He always obliged.

But not this time. When he saw Stevens's request, Rehnquist scribbled back a nasty note to his secretary: "I don't sign books." The secretary dutifully carried everything back to Stevens's chambers and dropped it off, but she was so embarrassed at the pettiness that she offered no further explanation.

Stevens did not let it go. He had the books sent right back to Rehnquist. "There must have been a failure of communication," Stevens wrote. "I am sending it again."

TWENTY-FOUR

"Bizarre Ideas and Outrageous Thoughts"

BY THE EARLY 1980S there was no doubt in Rehnquist's mind that he would retire when he could. Rehnquist had calculated his earliest possible retirement date—October 1, 1989—and it did not seem that far away. He could take on senior status and continue to have an office at the Court and a full paycheck. He could pick and choose his cases, and he wouldn't have to work hard. Potter Stewart had done exactly that, and it had worked out well for him.

Chafing under the Court's isolation, Rehnquist thought this sounded good. But there was at least one other reason for him to consider slacking off. Despite his reputation as an avid tennis player, the truth was that Rehnquist was in ill health. He had endured debilitating spinal surgeries in 1971 and 1982 (and would need a third operation in 1995). He had missed time from the bench due to numerous other hospitalizations, emergency and otherwise, for assorted maladies ranging from viral pneumonia to a problem with his big toe to his chronically bad back. His back was so weak that he dared not bend over and pick up anything but the lightest of objects.

Degenerative disc disease controlled him as only excruciating pain can. He couldn't sit or stand for long periods, and he couldn't exercise. Surgery hadn't helped. In almost constant pain and suffering from insomnia, Rehnquist was desperate for relief.

As a member of the Court, he qualified for treatment at the office of the Capitol physician. The doctor tried various cocktails of prescription drugs that included Butazolidin Alka, Darvon, Placidyl, Codeine, Valium, Dalmane, and Chloral Hydrate, among others. Rehnquist began living with a secret that he feared might get out: he was desperately, abusively addicted to prescription painkillers. Clandestine hospitalizations began as pain-management efforts and morphed into full-blown detoxification.

The most dangerous of the drugs Rehnquist was abusing was the hypnotic drug Placidyl. With unlimited pharmacy refills provided by his physician, Rehnquist had been taking three times the maximum dosage for many years. It was how Rehnquist got to sleep. Advertisements from the period show Placidyl's intended effects as a "gentle as a lullaby" way to knock out a patient for the night. The standard Placidyl dosage was 500 milligrams a night, at bedtime. Rehnquist started out at 200 milligrams in 1972, but by 1981 he was taking over seven times that amount—1,500 milligrams daily, three times the normal dosage. When he got a three-month prescription, it lasted only a month. Then he would get another.

Rehnquist was addicted, and he exhibited an addict's behavior. On the bench he slurred his speech, became tongue-tied when pronouncing long words, and sometimes had trouble finishing his thoughts.

Finally, Rehnquist checked himself into George Washington University Hospital in Washington. He knew the neurology staff at GW and felt comfortable coming in. The official diagnosis in the hospital records was that Rehnquist was being treated for "tension and anxiety," not back pain. But things quickly went from bad to worse once Rehnquist was hospitalized and could not get the massive doses of Placidyl that he still craved. Without the painkiller Rehnquist became delirious. In the words of his attending doctor, Rehnquist expressed "bizarre ideas and outrageous thoughts. He imagined, for instance, that there was a CIA plot against him." The curtains changed their colors and patterns when he looked at them. He heard scheming voices outside his room. He bolted from his hospital bed, running to the hospital lobby in his pajamas to escape.

Rehnquist was having such severe withdrawal symptoms that the doctors had to put him back on the drug. Only after that could they start slowly lowering his dosage. Rehnquist was dependent on Placidyl for a further six weeks; he finally was able to quit it altogether on February 7, 1982.

When Rehnquist returned to the bench on January 11, still on the lowered dosage, he seemed to be fine. It was business as usual on Rehnquist's first day back, and the contrast between his own situation and those he sat in judgment of couldn't have been starker: the Court upheld the constitutionality of a forty-year prison sentence imposed on a Virginia man for possession and distribution of nine ounces of marijuana worth about $200. The justices said that wasn't cruel and unusual punishment. The majority based its ruling on one of Rehnquist's opinions upholding the constitutionality of a life sentence for a Texan who committed three minor felonies involving $230.*

Rehnquist's addiction was severe—but the full extent of the madness wouldn't be known until after Rehnquist's death, when the FBI released the huge stash of data that its agents had amassed while investigating him for the chief justice's job. In typically stark bureau-speak, one FBI agent summarized his lengthy interview with one of Rehnquist's attending physicians at GW Hospital:

> Justice REHNQUIST had begun to express bizarre ideas and outrageous thoughts. He imagined, for instance, that there was a CENTRAL INTELLIGENCE AGENCY (CIA) plot against him and he also suffered from illusions, such as seeming to see the designed patterns on the hospital curtains change configuration. He had also gone to the hospital lobby in his pajamas in order to try to escape. In addition, he thought that he heard voices outside of his room discussing various plots against him. [The doctor] stated that [Rehnquist] probably heard voices in the hallway, but that his mental state was such that he jumped to unnecessary conclusions regarding the substance of the conversation. She stated that such actions were symptoms of metabolic encephalopathy, which she said could be generally defined as delirium.
>
> [The doctor] examined [Rehnquist] in the hospital. . . . She stated that the absolute worst diagnosis of someone exhibiting such behavior would be to conclude that that person was a drug addict, who simply "went crazy" when use of a particular drug was discontinued. She stated, however, that this was not the case and that she determined, during the

---

**Rummel v. Estelle,* 445 U.S. 263 (1980)

> course of treating [Rehnquist], that he was given a prescription drug, known as Placidyl, by a physician on Capitol Hill. . . . She stated that Placidyl is a highly toxic drug and she could not understand why anyone would prescribe it. She stated that she could think of no circumstances at all under which she would prescribe this drug for anyone. She stated that taking Placidyl in such large doses was dangerous and she felt that any physician who prescribed it was practicing very bad medicine, bordering on malpractice. She further stated that there appeared to be no restrictions on refills of this drug and she felt that this was very irresponsible also.

The GW physician wasn't the only one who excused Rehnquist's addiction on the ground that the drugs had been prescribed rather than bought on the street. All the other justices, as well as the regular members of the Supreme Court press corps, apparently did likewise—even though Rehnquist's problem was noticed by reporters who regularly covered the Supreme Court, and surely also must have been obvious to his fellow justices. No one said anything at the time. Then, as now, there were no cameras in the Supreme Court's ceremonial courtroom, no way for the average member of the public at that time to easily see the obvious effects of Rehnquist's addiction. Many years later, recordings from the Supreme Court's oral arguments finally entered the public domain. At my request, audio engineers from the Oyez Project at the Chicago-Kent College of Law analyzed all of Rehnquist's comments and questions from the bench during that era and concluded that the slurring began as early as October 1981. He was, in other words, incapacitated for at least three months. Who knew? The other justices didn't call him on it, and the press didn't report it until word leaked from George Washington University Hospital that Rehnquist was running around in his pajamas.

The usual checks and balances simply were not in place—nor are they now. Twenty years after Rehnquist's addiction, David Garrow made a strong case in the *University of Chicago Law Review* for a constitutional amendment imposing mandatory retirement for Supreme Court justices at age seventy-five. Garrow pointed out that he was simply restating a call for reform that had been seriously considered by Congress twice in the last century, the last time in 1954. Since then, Garrow contended, there have been at least four and perhaps as many as six justices* whose mental decrepitude should have disqualified them from hearing cases. To put it in Garrow's more gracious prose, these justices—and he included Douglas, Powell, and Marshall from the Rehnquist era—"overstayed the length of service their mental energies were capable of rendering."

Given the longevity and lifetime tenure of Supreme Court justices, having six impaired in a half-century is worrisome enough—and Garrow had not included Rehnquist in his list of justices who played with less than a full deck. He didn't put Rehnquist on the list because, in spite of the justice's obvious addiction, there was no evidence that he failed to keep up with his workload.

That doesn't mean Rehnquist's incapacity wasn't a matter for public inquiry, or concern. As Garrow saw it, even if Rehnquist and his fellow justices didn't feel compelled to reveal his addiction, Rehnquist's continuing public incoherence on the bench was so obvious that the knowledgeable journalists of the Supreme Court press corps should have exposed it. Not doing so until Rehnquist's hospitalization forced the matter into the public eye made the reporters "professionally remiss in the extreme."

The solution was clear to Garrow: Rehnquist's case, as well as the late-career infirmity of Thurgood Marshall, were just the two most recent "painful but undeniably important stories" that the Supreme Court press corps failed to reveal. And without the press as a barking watchdog, a constitutional age-limit for justices was needed. "History teaches us that a constitutional amendment mandating compulsory retirement at age 75 will strengthen the Supreme Court of the 21st Century and save it from predictable pain and embarrassment. However, the far more likely course is that five decades hence, some future scholar will [add] another half-dozen mentally decrepit justices to the sad and poignant roster our history already offers of jurists who harmed their Court and hurt their own reputations by remaining on the bench too long."

---

*Garrow is a law professor at the University of Pittsburgh. The post-1954 justices whose mental competency he questioned are Charles E. Whittaker, Hugo Black, William O. Douglas, Thurgood Marshall, and perhaps Sherman Minton and Lewis F. Powell, Jr.

TWENTY-FIVE

Bicentennial Bombshell

ON MAY 27, 1986, Chief Justice Burger arrived at the White House in the Court's black limousine. He had asked for a meeting with President Ronald Reagan near the end of the Court's term ostensibly to discuss the coming 1987 celebration of the 200th anniversary of the Constitution. It was a favored project of the chief justice, who was serving as the chairman of a special federal commission that was in charge of the bicentennial festivities.

The palace guard around Reagan had doubts about scheduling the meeting. The chief justice was constantly complaining that the celebration was short of funds and staff, and Reagan's White House team wanted to spare the president from having to listen to another plea for help. But in the end they extended the courtesy of a talk with the president, and Burger showed up on that Tuesday.

After about twenty minutes of chitchat about the bicentennial, Burger dropped a bombshell. He intended to resign. Balancing the duties of being chief justice and also running the bicentennial had just become too much for the seventy-nine-year-old. He wished to leave the Court so he could devote his full attention to the celebration.

Reagan was puzzled that the chief justice would choose the bicentennial over the Court, but he didn't try to change Burger's mind. The timing was opportune, coming far enough in advance of the 1986 elections to not cause undue political problems for the White House.

Reagan was already almost midway through his second term but had made only one Court appointment—Rehnquist's friend and Stanford classmate Sandra Day O'Connor. This was despite the fact that five of the Court's members were at least seventy-seven years old. Reagan was overdue to get another slot on the Court, and he was eager to make a statement with it. Burger's departure was, in other words, a welcome opportunity for Reagan to tilt the Court further to the right.

The president's new attorney general, Edwin Meese, had been pushing for that. Meese was a trusted conservative from Reagan's days as California governor and a skilled political brawler. After replacing the genteel Los Angeles corporate lawyer William French Smith at the head of the Department of Justice, Meese had begun preaching from his pulpit: the Supreme Court under Burger, with its four Nixon appointees, hadn't fulfilled its promise of rewriting the Warren Court's liberal agenda. Meese argued for a new approach in which the Supreme Court looked to the original intent of the men who wrote the Constitution and Bill of Rights. What the founders intended when they wrote the document in 1787 was what Meese insisted it meant now; he wanted no expansion of rights that hadn't been made explicit to begin with. The days of the liberal icons, Marshall and Brennan, clearly were waning. Even so, Brennan, frail at seventy-nine years of age, spoke out against Meese, calling his originalist approach "little more than arrogance cloaked as humility."

There was only one justice on the Court who was completely comfortable with Meese's originalist argument, and it was William Rehnquist.

The Reagan White House prided itself on running a tight, disciplined operation, and the selection of Burger's replacement was going to be completely in synch with that. There would be no surprises. Reagan was clear about wanting the next chief justice to have a well-established judicial track record. Thus, all candidates in the running to succeed Burger had to be either sitting Supreme Court justices or federal judges whose conservative credentials were unquestioned. Meese himself was out of the running.

The White House chief of staff, Donald T. Regan, a former Wall Street CEO, wanted to keep Burger's resignation a complete secret from all but Reagan's inner circle. Regan feared that premature disclosure would set off a lobbying war among judges and politicians vying for Burger's seat.

Two days later, Reagan pulled Regan, his counsel Peter Wallison, and Meese into the Oval Office to discuss what to do. Meese had been waiting for this opportunity. Arriving at Justice the year before, Meese had asked his friend (and assistant attorney general) William Bradford Reynolds to quietly begin compiling dossiers on prospective Supreme Court picks. Reynolds combed through the speeches and writings of potential nominees, looking for anything that was at odds with Reagan's agenda or could cause trouble with Senate confirmation. Meese now had the dossiers, which would be added to by Wallison and his lawyers at the White House. (There was the usual institutional rivalry among the senior aides; Wallison, aligned more closely to Regan than to Meese, didn't think much of the research done by Meese's team.) The three—Regan, Wallison, and Meese—decided they would cull down the resultant list themselves, to avoid press leaks.

The trio decided to first look to the current justices. By appointing a sitting justice as chief, Reagan would effectively get two appointees. Of the eight remaining justices, the group was taken by the idea of O'Connor becoming chief. Among the Court's cognoscenti, in fact, she had been a rumored replacement for Burger almost from the day she took her oath in September 1981. But even though the members of Reagan's inner circle saw political upside to appointing the first female chief justice, they also fretted about O'Connor's Arizona rancher's independent streak. She didn't always vote with the conservatives. So, she was too risky as a choice.

Almost by default, then, the group gravitated to Rehnquist as their private favorite to become chief justice. Unlike O'Connor, Rehnquist was completely, totally predictable; he was the most reliable and transparent of the Court's conservatives. Found in Wallison's files was a two-page talking-points memo, most likely prepared for Reagan, that summed up what the White House aides admired about Rehnquist: before and during his time on the Court, he was a "paradigmatic example" of judicial restraint, pushing the Court "to reverse the excesses of the Warren Court." The memo praised his "sheer cleverness" and listed case after case where Rehnquist had turned back the judicial clock to pre-Warren times, or dissented in trying to do so. "Moreover," the document went on, "virtually every beneficial decision listed above grew out of a small seed of legal principle that Rehnquist had planted in a prior, seemingly innocuous case, thus further demonstrating his mastery at looking beyond the facts of an individual case to gradually achieve fundamental reform in constitutional law. . . . Furthermore, Rehnquist possesses all the leadership qualities required to make a superb chief justice. No one can question the depth of his scholarship or intellect, the clarity of his philosophical vision or his ability to build a consensus to implant that vision in the Court's decisions."

So Rehnquist was the one. But Antonin Scalia and Robert Bork, both highly conservative federal appeals court judges, were also on the list as backups. After two weeks of staff work by the White House and the Justice Department, Reagan told his small selection team that he wanted to meet with Rehnquist and Scalia—and that Rehnquist should be brought in first. Wallison had the impression that the chief justice's job was Rehnquist's if he wanted it—but that if Rehnquist turned it down, Reagan would have no problem with Scalia.

The White House team got word to Rehnquist that Reagan wanted to meet with him for an interview on Thursday, June 12. The chief justice's job was in play. This was top secret; Rehnquist would have to make sure he wasn't spotted by anyone in the White House press corps. Wallison later boasted that both Rehnquist and Scalia had gotten through the White House gates without waking the "sleeping watchdogs" in the press room.

Rehnquist, although he had been contemplating a possible retirement, didn't intend to turn down the chief justice's job if Reagan proffered it. The two men were like-minded on the issues and certainly got along well in their Oval Office meeting, but Reagan had an important question for Rehnquist. Was he healthy enough to take on the job? Reagan was aware of Rehnquist's hospitalization a few years earlier for prescription drug addiction. Rehnquist decided to tackle the issue head-on, telling Reagan that he had long since kicked his addiction and could offer a clean bill of health from his doctors. That was good enough for Reagan. To the surprise of his White House aides, the president offered Rehnquist the chief's job on the spot, telling Rehnquist he was "the unanimous choice of all of us."

"It would be an honor," Rehnquist replied.

Reagan then mentioned that he was thinking of either Bork or Scalia to succeed him. What did Rehnquist think of them? The justice replied that he held both men in high regard; he didn't try to make a case for either of them.

Reagan told his aides to schedule Scalia for an interview the following Monday, June 16. Meese called Scalia with the news on Friday the 13th, and Scalia was jittery all weekend. He badly wanted the job. Reagan's choice of Scalia made sense. At age fifty, Scalia was nine years younger than Bork, and in better health. If this were going to be Reagan's last appointment—a distinct possibility at that time—then it had to be one for the ages. "There was enthusiasm for Bork from our standpoint," Meese later recalled in an interview with Joan Biskupic. "But the president had no idea whether he would get another appointment. He had to think about age and health." (Reagan would, in fact, get one more appointment, Anthony Kennedy in 1988.)

When Scalia had his Oval Office meeting with the president, the two men hit it off just as Reagan and Rehnquist had the week before. After trading a few anecdotes with the garrulous Scalia about old judges they had known, Reagan popped the question and Scalia accepted. "The tidiness of the selection process pleased the president's advisers," *Time* reported afterward. "Reagan was spared from ever having to say no."

Reagan made the announcement at the White House the next day at 2 P.M., with Burger, Rehnquist, and Scalia at his side. The other justices had learned about Burger's resignation, and all the rest of the drama to come, just ten minutes before that. Burger had messengers deliver a copy of his resignation letter to each of the other justices, who were then invited into a conference room to watch the event unfold on television. Wallison was ecstatic—not just that the selections had played out so naturally but that the press had been completely kept in the dark by a White House team that was, at least this time, totally leakproof.

TWENTY-SIX

A Score to Settle

Although Rehnquist was already an associate justice for life, having been confirmed by the Senate in 1971, he now would have to go through a new round of confirmation hearings in order to be confirmed as the chief. And the liberals were lying in wait, with a score to settle from 1971.

It quickly became apparent that Rehnquist was going to bear the brunt of the liberals' attack—a fact borne out by the Senate Judiciary Committee's votes on the two nominees on August 14. Approval of both men was never in doubt, but the committee's vote on Rehnquist was 13–5; for Scalia, 18–0. All the votes against Rehnquist came from Democrats who had questioned him rigorously when he appeared before the committee on July 30 and 31. The nays came from Joe Biden of Delaware, Edward Kennedy of Massachusetts, Patrick Leahy of Vermont, Howard Metzenbaum of Ohio, and Paul Simon of Illinois.

Kennedy had to wait his turn to speak, and when his turn came he spoke passionately. He began by saying that he adhered to his own version of "original intent," which was that the Senate had an obligation to scrutinize all judicial nominees carefully, but none more so than the chief justice.

"Mainstream or too extreme?" Kennedy asked, posing a rhetorical question about Rehnquist's views and their bearing on his fitness to serve.

That is the question. By his own record of massive isolated dissent, Justice Rehnquist answers that question. He is too extreme on race, too extreme on women's rights, too extreme on freedom of speech, too extreme on separation of church and state, too extreme to be Chief Justice. His appalling record on race is sufficient by itself to deny his confirmation. When he came to the Supreme Court, he had already authored a controversial memorandum in 1952 supporting school segregation; he had opposed public accommodation legislation in 1964; he had opposed remedies to end school segregation in 1967; he had led the so-called ballot security program in the sixties that was a euphemism for intimidation of black and Hispanic voters. On many of these issues, it now appears that Mr. Rehnquist was less than candid with the committee at his confirmation hearing in 1971.

America can be thankful that in the difficult and turbulent years since World War II, we have had a Supreme Court that has been right on race, right on equal rights for women, right on apportionment and the separation of power, right on free speech, and right on separation of church and state. Imagine what America would be like if Mr. Rehnquist had been the Chief Justice and his cramped and narrow view of the Constitution had prevailed in the critical years since World War II. The schools of America would still be segregated. Millions of citizens would be denied the right to vote under scandalous malapportionment laws. Women would be condemned to second class status as second class Americans. Courthouses would be closed to individual challenges against police brutality and executive abuse—closed even to the press. Government would embrace religion, and the walls of separation between church and state would be in ruins. State and local majorities would tell us what we can read, how to lead our private lives, whether to bear children, how to bring them up, what kind of people we may become.

In these ways and in so many others, a Court remade in the image of Justice Rehnquist would make the Constitution, whose bicentennial we celebrate next year, a lesser document in a lesser land.

Kennedy left no doubt how he would vote, and his comments presaged the grilling that Rehnquist would get from Biden and Metzenbaum as well, starting the next day. What particularly rankled Kennedy was the way he felt Rehnquist had dodged earlier questions about his *Plessy* memo during his original Supreme Court confirmation hearings, fifteen years before. Kennedy had been a member of the Judiciary Committee then, and he had never gotten over his belief that Rehnquist's record—including his explanation about the memo—was disqualifying on its face. When Rehnquist came before him again for confirmation as chief, Kennedy resurrected what he considered to be the two most damaging pieces of evidence from Rehnquist's 1971 hearings—that Rehnquist had harassed black and Hispanic voters in Phoenix during the 1960s, and that he had expressed racist views in memos to Justice Jackson.

In essence, these complaints against Rehnquist were the same that had been leveled at him in 1971—except for the facts added by my 1985 reporting for the *New York Times Magazine* that revealed two more racist memos authored by Rehnquist while he was Jackson's clerk. Those newly discovered memos added to the weight of the evidence, of course, but they didn't alter the overall picture of Rehnquist one way or the other. Kennedy knew the odds were overwhelmingly with Rehnquist. After all, Republicans controlled the Senate, and even if Rehnquist weren't confirmed as chief he would still be an associate justice for life.

Kennedy nonetheless was determined to do what he could. He kept a tenacious investigator, Walter Sheridan, on his Senate payroll whose ties to Ted and his late brothers Robert and John ran deep. Kennedy trusted Sheridan completely. As soon as Reagan nominated Rehnquist, Ted Kennedy put the family's personal private investigator on the case and told him to start digging.

Sheridan was a fascinating character in his own right. During the 1950s, he dug up all kinds of dirt for the Senate rackets subcommittee, of which Robert Kennedy was chief counsel and on which John Kennedy served as a senator. The subcommittee's principal target was Teamsters Union President Jimmy Hoffa. Young Robert Kennedy's relentless investigation of Hoffa and the Teamsters was a riveting national drama, broadcast live from the Senate Caucus Room in the early days of television. Sheridan was the committee's chief investigator, earning notoriety of his own.

Sheridan went where the Kennedys did. When John Kennedy became president and appointed his brother Robert to become attorney general, Sheridan moved with the younger Kennedy brother to Justice and continued his dogged pursuit of Hoffa. It was an epic struggle that finally resulted in Hoffa's conviction in 1964 for jury tampering. Sheridan got the credit for that. And when Robert Kennedy resigned as attorney general to run for the Senate from New York, he took Sheridan with him as his right hand in the campaign. Sheridan was never far from the Kennedys; when New Orleans district attorney Jim Garrison launched his whacked-out investigation of John Kennedy's assassination, Sheridan got himself arrested on witness-tampering charges. When Ted Kennedy published his memoir, I was curious what he would say about the man who'd done so many jobs for the brothers. Sheridan's name was not mentioned. It was just as he would have advised.

Rehnquist's opponents dredged up the litany of accusations that were by now well known: his outrageous early views on civil rights, allegations that he harassed Phoenix voters in the 1960s, the fact that two of his homes included restrictive covenants barring sales to nonwhites and people of "the Hebrew race."

When Rehnquist took his turn at the witness table after Kennedy and the others were done with their political posturing, he gave an unflappable performance in two days of testimony that was televised live. As senators shouted at each other, he sat impassively, arms folded. Privately, Rehnquist confided that the hearings took a personal toll. He was a proud man who couldn't abide the bruising accusations leveled against him. But he also wanted the job and obviously knew what he had to do to secure it. In essence, Rehnquist deflected every question and, by totally stonewalling, didn't allow his opponents any openings to land damaging blows. He said he couldn't recall participating in the Army's surveillance of lawful civilians; he had "no recollection" of a memo he wrote proposing the program. He said he wasn't aware of the property covenants on his summer home in Vermont and a former property in Phoenix.* He skated past an allegation that he had defrauded his ill brother-in-law by setting up a trust account for his care and then keeping it secret from him.

Rehnquist flatly denied that he had challenged Phoenix voters—even though the Democrats had ten witnesses to the contrary, including an ex-

---

*The deed for the home Rehnquist owned in Phoenix from 1961 to 1969 had a restriction, standard for that subdivision, barring possession by "anyone not of the white or Caucasian race." Rehnquist's summer home in Greensboro, Vermont, prohibited lease or sale to "a member of the Hebrew race." Although opposition senators acknowledged that both restrictions were legal vestiges, and unenforceable, they seized on the covenants as evidence of Rehnquist's flawed credibility and insensitivity to civil rights.

FBI agent who testified he'd been called to the scene of an election-day fracas and identified Rehnquist as the instigator. Rehnquist just said they all had the wrong man. It wasn't him. "I think they're mistaken. I just can't offer any other explanation."

And he stuck to his story that the views in the racist *Plessy* memo really belonged to his boss at the time, Justice Jackson. Was there anyone left who really believed that? Jackson's secretary, Elsie Douglas, repeated her 1971 assertion that Rehnquist was lying, smearing a great man. Rehnquist completely disowned the memo. "Senator, I don't think I reached a conclusion. Law clerks don't have to vote," he told Joe Biden. The frustrated senator shot back: "No, but they surely think."

The NAACP revved up its lobbying engine and tried to rally the opposition. Benjamin Hooks, the black civil rights activist, testified after Rehnquist. He cited Rehnquist's failure to disavow his *Plessy* memo. Hooks recalled watching segregationist "senators and Congress people, and mayors, with tears in their eyes, admit they made mistakes and that we were right, and they were wrong. But what I fail to see in any of Mr. Rehnquist's decisions is any acknowledgment that he was wrong then."*

With Strom Thurmond chairing the committee and the Republicans in charge of the ground rules, Rehnquist had arranged that he would not be questioned about his prescription drug addiction. When one of the senators tried to bring up even the *general* question of judicial health and disability, Rehnquist simply replied that "so long as I can perform my duties, I do not think I have any obligation to give the press a health briefing." Under the committee's ground rules, the questioning went no further.

After Rehnquist's two days in the witness chair, the Democrats tangled with the Reagan White House over gaining access to records from Rehnquist's

---

*The NAACP remained one of Rehnquist's most persistent critics throughout his long tenure on the Court. In 1998, after *USA Today* revealed that Rehnquist had never hired a black law clerk in twenty-seven years, the group led a protest of more than a thousand people outside the Court on the opening day of its new term. Kweisi Mfume, the NAACP's president, was among nineteen people arrested while trying to deliver résumés of minority law school students. The controversy about minority hiring continued during sharp questioning of justices Clarence Thomas and David Souter when they showed up as the Court's representatives at a congressional budget hearing the following year. But Rehnquist was unapologetic. In all the years that followed, he continued to rely on the clubby feeder system from top-tier judges and law schools that perpetuated an overwhelmingly white clerk pool.

days in the Nixon administration. They were fishing for evidence that might suggest Rehnquist was involved in Watergate. They wanted legal opinions, memoranda, or notes prepared by or for Rehnquist on a variety of subjects: surveillance by the military of radical political groups, investigations of leaks and treatment of classified documents, arrests of antiwar protesters, the 1970 shootings at Kent State University, judicial nominations, wiretapping, and Daniel Ellsberg and the Pentagon Papers. After going back and forth with Reagan counsel Wallison about whether to claim executive privilege, the Justice Department finally gave the committee access to twenty-five documents when it looked like they were about to be subpoenaed anyway. But there were no smoking guns—just the usual stuff from Rehnquist's days as the resident theorist for Nixon's law-and-order policies, and of course his unwitting duplicity in Nixon's efforts to embarrass the Kennedys about the Bay of Pigs and Vietnam.

Even though it seemed clear that Rehnquist would be confirmed, the Reagan White House took no chances. Reagan's aides wanted no surprises. FBI agents fanned out across Phoenix. The agents also interviewed Rehnquist's doctors and delved deeply into his hospitalization records. Days before the hearings, Reagan's counsel Wallison pored over summaries of the FBI's investigation and prepared his own notes advising how Rehnquist should deal with the various issues that were coming up. Wallison's handwritten notes in the White House files indicate that he counseled a more forthright approach than Rehnquist eventually took—particularly regarding the *Plessy* memo. Wallison thought that issue was bound to be the most explosive, and he advised what his notes called a "correction of record on 'Jackson's views' position"—advice that Rehnquist did not follow.

Wallison, in fact, thought Rehnquist should open with a prepared statement that hit all the tough issues square-on, including not just the racist *Plessy* memo but his failure to recuse himself in *Laird v. Tatum,* the "lone dissenter issue . . . challenges at polls in Arizona, civil rights issues, health, First Amendment questions, [and the] abortion issue." But Rehnquist did nothing of the sort, forcing the senators to raise those issues themselves. It turned out to be a good strategy. A bevy of influential politicos stood in the wings providing help, including one of the Democrats' own, Lloyd Cutler. Wallison turned to Cutler, his predecessor in Jimmy Carter's White House (and later the counsel for President Bill Clinton), for advice in the midst of the executive-privilege brouhaha. Tom Korologos, a legendary Washington fixer whose roots went back to the Nixon years, did spin-doctoring for the nominee, ran interference on the Hill, and counted votes. He was not worried about the eventual outcome and boasted of the help he gave Rehnquist.

It took five days of debate for all the senators to be heard, and in the end the most important vote was, as in 1971, the vote on whether to cut off debate. The Democrats might have wanted to talk the nomination to death, but there were 68 votes to dash any hopes of a filibuster—8 more than needed, including those of 16 Democrats. When the final vote came on September 17, Rehnquist won confirmation by 65–33. The 33 votes against Rehnquist were the largest number ever cast, up to that time, by the Senate against a Supreme Court nominee who won confirmation.*

The Senate was so wrung out by the drama of Rehnquist's confirmation that when it next took up the nomination of Scalia, there was only a smattering of floor speeches. The vote came quickly and it was unanimous, 98–0. In the ultimate of ironies, Biden, one of the few who spoke, commended Scalia—the Court's first Italian-American—for his open-mindedness. "There is a significant distinction between this nominee and the last one," Biden said. "One is that this nominee has demonstrated through his career that he has an intellectual flexibility. He is not a rigid man." It was a remark that Biden would grow to regret as the full extent of Scalia's unbridled conservatism became clear.

Biden called his vote for Scalia "the vote I most regret casting, out of all the ones I ever cast." As Biskupic described the Senate's unanimous vote on Scalia, "there was faint will to truly probe the nominee. . . . His Italian-American heritage created a strong motive to support him. The Democratic opponents of Rehnquist had just failed. As a result, although Scalia's record was, for all intents and purposes, in plain sight, he barely had to defend or explain it. Scalia took his seat with hardly a glance at the substance of his views."

Rehnquist saw the Senate's vote on his own nomination as the public rebuke that it was intended to be, and he took it hard. He felt that the Judiciary Committee, in particular, had treated him badly. Rehnquist wrote to his eighty-nine-year-old mother that he was "breathing a sigh of relief after the three months of turmoil in connection with my confirmation."

*In 1991, Clarence Thomas was confirmed by an even thinner margin, 52–48.

He confessed to having ambivalence each fall as the Court's new term approached—"I am somewhat downcast because we have just finished our vacation, and must look forward to going back to work as another term of the Court begins." But this time, he added, "I am so pleased to have all of the hassle in connection with the confirmation over that the prospect of mere Court work actually seems quite inviting by comparison."

Rehnquist and Scalia had a double swearing in nine days after the Senate vote. One of Wallison's White House aides wrote his boss a memo urging that all of the other justices should attend; it would "enhance the image of Chief Justice Rehnquist as a leader and the perception of his ability to bring the Court together." Favored senators would be invited, but those who engaged in "reprehensible" attacks on Rehnquist were snubbed. Meanwhile, Reagan's chief lobbyist on Capitol Hill put together talking points for the president to use in phone calls thanking key senators for their help. Both confirmations were a huge win for Reagan, and the unanimous vote on Scalia was almost too good to be true. The weekend of festivities that followed put Rehnquist in a decidedly better mood. "It was almost like a wedding," he gushed.

TWENTY-SEVEN

High Expectations

WITH THE CONFIRMATION BEHIND HIM, Rehnquist seemed to perk up as he reveled in the attention he received as the new chief justice. A few weeks after the new term began in October, he and his wife Nan were invited by the Reagans to a state dinner at the White House honoring German Chancellor and Mrs. Helmut Kohl, and the next evening the Kohls reciprocated with an invitation to dinner at Decatur House. "Both were black tie—fun to do once in a while."

But the satisfaction Rehnquist took from the new attention was tempered by a new reality. Nan, fifty-seven years old, had been diagnosed with ovarian cancer. Typically, the private Rehnquist had not made an issue of it during the confirmation hearings. But within the year that followed, Nan was undergoing the first of many difficult bouts with chemotherapy. She was a patient at the National Institutes of Health, just outside Washington, and was receiving the best possible care. But even Rehnquist, normally a stoic, described her travail as "a tough time." In a November 1988 letter to his sister, Jean, he described Nan's ordeal in detail and made no effort to soften the news that his wife was in dire straits.

Nan's struggle with cancer was an emotional blow for Rehnquist. She had been his soul mate, a rock-steady influence for most of his adult life while remaining almost completely invisible to the outside world as Rehnquist carried out his public duties alone. Throughout their lives, he and Nan had read favorite books aloud to each other in the evening before bedtime; now Rehnquist put on headphones and listened to his Walkman before falling asleep, so as not to disturb Nan. Rehnquist found some solace in writing long, descriptive letters to his family, and occasionally to the other justices, that updated them on her latest operations, or hospitalizations, or treatments. Her illness dragged on for years.

There was a certain poignancy about what were, for Rehnquist, deeply affecting letters describing his wife's courageous battle against cancer. Rehnquist was otherwise not much for showing emotion of any sort. In fact, despite the professed importance of family to Rehnquist, his missives to his children and close relations were formalistic, civil if reserved, and could take on a decidedly hectoring quality.

If one of his children disappointed him, Rehnquist would dictate a stern letter, give it to his secretary to type out on Supreme Court stationery, and mail it off. There was no softening his displeasure, no watering down of his expectations. One summer he and Nan allowed their oldest, Jim, then twenty years old, to stay at the family home in suburban Virginia as a caretaker while the rest of the family summered in Vermont. Rehnquist was aghast at the mess they came back to, and said so in a letter to Jim that described the carnage in detail—moldy food and all. Rehnquist's sole concession to his son was to acknowledge that "I also know that you are less of a slob about those things than you used to be."

Rehnquist was just as punctilious with his children about money. He loaned Jim $5,000 in 1988, at an interest rate of 10 percent—and Rehnquist expected to collect everything he was owed. Over the course of the next year, Jim repaid every penny of the $5,000 on schedule. Rehnquist then sent his son a letter asking for the accrued interest—$289 in all, carefully calculated and thoroughly documented by Rehnquist. All three children were expected to earn money for college; dollars mattered in a household getting by solely on Rehnquist's salary, which, in 1980, was $88,700 a year. On another occasion, when twenty-year-old Jim didn't pay back $200 that he owed his father and mother, Rehnquist vented about it in a letter to his youngest daughter Nancy: "More of his carelessness."

Rehnquist also didn't disguise his disappointment when, after pressuring his son to go to law school, Jim was turned down by Harvard but admitted to the law schools at Boston College and Boston University (where he ended up going).* Both "are perfectly good, but not really first rate, law schools," Rehnquist wrote to his sister, Jean. When a friend of Jim's from his undergraduate days at Amherst asked for a letter of recommendation to a law program at Georgetown, Rehnquist didn't hesitate, saying he knew Jim's friend well and vouching that he "was somewhat more diligent than my son in applying himself to the academic side of the program" at Amherst. (Jim, a public-school kid like his two younger sisters, was a basketball star at Amherst who set numerous scoring records that still stood thirty-five years after his 1977 graduation.) Rehnquist took to calling Jim "Weakfish," after a character in Al Capp's *Li'l Abner* comic strip. In the strip, Rehnquist explained to Jim, Weakfish was the timid son of the great General Bullmoose, and he was everything that Bullmoose was not: "He's kind, he's generous, he's—ugh!—decent! In other words, he's no businessman."

Youngest daughter Nancy followed Jim's lead and went to Amherst (the middle daughter, Janet, graduated from the University of Virginia and its law school). With two years to go at Amherst, Nancy announced to family and friends that she intended to marry. She was head over heels in love. The wedding would be held at the Rehnquist's summer home in Vermont, the August following her graduation.

Rehnquist was all for the idea and even bought a new suit (on sale) for the occasion. Nancy's fiancé was "a very nice, stable guy with good expectations," and he "had really done it all himself." Rehnquist admired the man's gumption. But there was also the matter of whom *not* to invite to what would necessarily be a small ceremony.

There was one particular cousin Rehnquist wanted to make sure was excluded. Rehnquist told his sister Jean that the undesirable cousin had slighted him—"from the time that Nan and I were married until the time I was appointed to the Supreme Court, we did not even receive return Christmas cards from them—they were on our list, but we were not on theirs, so to speak." Rehnquist took this as a grievous insult and saw the wedding as a chance to snub him back—but obliquely. Jean was to "be as vague as possible about the date, place, and the like," lest the cousin drop in and spoil the festivities. To make doubly sure his cousin didn't show up,

---

*Jim Rehnquist was editor in chief of the *Boston University Law Review.* He served four years as a federal prosecutor in Boston and then switched to representing defendants accused of white-collar crimes.

Rehnquist sent a letter himself that, in so many words, told the unwanted cousin to stay home, not to even think about crashing the wedding. As it turned out, Nancy fell out of love with the bridegroom shortly before the event, and the wedding was called off anyway. Rehnquist confessed he was disappointed. He genuinely liked the guy and was looking forward to being his father-in-law.

BY 1990, THE CANCER THAT NAN had been battling for years had spread despite the best efforts of her team at NIH. She spent six hours in surgery at NIH on September 20, 1990, and Rehnquist sent a note to the conference telling his fellow justices that "the surgeon's report is encouraging." But within two months her doctors found that the cancer had spread to her liver, a death sentence for sure. Nan died at NIH the following year, October 17, 1991, at age sixty-two.

The next day, the Court's newest justice, Clarence Thomas, was to be ceremonially sworn in as the replacement for Thurgood Marshall. The confirmation hearings for Thomas had dragged on for months in a long-running and tawdry circus, replete with allegations of sexual misconduct and Thomas's lying about it. The Court's second African-American justice had survived by the slimmest of margins, but his supporters savored the hard-fought victory and wanted to make a point of having bested the Democrats. The White House threw an elaborate party on the South Lawn on October 18 for a thousand guests and put the Marine band in the Truman balcony to play patriotic tunes—all this on the day after Nan Rehnquist's death.

There were those at the Court who couldn't believe the audacity of Thomas's supporters in the administration of George H. W. Bush. For a justice to become a full-fledged member of the Court, two oaths were required. Protocol dictated that the chief justice administer the second oath in a ceremony at the Court; that had been previously scheduled for October 22, but now Rehnquist was in mourning, with Nan's funeral scheduled to take place on that day. When the justices took the bench in the main courtroom the following Monday, Byron White read a tribute to Nan. Harry Blackmun sent a $50 check in her honor to the National Lutheran Home, where Nan had worked on the staff as the director of volunteer service.

None of this mattered to the White House, which rushed to stage the festival for Thomas as a demonstration of its triumph over the Democratic senators and liberal interest groups who had opposed him in the vitriolic televised hearings.

The matter of Nan Rehnquist's death, a solemn occasion in which the justices supported one of their own, thus became an arcane drama in the uneasy relations between branches of government. Thomas would, indeed, have his ceremonial swearing in at the White House—Byron White agreed to do the job. But the justices wanted it made clear that Thomas wasn't really a justice—not until he took the judicial oath, at the Court itself. That ceremony had been rescheduled for November 1.

White carried the message to the White House ceremony. He pointedly told Thomas as he squared up to administer the oath that "when, at 10 o'clock on November 1, you take the judicial oath that is required by statute, you will become the 106th justice to sit on the Supreme Court, and we look forward to that day."* The justices were honoring not only their colleague but the sanctity of tradition. Thomas had struggled for 110 days to get to the Court, and as far as they were concerned he could wait a few weeks more.

---

*Thomas ended up being sworn in on October 23. Although delaying the swearing in until November 1 would not have posed a problem because the Court was in recess until November 4 and no official business would be conducted in the meantime, the White House was concerned about that delay. Investigative reporters were still digging, and the White House wanted to get Thomas legitimized as a justice before another bomb dropped. Thomas called Rehnquist the day after Nan's funeral and asked to be sworn in immediately. Rehnquist agreed to do it. At noon that same day, Wednesday, October 23, the chief justice officiated at a secret ceremony in one of the Court's conference rooms. Rehnquist recited the judicial oath, which Thomas repeated, swearing to "do equal right to the poor and to the rich." The only witnesses were Thomas's wife, Virginia; his friend and supporter Senator John Danforth (R-MO); and Robb Jones, Rehnquist's administrative assistant. The speeded-up swearing in turned out to be wise. Almost at the same instant, editors across town at the *Washington Post* were debating whether to publish new allegations of misconduct against Thomas. Since Thomas had already been sworn in, they decided not to.

TWENTY-EIGHT

The Brennan Court

IN HIS FIRST YEAR AS CHIEF JUSTICE, Rehnquist was reluctant to abandon his Lone Ranger role for that of consensus builder. Dependably on the rightward fringe, Rehnquist could not get the votes to overrule the abortion and criminal-law precedents that he disliked. The result was that the senior justice on the other side, William J. Brennan, directed the opinion writing. The Rehnquist Court appeared to have become a liberal bastion. Rehnquist could not (or did not try to) win over the moderates who represented the swing votes in close cases. Thus, in short order, the "Brennan Court," with Rehnquist dissenting each time, mandated: pregnancy disability leaves for women;* new trials for blacks who were convicted by all-white juries;** a challenge under the Voting Rights Act to an Alabama town's annexing an all-white area;† lawsuits by low-income public-housing tenants who were

---

**California Federal Savings & Loan v. Guerra*, 479 U.S. 272, decided by a 6–3 vote, January 13, 1987. Marshall wrote the opinion; White, Rehnquist, and Powell dissented.

***Batson v. Kentucky*, 476 U.S. 79, decided by a 7–2 vote, April 30, 1986. Powell wrote the opinion; Burger and Rehnquist dissented. The Court also provided greater protections for defendants indicted by a grand jury selected in a racially discriminatory fashion in *Vasquez v. Hillery*, 474 U.S. 254, decided by a 6–3 vote, January 14, 1986. Marshall wrote the opinion; Powell, Burger, and Rehnquist dissented.

†*City of Pleasant Grove v. United States*, 479 U.S. 462, decided by a 6–3 vote, January 21, 1987. White wrote the opinion; Powell, Rehnquist, and O'Connor dissented.

angry about utility rates;* unemployment pay for a Seventh-Day Adventist fired for refusing to work on Saturdays;** handicapped-worker protections for people with contagious diseases such as AIDS;† half of future police promotions in Alabama for blacks, to overcome past egregious discrimination;†† relaxing asylum standards for aliens;‡ and a hands-off policy against sexually explicit programming on cable television.‡‡

Those were not the results that Reagan and his minions had hoped for or expected. They had relished seeing Rehnquist take the center chair in place of what they saw as Burger's anemic conservatism—and they wanted to see a quick turnaround. The situation that Rehnquist was expected to clean up—and didn't—was well summarized by Bruce Fein, a perennial scold on the right. Fein had characterized the major decisions of Burger's final year on the Court as "the most significant defeats for the policy objectives of a chief executive [Reagan] in a half a century." Fein had testified for Rehnquist at his confirmation hearings. Like so many others, he was a true believer in Rehnquist's conservative instincts. And all true believers knew that the president had elevated Rehnquist in order to bring a semblance of conservative leadership to the chief justice's chair.

But based upon the results of his first term as chief justice, Rehnquist had failed. The Court itself had not changed in essence: Scalia was swapped for Burger; the rest of the cast was the same. Rehnquist's leadership (or the lack thereof) could be demonstrated by the extent to which the Court acted

---

* *Wright v. City of Roanoke Redevelopment and Housing Authority,* 479 U.S. 418, decided by a 5–4 vote, January 14, 1987. White wrote the opinion; O'Connor, Rehnquist, Scalia, and Powell dissented.

** *Hobbie v. Unemployment Appeals Commission of Florida,* 480 U.S. 136, decided by an 8–1 vote, February 25, 1987. Brennan wrote the opinion; Rehnquist dissented.

† *School Board of Nassau County, Fla. v. Arline,* 480 U.S. 273, decided by a 7–2 vote, March 3, 1987. Brennan wrote the opinion; Rehnquist and Scalia dissented.

†† *Local #93, International Association of Firefighters v. City of Cleveland and Cleveland Vanguards,* 478 U.S. 501, decided by a 6–3 vote, July 2, 1986. Brennan wrote the opinion; White, Burger, and Rehnquist dissented. The Court also approved union quotas favoring minorities in *Local #28 of the Sheet Metal Workers' International v. Equal Employment Opportunity Commission,* 478 U.S. 421, decided by a 5–4 vote, July 2, 1986. Brennan wrote the opinion; White, Burger, Rehnquist, and O'Connor dissented.

‡ *Immigration and Naturalization Service v. Cardoza-Fonseca,* 480 U.S. 421, decided by a 6–3 vote, March 9, 1987. Stevens wrote the opinion; Powell, Rehnquist, and White dissented.

‡‡ *Community Television of Utah, Inc. v. Wilkinson,* aff'd mem., 480 U.S. 926 (1987); O'Connor and Rehnquist dissented.

differently from the year before and overturned liberal precedents. If Rehnquist were the superior leader, the results would speak for themselves as he led the justices rightward.

But the opposite happened, and Rehnquist found himself in the minority in some of the most important cases of the term. He had not produced a discernible conservative shift. Cagily, Brennan had prevailed. Rehnquist's 1986–1987 inaugural term as the chief, his star turn, had been botched. He would never get another chance to so clearly demonstrate that he had the power of persuasion or personality to move the Court. He did not abandon his core conservative beliefs, preferring to be in the minority rather than to compromise his worldview, but his stand made little impression on the justices who were not already disposed to agree with him.

On an aging Court like the one Rehnquist inherited—the average age of the justices was almost sixty-nine, virtually unchanged from five years earlier—turnover was bound to accelerate. The changing composition of the Court was a wild card, making future speculation about the impact of Rehnquist's leadership far less reliable. And a change in the Court's membership would come quickly. But anyone who wanted to gauge the true scope and impact of Rehnquist's leadership skills—his capacity for moral suasion—had the answer in that first year. Conciliation was not something the new chief was interested in. Rehnquist wanted to win, but only on his own terms. More than half of the decisions of the term came from a deeply divided Court in votes of 5–4 or 6–3.

At the end of Rehnquist's first term as chief, Lewis Powell announced his retirement. Powell had sent a kind note to Rehnquist when his confirmation twin became the chief. Powell truly liked Rehnquist, although he did not always agree with his ways. Powell told his younger colleague that he looked forward to serving under his leadership. But the truth was that Powell, at seventy-nine, was old, sick, and tired.

Powell's departure would turn out to be a pivotal moment not only for Rehnquist and the Court but for the Reagan administration as well. Powell was a critical swing vote. When he voted with the conservatives, typically in economic and property rights cases, the conservatives won. But on matters of individual and civil rights, Powell could (and often did) tilt the Court toward the liberals. It was not too much to say that Powell's vote was what had determined whether the Court was liberal or conservative on an issue.

And on no issue was Powell's influence more salient than abortion. Powell had split with Rehnquist in 1973 and voted with the majority in *Roe v. Wade.* But the seven-man majority from *Roe* had slipped to six by 1983, when the Court reaffirmed *Roe* in 1983 in an opinion written by Powell.* Sandra Day O'Connor, new to the Court, voted against *Roe.* By 1986, in the waning days of the Burger Court, the majority for *Roe* had slipped to five as Burger moved to the other side.** His replacement by the ultra-conservative Scalia didn't change the balance. Powell was the deciding vote. Whoever replaced him would decide the fate of *Roe.*

Reagan did not have to look far for another thoroughbred conservative who would be certain not only to finish off *Roe* but also to reverse the horrendous start that Rehnquist had in his first term as chief justice. Robert Bork, sixty years old and Reagan's number-two choice from the year before, was ready to go.

But Democrats had regained control of the Senate in the 1986 election and confirming a hard-core conservative would not be so easy. With the stakes high and the future of *Roe* at stake, civil rights and women's groups went all out to defeat Bork. Within an hour of Bork's nomination, Ted Kennedy was on the Senate floor inveighing against him: "Robert Bork's America is a land in which women would be forced into back-alley abortions, blacks would sit at segregated lunch counters, rogue police could break down citizens' doors in midnight raids . . . and the doors of the federal courts would be shut on the fingers of millions of citizens for whom the judiciary is often the only protector of the individual rights that are the heart of our democracy."

The partisan battle over Bork lasted three and a half months. With the Democrats holding on to all but 2 of their 54 votes, Bork was defeated 58–42. Six Republicans crossed over and voted against Bork in the first outright defeat of a Supreme Court nominee since Carswell in 1970. Following Bork's defeat, Reagan nominated Douglas H. Ginsburg, a forty-one-year-old colleague of Bork's on the federal appeals court. Within days, Ginsburg, too, was in trouble amid allegations of ethics breaches. But what really killed his nomination was Ginsburg's own admission that he had smoked

---

**Akron v. Akron Center for Reproductive Health, Inc.*, 462 U.S. 416 (1983)

***Thornburgh v. American College of Obstetricians & Gynecologists,* 476 U.S. 747 (1986)

marijuana in the 1960s and 1970s. That did it for Reagan. Ginsburg's nomination was withdrawn. Reagan finally found his man in Anthony Kennedy, fifty-one, a Meese crony who was a federal appeals judge from California. He was confirmed 97–0.

For the Reagan White House, the key thing about Anthony Kennedy was that he was a relatively young and highly reliable conservative who was confirmable. Unlike Bork, Kennedy's writings and opinions were careful and narrow, giving the liberals a much smaller target. Importantly, the new Justice Kennedy was, like Scalia, a Roman Catholic. Conservatives did not doubt he would vote to overturn *Roe.*

Indeed, the Court soon was confronting anew the threat of *Roe*'s evisceration. This time, Powell's absence loomed large. Faced with a challenge to the constitutionality of a Missouri law regulating abortions, five justices—Kennedy, Scalia, O'Connor, White, and Rehnquist—voted to uphold the state law.* Rehnquist at last found himself in the majority, and he assigned the opinion writing to himself. It would be easy to credit Rehnquist for leading a conservative revolution that had finally succeeded in taking *Roe* to the brink. But that would be wrong. As the vote plainly showed, the Court was shifting under Rehnquist. It was Kennedy's arrival that had made all the difference. Rehnquist was simply the beneficiary of a Republican president's conservative choices—he now had five votes against *Roe.* The question was what he would, or could, do with them.

The answer defied Rehnquist, who by now clearly was a more or less passive actor in the drama going on. The chief justice's opinion took a broad swipe at *Roe,* but in spite of getting five votes for upholding Missouri's law he could not corral the increasingly restive O'Connor or the staunchly conservative Scalia to agree with everything he had written. Nor did he try. Lacking five justices to sign on to his opinion, Rehnquist spoke only for a plurality of three. The opportunity to write a majority opinion that might form the basis for the outright overruling of *Roe* was squandered.

Scalia, by now the real standard-bearer of the right wing of the Court, did what Rehnquist was unwilling to do and lashed out publicly and privately at the justices he thought were wrecking any chance of overturning *Roe.* Scalia tried to muscle the conservative fence-sitters back into line, to

* *Webster v. Reproductive Health Services,* 492 U.S. 490 (1989)

no avail. Blackmun, now almost eighty-one years old and suddenly in the minority defending the most important case of his life, could see what was coming. *Roe,* he said, was not secure. "I fear for the liberty and equality of the millions of women who have lived and come of age in the 16 years since *Roe* was decided. I fear for the integrity of, and public esteem for, this Court."

The waiting game to see how the Court would next shift began anew. Within a year, the liberal William J. Brennan retired, replaced by George H. W. Bush's first appointee, David Souter.* Souter was pro-choice, so the balance of power in *Roe* was unchanged. Then, a year later, Thurgood Marshall stepped down, and Bush's choice of Clarence Thomas all but ensured another vote against *Roe.*

The test came in *Planned Parenthood v. Casey.*** The Pennsylvania statute whose constitutionality was before the Court was, in almost every respect, a perfect test of *Roe*'s continued viability. The state law was clearly aimed at stopping abortions. It contained just about every restriction that abortion opponents could think of: parental consent for minors, a husband's consent for married women, a waiting period, and so forth. A federal district court had invalidated the law, citing *Roe* as binding precedent. But a federal appeals court had reinstated the law and declared that, contrary to *Roe,* abortion was no longer a fundamental constitutional right. The case had to be taken up by the Supreme Court, and it presented the constitutional issue squarely. With Marshall gone and Thomas coming over to their side, conservatives fully expected the Court to affirm the appeals court and finally overrule *Roe.*

But the result showed the improbability of predicting outcomes based on past performance, let alone the leadership skills of the chief justice. By the time *Casey* came down, Kennedy and O'Connor had moved out of the

---

*Rehnquist wrote to his sister, Jean, a few weeks after Souter arrived: "The rest of us were very anxious that he come on board as soon as possible, so that we would not hear cases argued to a bench of just eight Justices with the attendant possibility of dividing equally on any particular case. . . . [The result] was that he sat the first week having barely read the briefs, with only one law clerk and still looking for a place to live. I don't envy him. He seems like a very decent fellow, with a certain amount of New England reserve, but by no means lacking confidence in his own abilities. He is not only a bachelor, but an only child, and so far as I could tell, he had no family members at the reception following his swearing-in. But a number of friends from New Hampshire did come down for the occasion."

**505 U.S. 833 (1992)

dependably conservative bloc. With new Justice Souter, they formed a troika that not only reaffirmed the constitutional right to abortion but also put a brake on any significant dampening of *Roe*'s protections for at least the following two decades. When the three justices wrote eloquently about *stare decisis,* the effect was to provide reassurance that Blackmun's worst fears—"I fear for the integrity of, and public esteem for, this Court"—wouldn't be realized.

TWENTY-NINE

Federalism, Occasionally

REHNQUIST, SCALIA, AND THOMAS were relegated to the fringe during the formative 1991–1992 term. When O'Connor, Kennedy, and Souter voted together on any case that term, they were never in the minority.

This is not to say that the changes of membership on the Court didn't have any effect. It was a more conservative court, particularly in criminal cases, and Rehnquist now stood closer to the ideological center as a result. Rehnquist did, indeed, shatter the cherished doctrine of *stare decisis* as he authored majority opinions that made it easier for states to execute people. "*Stare decisis* is not an inexorable command," he wrote in *Payne v. Tennessee.**

Rehnquist also received credit for a resurgence of a certain strain of federalism that took away some economic regulatory power from the federal government and gave it back to the states. Federalism was susceptible to many meanings, but at its core it meant states' rights. As such, it was also a loaded term—"states' rights" was a code phrase for southern segregation in the 1950s. But as a core conservative tenet, federalism meant strictly interpreting the Constitution and keeping the federal government out of affairs that rightly belonged with the states.

*501 U.S. 808 (1991)

Rehnquist's federalism revolution was really enabled by the arrival of Clarence Thomas in 1991. The resolute conservative who replaced the liberal Thurgood Marshall finally provided the crucial fifth vote for an array of 5–4 decisions that diminished federal power.

The so-called federalism revolution started in earnest in 1995, almost a full ten years into Rehnquist's tenure as chief. It took that long for the Court's new cast of characters to have the right cases in front of them. Rehnquist had waited a lifetime for the opportunity to make his point. With each arrival of O'Connor, Scalia, and Kennedy at the Court, he had gotten progressively closer to realizing his ambition. Finally, when Thomas got there, the stage was set. The first federal statute to fall, in a 5–4 decision in *U.S. v. Lopez,*[*] was the Gun-Free School Zones Act. Congress had made it a federal crime to possess a gun within a thousand feet of a school. Who could argue with keeping kids safe? The answer was: conservatives, who didn't believe that the commerce clause of the Constitution conferred a general police power on Congress.

It was the first time since the New Deal that the Court had struck down a federal law on the grounds that it exceeded Congress's commerce power, and Rehnquist underscored the importance of the occasion by assigning the majority-opinion writing to himself. Eventually, federal statutes were invalidated in whole or in part on federalism grounds in nine cases that were decided between 1995 and 2001.[**] By then, among other things, the Rehnquist Court also had overruled one of its own federal affirmative-action precedents from only five years earlier; upheld random drug testing of high-school athletes in the biggest exception ever to the 4th Amendment's requirement that the government have some suspicion of wrongdoing before conducting a search; took away the right of victims of gender-motivated violence to sue their attackers in federal court under the Violence Against

---

*514 U.S. 549 (1995)

**See Lori A. Ringhand, "The Rehnquist Court: A By the Numbers Retrospective," 9 *University of Pennsylvania Journal of Constitutional Law* 1033, 1055 (2007). The nine cases are *U.S. v. Lopez,* 514 U.S. 549 (1995); *Seminole Tribe of Florida v. Florida,* 517 U.S. 44 (1996); *Printz v. U.S.,* 521 U.S. 898 (1997); *Florida Prepaid Postsecondary Education Expense Bank v. College Savings Bank,* 527 U.S. 627 (1999); *College Savings Bank v. Florida Prepaid Postsecondary Education Expense Bank,* 527 U.S. 666 (1999); *Alden v. Maine,* 527 U.S. 706 (1999); *Kimel v. Florida Board of Regents,* 528 U.S. 62 (2000); *U.S. v. Morrison,* 529 U.S. 598 (2000); and *Board of Trustees of the University of Alabama v. Garrett,* 531 U.S. 356 (2001).

Women Act; and, for the first time, upheld the use of public money for religious-school tuition. From the Fall 1994 term until O'Connor's retirement and Rehnquist's death in 2005, the membership of the Court didn't change. The Rehnquist Court retained a tenuous conservative majority—but only if the chief justice could keep O'Connor, Kennedy, Scalia, and Thomas with him. Lose any one of them, and Rehnquist's conservative Court would pitch leftward.

The elusive nature of this majority made the so-called federalism revolution decidedly less than world-shaking. Over seven terms, the federalists averaged about one win per year. No major federal programs got the ax. Die-hard federalists who wanted to see Rehnquist put a stake in the heart of the big initiatives of the New Deal and the Great Society were not impressed. "The Rehnquist Court has revived the doctrine of federalism, albeit only at the edges and in very easy cases," said Roger Pilon, the founder and director of the Cato Institute's Center for Constitutional Studies and a former Reagan administration official. "It hasn't gone after Social Security or Medicare or Medicaid and tried to argue they are unconstitutional, although they are." O'Connor and Kennedy carved such an increasingly liberal path that, by 2003, it was clear that the federalism boomlet was over.

Because the federalism epoch coincided with historic stability in the Rehnquist Court's makeup,* the vast trove of outcomes and alignments among an unchanged lineup of justices enabled a kind of sabermetric analysis. A huge data set—of cases and votes—made it possible to rate how the nine teammates played together over time. What Billy Beane was doing for the Oakland A's, Supreme Court analysts could do for the Rehnquist Court. So who were the Court's power players during this long stretch? The metrics actually provided a highly objective means of evaluating Rehnquist's leadership as chief justice during this historic period of stability among its members. The pivotal effects of O'Connor and Kennedy were evident from the 1994 term—the term of *Lopez,* which started the federalism epoch—until the end of Rehnquist's tenure in 2005. During those eleven years, the Court decided 1,007 cases.** In well over a third of those—

---

*The last eleven years of Rehnquist's tenure as chief justice constituted the second-longest period of Supreme Court membership stability, and the longest for a nine-justice Court. The longest in history was from November 1811 to March 1823, when the law provided for only seven justices.

**This analysis uses the data set from the CQ Press Supreme Court Collection.

391 decisions, to be exact, or 38.8 percent—there was no disagreement at all; the justices were *unanimous.*

That left 616 cases during those eleven years in which the justices didn't see eye to eye. In a third,* the disagreement split cleanly and closely along conservative-liberal lines, resulting in 5–4 or 6–3 decisions. In other words, the justices were so ideologically factionalized during Rehnquist's federalism epoch that one out of every three votes was, in essence, too close to call. The decision could have gone either way, depending on whether one or two justices swung to the right or left.

A certain kind of chief justice might have played the ideological opposites against each other to gain the best result attainable. Earl Warren seldom found himself on the losing side; the same was true of Warren's predecessor as chief justice, Fred Vinson, and his successor, Burger. Even Brennan was an old master at this game of chess when it suited his liberal agenda.

Based on the eleven years worth of statistics spanning 1994 to 2005, it is clear that, from the chief down, few on the Rehnquist Court had any desire for compromise. The two most dogmatic conservatives, Scalia and Thomas, had almost no interest in finding common ground with their liberal brethren. Of the 210 close cases decided during the eleven-year span, Thomas cast the deciding vote to give the liberal bloc a 5–4 win in a mere *three* cases, and Scalia gave the liberals a 5–4 win exactly *one* time (in a mundane contract arbitration case) during the same period.

The liberals were only slightly more tolerant of their conservative benchmates. Stephen Breyer, the Clinton appointee who replaced Blackmun at the start of the 1994 term, voted with the conservatives in eighteen out of the 210 close cases; David Souter in nine; and John Paul Stevens in three. Ruth Bader Ginsburg sided with the conservatives in just *one* case, voting on the side of the University of Minnesota in an age-discrimination lawsuit.

And Rehnquist? He certainly was not trying to unite the two factions. The vaunted "leader" of the federalism revolution moved over to give the liberals a majority in *two* out of 210 close cases—in other words, a little less than 1 percent of the time. Both cases were hot-button federalist issues that would have offended an original-intent purist, and thus both represented

*The exact number is 210 cases out of 616, or 34.1 percent.

for Rehnquist an expenditure of ideological capital: the chief justice sided with the liberals in permitting the Census Bureau to use statistical sampling to estimate population, rather than requiring the agency to conduct an "actual enumeration" as specified in the Constitution; and he was willing to let a federal court approve a Florida legislative redistricting plan when it seemed like the state itself wasn't going to act promptly to do so. But that was it. Rehnquist had, indeed, played against type in both cases—in votes that were five years apart—but together the two decisions hardly constituted an olive branch to the liberals.

Statistics may not make for colorful history, but they do not lie. What the tally makes clear is that to the end Rehnquist hung on to the role he had carved out for himself many years before, when he was the Lone Dissenter. Back in the early days it was fun for him; he played a kind of parlor game of using clever dissents to plant the seeds for future havoc. But as he aged in the job, Rehnquist was no longer alone in his ideological cloak. After Scalia and then Thomas moved in alongside him, precedents began to fall. But that happened because the loner finally had fellow travelers, not because Rehnquist had somehow acquired the leadership gene.

The poet Robert Pinsky wrote of mules: "A creature willing to labor for you patiently many years, just for the privilege to kick you once." That was Rehnquist, the tenacious, stubborn conservative. Throughout his long career, Rehnquist saw the world in the same shades of black and white. By his own admission, he never changed. And a chief justice with a worldview as rigid as Rehnquist's could kick hard, but he could never truly lead; could not be a judicial statesman. The man who had been put on the Court by Richard Nixon because of his fanatical conservatism—and who had been elevated to the chief justiceship by Ronald Reagan for the same reason—had an ideology that controlled him. Moving from one conservative perch to another, Rehnquist was ever the predictable, available man: an expedient conservative, devoted to a value system that was all his own.

Paeans to Rehnquist came from all over the conservative community when his life and career neared its close. The tributes to his supposed bridge-building skills were repeated so often that they assumed their own reality. A posting on FoxNews.com a few months before he died was typical. Rehnquist, the commentary said, had a "willingness to accept majority opinion and to compromise [that] has set him apart from Scalia and Thomas, both hardliners when it comes to constitutional interpretation."

The numbers, of course, irrefutably prove otherwise. But the comment encapsulated conventional right-wing wisdom about Rehnquist's long tenure. His career was a conservative's fantasy—dedicating thirty-three years to creating a liberal's hell. Every 5–4 or 6–3 case had the potential for anointing him as a conciliator. But in the long grey shadow of an unchanged bench, Rehnquist proved he could not be both an ideologue and a leader. Stubbornly, even defiantly, he did not seem to care. The ideologue won out.

On Rehnquist's Court, the swing vote, or votes, in crucial cases had to be found elsewhere—with O'Connor and Kennedy. They, and not Rehnquist, held the true power to carry a decision. Without them, Rehnquist could not win a close case. To the extent there was a revolution of the federalist variety or any other, O'Connor and Kennedy were its real strategists—not Rehnquist.

To illustrate the power of O'Connor and Kennedy as shifting centrists during the eleven years from 1994 to 2005, consider this: two-thirds of the close cases during that period—139 cases out of 210—were 5–4 decisions in which all but O'Connor and Kennedy lined up strictly along ideological lines. In 89 of those cases, O'Connor and Kennedy voted as a bloc with the three conservatives[*] to provide a 5–4 margin. In 32 others, O'Connor switched sides and gave the liberal bloc[**] a 5–4 margin of victory. Eighteen times, it was Kennedy who joined the liberals to give them a 5–4 win. (In 30 other cases, *both* O'Connor and Kennedy voted with the liberals for a 6–3 result.)

The votes of O'Connor and Kennedy were dispositive—for one side or the other—in almost every close case. So much so that the conservative troika of Rehnquist, Scalia, and Thomas were victorious in just *one* case[†] during those eleven years when O'Connor and Kennedy lined up on the other side.

The three predictable conservatives could prevail in a case only if O'Connor and Kennedy deigned to allow it. Rehnquist wasn't a factor because he was voting as the same hard-line conservative he always had been, unevolved since his 1950s fights against *Brown* and everything else the liberals stood for.

---

*Rehnquist, Scalia, and Thomas.

** Stevens, Souter, Ginsburg, and Breyer.

†*Richardson v. United States,* 526 U.S. 813 (1999)

Rehnquist's expedient and unyielding conservatism, which marginalized him as a leader and negated his ability to influence the outcome in any close case, did cast an enduring legacy. The politicization of the Court—a focus on finding nominees so reliably ideological that they could be considered an extension of the president's cabinet—began with Rehnquist and continues unabated. Earlier choices among Rehnquist's contemporaries—Burger, Blackmun, and Powell—ultimately disappointed their conservative patrons, but Rehnquist fully delivered, as have his conservative successors on the current Court: John Roberts, Antonin Scalia, Clarence Thomas, and Samuel Alito. Rehnquist was the model nominee for the Court's modern era, his doctrinaire beliefs fully formed and road-tested before arrival. The Roberts Court is Rehnquist's true legacy, and Roberts himself—once a Rehnquist clerk—is Rehnquist's natural heir.

And that is a potent bequest, because the Roberts Court is even more ideologically partisan and conservative than Rehnquist's. The evidence is incontrovertible: in 491 decisions of the Roberts Court through the end of calendar 2011, Roberts was such a predictable, reliable conservative that he *never* provided the crucial fifth vote for the liberal bloc. The same was true for O'Connor's replacement, Alito. For either of them, identifying with the liberals was anathema. On the Roberts Court, even Scalia and Thomas (and Ginsburg and Stevens) occasionally crossed the aisle.

So totally did Rehnquist's heir stick to his ideology and maintain solidarity with the conservative bloc that in his first six terms, Roberts voted against his conservative brethren a mere seven times—on average, about once each year. The metrics show that the difference between Rehnquist and Roberts is just one of personality (Roberts: deft and disarming) and degree of conservatism (Roberts: more so).

Roberts's first and only vote with the liberals was indeed a momentous one as he authored the Court's 5–4 opinion upholding the Affordable Care Act. But when Roberts handed President Obama that signature victory on June 28, 2012 he planted a Rehnquistian seed: the new health care law, the natural heir wrote for his majority, could not be justified by Congress's broad power to regulate commerce. Two centuries of precedent were called into question.

THIRTY

A Fragile Majority

PAUL BENDER WAS A CONTEMPORARY of Rehnquist's and the dean emeritus at the Sandra Day O'Connor School of Law at Arizona State University. Long before that sinecure, Bender had worked both sides of the Court, first as a clerk for Rehnquist's icon Felix Frankfurter and, decades later, as principal deputy solicitor general in the administration of President Bill Clinton.

Bender saw Rehnquist for what he really was—"the first true conservative justice, the one who marked the beginning of a conservative Court. His ideas set the tone." In emphasizing Rehnquist's "ideas" Bender was recognizing two things: Rehnquist was not a persuasive chief justice but one whose opinions were the reference points for conservative judgments of the future. They were seeds. In that way, although the federalism of the Rehnquist Court was not overambitious, it contained revolutionary potential. To Bender, "*Lopez* really was the beginning of the revolution, and Rehnquist's ideas set the tone for future debate. The Obama health care case, for example, will have to draw from *Lopez.* Rehnquist was a clear writer, and he wrote short, readable opinions that contained 'big ideas' that the Court could use later." Even though in his last years, according to Bender, Rehnquist "was the *third* most conservative behind Scalia and Thomas, now Roberts and Alito are more conservative than Rehnquist ever was." Some of Rehnquist's most important conservative thoughts just needed other conservatives on the Court before they could become law.

Because Rehnquist always voted for what he considered "the better point of view," his thin majorities were, as Bender pointed out, inherently fragile. Thus, when the so-called federalism revolution seemed to have run its course by 2003, the end was heralded by a Rehnquist decision that seemed to go against his entire previous judicial career—and yet which made perfect sense given Rehnquist's pragmatic conservatism. When Rehnquist wrote the 6–3 majority opinion in *Nevada Department of Human Resources v. Hibbs,** he surprised his critics by affirming Congress's right to make state governments give their employees the benefits of the federal Family and Medical Leave Act.

Rehnquist's opinion in *Hibbs* was inconsistent with his views—a dramatic departure for a man who was if nothing else set in his view of the world. It also went against his own Court's earlier precedents that said Congress couldn't legislate such requirements for state employers. But the chief justice said "a self-fulfilling cycle of discrimination" had to be broken. What was going on? Some declared that *Hibbs* was the end of the federalism revolution—and scholars who made it a sport to study such things puzzled over how Rehnquist could so cavalierly have brought it about.

Another view was that Rehnquist was simply a situationist—voting with his gut for "the better point of view"—and that *Hibbs* had struck a chord with a grandfather who occasionally helped his daughter, a single mother, with child care. It made as much sense as any other explanation, because this certainly wasn't the only time that Rehnquist confounded the conservative pundits.

No opinion was more illustrative of that than his 2000 opinion upholding the constitutionality of *Miranda*** after almost a lifetime of opposing it. Rehnquist had been campaigning to erase *Miranda* since his earliest days in the Nixon administration, when he wrote the memo to John Dean proposing a constitutional amendment to take away safeguards that the Warren Court had provided to criminal defendants.

As a new justice at the Court, Rehnquist had revved up an unrelenting campaign against *Miranda.* Soon after he arrived at the Court, Rehnquist

---

*538 U.S. 721 (2003)

***Miranda v. Arizona,* 384 U.S. 436 (1966)

got his first chance to plant what he probably expected would be the seeds of *Miranda*'s eventual destruction. The case was *Michigan v. Tucker,** and it raised for the first time the question of whether the Warren Court's protections in *Miranda* would stand or fall. A suspect had tipped off the police about a witness to his crime. The tip-off came before the suspect received a *Miranda* warning. Could the prosecution still use the witness? A hawkish new majority not only said yes but seemed to line up against *Miranda* itself. When young Mr. Rehnquist was asked to write the 8–1 opinion in *Tucker* (with only Douglas dissenting) it contained a hidden bomb: *Miranda* warnings, Rehnquist said, were only "procedural safeguards [that] were not themselves rights protected by the Constitution." That was ominous. If they weren't constitutionally protected, the *Miranda* warnings were on shaky ground. Indeed, given the chance to further cut back on *Miranda* safeguards a decade later in two other cases,** the Court each time used Rehnquist's opinion in *Tucker* as a touchstone.

A federal appeals court finally invited the Rehnquist Court to finish the job. In an opinion allowing the confession of a bank-robbery getaway driver to be admitted into evidence despite the absence of a *Miranda* warning, the appeals court quoted Rehnquist's opinions. *Miranda* was on the brink.

The Rehnquist Court finally got its chance to deal head-on with the constitutionality of *Miranda.* But in the case of *Dickerson v. United States,*† the seven justices in the majority—with Rehnquist leading—acted as if they had never heard of *Tucker* and its progeny, let alone Rehnquist's more than three decades of public and private opposition to *Miranda.* Instead of wiping out thirty-four years of confession jurisprudence, Rehnquist wrote a 7–2 majority opinion wiping away his own precedents.

The die-hards Scalia and Thomas blasted the majority for its "foolish" decision in *Dickerson,* but Rehnquist knew exactly what he was doing. By 2000, the police and public were so accustomed to the strict procedures of *Miranda* that overruling it would only have led to chaos. As Dennis Hutchinson of the University of Chicago put it: "For the Court to suddenly say, after years of the public hearing 'You have the right to remain silent'

---

*417 U.S. 433 (1974)

***New York v. Quarles,* 467 U.S. 649 (1984), an opinion also written by Rehnquist; and *Oregon v. Elstad,* 470 U.S. 298 (1985)

†530 U.S. 428 (2000)

on *Dragnet* and *Law and Order* and all the courtroom procedural shows, that the *Miranda* warning isn't required? When the Supreme Court overrules itself, it's like the clock that strikes 13. People ask, 'Have they got anything else right?' Plus, cops like *Miranda*! Once they Mirandize someone, and the person keeps talking, as they often do, you've got 'em!" The decision actually comported with Rehnquist's law-and-order credo in some way. Although *Miranda* was supposed to favor the suspect, in practice the warnings helped the police get confessions and convictions. "The better point of view" was one that supported law enforcement, even if it went against everything Rehnquist had ever said or written about *Miranda.*

Still, he needed to explain the about-face. Although Rehnquist never tried to hide his distaste for *stare decisis,* there was no other way to explain his changed view of *Miranda.* He thus called forth the demon:

> Whether or not we would agree with *Miranda*'s reasoning and its resulting rule, were we addressing the issues in the first instance, the principles of *stare decisis* weigh heavily against overruling it now. . . . *Miranda* has become embedded in routine police practice to the point where the warnings have become part of our national culture.

"I doubt that any justice in Supreme Court history has dismissed his own majority opinions more summarily or nonchalantly," observed University of Michigan Law Professor Yale Kamisar.

But when the same thing happened four years later in another end-of-federalism case, *Locke v. Davey,*[*] it showed how Rehnquist could lose his fragile majority as Kennedy and O'Connor increasingly went their own way. The question in *Locke* was whether a state that underwrites college scholarships for secular study must also subsidize students who want to study for the ministry. Just two years earlier, Rehnquist had commanded a 5–4 majority, with the votes of Kennedy and O'Connor, for his historic opinion holding that states could give parents vouchers to pay religious-school tuition.[**] *Locke* presented the logical next question: whether states with such a school-choice voucher program were *required* to extend the payments to religious study.

---

*540 U.S. 712 (2004)

***Zelman v. Simmons-Harris,* 536 U.S. 639 (2002)

That was where Kennedy and O'Connor drew the line. In *Locke,* they voted with the liberals and, by so doing, proved that for Rehnquist, nearing eighty, the federalism revolution was indeed over. But the case illustrated something else about Rehnquist, who—knowing he'd lost his majority—had to decide whether to take a principled stand and go down in defeat along with Scalia and Thomas (allowing John Paul Stevens to control the assignment) or to vote with the liberals and thus assign the majority opinion to himself. Doing the latter would be the best way to ensure a narrow, damage-limiting holding in the case.

And that is what Rehnquist did. In *Locke,* "the better point of view" dictated that Rehnquist throw Scalia and Thomas under the bus. Rehnquist wrote a 7–2 opinion saying that just because states provide tuition assistance for needy and worthy students doesn't mean the states must extend that privilege to those studying for the ministry. The clarions sounded as Scalia and Thomas angrily dissented—and others once again foretold the end of the revolution Rehnquist was supposed to have been leading.

In fact, *Hibbs, Dickerson,* and *Locke* proved the kind of conservative that Rehnquist really was. Rehnquist did not accord higher value to *stare decisis,* or to the tenets of a certain body of law, if some other outcome suited him. And *Bush v. Gore** certainly demonstrated that.

When *Bush v. Gore* came to the Court in the midst of what was still being called Rehnquist's federalism revolution, the Court's conservative bloc—Rehnquist, O'Connor, Scalia, Kennedy, and Thomas—called a halt to the state of Florida's counting of the disputed presidential ballots. With George W. Bush ahead in the count, the effect of the Court's action was to hand the state's electoral votes, and thus the presidential election itself, to Bush. In any other routine case involving state actions by the people's representatives, those same five justices, to varying degrees, would have been the *least* likely to interfere. The structural pillar of Rehnquist's federalism orthodoxy was that state actions shouldn't be overruled or interfered with by the Court. Federalists would have left the state alone to do its job. Of course, *Bush v. Gore* was a case unlike any other, turning everything upside down: federalists became interventionists, liberals wanted to keep hands off. Five justices, Rehnquist among them, decided Bush represented the better point of view.

---

*531 U.S. 98 (2000)

The majority conceded the messy politics of its decision by cautioning that *Bush v. Gore* would have no precedential effect. The ruling, said the majority, was "limited to the present circumstances." It was good for one ride only, a ticket for Bush but otherwise not what jurists euphemistically call "good law."

The shelves full of books and law review articles that have since been written about this case, pro and con, collectively stand for the proposition that *Bush v. Gore* defies explanation as anything other than what it was: a purely political decision decided strictly along ideological lines. Alan Dershowitz called the majority's "limited-to-the-present-circumstances" clause the "one telltale line that revealed [*Bush v. Gore's*] true purpose":

> The purpose of the remarkable cautionary line—which is virtually an admission that this decision does not fit into a line of continuing precedents—was to cobble together a majority for Bush consisting of justices who almost never find equal-protection violations (except, perhaps, when white people are "discriminated" against by affirmative action) and who do not want a broad equal-protection decision waiting out there to be used as a precedent in other cases in which the result would be inconsistent with the political or ideological results they generally prefer.

When Rehnquist privately wrote, shortly after becoming chief justice, that "*stare decisis* in constitutional law is pretty much of a sham," he was being surprisingly honest not only about his own partisanship but about the nature of important ideological fights at the Court in general. There was nothing in the Constitution that gave the Supreme Court the authority to decide an election.

Rehnquist refused ever to discuss the decision, and in keeping with the majority's admonition *Bush v. Gore* was never cited by a justice in an opinion, a concurrence, or a dissent. If nothing else, *Bush v. Gore* proved that Rehnquist was not alone in his partisanship, and that he wasn't always the only results-oriented jurist on the Court. A year after Rehnquist's death, nineteen scholars contributed weighty chapters to an opus titled *The Rehnquist Legacy.* The number of mentions of *Bush v. Gore*? Exactly two. It was a political decision by a politicized Court. There was really no point in trying to explain it further.

When *Bush v. Gore* came down, Rehnquist was simply one of five. The Court offered no signed opinion. There were no statements from the bench. It was a metaphor for how Rehnquist ran the Court. By and large Rehnquist did not feel impelled to lead the majority, nor did he give ground when the landscape shifted beneath him. He was what he was, and if there were four others with him, well, that was a majority for doing something. Regardless, he quickly moved on.

Rehnquist took the long view when it came to his personal endurance: he would have bested the longevity record of Bill Douglas, whom he always admired, if he could have. But otherwise, Rehnquist disciplined himself to become an efficient master of the short game. In a career that was one of the longest in the Court's history, he participated in 4,353 cases and was in the majority in more than three-fourths of them (many of which were mundane and agreed upon unanimously).* The sheer volume of work he cranked out was mind-numbing: 440 opinions, 330 dissents. "They're all kind of a long, grey line," he had said in 1985. "I can't remember back for the whole thirteen years." Twenty more unmemorable—to Rehnquist—years had followed.

With so many routine cases, Rehnquist did not care to look very far forward or very far back. Of course, Rehnquist tallied his wins. He was, after all, a wagering man and he did not like to lose. But winning had to be on his terms. If he sacrificed a principle to win a point, there had to be a good reason. The Court was his job. He made quick work of whatever was before him. He always had time for his other diversions, and for occasional flights of fancy that suggested his mind wasn't fully occupied with fine points of jurisprudence. Indeed, he even had time for fashion. Which was where the stripes came in.

*Rehnquist was in the majority in 3,351 of the 4,353 cases he participated in.

THIRTY-ONE

Splendor of Stripes

REHNQUIST MUST HAVE BEEN FEELING particularly sprightly when he took the bench on the Tuesday after Martin Luther King Day on January 17, 1995, a day ordinary in every respect save one. Rehnquist began it wearing stripes.

Rehnquist, it was later said by the Court's public information office, had designed the quasi-imperial adornments after seeing something similar on the Lord Chancellor's robe in a community-theater production of Gilbert and Sullivan's *Iolanthe.* Rehnquist took a fancy to it. He affixed four gold stripes to each sleeve of his own robe, and he intended to keep them.

It was another of Rehnquist's private whimsies, and as always with such things there was a backstory. Only the first chief justice, John Jay, had dared to do something similar. Jay wore a scarlet-and-black robe with silver trim. The great John Marshall reverted to black silk in 1801. There the fashion had remained, more or less—with the exception of a brief Bicentennial interlude when the pompous Burger wore a reproduction of Jay's first robe—until Rehnquist decided it was time for a change. Perhaps it was a tweak, or a private joke; Rehnquist never gave a reason. Was it a play for attention, or a snub, or a bit of music-hall variety to liven up the Court, a habit Rehnquist had revealed in his earliest days as an associate justice, often bored by the drabness of it all?

Privately, some of the justices grumbled about this and other vestiges of Rehnquist's idiosyncratic—and highly arbitrary—pronouncements about Supreme Court protocol. Stevens later recalled in his memoir how Rehnquist had been quite taken with the colorful robes worn by some judges at an international conference that the chief attended; when Rehnquist got back home he had tried, unsuccessfully, to get his brethren to change their attire. "We had immediately and uniformly given him a negative response to that suggestion. Nevertheless, with regard to his own robes, he went right ahead."

Rehnquist could be a stickler for the rules as long as they did not apply to him. He insisted that the Court's annual holiday party be called a Christmas party, and when there were objections on religious grounds to the caroling that the chief justice enjoyed leading in the Great Hall, he moved the Christmas festivities to a conference room and kept right on singing.

Terse and no-nonsense when he was conducting business on the bench, Rehnquist was finicky about punctuality and obeying time limits—and never more so than during oral arguments. Rehnquist conducted judicial business with an innate impatience. As Clarence Thomas soon learned when he got to the Court, Rehnquist "could get things done with a glare."

A series of lights on the lectern warned an advocate when his or her time would expire; if Rehnquist were presiding he would immediately cut the person off, even in mid-sentence, when the light turned red. He also rebuked advocates who referred to the justices as "judges" or, later on, to Rehnquist as anything other than "chief justice."

John Paul Stevens didn't understand the petulance, or why Rehnquist was so bristly about being addressed as chief justice. After all, "in addition to sitting in the middle of the bench and presiding over arguments, Bill had affixed four gold stripes on each sleeve of his robes. Any observer could tell that he held a unique position among the nine of us."

Rehnquist insisted on a rigid dress code for those who appeared before the Court as well. No gold stripes for them! It was customary for the government's lawyers, who worked in the solicitor general's office, to appear before the justices in full formal regalia—a cutaway morning coat with tails, striped trousers, and a grey ascot. Paul Bender, the principal deputy solicitor general during Bill Clinton's presidency, recalled Rehnquist writing an officious letter to the solicitor general, complaining about the "inappropriate" dress of one of the women from the solicitor general's office who had just argued a case. The woman had worn a businesslike dark-lavender suit to the Court. She was upset when she saw the letter. The acting solicitor general at the time, Walter Dellinger, wondered what in the world Rehnquist was complaining about. Dellinger wrote back asking for guidance. Did Rehnquist's complaint mean that henceforth all women from the office would have to appear before the justices dressed in a cutaway morning coat and striped trousers, like the men? No, Rehnquist replied. What was inappropriate was the color. The women should wear black, navy, or charcoal grey. No other color. Burger, Rehnquist's supposed opposite, had once chastised the solicitor general's office about the color of a vest; it was the wrong shade of grey.

Rehnquist's intolerance particularly bothered Blackmun, who agonized about it and jotted notes to himself—and for posterity—when he thought Rehnquist was being abusive to advocates or was disrespecting the other justices. Blackmun took notice when Rehnquist shushed one of his brethren, or when he did not honor a tradition such as the justices shaking hands before they took the bench for oral arguments. Fastidiously, sometimes he even cross-referenced his notes so as not to lose track of the slights. Blackmun also filed away newspaper clippings that bore out his own experiences, including one titled "Invoking the wrath of Rehnquist."

When Blackmun felt the sting of Rehnquist's lash, he would get bitter and resort to sarcasm. After someone fired a bullet through the window of Blackmun's apartment in February 1985, Blackmun had stopped driving himself to the Court and switched to having a Court car pick him up and take him back home. Blackmun had received death threats ever since *Roe.* The police wanted Blackmun to have an added measure of security, and Burger approved; the chief had a car and driver, too. But when Rehnquist took over the following year, he wanted to know why Blackmun was getting special treatment—and told him to justify it in writing. Blackmun testily replied in four single-spaced paragraphs that ended: "I shall abide by your judgment on this. I do not wish to embarrass you in any way. I can take the subway. . . ."

THIRTY-TWO

Clinton's Trial

On May 26, 1997, President Bill Clinton was buoyant: he had just negotiated an agreement with Republican congressional leaders promising to balance the federal budget in five years. The economy was way up, along with his approval ratings. And he was on his way to Paris for a North Atlantic Treaty Organization summit, expecting to win agreement on his plan to expand NATO by adding three of the former communist countries in Eastern Europe.

As Clinton jetted to Paris, back in Washington the Supreme Court on May 27 had prepared an unwelcome surprise. It ruled unanimously that Paula Corbin Jones, a former Arkansas state employee, could go ahead with her embarrassing civil lawsuit against Clinton accusing him of making a crude sexual advance toward her while he was the Arkansas governor.

What Clinton could not yet know was that the Supreme Court had just set him on the road to impeachment.

Free to move ahead with their lawsuit against the president, Jones's lawyers pressed Clinton—who was denying Jones's allegations—about his other rumored extramarital affairs. When Clinton lied under oath about his relationship with former White House intern Monica Lewinsky, the stage was set for perjury charges. Clinton's presidency was under siege, his personal reputation was in shreds, and his enemies finally had their evidence of his "high crimes and misdemeanors." Rehnquist, striped robe and all, would preside over the judgment that would be determined by the Senate.

There was a certain irony to Rehnquist's assuming that role in the Senate after a career dedicated to reducing its power. Indeed, just a few weeks after the Court's unanimous decision in *Clinton v. Jones,** the Rehnquist Court issued three rulings striking down laws that Congress had passed over the previous four years: the Religious Freedom Restoration Act was enacted in the name of religious liberty; the Communications Decency Act sought to control sexual materials on the Internet; and the Brady Act required local law enforcement to conduct background checks on gun buyers. All three, the Rehnquist Court said, were infringements either on the prerogatives of the states or on those of the Court itself.

Throughout the summer of 1998, even as Clinton's political troubles multiplied, Rehnquist doubted the will of the House of Representatives to actually move ahead and impeach the president. But Rehnquist underestimated the partisanship that infected the House.

On January 7, 1999, Rehnquist began presiding over the twenty-day Senate trial of Clinton. Given the scant likelihood that the Senate would come up with the 67 votes needed to convict Clinton, Rehnquist's job in the secret proceedings was mainly ceremonial.

Even so, Rehnquist, stripes and all, cared about how history would treat him. He was such a student of the Senate's only other presidential impeachment trial (that of Andrew Johnson, 131 years earlier) that he'd written a book about it, and he knew that any hint of favoritism toward either Clinton or his prosecutors would be judged harshly. He took a firm hand to reduce the rancor and partisanship that had earlier beset the House in its debate on the articles of impeachment. He ruled, for example, that the senators were not merely "jurors," as in a typical trial, but "a court" constituted to determine matters of law as well as fact. That meant the senators—not Rehnquist—would decide by their own vote who would speak, and who (if anyone) would be sworn as a witness for or against Clinton. It was a shrewd move on Rehnquist's part, because even though it seemingly reduced his authority it inoculated him against complaints about even-handedness from one side or the other. If the proceedings devolved, the senators had only themselves to blame.

Rehnquist sat through the deliberations and the speeches by the senators. Finally, shortly after noon on February 12, 1999, the senators served

---

*520 U.S. 681 (1997)

notice that they were ready to vote on the impeachment articles, and the doors to the Senate chamber were thrust open for the first time in a month. There was Rehnquist, posing the final question of the trial: "Senators, how say you? Is the respondent, William Jefferson Clinton, guilty or not guilty?"

When the impeachment articles had failed and everyone had gone back to their regular jobs, Rehnquist set aside for his grandchildren five sets of tickets to the proceedings ("might even acquire intrinsic value by the second half of this century") and made light of his own participation in the proceedings. He had another flight of fancy, deciding to donate the robe he wore, with its distinctive gold stripes, to the Smithsonian Institution—and to value the donation for tax purposes at $30,000, courtesy of an appraisal by Sotheby's.

THIRTY-THREE

"Never Let the War End Until You've Won It"

BECAUSE REHNQUIST HAD MADE NO SECRET of his distaste for a long life on the Court, most thought he would retire sooner rather than later. His elevation to chief justice stopped the rumors, but once George W. Bush was in the White House, speculation as to his departure began anew. Although Rehnquist did nothing to dispel or encourage the rumors (with life tenure, he didn't have to), privately he had come to a different view. One of the things that changed Rehnquist's outlook was Nan's death in 1991. Her long struggle with ovarian cancer left him bereft. Her death turned him from being simply a loner on the Court to someone who seemed simply alone.* The Court represented familiarity. He was no longer so interested in leaving it.

*Rehnquist's longtime friend Cynthia Holcomb Hall, a federal appeals-court judge in Pasadena, California, became closer to him after Nan's death. Hall's husband had died in a plane crash in 1980. Rehnquist and Hall found opportunities to see each other in Washington and California, although on at least one occasion Rehnquist dodged her in favor of his regular poker game. Hall was an enthusiastic planner of birthday parties for the chief. When a Washington gossip column carried a blurb about their budding friendship, Justice Harry Blackmun clipped out the item and saved it. Hall told Rehnquist later that she hadn't liked such attention being paid to their friendship. It "made my life miserable. . . ."

Eight months after Nan's death, Rehnquist was still hewing to the party line that while he enjoyed his job "I wouldn't want to hold it forever." But the reality was different. Once Bill Clinton gained the White House in the 1992 election, those who thought they knew Rehnquist well correctly predicted he would never leave of his own volition with a Democrat in the White House.

What was harder to comprehend, though, was the tenacity with which Rehnquist hung on even after his Court handed the election of 2000 to George W. Bush. Those events created a situation tailor-made for Rehnquist's retirement—having helped Bush to the White House, Rehnquist could make a graceful exit in favor of whichever young conservative Bush anointed. Even Bush expected this. But anyone who thought Rehnquist would step down from the Court had underestimated him. Stubbornly, Rehnquist simply refused to go. He thought retired justices just went on to die.

When Rehnquist returned to the Court in October 2004 for the start of the new term, he was bothered by a persistent sore throat. The chief was also having trouble singing hymns. Finally, he went to a doctor. The eighty-year-old chief justice, a lifelong smoker, had anaplastic thyroid cancer—a type that was aggressive and usually rapidly fatal. Surgeons at Bethesda Naval Hospital moved quickly. They performed a tracheotomy, cutting a hole in his throat through which Rehnquist breathed and spoke.

By the time Rehnquist came out of the hospital on October 29 after a one-week stay, the presidential election was just days away. It made manifest the big stakes looming at the Court: whoever won the election soon would have Rehnquist's seat to fill.

The justices rallied around their chief, sending him notes of encouragement that ranged from perfunctory (Souter and Thomas) to heartfelt (O'Connor). Ginsburg, a cancer survivor, sent Rehnquist her own radiation-therapy "completion certificate." Breyer penned a note telling the chief he was "missing nothing" and reporting the payoff of a $1 bet to Thomas.

Too weak to climb stairs, Rehnquist had a room fixed up in the basement of his Virginia townhouse. Unable to eat, he was fed through a pump directly into his stomach. Chemotherapy only made him more frail. Friends brought him lollipops so that he could have the sensation of taste, but he began refusing them because he did not have the satisfaction of chewing and swallowing food. His weight loss was rapid; his booming baritone voice was gone.

Rehnquist was so debilitated he could not return to the Court, but against all odds and speculation he was determined not to retire. He listened to oral arguments on tape and cast his votes by memo. Staff and clerks ferried mail. Doctors who heard about his plight e-mailed and phoned his office with hopes to involve him in clinical trials, but Rehnquist pushed them aside. Instead, as his sounding boards for second opinions, Rehnquist relied on two trusted, elderly Stanford classmates—one a doctor, the other a lawyer.

With the second inauguration of George W. Bush looming, retirement speculation about Rehnquist ratcheted up again in January 2005. Rehnquist had not been to the Court in the two months since his surgery; Stevens, the senior associate justice, ran the conferences and presided at oral arguments. But Rehnquist was determined to carry on, and to demonstrate that he was well enough not only to serve but also to swear in Bush for his second term on January 20.

The justices' first conference of 2005 was scheduled for Friday, January 7—coincidentally, the thirty-third anniversary of Rehnquist's swearing in as an associate justice. Rehnquist told the other justices that he planned to be there in person. Typically, there would be a small celebration. Stevens, courtly to a fault, dictated a note and had it typed up and delivered to Rehnquist, complimenting the chief "on your fine year-end statement." As usual, Rehnquist had gotten out his annual New Year's Day report about the Court's business right on time, never once mentioning his illness. He was fanatical about hitting his deadlines.

"May I tell you how happy I am that you are going to be at the next Conference," Stevens added.

Getting back to the Court would require energy and orchestration. Rehnquist planned to spend the prior afternoon seeing various doctors at Johns Hopkins University Hospital. He had also made a decision to have the Supreme Court's public information office announce that he wouldn't be on the bench the following Monday for the first oral arguments of the year, due to problems he continued to have with his tracheotomy. Still, Rehnquist maintained an impressive front, and the Supreme Court press corps took note. When reporters started asking questions, a staffer in the Court's press office asked for guidance. What should she tell those who were asking for confirmation of Rehnquist's return to the conference, and about whether the justices had celebrated the chief's anniversary?

Rehnquist's secretary typed up the press-office query and gave it to him. Ever at odds with the media, Rehnquist scrawled a reply: "I have no further comment."

On January 20, Rehnquist made sure that he was present to administer the oath to Bush. In a carefully orchestrated appearance that took all of thirteen minutes, Rehnquist swore in the president in a steady if reedy voice and firmly told him "Congratulations" once the oath was taken.* Then Rehnquist made a quick exit. It would be two more months before Rehnquist would finally return to the bench.

Once the chief returned in March, O'Connor sought him out for a heart-to-heart talk about retirement. O'Connor had already decided that she would soon retire. She was seventy-five years old, and was nearing twenty-four years on the Court. Her husband, John, had Alzheimer's and required care. Rehnquist counseled that both of them shouldn't step down at the same time: "We don't need two vacancies." O'Connor had inferred from their talk that Rehnquist, wracked by cancer, would retire first. Then, she would go a year later. It made sense.

Photographers and television cameras were staked out in front of Rehnquist's Virginia townhouse. Images of the gaunt chief justice in a wheelchair, reminiscent of Douglas's last days at the Court, were splashed all over. When a Fox News producer shouted a question at him about the timing of his possible retirement, Rehnquist replied testily: "That's for me to know, and you to find out."

As the Court's term ended in June 2005, O'Connor went to see Rehnquist again. His illness had placed an extra burden on the others—they had to pick up the slack in opinion writing and felt constrained from engaging in vigorous debate at conferences when the obviously feeble Rehnquist was presiding. But O'Connor was convinced that Rehnquist had made whatever point he intended by sticking out the term. Surely the chief, now safely at the term's end, would be retiring.

Confident of that, O'Connor had already hired her law clerks for the coming year. The transition to a new chief would be hard enough for

---

*Rehnquist had told Bill Clinton "Good luck" after administering the oath at his 1997 inauguration. Exactly one week before, the Court had heard oral arguments in *Clinton v. Jones,* 520 U.S. 681 (1997), the case that would lead to Clinton's impeachment.

the Court without the complications of filling a second vacancy; O'Connor's staying on the extra year would enable a smoother transition.

But when O'Connor spoke to Rehnquist about his plans, she got a surprise. Notwithstanding his rapid decline, Rehnquist stubbornly had not given any consideration to retiring. The chief was emphatic: "I want to stay another year." It really was all about him. In spite of the media's death watch—or, perhaps, *to spite* it—he was going to hang on.

Rehnquist also reminded her about their earlier discussion. He used almost the exact same words: "I don't think we need two vacancies." But now it was clear to O'Connor that she had been wrong all along. Rehnquist was expecting her to step aside. He would die in office. On the spot, she told her old friend that she would call it quits: "Well, okay, I'll retire then."

O'Connor wrote out a letter to the president two days after the Court's term ended. She gave it to the Court's marshal for safekeeping. The marshal was to hold the letter in the Court's safe and then personally deliver it to the White House at the end of the week, Friday, July 1. O'Connor revealed nothing else about the letter or its contents.

The day before the scheduled delivery, the marshal called the White House, proffering the exact message prescribed by O'Connor: "I need to deliver something, a letter, from a justice."

Thus the letter's journey was begun. The marshal would take it to the White House at 10:30 the following morning. By then, O'Connor would be safely out of town. She didn't want to be victimized by the same sort of media feeding frenzy that had swirled around Rehnquist for months.

George W. Bush was not surprised at the call; the White House had been expecting a vacancy and John Roberts already was short-listed. Rumors were rampant. But the inevitable departure was thought to be Rehnquist's, not O'Connor's. Her decision caught everyone by surprise.

In Rehnquist's final months, frail and sick, it would be hard for most to envision him as the young, idealistic partisan that he was when he came to the Court. He had dreaded becoming old and infirm, wondering what it would be like if he were unfortunate enough to live as long as his ninety-one-year-old mother. "Leave the party while you're still having fun," he would counsel. Rehnquist had watched as Bill Douglas finally retired at age seventy-seven after being ravaged by a stroke, with almost everyone but Douglas himself knowing that the old man's retirement was past due. Now Rehnquist was almost eighty-one and desperately ill himself.

But partisans do not quit. "Never let the war end until you've won it," Rehnquist said. Now the chief took his own advice. He was in it to the end.

Somehow, in the midst of the media circus that surrounded his death watch, Rehnquist remembered something: this was just his day job, still the short game. The real zest of life was everything else. There had to be some diversions.

Nearing death, unable to speak, Rehnquist could still communicate by e-mail. Calling himself Felix (as in Frankfurter), the nickname by which he closed his letters to family, had always imparted a humanizing, endearing touch (sometimes the only one) to a man who seemed so brittle. Now, to this partisan who was old and infirm and alone, the nickname became his way of reaching back out. There was a statement to be made. This ending was different.

Out went a surprise message to his family from his new address: felix@sc-us.gov. Henceforth, Rehnquist typed, that was how to reach him.

His son, Jim, could not believe it. He thought he was being spoofed.

"Dad, is this really you?"

"Yes," Rehnquist typed back. "It is really me."

It always was.

ACKNOWLEDGMENTS

THIS BOOK IS DEDICATED TO three editors who believed in me when I was a young journalist starting out. They took a chance on me, and with this book I thank them.

Daryl Royster Alexander was my first editor at the *New York Times Magazine.* She contacted me out of the blue. Someone told her I might be just the ticket for an article that had already hit a shoal in the newsroom by the time we first spoke. After that I was always the one pestering her with ideas, hoping one would catch fire. Three years later I had all but given up on realizing my dream—yes, it was—of writing for the *Times Magazine.* Then came a letter. Daryl had an assignment for me: get an interview with Justice Harry Blackmun. I wondered why no one on the *Times* staff wanted it, even though I could have guessed. Had any justice, let alone Blackmun of *Roe v. Wade* fame, ever granted an interview?

Of course I took it. The Blackmun article that appeared in 1983 was the first of my four cover stories (among many others) for the *Times Magazine.* How I got it is a story unto itself, for another day. But in the course of four hectic months in late 1982 and early 1983 I brought my game up as the Blackmun story came together. I watched and learned from Daryl, my unflappable editor. When the magazine was ready for another story about the Court, it was Daryl's idea to seek out Rehnquist. My *Times Magazine* cover story entitled "The Partisan" led me, twenty-seven years later, to this book. As usual, the best ideas were Daryl's. I owe her.

When Daryl moved over to the national desk, Alex Ward became my new editor at the magazine. I knew Alex only by phone at first. His bluntness came across as hard-bitten cynicism and it made me wary, but I soon realized what a friend and talent he was. I learned to take his advice, and to this day I continue to seek him out and value his mentorship. Alex was the person I called in 1986 when Walter Sheridan, Ted Kennedy's investigator, asked for my help in the Rehnquist confirmation hearings. "Everything you had to say was in that story!" Alex shot back. "Tell him that! Don't become the story! Stay out of it." That was valued advice. I continue to heed it. Alex scored a direct hit, as always.

Michael VerMeulen was a brilliant editor who was twenty years old, if that, when we met. Michael was the dissolute junior on the ragged two-man staff of *Student Lawyer* magazine, published out of Chicago by the American Bar Association, but as far as Michael was concerned it was the *Paris Review* and he was George Plimpton. Michael dreamed big. More to the point, he could pull it off, and he soon persuaded me to write for him. Michael moved on to a storied future as the editor of *British GQ*, and he was the font of many assignments that were out-and-out adventures for me. He died way too soon, at age thirty-eight in 1995, but it still feels like he is on this ride.

I am now three-for-three with my longtime agent Jane Dystel, and her friendship and wise counsel has seen me across the finish line once again. Jane is as no-nonsense as they come, even by New York standards, but I will confess that when she told me in 1986 that she would, indeed, sell my first book, I didn't believe it. Now I know better. I am looking forward to number four.

Clive Priddle of PublicAffairs recognized the potential of this book and showed great patience as I labored to finish it. Once he got his hands on the manuscript, he spent a lot more time with it than I had any right to expect, and he helped to make it a whole lot better. The polishing continued once Sandra Beris and Christine Arden began applying their considerable editorial production and copyediting skills. Each has an eye for detail that is evident throughout.

Carmen Jones-Clad, my valued assistant and closest coworker for nearly all of my fourteen years at CQ Press, was in on this from the beginning, running interference and taking care of whatever arrangements were required. Midway through, I told her she was my own Della Street. Such a class act you are, Carmen.

During the course of this long endeavor, I had three Washington-based research assistants—all of them graduate students at George Washington University—whose tenacious digging yielded many of the documents upon which this book is based. Amanda Rogers put together the initial road map for researching the Rehnquist papers and also mined the FBI's Rehnquist files. Alyssa Hellman spent a week on the scene at Stanford University, and weeks more at the Library of Congress, and brought back a trove of material from each. Chelsey Goff wheedled documents out of archivists at other presidential and university libraries where important things were buried. Chelsey was also my first reader and sounding board. She totally understood this project and stayed with it until it was finished.

When I needed more feet on the ground in Palo Alto, I called Alex Ward for a recommendation. Back came Malia Wollan's name, and she turned out to be both quick and perceptive in combing through files at the Hoover Institution and the Stanford Library. She really had a way of finding things. I was fortunate to have her.

Special thanks to others whose efforts at locating people, documents, and photographs were invaluable: Olu Davis and Joel Treese at CQ Press; Jerry Goldman and Pat Ward of the Oyez Project, Chicago-Kent College of Law; Andrea Hackman, curatorial assistant at the Supreme Court; Susan Hilpisch, assistant to the director at the Center for Advanced Study in the Behavioral Sciences at Stanford University; John Jacob of the Lewis Powell Archives, Washington and Lee University School of Law; Judith Romero, associate director of media relations at Stanford University; Abigail Malangone at the Nixon Presidential Library; and Doug Gavel, associate director of media relations and public affairs at the Harvard Kennedy School of Government. Special thanks, also, to Mark Tushnet at Harvard Law School for his kind permission to reprint footnoted material in Chapter Ten.

I wish to express my thanks, also, to the many friends and colleagues who encouraged me along the way, particularly Ken Allen, Mitch Tropin, Milo Cividanes and Bob Merry. They listened to a lot of stories as my work progressed and always urged me on. Mary Rose Synek and the hundreds of young actors she has taught through the Broadway Bound Fund provided a very special creative inspiration and were a rejuvenative force. Finally, I owe huge thanks to my wife, Susan, and to our children, Jenny, Christie, and Greg. Looking back, their patience and understanding seems nothing short of remarkable. How lucky I am.

CHRONOLOGY

1924 OCTOBER 1: William Donald Rehnquist born in Milwaukee. Changes his middle name to Hubbs in 1943 due to superstition.

1942 JUNE: Rehnquist graduates Shorewood High School. Earns a four-year scholarship to Kenyon College, but quits after one semester.

OCTOBER: He is arrested for vagrancy, Ravenna, Ohio; spends a night in jail.

1943 APRIL 13: He enlists in the Army in Columbus, Ohio. Mainly serves stateside, but gets various exotic North Africa postings in the waning days of the war. Discharged in 1946.

1946 SEPTEMBER: Enters Stanford University. A registrar's snafu starts him off as a second-semester junior.

1948 JANUARY: Receives undergraduate degree from Stanford.

AUGUST: Receives master's degree in political science from Stanford. Begins PhD studies the following month at Harvard.

1950 MARCH: After dropping PhD plans, Rehnquist converts Harvard coursework to a second master's degree in political science. Disgruntled with the Ivy League, he had already returned to Stanford Law School in fall 1949.

1951 DECEMBER: Receives law degree from Stanford.

1952 FEBRUARY: Arrives at the Supreme Court midterm as a clerk for Justice Robert Jackson. Serves until the end of the following term in June 1953.

1953 Marries Natalie (Nan) Cornell in San Diego. The couple moves to Phoenix, Arizona. Rehnquist practices law with various firms for the next sixteen years.

1955 Birth of James (Jim) Rehnquist.

1957 Birth of Janet Rehnquist.

1959 Birth of Nancy Rehnquist.

1969 January 29: Joins Nixon administration as assistant attorney general in the Justice Department's Office of Legal Counsel.

1971 October 21: Nominated by President Richard Nixon to become the Supreme Court's one hundredth member, and its eighty-ninth associate justice.
December 10: Confirmed by the Senate, 68–26.
December 13: Seven sitting justices hear first oral argument in *Roe v. Wade*. Rehnquist and Lewis Powell are not yet sworn in.

1972 January 7: Takes oath of office as associate justice.
October 11: *Roe v. Wade* re-argued before all nine justices. The case is decided on January 22, 1973 by a vote of 7–2, with Rehnquist and Byron White dissenting.

1986 June 17: President Ronald Reagan nominates Rehnquist to become the sixteenth chief justice.
September 17: Rehnquist is confirmed by the Senate, 65–33.
September 26: Takes oath of office as chief justice.

1991 October 17: Wife Nan dies after a five-year battle with ovarian cancer. She is sixty-two years old.

1995 January 17: Rehnquist begins wearing four gold stripes on each sleeve of his judicial robe.

1999 January 7: Presides over twenty-day Senate impeachment trial of President Bill Clinton.
February 12: Impeachment articles fail. Rehnquist declares the proceedings over and returns to the Supreme Court.

2000 December 12: *Bush v. Gore* decided by a vote of 5–4.

2004 October 22: Rehnquist hospitalized for thyroid cancer. Press and public are told on October 25. He does not return to the Court for the remainder of the year.

2005 January 20: Despite his illness, Rehnquist swears in President George W. Bush for a second term.
July 1: Sandra Day O'Connor resigns unexpectedly after Rehnquist tells her he does not intend to quit.
July 19: Bush nominates John Roberts to fill O'Connor's vacancy.
September 3: Rehnquist dies in Arlington, Virginia. He is buried on September 7, at Arlington National Cemetery, next to his wife. Bush changes Roberts's nomination to chief justice two days after Rehnquist's death.

NOTES ON SOURCES

I FIRST MET WILLIAM REHNQUIST in his chambers at the Supreme Court on December 13, 1984, on assignment for the *New York Times Magazine*. Two years earlier, I had conducted lengthy interviews with Justice Harry Blackmun, author of the opinion in *Roe v. Wade,* for the *Times Magazine.* It was time to look at the Court again, through the eyes of a different justice. When my editor, Daryl Royster Alexander, asked which one, I recollect that I didn't give the answer she was looking for. Daryl really needn't have asked at all, because she already had a subject in mind. "I think it just has to be The Dissenter," she told me. "He's the one with the agenda." And so off I went on my next mission.

I wrote a letter to Rehnquist and soon received a reply inviting me to meet with him. He did not promise an interview, or even much of his time. But he was willing to sit down for a chat, and he said he would decide the extent of his involvement in my story once he met me. I resolved to go into that first meeting fully prepared, tape recorder at the ready. When I was inside his office, I turned on the recorder and we began what would turn into two hour-long conversations. The second meeting occurred in his chambers a week later, on December 19. Our final interview, by phone, took place on February 19, 1985, shortly before my *Times Magazine* article was to go to press. All three conversations were recorded with Rehnquist's approval. The interviews were on the record and Rehnquist placed no subject off-limits, although when I asked questions about his health he bristled and refused to answer. I came in with dozens of questions and was able to ask them all.

"The Partisan: A Talk with Justice Rehnquist" appeared in the *New York Times Magazine* on March 3, 1985. The article contained a bombshell: Rehnquist had written not one (as the interlocutors at his 1971 confirmation hearings believed) but *three* segregationist memos while a law clerk at the Court during the term in which *Brown v. Board of Education* was decided. The memos raised new questions about Rehnquist's truthfulness during his confirmation hearings, and would dog him at his future confirmation hearings to become chief justice. Rehnquist didn't like my article (nor did he care for the magazine's cover photograph that he deemed "grim"), but it did make an impression on him. On May 28, 1996, he wrote to the editor of the *Times Magazine* that he would never give another interview because of it—a resolution that he mostly honored for the rest of his life. Rehnquist was not one to seek the limelight, and he felt no need to explain himself. He didn't keep a diary of his Washington years, and he did not write a memoir. Although our paths in Washington sometimes crossed, I never had the occasion or opportunity to speak with him again.

Thus, this investigative biography is based mainly upon the extensive public records documenting Rehnquist's life. Following Rehnquist's death in 2005, much new material became available, including thousands of pages of FBI investigative files (compiled by the bureau for Rehnquist's 1971 and 1986 confirmation hearings) and tens of thousands of pages of Rehnquist's official papers at the Hoover Institution Archives at Stanford University. The Rehnquist collection at Stanford comprises 893 boxes (548 linear feet), of which 349 are open for research. Remaining boxes are closed during the lifetime of any member of the Court who served with Rehnquist. An index of the Rehnquist papers can be found here: http://findingaids.stanford.edu/xtf/view?docId=ead/hoover/rehnquis.xml;query=;brand=default. Documents from the Rehnquist collection at Stanford are identified as *WHR Papers* in the citations below.

Alyssa Hellman, Malia Wollan, and I spent a total of nine days at Stanford reviewing documents in the Rehnquist collection. In addition, I obtained materials from the Richard Nixon Presidential Library in Yorba Linda, California; the Ronald Reagan Presidential Library in Simi Valley, California; the NAACP records at the Library of Congress; the papers of justices Robert Jackson, William O. Douglas, Thurgood Marshall, and Harry A. Blackmun at the Library of Congress in Washington; and the papers of Justice Lewis Powell at Washington and Lee University in Lexington, Virginia. Citations to each justice's papers are keyed to that justice's initials (*RJ, WOD, TM, HAB,* and *LP*). Citations to these papers are given as a box number, followed in some cases by a folio number (e.g., *172/4*). From these and other sources I amassed 12,900 pages of documents that comprise the foundation of this book. Documentary research was supplemented by interviews with law clerks, law professors, and others who knew

Rehnquist or had experiences with him. Interview notes from my earlier *Times Magazine* reporting were pulled from storage and proved useful. Other than interviewing Rehnquist's sister, Jean Laurin, during my research for the *Times,* I did not interview Rehnquist's family. I did seek his children's assistance during fact checking for this book. Rehnquist's son Jim, a Boston attorney, stated that he would act as the family's liaison for this purpose, but thereafter he failed to respond to repeated inquiries.

Rehnquist often addressed family members by nicknames in his letters to them. (He dictated the letters and had a secretary retype them on his Supreme Court letterhead.) If nicknames were used in a letter, they are retained in the citations below, with the given name of the recipient in a parenthetical in the first mention.

I found some books and articles to be particularly influential in my own writing and thus worthy of more than just citation below. Linda Greenhouse, the former Supreme Court reporter for the *New York Times,* wrote numerous articles and blog postings that comprise a valuable body of work about Rehnquist and his decisions. John Dean's *The Rehnquist Choice* provided insight into Nixon's selection of Rehnquist to become associate justice, and its comprehensive source notes were a roadmap for future research. Herman J. Obermayer's *Rehnquist: A Personal Portrait,* written from a friend's perspective, showed a seldom-seen side of Rehnquist. Joan Biskupic's *American Original: The Life and Constitution of Antonin Scalia* contained excellent reporting about Rehnquist's selection by Ronald Reagan to become chief justice in 1986. *Supreme Conflict,* by Jan Crawford Greenburg, has the best account I found anywhere of the interplay between Rehnquist and Sandra Day O'Connor during the final months of Rehnquist's life. See the bibliography for other books and articles that proved useful. Books and articles are cited below with the author's last name and relevant page numbers.

There are numerous sites on the Web that provide access to the White House tapes of Richard Nixon. I found two sites to be especially useful: the Presidential Recordings Program at the Miller Center of Public Affairs, University of Virginia (http://whitehousetapes.net), and American Public Media (http://americanradioworks.publicradio.org/features/prestapes). Tapes and transcripts from the Miller Center are referenced as *MC* and from American Public Media as *APM.* The Nixon Library has a special link for taped White House conversations about or with Supreme Court justices:

http://nixonlibrary.gov/forresearchers/find/subjects/supreme-court.php. Special thanks to Abigail Malangone at the Nixon Library for fact checking and verification of all Rehnquist-related conversations.

Chelsey D. Goff checked Rehnquist's educational dates and records at the various institutions he attended, and any discrepancies that she found are noted in these source notes, or in footnotes.

Citations to Supreme Court cases were verified using *The Oxford Companion to the Supreme Court,* 2nd edition.

Where someone's age is listed, it is that person's age at the time the events being described were taking place.

Where a person is said to have "thought" or "believed" something, such an attribution is based on a comment by that person, either to me or to someone I subsequently interviewed, or previously in print.

No one who was interviewed received payment; no person received any assurances as to how he or she would be portrayed or how his or her comments would be used; and no one who was interviewed reviewed the manuscript before publication.

All significant citations can be found below except when, in deference to a source, I have preserved confidentiality.

In the notes that follow, *WHR* stands for William H. Rehnquist. A list of researchers appears in the front of this book. Where someone who performed research is cited, initials are used: *CDG* stands for Chelsey D. Goff and *AH* stands for Alyssa Hellman. They, along with Amanda Rogers and Malia Wollan, performed amazing feats in gathering documents, and this book could not have been written without them.

INTRODUCTION

xiii **"I'll give you one last bit of advice":** Nixon phone call to WHR, December 10, 1971, 5:18 P.M. APM. Note: According to White House logs, this call lasted two minutes.

xiv **Only seventeen men have presided:** Useful context is provided by the opening remarks of Senator Edward M. Kennedy at Rehnquist's 1986 confirmation hearings. General link to hearings: http://gpo.gov/fdsys/pkg/GPO-CHRG-REHNQUIST/content-detail.html. Kennedy's remarks: http://gpo.gov/fdsys/pkg/GPO-CHRG-REHNQUIST/pdf/GPO-CHRG-REHNQUIST-2-10.pdf.

xv **"John Roberts is proving to be an absolutely first-rate law clerk" (fn 1):** Snyder, "The Judicial Genealogy (and Mythology) of John Roberts," p. 1223.

xv **left behind no memoir:** "Head of the Class," by Charles Lane, *Stanford Magazine,* July/August 2005, quoting an interview between Rehnquist and Charlie Rose of PBS in 2001.

xvi **participation was "under duress":** Author interview with WHR, December 19, 1984. Because he believed the *Times Magazine* story would be written regardless, Rehnquist added: "I don't regard [the interview] as a voluntary thing."

xvi **Nixon telephoned his attorney general:** Nixon phone call to John Mitchell, October 21, 1971. APM.

xvii **"a reactionary bastard":** Nixon phone call to John Mitchell, October 21, 1971. APM.

xvii **Rehnquist privately grumbled about the liberal media:** Author interview with WHR, December 19, 1984.

xvii **"If you're bothered by what the press says about you":** Author interview with WHR, December 13, 1984.

xviii **"Justices fall into three types":** Author interview with Margaret Hermann, October 15, 2011. Also, "Supreme Court Justices' Leadership Styles: What Kind of Leader and Why?" unpublished AP/LS Conference Proposal, received October 26, 2011, by Jeremy A. Blumenthal, Azmat Sakiev, and Margaret G. Hermann.

xviii **results and efficiency are what matter:** See Snyder, "The Judicial Genealogy (and Mythology) of John Roberts," p. 1224.

xviii **She was a University of Wisconsin English literature major who spoke five languages:** Author interview with Jean Laurin (WHR's sister), February 18, 1985.

xviii **In 1939, his parents defaulted:** This and other information from county records was first reported in "A Chief Justice-Designate with Big Ambitions," by George Lardner, Jr., and Saundra Saperstein, *Washington Post,* July 6, 1986.

xviii **entries in the first of several journals:** WHR Papers, Box 1.

xix **"Next week I will be 62 years old":** WHR Papers, Box 172/6.

xx **Harry Blackmun . . . wrote to the young justice:** HAB Papers, Box 1407/7.

xx **"I did nothing in particular, and I did it very well" (fn):** Quoted in Barrett, "A Rehnquist Ode on the Vinson Court," p. 297.

xx **attributes authorship of the majority opinion to Justice Anthony Kennedy (fn):** Toobin, *The Nine,* p. 205.

xxi **Rehnquist quixotically would compare himself:** Author interview with WHR, December 19, 1984.

xxi **"arguments we would get into as law clerks":** Author interview with WHR, December 19, 1984.

xxi **"You equate *change* with *growth*?":** Author interview with WHR, December 13, 1984.

CHAPTER ONE: SHOREWOOD

1 **Rehnquist was born in Milwaukee on October 1, 1924 [birth date, other biographical information]:** Security clearance form and passport applications in WHR Papers, Box 353.

1 **"I feel sad to get no more translations" (fn 2):** Margery Rehnquist letter to WHR, WHR Papers, Box 172/6.

1 **Rehnquists settled in Shorewood . . . "village full of Republicans" . . . "no blacks":** Lardner and Saperstein, "A Chief Justice-Designate with Big Ambitions."

2 **"Everybody we knew was pretty much Republican":** Lardner and Saperstein, "A Chief Justice-Designate with Big Ambitions."

2 **recalled memorable experiences for his grandson in a 2003 letter . . . "My [fifth-grade] homeroom teacher was named Miss Wild":** WHR letter to Thomas (Rehnquist, WHR's grandson), October 6, 2003, in WHR Papers, Box 172/8.

2 **He showed a competitive streak early on:** WHR letter to Thomas (Rehnquist), October 6, 2003, in WHR Papers, Box 172/8.

2 **"one of the ten best in the country":** Author interview with Roy Genskow, February 13, 1985.

2 **Charlotte Wollaeger, who taught English and speech to Rehnquist:** Author interview with Charlotte Wollaeger, February 12, 1985.

3 **Genskow came up two years behind Rehnquist at Shorewood:** Author interview with Roy Genskow, February 13, 1985.

3 **Shorewood High reflected its all-white community . . . spring prom featured a Harlem theme:** Lardner and Saperstein, "A Chief Justice-Designate with Big Ambitions."

3 **"blacks weren't a factor in his life at all":** Author interview with Roy Genskow, February 13, 1985.

4 **Rehnquist's sister, Jean, was three years younger than Bill:** Author interview with Jean Laurin, February 18, 1985.

4 **Politics permeated the household:** That comment and others in this paragraph are from author interview with Jean Laurin, February 18, 1985.

4 **neighbor from across the street, Guy Scrivner:** Author interview with Guy Scrivner, February 13, 1985.

5 **"I can still remember all of us being herded into the auditorium":** WHR speech at Shorewood High School, May 24, 2002, found in WHR Papers, Box 262.

5 **appointed 15 block captains, including Rehnquist:** *Shorewood Ripples,* student newspaper, January 16, 1942, author research at Shorewood High School library.

5 **for one final celebration:** WHR speech at Shorewood High School, May 24, 2002, found in WHR Papers, Box 262.

CHAPTER TWO: A CHANGE OF NAME AND PLACE

7 **Rehnquist's full scholarship to Kenyon College:** *Shorewood Ripples,* April 24, 1942.

8 **spending his Saturday night in jail:** From Security Investigation Data for Sensitive Position, filled out by WHR on January 30, 1969, in WHR Papers, Box 353/4.

8 **Kenyon reciprocated, never claiming him as its own:** "A Political Omission," *Kenyon College Alumni Bulletin* 28, no. 4 (Spring/Summer 2006).

9 **changed his middle name to Hubbs:** Roberts, "William H. Rehnquist: A Remembrance," p. 432, tells the story of the numerologist. Rehnquist also explained

the Hubbs ancestry in a letter to Doyle Hubbs dated June 9, 1998, which was posted on the Hubbs Family Genealogy Forum. Rehnquist confessed to being "naturally superstitious" in a note to Blackmun, HAB Papers, Box 1407/12.

9 **Rehnquist was definitive about the timing of the name change—"at time of entry into the Army" (fn 1):** From Security Investigation Data for Sensitive Position, filled out by WHR on January 30, 1969, in WHR Papers, Box 353/4.

9 **Denison has no record of this (fn 2):** CDG research, Dennison University Office of Communications, August 1, 2011.

10 **The program closed down . . . "I had had enough spit and polish":** WHR speech to American Meteorological Society, October 23, 2001.

10 **It was still a time of racial segregation—the US military would not integrate its ranks until 1948. White soldiers received what were seen as preferential assignments:** "Veteran Remembers Army Integration Sixty Years Ago," by Elizabeth M. Lorge, Army News Service, July 22, 2008, found at http://www.army.mil/article/11071/veteran-remembers-army-integration-60-years-ago/. Note: This article is posted to the Army's official website and constitutes an authorized history, with contributions from the US Army Center for Military History. The article states: "Sixty years ago, the United States had two armies—a white Army and a black one. . . . Integration was possible because of Executive Order 9981, signed by President Harry Truman on July 26, 1948. It called for equal treatment and opportunity for black servicemen."

10 **Rehnquist was sent to Will Rogers Field:** WHR speech to American Meteorological Society, October 23, 2001.

CHAPTER THREE: "HATE BLACK"

13 **"if you lived in the right climate":** WHR speech at Shorewood High School, May 24, 2002, found in WHR Papers, Box 262.

13 **"a more equable climate":** Typewritten notes dated June 20, 1973, for WHR speech to State Bar of Wisconsin, AH research, WHR Papers, Box 200/3.

13 **"I wanted to find someplace like North Africa to go to school":** Author interview with WHR, February 19, 1985.

14 **"I think they gave me credit for all sorts of very non-academic stuff":** Author interview with WHR, December 19, 1984.

14 **As a soldier in North Africa, Rehnquist had read *The Road to Serfdom*:** *Stanford Magazine,* quoting a 2001 interview with Brian Lamb of C-SPAN.

14 **Hayek's book had an impact on Rehnquist:** letter to Weakfish (Jim Rehnquist) dated June 14, 2004, WHR Papers, Box 172/4.

14 **Fairman became Rehnquist's mentor and role model:** Lane, "Head of the Class."

14 **It was the first book Rehnquist ever read about the Constitution:** Author interview with WHR, December 19, 1984.

15 **The Stanford professor became a darling of the political right:** Lane, "Head of the Class," contains excellent background information about Fairman's influence on Rehnquist. For further context about Fairman and his views, see Wildenthal, "Nationalizing the Bill of Rights."

16 **Fairman's shadow seemed always to lurk:** Lane, "Head of the Class."

17 **"the Black group" penned the words "Hate Black" . . . :** WHR Papers, Box 1.

17 **Frankfurter—Black's opponent on and off the bench:** See Aynes, "Charles Fairman, Felix Frankfurter, and the Fourteenth Amendment."

17 **Rehnquist would adopt Frankfurter's first name:** WHR Papers, Box 353/12.

17 **"there was no way you could go about it":** Interview with Brian Lamb on C-SPAN, 2001.

18 **"What now, Hon. W. H. Rehnquist?":** WHR Papers, Box 1.

CHAPTER FOUR: BASIC MORAL RIGHTS

19 **Stanford's founder actually had modeled Encina Hall:** *Stanford Magazine,* September/October 1998, "The Bad Boys of Encina Hall," by Karen Bartholomew.

21 **"arranged to get a Master's degree":** Author interview with WHR, December 19, 1984.

22 **post-Stanford stasis of Rehnquist's views . . . *DeShaney*:** Kmiec, "Young Mr. Rehnquist's Theory of Moral Rights—Mostly Observed," p. 1856: "It is quite obvious that the *DeShaney* opinion tracks the young Rehnquist's distinction between negative and positive liberties."

23 **drive back to Wisconsin:** WHR Papers, Box 3, Notebook 1.

24 **"whether I had arranged the bibliography":** Letter to Bombna (Nancy Rehnquist), April 30, 1981, WHR Papers, Box 172/11.

24 **intended to begin working on a PhD in political theory:** Letter to Weakfish (Jim Rehnquist), February 13, 1979, WHR Papers, Box 172/4.

24 **Rehnquist simply admired the professor for bringing the characters to life:** Letter to Weakfish (Jim Rehnquist), February 22, 1982, WHR Papers, Box 172/4.

24 **Harvard would prepare him . . . to be a political philosopher:** Letter to Weakfish (Jim Rehnquist), February 13, 1979, WHR Papers, Box 172/4.

24 **quickly led to disappointment and despair:** Letter to Tim Spears (son-in-law), February 14, 1989, WHR Papers, Box 172/9.

24 **"I had a feeling there was more preciousness":** Letter to Weakfish (Jim Rehnquist), February 13, 1979, WHR Papers, Box 172/4.

24 **admitted that he was depressed:** Letter to Tim Spears, February 14, 1989, WHR Papers, Box 172/9.

24 **"liberal blatherers":** Lane, "Head of the Class," quoting former Rehnquist clerk Craig Bradley.

24 **"I did not very much cotton":** Letter to Tim Spears, February 14, 1989, WHR Papers, Box 172/9.

24 **"He said he just couldn't take Harvard liberalism":** Lardner and Saperstein, "A Chief Justice-Designate with Big Ambitions."

25 **"took some vocational tests . . . so I decided to go to law school":** Letter to Tim Spears, February 14, 1989, WHR Papers, Box 172/9.

25 **Harvard was "a blessing in disguise":** Letter to Tim Spears, February 14, 1989, WHR Papers, Box 172/9.

25 **Cornell was five years younger than Bill Rehnquist; he met her during the summer of 1951 (fn 2):** Lane, "Head of the Class."

25 **"intellectual awakening":** Letter to Weakfish (Jim Rehnquist), February 28, 1981, WHR Papers, Box 172/4.

26 **"outlandishly conservative and outlandishly bright":** Lane, "Head of the Class."

26 **"Articulate and abrupt" was Baxter's characterization":** Lardner and Saperstein, "A Chief Justice-Designate with Big Ambitions."

26 **Stanford did not rank its law school classes:** CDG interview with Judith Romero, associate director of media relations, Stanford University, July 7, 2011.

CHAPTER FIVE: ON TO WASHINGTON

I relied on Rehnquist's book, *The Supreme Court,* for its reminiscences of the events leading to his clerkship interview with Jackson, the interview itself, and his 1952–1953 clerkship at the Supreme Court. I also drew on Rehnquist's characterizations of the various justices who were on the bench during his clerkship, and of Felix Frankfurter's mentorship. The correspondence between Rehnquist and Jackson is from the Jackson Papers at the Library of Congress, Box 19/3. Phil C. Neal's recollection of Rehnquist—"He was a very strong student, a pretty mature fellow"—came from Charles Lane's excellent article in *Stanford Magazine.* Lane also provides a detailed account of the events leading up to Rehnquist's getting the clerkship with Jackson.

CHAPTER SIX: AN "UNHUMANITARIAN POSITION," AND OTHER MEMOS

34 **clerks as a group harbored "extreme solicitude for the claims of communists":** The quote is from Rehnquist's article, "Who Writes Decisions of the Supreme Court," *U.S. News & World Report,* December 13, 1957.

34 **how delighted all seven of Rehnquist's colleagues were . . . "almost a unanimous feeling of joy":** "The Rehnquist Years," by David J. Garrow, *New York Times Magazine,* October 6, 1996. Direct url: http://www.nytimes.com/1996/10/06/magazine/the-rehnquist-reins.html?pagewanted=all&src=pm.

35 **At issue in *Plessy* . . . *Brown* had its origins . . . Another case, *Terry v. Adams:*** *Oxford Companion to the Supreme Court,* 2nd ed.

38 **"A Random Thought on the Segregation Cases":** See Kluger, *Simple Justice,* p. 605. The memo is also contained in the Jackson Papers, Box 184.

40 **Jackson had his own concerns:** Kluger, *Simple Justice,* p. 609.

40 **The justices called a second round of arguments:** *Oxford Companion to the Supreme Court,* p. 111. For a *Brown* timeline, also see http://archives.gov/education/lessons/brown-v-board/timeline.html.

40 **Rehnquist wrote two revealing memos about *Terry* . . . "recommend a grant":** Undated memo (first of two) from WHR to Jackson, in author's files.

41 **wrapped up his argument with a recommendation that Jackson file a dissent:** Undated memo (second of two) from WHR to Jackson, in author's files.

42 **Hutchinson told me that after inspecting all of the justice's papers:** Author interview with Dennis Hutchinson, January 16, 1985.

42 **Adding to the weight of the evidence was a letter that Rehnquist wrote to Felix Frankfurter in 1955:** See Snyder and Barrett, "Rehnquist's Missing Letter." Rehnquist's 1955 letter to Frankfurter is missing from the Frankfurter Papers at the Library of Congress and is presumed to have been stolen. The authors were able to reconstruct Rehnquist's letter based upon a contemporaneous account of it in a letter to Frankfurter from E. Barrett Prettyman, Jr., who succeeded Rehnquist as Jackson's clerk. The Prettyman letter of October 13, 1955, is reprinted at Snyder and Barrett, "Rehnquist's Missing Letter," p. 28. Snyder and Barrett "conclude[d] that Rehnquist's letter to Frankfurter primarily reflects Rehnquist's disappointment with *Brown* and the Warren Court. . . . In our view Rehnquist's disappointment with Brown provides the most plausible motivation for his harsh 1955 letter about Jackson." See also "Memo Adds to Doubts on Rehnquist's Denials," by Adam Liptak, *New York Times,* March 20, 2012. Liptak quotes Prettyman that "there is absolutely no doubt in my mind" that Rehnquist's 1952 *Plessy* memo represented Rehnquist's own views, not Jackson's. Prettyman told Liptak that he thought Rehnquist's harsh assessment of Jackson in the 1955 letter to Frankfurter reflected the rocky relationship between Jackson and Rehnquist. Prettyman was even blunter in comments to Synder and Barrett, as they explain in footnote 14 of their article: "Prettyman recalled the look on Jackson's face and the tone of his voice . . . indicating that Jackson thought that Rehnquist had deliberately undermined and disrespected him. According to Prettyman, Rehnquist disapproved of Jackson even before the Court decided *Brown* because Rehnquist foresaw the possibility that Jackson would support the Court's decision. Prettyman suggested that Rehnquist praised Jackson following Rehnquist's clerkship for reasons of expediency and to protect his future. Jackson's death, Prettyman concluded, liberated Rehnquist to reveal his true anti-Jackson feelings to Frankfurter." At footnote 13, the authors also quote another former Jackson clerk, the late James M. Marsh, who recalled friction between Jackson and Rehnquist, as well as between Rehnquist and his co-clerk Donald Cronson. After Rehnquist and Cronson, Jackson returned to the practice of hiring only one clerk per term.

43 **"Well, I think before, there was a perfectly reasonable argument the other way." For the first and only time in his public life, he owned up to the segregationist stance he'd taken while a law clerk:** Author interview with WHR, February 19, 1985.

45 **A "rather grim visage of me on the front cover," he wrote his sister Jean:** Letter to Jean Laurin, March 11, 1985, WHR Papers, Box 172/3. Rehnquist continued: "John Jenkins, the author, told me that he had talked to you on the telephone, and I can see from some of the information that he got about our dinner table conversation at home that your recollections were not too different from mine."

CHAPTER SEVEN: "LIKE A BUNCH OF OLD WOMEN"

Background on the *Rosenberg* case comes mainly from contemporaneous accounts in the *New York Times,* from the justices' own writings in the *Rosenberg* case, and from historical accounts in *The Oxford Companion to the Supreme Court* and *The American Judicial Tradition* by G. Edward White.

Sources other than the above follow:

45 **took the communist threat seriously:** Rehnquist made this quite clear in "Who Writes Decisions of the Supreme Court," *U.S. News & World Report,* December 13, 1957.

46 **"in an atmosphere in which the barbarity of capital punishment coalesced with the hysteria of anti-Communism":** White, *The American Judicial Tradition,* p. 350.

47 **"recited the history of this unusual case at length because we think a full recitation is necessary" (fn):** The quoted comments appear at *Rosenberg v. United States,* 346 U.S. 273, 285 and 346 U.S. 273, 287.

47 **Rehnquist was elated . . . he wrote back to Jackson . . . "I admired the opinion that you wrote":** Undated letter from WHR to Jackson, Jackson Papers, Box 19/3. Rehnquist's letter had to have been written sometime before July 13, 1953, the date of Jackson's reply.

48 **Jackson told him to go right ahead:** Jackson letter to WHR, July 13, 1953, Jackson Papers, Box 19/3.

CHAPTER EIGHT: HANGING JUDGE

Rehnquist's admiration for "Hanging Judge" Parker and the account of his trip to Ft. Smith are from his speech titled "Isaac Parker, Bill Sykes, and the Rule of Law," delivered at the University of Arkansas at Little Rock, September 23, 1983. Rehnquist's disillusionment with excessive appeals in criminal cases, and with the case of Jimmy Lee Gray in particular, also is vividly set forth in this speech. To the best of my knowledge this speech is not in Rehnquist's papers at Stanford and is not available from the Supreme Court. It is in my files.

Sources other than the above follow:

53 **"He likes to get his work done and get home":** Author interview with Ron Blunt, January 7, 1985.

54 **Among Jackson's papers, wrote author Garrow, was another Rehnquist memo:** Garrow, "The Rehnquist Years," *New York Times Magazine,* October 6, 1996.

55 **In *McCleskey,* another *habeas* case from Georgia, the Court accepted the validity of a study prepared by David C. Baldus . . . Powell was asked by his biographer whether there was any vote he would have liked to change (fn 3):** The description of Baldus's role in *McCleskey,* and of Powell's later regret, is from Baldus's obituary, "David C. Baldus, 75, Dies; Studied Race and the Law," by Adam Liptak, *New York Times,* June 15, 2011. Note: Toward the end of his opinion in *McCleskey,* Powell suggested that state legislatures were more qualified to judge how statistics should be used in death-penalty cases. Twenty-five years later, two states—Kentucky and North Carolina—had laws that allowed statistical studies of racial disparity to be used by those facing the death penalty. A landmark 2012 judicial ruling in North Carolina marked the first time that state's law had resulted in a death sentence being commuted to life without parole. See "Bias Law Used to Move a Man off Death Row," by Campbell Robertson, *New York Times,* April 21, 2012.

56 **"the entire pace of death-row executions all across America":** Garrow, "The Rehnquist Years," *New York Times Magazine,* October 6, 1996.

57 **"often appeared to be remarkably mean spirited, more so perhaps than any member of the modern court" . . . wanted "corpses to pile up" . . . "the very nature of the nominee":** "Cold, Cold Heart," by Nat Hentoff, *Washington Post,* August 6, 1986.

57 **The punishment Rehnquist considered cruel and unusual, "and rightly so": hard labor while in chains:** Author interview with WHR, December 19, 1984.

57 **Rehnquist had high praise for the British practice of allowing few appeals from trial-court judgments in criminal cases, and of punishing those whose appeals are later deemed frivolous:** From a speech delivered by Rehnquist on October 20, 1983, at the Grand Opera House, Macon, Georgia. The speech is reprinted at 35 *Mercer Law Review* 1015 (1984).

57 **reminisce about his early days practicing law in Phoenix . . . only federal judge was an FDR appointee named Dave Ling:** From a speech entitled "Seen in a Glass Darkly: The Future of the Federal Courts," delivered by Rehnquist at the Fourth Circuit Judicial Conference on June 26, 1993. WHR Papers, Box 237/1.

CHAPTER NINE: RUGGED LIBERTARIANISM

59 **four hundred lawyers in all of Maricopa County:** Lardner and Saperstein, "A Chief Justice-Designate with Big Ambitions."

59 **arrived there in July 1953:** WHR letter to Jackson, July 13, 1953, Jackson Papers, Box 19/3.

59 **More than half the streets were unpaved:** Obermayer, *Rehnquist: A Personal Portrait,* p. 36.

59 **had no friends, and knew exactly one person:** Letter to Jim Rehnquist, October 17, 1988, WHR Papers, Box 172/4.

59 **Roberts added some grace notes to the legend:** Roberts, "William H. Rehnquist: A Remembrance," p. 433.

60 **flipped a coin to make his decision:** "Rehnquist Is Described as a Firm Conservative," by Martin Waldron, *New York Times,* October 28, 1971.

60 **Nan grew up in Phoenix:** Natalie Cornell Rehnquist obituary, *Arizona Republic,* October 18, 1991.

60 **name partner was Denison Kitchel:** Denison Kitchel obituary, *New York Times,* October 22, 2002; also Obermayer, *Rehnquist: A Personal Portrait,* pp. 33–35 and 186.

61 **"appearance on the national scene can be traced directly to an obscure political machine in the Sun Belt city of Phoenix, Arizona . . . Luck put Bill in right place":** Obermayer, *Rehnquist: A Personal Portrait,* p. 33.

61 **Kitchel's connections:** Obermayer, *Rehnquist: A Personal Portrait,* p. 34.

61 **"Barry Goldwater was his philosophical soul mate":** Obermayer, *Rehnquist: A Personal Portrait,* p. 35.

61 **earned $300 a month:** Letter to Jim Rehnquist, June 19, 1989, WHR Papers, Box 172/4.

61 **tried and failed to get Kitchel to raise his salary by $50 a month:** Roberts, "William H. Rehnquist: A Remembrance," p. 433.

62 **When the work finally did start coming, it wasn't exactly the kind that Rehnquist desired. He wanted to get into the courtroom:** Letter to Jim Rehnquist, October 17, 1988, WHR Papers, Box 172/4.

62 "**was much too ambitious and independent to remain the protégé of a domineering intellectual for long":** Obermayer, *Rehnquist: A Personal Portrait,* p. 39.

62 **"It was a revelation to talk to someone [conservative] who had thought out positions":** Quoted in Lardner and Saperstein, "A Chief Justice-Designate with Big Ambitions."

62 **James in 1955, Janet in 1957, and Nancy in 1959 . . . spacious home at 1617 Palmcroft Drive . . . Rehnquist's Arizona investments . . . Rehnquists in 1954 built a small tract home (fn):** From Rehnquist's security clearance form and financial disclosure form, prepared and sworn to when he joined the Nixon administration, WHR Papers, Box 353.

CHAPTER TEN: "WHAT THE COURT REALLY NEEDS IS A CHIEF JUSTICE"

Rehnquist's early political activism is well documented in the NAACP Records at the Library of Congress, and much of the material in this chapter comes from that collection. The NAACP conducted investigations into Rehnquist's past and gathered other materials about Rehnquist during his 1971 and 1986 confirmation hearings.

Sources other than the above follow:

66 **last letter to his former boss Jackson:** WHR letter to Jackson, April 16, 1954, Jackson Papers, Box 19/3.

69 **"I am a lawyer without a client tonight":** 1971 confirmation hearings, p. 305. Also available at http://gpo.gov/fdsys/pkg/GPO-CHRG-REHNQUIST-POWELL/pdf/GPO-CHRG-REHNQUIST-POWELL-7-4-4.pdf.

70 **"The ordinance, of course, does not and cannot":** 1971 confirmation hearings, p. 307. Also available at http://gpo.gov/fdsys/pkg/GPO-CHRG-REHNQUIST-POWELL/pdf/GPO-CHRG-REHNQUIST-POWELL-7-4-5.pdf.

70 **"We are no more dedicated to an 'integrated' society than we are to a 'segregated' society":** 1971 confirmation hearings, p. 309. Also available at http://gpo.gov/fdsys/pkg/GPO-CHRG-REHNQUIST-POWELL/pdf/GPO-CHRG-REHNQUIST-POWELL-7-4-6.pdf.

73 **Goldwater . . . would vote *against* the bill:** Obermayer, *Rehnquist: A Personal Portrait,* p. 42, states flatly that Goldwater's opposition to the Act was Rehnquist's idea. Goldwater's views were closely followed and catalogued at the time by the *New York Times,* January 19, 1964, and February 17, 1964.

74 **Rehnquist wrote Goldwater's unapologetic concession remarks:** Obermayer, *Rehnquist: A Personal Portrait,* p. 4.

CHAPTER ELEVEN: COWBOYS IN WASHINGTON

Background on Richard Kleindienst, the description of his involvement with Richard Nixon's 1960 and 1968 presidential campaigns, his recruitment of Rehnquist to join the Justice Department, and John Mitchell's initial opposition to Rehnquist comes from

Justice: The Memoirs of Attorney General Richard G. Kleindienst, published in 1985. John Dean's recollections of Rehnquist's early days at Justice come from Dean's book, *The Rehnquist Choice.*

Sources other than the above follow:

76 **The two men shared the same conservative outlook and resentment toward the Eastern elite:** Obermayer, *Rehnquist: A Personal Portrait,* p. 44.

77 **Phoenix public library to determine what the Office of Legal Counsel actually did:** Roberts, "William H. Rehnquist: A Remembrance," p. 434.

77 **submitted his paperwork to Egil Krogh and John Ehrlichman:** WHR Papers, Box 353.

77 **Mitchell fought, went to prison, lost everything, but never ratted out Nixon:** Mitchell obituary, *New York Times,* November 10, 1988.

77 **Mitchell's photograph Rehnquist kept on view:** Author interview with WHR, December 19, 1984.

77 **The rent suited the frugal Rehnquist:** WHR Papers, Box 3.

77 **Rehnquist wrote to a mutual friend that he hoped Kleindienst would be acquitted (fn):** Letter to Cynthia [presumably Judge Cynthia Holcomb Hall], September 21, 1981, in WHR Papers, Box 172.

78 **objection the NAACP had raised:** Waldron, "Rehnquist Is Described As a Firm Conservative," *New York Times,* October 28, 1971.

79 **"The world of his youthful ideals had turned sour and neurotic . . ." (Holroyd quote from Strachey biography):** Holroyd, *Lytton Strachey,* p. 28.

80 **Did Rehnquist seek acceptance yet absorb the private pain of criticism?:** Rehnquist acknowledged on the record during our December 13, 1984, interview to being "a little bit" bothered by the public criticism of his prescription drug addiction. The admission is significant given his otherwise steadfast refusal ever to discuss the incident.

80 **Rehnquist cut quite a figure upon his return to the Nation's Capital:** Although many have commented on this, see in particular the observations of Roberts, "William H. Rehnquist: A Remembrance," p. 435.

80 **"I did not think moving to Washington would be like moving to Boston":** Letter to Jim Rehnquist, February 22, 1982, WHR Papers, Box 172/4.

80 **"This is in truth a 'one industry' town":** Letter to Jean Laurin, January 14, 1981, WHR Papers, Box 172/3.

80 **Rehnquist put together a nineteen-page memorandum for John Dean:** Dean, *The Rehnquist Choice,* p. 268. Note: Although Dean had the April 1, 1969, memo and wrote about it in his 2001 book, the memo was marked "administratively confidential" and was not revealed to the senators who voted twice to confirm Rehnquist to the Supreme Court. Thomas W. Davies, a professor at the University of Tennessee College of Law and a legal historian, later succeeded in obtaining the document from the National Archives. I have relied on Dean's account here, although commentators who also later obtained it, such as Yale Kamisar, give similar descriptions.

80 **"it was more like a smoking cannon" . . . "a brutal critique":** Dean, *The Rehnquist Choice,* pp. 268–269.

82 **"new barbarians":** Quoted in Lynn Pearle memorandum, November 4, 1971, NAACP Records, Box IX:17/5.

82 **"original barbarians":** Quoted in Lardner and Saperstein, "A Chief Justice-Designate with Big Ambitions."

83 **"Law and order will be pursued at whatever cost in individual liberties and rights":** Quoted in the *Boston Globe,* February 16, 1975, WHR Papers, Box 3.

83 **"I was offering this as a dire prediction of what might happen":** Letter to Jim Rehnquist, April 2, 1975, WHR Papers, Box 172/4.

83 **He made plans to visit fifty college campuses, "trying to get live human beings on the other side of the discussion table":** *Albuquerque Tribune,* November 17, 1970, WHR Papers, Box 3.

83 **"Cost versus value is something that will have to be evaluated":** *Arizona Republic,* November 19, 1970, WHR Papers, Box 3.

84 **Rehnquist styled himself as the administration's resident constitutional theorist:** Lardner and Saperstein, "A Chief Justice-Designate with Big Ambitions."

84 **the *Washington Post* editorialized against G. Harrold Carswell . . . letter to the paper from Rehnquist . . . lectured government whistleblowers in the *Civil Service Journal:*** Quoted in Lynn Pearle memorandum, November 4, 1971, NAACP Records, Box IX:17/5.

85 **"The overall implication of the equal rights amendment":** Reagan Library, Peter Wallison Files, OA 14287.

85 **Rehnquist to be the spokesman . . . "no-knock searches":** "The Rehnquist Court," by David G. Savage, *Los Angeles Times,* September 29, 1991.

86 **Any system that "permits a convicted defendant to spend the next ten or twenty years litigating the validity of the procedures used in his trial is a contradiction in terms":** Quoted in Lynn Pearle memorandum, November 4, 1971, NAACP Records, Box IX:17/5.

87 **Charges against most of the protesters were dropped and the government eventually paid millions of dollars in damages:** Lardner and Saperstein, "A Chief Justice-Designate with Big Ambitions."

87 **But Nixon and Attorney General Mitchell were pleased:** MC, White House Conversation Number 492-003, with Nixon, Mitchell, and Rep. Gerald R. Ford, May 5, 1971. Direct url: http://whitehousetapes.net/clips/1971_0505_ford/index.htm.

87 **The protesters, according to Rehnquist, had "Communist-oriented or related backgrounds":** Quoted in Lynn Pearle memorandum, November 4, 1971, NAACP Records, Box IX:17/5.

87 **"The doctrine which there obtains is customarily referred to as 'qualified martial law'":** Lardner and Saperstein, "A Chief Justice-Designate with Big Ambitions."

88 **outcry so stung Rehnquist that over the summer he wrote letters to three of his fellow justices:** "Papers Offer Close-Up of Rehnquist and the Court," by Adam Liptak and Jonathan D. Glater, *New York Times,* November 18, 2008.

88 **Holtzman filed a motion to recuse Rehnquist from participating in the case (fn 2):** WHR Papers, Box 6.

CHAPTER TWELVE: CHANGES ON THE COURT

A general note about Chapters Twelve through Sixteen: John Dean was in a unique position to witness Rehnquist's role in the Supreme Court selection process in the early days of the Nixon presidency. Dean served first as a Justice Department official working for John Mitchell and later as the White House counsel to Nixon. From 1969 through 1971 Nixon appointed four justices to the Court and was deeply involved in the details, including plotting with Mitchell to force the departures or resignations of justices Nixon didn't like. Dean's well-sourced book, *The Rehnquist Choice,* devotes 318 pages to this two-year span of Rehnquist's career and constitutes a definitive historical work. This chapter and the five that follow draw significantly from Dean's book.

Sources other than *The Rehnquist Choice* are shown for Chapters Twelve through Sixteen:

90 **"It wouldn't surprise me if he was robbing banks on the side or writing novels under another name":** Williamson, "A Question of Judgment," p. 762.

91 **Lambert was a tough investigator and a Pulitzer Prize winner:** William Lambert obituary, *New York Times,* February 16, 1998.

91 **but he also was a reliable, trusted conduit when the White House wanted to get a story out:** Reagan Library, Peter Wallison Files, OA 14287.

91 **Fortas kept the money for eleven months but returned it after Wolfson was indicted on federal stock fraud charges (fn):** Lambert obituary, *New York Times,* February 16, 1998.

93 **"Mitchell's bluff had succeeded beyond his wildest expectations":** Dean, *The Rehnquist Choice,* p. 10.

CHAPTER THIRTEEN: SOUTHERN STRATEGY

In *The Rehnquist Choice,* John Dean provides a first-person account of Nixon's abortive efforts to find a replacement for Fortas, the president's southern strategy, and Rehnquist's role in the selection process.

Sources other than *The Rehnquist Choice* follow:

97 **Haynsworth protested that the 1950s were a different time, "when none of us was thinking or writing as we are today":** *CQ Almanac Online Edition,* direct url: http://library.cqpress.com/cqalmanac/document.php?id=cqal69-1248180&type=query&num=Clement+Haynsworth&.

97 **John P. Frank, a distinguished Phoenix constitutional lawyer:** Frank obituary, *Los Angeles Times,* September 12, 2002.

97 **all three of the top Republican leaders in the Senate voted against confirmation . . . "An outstanding jurist":** *CQ Almanac Online Edition,* direct url: http://library.cqpress.com/cqalmanac/document.php?id=cqal69-1248180&type=query&num=Clement+Haynsworth&.

100 **Carswell was arrested in 1976 (fn):** "Carswell Arrested by Vice Squad," *New York Times,* June 27, 1976; "Carswell Arrest Reports Reviewed," Lakeland (Florida) *Ledger,* June 28, 1976; "Judge Carswell Beaten by Youth in Hotel Room," *Los Angeles Times,* September 11, 1979.

101 **Twelve days later, Carswell resigned and ran unsuccessfully for a seat in the Senate from Florida:** "Carswell Resigns as Judge to Seek U.S. Senate Seat," *New York Times,* April 21, 1970.

101 **Not since the Civil War had there been such a long stretch without a full Court:** *Oxford Companion to the Supreme Court,* Chronology of Succession, p. 1146; verified in *CQ Almanac Online Edition,* direct url: http://library.cqpress.com/cqalmanac/document.php?id=cqal70–1292788&type=query&num=Blackmun+Nomination+1970+Almanac&.

CHAPTER FOURTEEN: TWO MORE VACANCIES

105 **recuperating from the first of what would be many operations on his spine:** 1971 confirmation hearings, p. 484. Direct url: http://gpo.gov/fdsys/pkg/GPO-CHRG-REHNQUIST-POWELL/pdf/GPO-CHRG-REHNQUIST-POWELL-8-1.pdf.

105 **there was "a reasonable possibility that the government would succeed in the action":** 1971 confirmation hearings, p. 484. Direct url: see above.

106 **still at the beach:** 1971 confirmation hearings, p. 484. Direct url: see above.

107 **Nixon could paint the war in Vietnam as Kennedy's responsibility:** "Word for Word/Presidential Tapes: Nixon Wanted to Show Up JFK and Wouldn't Let It Go," by Tim Weiner, *New York Times,* February 28, 1999.

107 **"Of course. Whizzer White is of the old Kennedy crowd":** "Nixon, Hoover Bashed Justices in '71 Phone Call," by Walter Pincus, *Washington Post,* September 28, 2007.

107 **Diem's killing ended what little vestige of democracy remained . . . "This is a conspiracy":** MC, White House conversation between Nixon and Bob Haldeman, July 1, 1971, 8:45 A.M. to 9:52 A.M. Direct url: ttp://whitehousetapes.net/transcript/nixon/conspiracy

108 **pep talk to the various representatives of the defense and intelligence agencies who were supposed to be declassifying the materials:** Nixon Library, Presidential Daily Diary for July 1, 1971. The daily diary shows that Nixon went to his office in the Old Executive Office Building at 2:05 P.M. and initially met privately for thirty minutes with Henry Kissinger, his national security adviser. At 4:13 P.M., he met with the group that Rehnquist chaired, which was called the Security Classification Procedures Study Group. In addition to Nixon, Rehnquist, and Dean, the other attendees at the meeting were Bob Haldeman, John Ehrlichman, Ron Ziegler (press secretary), Joseph J. Liebling (deputy assistant secretary of defense), William D. Blair (director of the Office of Media Services, Department of State), N. Harris Lyon (executive director, Office of Security, CIA), Howard C. Brown, Jr. (assistant general manager, Atomic Energy Commission), and Thomas K. Latimer (staff member, National Security Council). Judging from the mid-echelon titles of the regulars at the meeting, the agencies and departments they represented probably did not expect their attendees to be getting face time with the president and all four of his top aides (Dean, Haldeman, Ehrlichman, and Ziegler). Nixon and his entourage spent just short of an hour with the group.

109 **"We've got to follow up on this thing . . . Rehnchburg and that group?":** Transcript of meeting on July 24, 1971, Reagan Library, Peter Wallison Files, OA 14287.

109 **Nixon started working on an end-around:** Summary of White House surveillance activities prepared by House Judiciary Committee, May–June 1974, in files at Reagan Library, Peter Wallison Files, OA 14287.

109 **Ehrlichman suggested Colson:** Conversation from October 8, 1971, reported in "Word for Word/Presidential Tapes: Nixon Wanted to Show Up JFK and Wouldn't Let It Go," by Tim Weiner, *New York Times,* February 28, 1999.

109 **Colson sent an Eyes Only memo to the president:** Colson memorandum dated September 24, 1971, in files at Reagan Library, Peter Wallison Files, OA 14287. E. Howard Hunt, a White House operative, testified that he was instructed by Colson to fabricate cables designed to implicate the Kennedy administration in the assassination of Diem and his brother. Although Hunt completed the mission, Colson denied involvement. See summary of White House surveillance activities prepared by House Judiciary Committee, May–June 1974, in files at Reagan Library, Peter Wallison Files, OA 14287. More about Colson: "Charles Colson, 80, Watergate Felon Reborn as Evangelical Leader, Dies," by Tim Weiner, *New York Times,* April 22, 2012.

CHAPTER FIFTEEN: "YOU MIGHT CONSIDER BILL REHNQUIST"

111 **Congressman Richard H. Poff, a Republican:** Poff obituary, *New York Times,* July 1, 2011.

111 **Dean knew Poff very well:** John Dean interview with APM, direct url: http://americanradioworks.publicradio.org/features/prestapes/johndean.html

112 **As a young congressman, Poff had signed the Southern Manifesto . . . the interview transcript soon was circulating:** Poff obituary, *New York Times,* July 1, 2011.

114 **Nixon saw it as a way to rub the Senate's nose in the mess he thought the Democratic leadership had created:** Dean, *The Rehnquist Choice,* p. 22, called Nixon's plan "the equivalent of throwing a stink bomb into the Senate."

114 **allowing an obviously unqualified candidate like Carswell to easily slip through:** For an excellent explanation of the ABA vetting process, see Yalof, *Pursuit of Justices,* p. 214, note 48.

115 **Nixon—acting through Mitchell—gave the ABA his list:** "Court Nominees: Powell and Rehnquist Confirmed," *CQ Almanac, 1971 Edition.*

115 **Powell signaled he was ready:** John Dean interview with APM, direct url: http://americanradioworks.publicradio.org/features/prestapes/johndean.html.

116–119 **Nixon seemed genuinely surprised when the names were revealed by the Dow Jones newswire . . . "I want the positive stuff first" . . . "Get 'em off on a red herring" . . . "Then we get the goddamn story out first, and then we're way ahead of them":** APM, transcripts of Nixon-Mitchell telephone calls. Direct url: http://americanradioworks.publicradio.org/features/prestapes/rmn_jm_101471.html. Note: This APM site contains recordings and transcripts of all conversations referenced in these pages.

118 **"Most Not Well Known; Potential Choices Do Not Include Leading Judicial Figures":** "President Asks Bar Unit to Check Six for High Court," by Fred P. Graham, *New York Times,* October 14, 1971,.

119 **Dershowitz could see what was coming . . . another piece in the *Times:*** "Senate's Role: It Need Not Allow the President a Partisan Victory," by Alan Dershowitz, *New York Times,* October 17, 1971; "Of Justices and Philosophies," *New York Times,* October 24, 1971.

120 **"I'd say that two years of Powell is worth 20 of somebody else, and that's the damn truth" (fn 1):** See APM transcripts of Nixon-Mitchell cited above.

121 **"We sort of knocked Howard off his feet" . . . Mitchell quickly got into selling mode . . . "I still haven't heard back from Howard Baker" . . . "you might consider this Bill Rehnquist" . . . "I may reevaluate" . . . "Well, anyway, whatever he is, get him changed":** See APM transcripts of Nixon-Mitchell cited above for all conversations recounted in these pages.

126 **Rehnquist slumped in a chair:** Lardner and Saperstein, "A Chief Justice-Designate with Big Ambitions."

126 **"I'm not a woman, black, or mediocre":** *CBS Evening News,* Roger Mudd reporting, October 22, 1971.

126 **Mitchell telephoned Nixon . . . "go the other way" . . . "Okay, take him off":** See APM transcripts of Nixon-Mitchell cited above.

127 **The president had never talked to Rehnquist about the nomination:** CDG verified with Abigail Malangone at Nixon Library, March 23, 2012. At my request the Nixon Library searched all Nixon White House transcripts and records. The search turned up three meetings or conversations between Nixon and Rehnquist; there were no surprises. The first meeting of the two was the July 1, 1971, declassification meeting at the EOB; Rehnquist was present along with many others. There was no further contact between the two men until Nixon's two-minute telephone call to Rehnquist at 5:18 P.M. on December 10, 1971, the day Rehnquist was confirmed by the Senate. A final meeting between Nixon and Rehnquist, Powell, and their wives took place on December 22, 1971. It was a photo opportunity, eighteen minutes long, during which Nixon ceremonially signed presidential commissions for the two justices. The photograph of Nixon that Rehnquist displayed in his chambers was from that ceremony.

127 **"Rehnquist had never been on anybody's radar . . . because Rehnquist was *running* the radar machine":** John Dean interview with APM, direct url: http://americanradioworks.publicradio.org/features/prestapes/johndean.html.

128 **Kleindienst, who actually had nothing at all to do with the closely held decision, later would take credit:** Kleindienst, *Justice: The Memoirs of Attorney General Richard G. Kleindienst,* p. 123.

128 **Nixon was immensely satisfied with his short televised address that evening:** Address to the Nation, October 21, 1971, American Presidency Project, direct url for full text of address: http://www.presidency.ucsb.edu/ws/index.php?pid=3196#axzz1qorqN5rO.

128 **"really threw a bombshell at these bastards" . . . "And he's on our side" . . . "We kept it quiet!":** See APM transcripts of Nixon-Mitchell cited above.

CHAPTER SIXTEEN: "WHAT NOW, HON. W. H. REHNQUIST?"

131 **no immediate negative backlash among senators:** "Court Nominees: Powell and Rehnquist Confirmed," *CQ Almanac, 1971 Edition.*

132 **He denied that he was ever a member of the John Birch Society. He said he had never harassed voters. He now realized "the strong concern of minorities for the recognition of these rights." And so on:** "Court Nominees: Powell and Rehnquist Confirmed," *CQ Almanac, 1971 Edition.*

132 **"She came to me as a good citizen":** Author interview with Dershowitz, January 3, 2011.

132 **Bok had been an ardent, and vocal, opponent of the Carswell nomination:** Author interview with Derek Bok, March 22, 2012: Bok was asked to get into the fray by Joseph Califano, Lloyd Cutler, and some other establishment lawyers. "I just thought he [Carswell] was enormously undistinguished, at a time when there were some very distinguished candidates out there. I was not a serial activist. Just on Carswell, and, really, only because those lawyers, whom I deeply respected, asked me to get involved." For excellent background on the role Bok and other distinguished academics played in defeating the Carswell nomination, see "Annals of Politics: Judge Carswell and the Senate, Part II," by Richard Harris, *The New Yorker,* December 17, 1970, at p. 54.

133 **Dershowitz said he instructed Klein to track down "Jewish Stanford graduates":** Author interview with Dershowitz, January 3, 2011.

133 **Stanford's commencement speaker, Justice Stephen Breyer, noted:** *Stanford Today,* July/August 1997.

133 **That was just a shot in the dark, and it went nowhere:** Author interview with Joel Klein, March 26, 2012. Klein did not recollect being assigned by Dershowitz to track down the rumor about Rehnquist, although "I am not saying it didn't happen. But it was forty years ago. I just don't remember."

133 **The Harvard president knew nothing about it:** Author interview with Bok, March 22, 2012. Although Bok didn't recollect anything about Dershowitz's story, he did remember Rehnquist. "We were both there at the same time. I was the head proctor at Encina [in 1950–1951] when Bill Rehnquist was an adviser there. He was a law student, and he was getting free housing at Encina in exchange for acting as an adviser. I was in charge of keeping order. He [WHR] was there in a semi-official capacity." Bok said he would have had no knowledge of any shenanigans that happened earlier, because Bok didn't get to Stanford until the fall of 1947, when Rehnquist was already an upperclassman. But Bok had an impression of Rehnquist the law student: "We thought he was a nerd, kind of a nerdy type. He had to work hard as a law student, unlike the fun-loving undergrads, and he was on the law review which meant he had to work even harder. He was very studious, very serious. I don't recall ever having much to do with Rehnquist except on one memorable occasion. I was trying to decide where to go to law school. My mother had told me she would only support me in law school if I went someplace else, other than to Stanford. Because she thought there was a lot more to the world than what I would see just at Stanford. Stanford then was comprised mostly of Westerners. So I went upstairs to see Rehnquist. And his advice to me was, 'Go to Harvard.' That's what he told me. 'Go to Harvard Law School. It's an excellent place.' That's the only time I can recall having a real conversation with him." Told that Rehnquist actually didn't care for Harvard, Bok didn't miss a beat: "Maybe he didn't like me!"

133 **In the end, Dershowitz held off and didn't recount the details until after Rehnquist's death:** "Telling the Truth About Chief Justice Rehnquist," *Huffington Post,* September 4, 2005.

133 **The usual Democratic liberals . . . parliamentary maneuver to delay the Rehnquist vote . . . Bayh was furious:** "Court Nominees: Powell and Rehnquist Confirmed," *CQ Almanac, 1971 Edition.*

134 **vote on Powell went ahead as planned . . . "not very exciting":** "Court Nominees: Powell and Rehnquist Confirmed," *CQ Almanac, 1971 Edition.* For a record of the vote, designated CQ Senate Vote #408, see *CQ Almanac, 1971 Edition,* p. 65-S.

134 **Brooke, the only black man in the Senate, criticized Rehnquist's "narrow view of the rights of man":** "Court Nominees: Powell and Rehnquist Confirmed," *CQ Almanac, 1971 Edition.*

135 **Rehnquist's story, in his letter to Eastland, was that the memo was a reflection of Jackson's views, not his own . . . Elsie Douglas, forcefully went the other way:** In addition to *CQ Almanac* cited above, see Kluger, *Simple Justice,* p. 606 (fn).

136 **"The only way they were sure they could get enough people there":** Author interview with WHR, December 19, 1984.

136 **the motion to cut off debate fell 11 votes short . . . Bayh's proposal was crushed:** The cloture vote, CQ Senate Vote #413, is recorded on p. 66-S of the *CQ Almanac, 1971 Edition.* Senate Minority Leader Hugh Scott (R-PA) introduced the motion. Bayh's motion to postpone the vote on Rehnquist until January 18, 1972, CQ Senate Vote #414, also is recorded on p. 66-S of the *CQ Almanac, 1971 Edition.*

136 **vote was straight up-or-down on Rehnquist, and the margin comfortable enough if well short of a ringing endorsement:** CQ Senate Vote #417, *CQ Almanac, 1971 Edition,* p. 67-S.

CHAPTER SEVENTEEN: *ROE V. WADE*

Dates of various events in this chapter, including the swearing in of Rehnquist and Powell and the timing of the oral argument in *Roe v. Wade,* come from *The Oxford Companion to the Supreme Court.*

137 **Blackmun called it a "bobtailed Court" . . . chief justice, still new to his job, gave Potter Stewart responsibility for figuring out which cases could be adequately heard by seven justices:** HAB to WHR, July 20, 1987, Blackmun Papers, Box 151/3.

138 **The Court, with its constantly changing cast in the early Nixon years, had been struggling with that question, too, in a case called *Younger v. Harris:*** *Oxford Companion to the Supreme Court,* p. 1111.

138 **Stewart told the chief that *Younger* paved the way for the Court to quickly dispose of the abortion cases:** HAB to WHR, July 20, 1987, Blackmun Papers, Box 151/3.

138 **But as Blackmun saw it, Stewart had muffed his assignment:** HAB to WHR, July 20, 1987, Blackmun Papers, Box 151/3.

138 **On the assignment sheet that he circulated the following Friday, December 17, Burger put Blackmun's name alongside *Roe* and *Doe:*** For background, see Bob Woodward and Scott Armstrong, *The Brethren,* p. 204.

139 **"There were, literally, not enough columns [in the conference's tally sheet] to mark up an accurate reflection of the voting in either" case:** Ball and Cooper, "Fighting Justices," p. 17, quoting Burger to Douglas, December 20, 1971, in William Brennan Papers, Library of Congress, Box 281.

139 **Burger insisted on taking a vote of the justices as to which cases should be held over . . . Again, Douglas objected:** Woodward and Armstrong, *The Brethren,* p. 212.

139 **Powell didn't intend to have anything to do with the abortion cases:** Powell to WHR, June 1, 1972, WHR Papers, Box 8.

140 **Blackmun circulated his draft on May 18:** WOD to HAB, May 25, 1972, in WHR Papers, Box 8.

140 **the Blackmun approach was problematic:** *Oxford Companion to the Supreme Court,* p. 863.

140 **In an orchestrated move, Douglas, Brennan, and Marshall decided it was best to take the win and move on:** Memos from all three justices, each dated May 25, 1972, are in WHR Papers, Box 8.

140 **Then Stewart also came around a few days later:** Potter Stewart to HAB, May 31, 1972, in WHR Papers, Box 8.

140 **Blackmun had what Douglas called "a firm 5":** WOD to HAB, May 31, 1972, in WHR Papers, Box 8.

140 **Blackmun, who circulated a memorandum to the justices telling them that he now favored pushing the abortion cases into the next term, with reargument as early as possible:** HAB to Conference, May 31, 1972, in WHR Papers, Box 8.

141 **Powell sent a carefully worded memo to the conference on June 1:** Powell to Conference, June 1, 1972, WHR Papers, Box 8. The carbon-paper copy with Powell's note to Rehnquist is also in this box.

142 **"I will file a statement telling what is happening to us and the tragedy it entails":** WOD to Burger, June 1, 1972, WHR Papers, Box 8.

142 **The next day Douglas did just that:** Woodward and Armstrong, *The Brethren,* p. 226.

142 **Burger sent him a four-page single-spaced rebuke:** Burger to WOD, July 27, 1972, WHR Papers, Box 8.

142 **Blackmun announced in a memo to the justices on June 3 that he was withdrawing his draft opinion . . . he hadn't switched sides:** Woodward and Armstrong, *The Brethren,* pp. 224 and 225. Note: Blackmun referred to the "spring" and "fall" editions of his opinions in a memo to WHR, November 27, 1972, HAB Papers, Box 151/5.

142 **Two months before *Roe* was handed down, Rehnquist wrote to Blackmun:** WHR to HAB, November 24, 1972, HAB Papers, Box 151/4.

143 **three of the five justices appointed by Republican presidents Ronald Reagan and his successor George H. W. Bush turned out to have the controlling votes that preserved the constitutional right to abortion:** "A Telling Court Opinion," by Linda Greenhouse, *New York Times,* July 1, 1992.

144 **Because of the way the two men had come to the Court, they continued to share a special bond:** Noteworthy exchanges between the two justices are in the author's possession and may be found in the LP Papers, Series 10.2.2.

145 **For Stevens, indignation about the episode ran so deep that thirty years later he was still complaining about it in his memoir:** Stevens, *Five Chiefs,* pp. 184–185.

145 **Powell also had misgivings about Rehnquist's intended public rebuke of his brethren . . . he wrote a long memorandum:** LP to WHR, April 3, 1981, in LP Papers.

146 **Rehnquist ignored Powell's counsel . . . asked the newly retired Powell to chair a committee of judges whose mandate was to speed up death-penalty litigation:** Jeffries, *Justice Lewis F. Powell, Jr.*, pp. 447, 449.

CHAPTER EIGHTEEN: "THE BETTER POINT OF VIEW"

Rehnquist's comments in this chapter come from interviews with the author on December 13, 1984, and December 19, 1984, unless otherwise noted below.

151 **poet Matthew Arnold's description of Sophocles . . . Rehnquist would use the quote again in 2002 (fn):** Rehnquist is quoted in "Ex-Supreme Court Justice Byron White Dies," by Joan Biskupic, *USA Today,* April 15, 2002.

151 **"Welcome, and congratulations . . . It will be very nice, I assure you, to have you here on a permanent basis":** WOD to WHR, December 10, 1971, WOD Papers, Box 1782.

152 **Rehnquist told the Maricopa Young Republican League:** Lynn Pearle memorandum, November 4, 1971, NAACP Records, Box IX:17/5.

152 **Rehnquist suggested a rain check:** WHR letter to WOD dated July 24, 1972, WOD Papers, Box 1782.

152 **"Happily for you. . . . No kids":** WHR letter to WOD dated August 7, 1972, WOD Papers, Box 1782.

152 **"three teenagers at home":** WHR letter to WOD dated June 29, 1972, WOD Papers, Box 1782.

152 **took a mountain hike . . . looked for anemones:** Handwritten note from Nan (Rehnquist) to "Cathy and Bill" (Douglas) on "NCR" stationery, August 16, 1972, WOD Papers, Box 1782.

152 **Rehnquist promised copies but then misplaced the negatives:** WHR handwritten memo-pad note to WOD, undated (but presumably 1972), WOD Papers, Box 1782.

152 **Bill Douglas invited Nan and her sister:** WHR letter to WOD, July 11, 1972, WOD Papers, Box 1782.

152 **"Bill mentioned to me that when he looked at Rehnquist he saw himself," Cathy Douglas recalled:** Author interview with Cathy Douglas, January 4, 1985.

153 **Martin said Douglas told her he'd never seen anyone on the Court who was as bright as Rehnquist (fn):** Author interview with Joan Martin, July 5, 2010

153 **"We saw your interview with Eric Sevareid":** WHR letter to WOD, September 7, 1972, WOD Papers, Box 1782.

154 **missed the president's State of the Union address:** See Roberts, "William H. Rehnquist: A Remembrance," p. 434.

154 **marveling at the "theatricality" of Aaron Burr:** Notes for Remarks to Whig-Cliosophic Society, Princeton University, October 26, 1972, WHR Papers, Box 198/15. Note: The group Rehnquist addressed is the oldest debate union in the United States. Burr was one of its co-founders.

154 **Jefferson as a good president but a "skulker":** Remarks to American University of Cairo, draft dated January 26, 1993 (the speech was given on February 3, 1993), WHR Papers, Box 234/6.

154 **applauding the "underrated" William Howard Taft:** Speech to University of Virginia Law School, October 27, 2001, WHR Papers, Box 261/2.

156 **"this guy is going to be around for a millennium, making bad sound good":** Lardner and Saperstein, "A Chief Justice-Designate with Big Ambitions."

156 **furious if he thought the chief justice slighted him . . . used Burger as the model of what *not* to do:** See Greenhouse, "The Apprenticeship of William H. Rehnquist," generally, and specifically on p. 1368 for discussion of how Burger slighted Rehnquist in swearing in the Reagan cabinet in 1981.

157 **Burger, already deeply insecure:** See Greenhouse, "The Apprenticeship of William H. Rehnquist," p. 1367.

157 **Powell was recuperating from surgery at Bethesda Naval Hospital:** Jeffries, *Justice Lewis F. Powell, Jr.*, p. 536.

157 **Rehnquist scribbled a note to the ailing justice, revealing that he didn't believe Burger was adequately supporting their cause:** WHR letter to LP, March 19, 1979, LP Papers, Series 10.2.2.

158 **"The April argument calendar came out":** WHR letter to LP, March 20, 1979, LP Papers, Series 10.2.2.

159 **article in *Newsweek* headlined "A Rudderless Court":** "A Rudderless Court." *Newsweek,* July 23, 1979.

159 **"The piece on 'A Rudderless Court' is sophomoric":** LP letter to WHR, July 23, 1979, LP Papers, Series 10.2.2.

159 **Powell decided to enlist Rehnquist and Byron White in an off-the-record effort . . . to plant a story in *Time:*** See Powell's notes titled "David Westin" and "Ground rules laid down by David," dated October 10, 1979, LP Papers, Series 10.2.2.

160 **resulting article in *Time:*** "Inside the High Court," *Time,* November 5, 1979.

160 **routine surgery for prostate cancer had gone terribly awry:** Jeffries, *Justice Lewis F. Powell, Jr.*, p. 539.

160 **"We have now finished our January argument calendar":** WHR letter to LP, January 18, 1985, LP Papers, Series 10.2.2.

161 **Burger's perceived failings would motivate Rehnquist to do things differently:** See Greenhouse, "The Apprenticeship of William H. Rehnquist," for elaboration on her theory that Rehnquist took Burger as a negative model.

161 **Rehnquist complained about the administrative burden of his new role (fn 2):** WHR to Nancy and Tim Spears (daughter and son-in-law), October 27, 1986, WHR Papers, Box 172/11.

CHAPTER NINETEEN: LONE DISSENTER

164 **"His vote could almost always be predicted":** "Telling the Truth About Chief Justice Rehnquist," *Huffington Post,* September 4, 2005.

165 **Chemerinsky of the University of Southern California Law School uses the term "ahistorical" (fn 3):** Chemerinsky, "Politics, Not History, Explains the Rehnquist Court," p. 648.

166 **In the 1970s, he did not think discrimination against women violated the Constitution:** "The Rehnquist Court," by David G. Savage, *Los Angeles Times,* September 29, 1991.

167 **He explained it all with a whimsical cover memorandum:** Barrett, "A Rehnquist Ode on the Vinson Court," p. 294.

167 **"He's the one with the agenda":** Author interview with A. E. Dick Howard, January 4, 1985.

167 **"he could have an enormous impact, particularly if he were elevated to Chief Justice":** Author interview with Laurence Tribe, January 10, 1985.

CHAPTER TWENTY: BORED AT THE COURT

169 **cigar-and-poker nights with his buddies . . . Berns served as the unofficial "corresponding secretary" (fn 1):** BLT, Blog of Legal Times, August 29, 2009.

169 **two-page, single-spaced memo onto the desk of the chief justice (with copies to all the other justices) asking him to please, please do something about all the dreariness:** WHR "Dear Chief" memorandum to Burger, September 24, 1973, WHR Papers, Box 8, and Burger's "Dear Bill" reply to WHR, September 25, 1973, WHR Papers, Box 8.

171 **tried and failed to get the Supreme Court press corps to put on a satirical show:** Greenhouse, "The Apprenticeship of William H. Rehnquist," p. 1371.

171 **quizzed his clerks about their college fight songs, most of which Rehnquist had memorized:** Barrett, "A Rehnquist Ode on the Vinson Court," p. 294.

171 **wrote limericks . . . scribbled notes to his seatmate Blackmun . . . and translated English phrases into rough, schoolboy Latin:** See various notes passed between HAB and WHR, HAB Papers, Box 116/5.

171 **served as the choral director for the annual Christmas sing-along at the Court, as well as at judicial conferences—where his fondness for leading the Southern anthem "Dixie" earned him a tongue-lashing:** "Rehnquist's Inclusion of 'Dixie' Strikes a Sour Note," by Craig Timberg, *Washington Post,* July 22, 1999.

171 **life-sized cardboard cutout of Burger:** Lardner and Saperstein, "A Chief Justice-Designate with Big Ambitions."

171 **In the choral performance that angered Burger, Rehnquist and his law clerk Craig Bradley changed the lyrics to "Angels from the Realms of Glory" (fn 3):** Barrett, "A Rehnquist Ode on the Vinson Court," p. 292.

172 **he assigned Rehnquist only one opinion:** Garrow, "The Rehnquist Years," *New York Times Magazine,* October 6, 1996.

173 **Rehnquist saw Marshall's dissent for the personal rebuke that it was intended to be, and he decided to respond in kind:** This account is based in part upon author interview with Ron Blunt, 1/7/85; author interviews with David Jaffe, January 7 and 9, 198; and author interview with Cory Streisinger, January 10, 1985.

173 **Marshall, seventy-four years old at the time, already had a reputation among the clerks and justices as someone who was beginning to lose his mental edge . . . watching daytime television:** Garrow, "Mental Decrepitude on the

U.S. Supreme Court," p. 1072 (characterizing Marshall as "disengaged," watching daytime television).

CHAPTER TWENTY-ONE: AN ASPIRING NOVELIST

This chapter is based upon correspondence between Rehnquist and Robert Lantz, correspondence between Rehnquist and Sidney Davis, correspondence between Lantz and numerous editors and publishers, and unpublished WHR manuscripts—all found in WHR Papers, Box 193.

Sources other than the above follow:

178 **Douglas was a prolific author:** "350 Books by Supreme Court Justices," by Ronald Collins, *ScotusBlog,* March 12, 2012, posted at scotusblog.com. Douglas's fifty-one books gave him another record at the Court: the most prolific author in its history.

178 **scramble for money from outside speaking and writing. He had even moonlighted as the president of the Albert Parvin Foundation:** Woodward and Armstrong, *The Brethren,* pp. 14 and 87; Dean, *The Rehnquist Choice,* p. 24.

178 **Douglas's outside income from books, and his writing for the counterculture journal *Evergreen Review,* had already drawn the attention of Attorney General Mitchell and President Nixon (fn):** Dean, *The Rehnquist Choice,* pp. 208 and 227.

178 **Douglas put Rehnquist in touch with his personal attorney and literary lawyer, a New Yorker named Sidney Davis:** Background on Davis is from "Sidney M. Davis, 69, Aide to Senate Panels," unbylined *New York Times* obituary, May 18, 1988; and Oral History of Walter F. Murphy, found at http://www.princeton.edu/~mudd/finding_aids/douglas/douglasintro.html.

179 **Lantz was sixty years old and at the top of his game:** Background on Lantz is from "Robert Lantz, 93, Agent to the Stars, Dies," by Tim Weiner, *New York Times,* October 20, 2007; "Robert Lantz, 93, Talent Agent," unbylined obituary, *Variety,* October 22, 2007; and Lantz's biography at www.filmreference.com/film/83/Robert-Lantz-html.

179 **Rehnquist sent a handwritten note to Bill Douglas thanking him for the introduction to Lantz: "He is delightful" (fn):** Handwritten note, WHR to WOD ("Dear Bill"), July 2, 1975, WOD Papers, Box 1782.

181 **No Supreme Court justice had ever published a novel:** Verified by Professor Dennis Hutchinson of the University of Chicago Law School in e-mail correspondence with author, March 23, 2012, in author's files. For additional context, see also *ScotusBlog,* cited above, and Krugman, "Judicial Fictions: Images of Supreme Court Justices in the Novel, Drama, and Film."

182 **"presently somewhat taken with the idea of extracting a title from this couplet found in Pope's 'Rape of the Lock'":** In addition to mentioning this couplet in his letter to Lantz on December 26, 1974, WHR passed a bench note to HAB on April 27, 1992 (quizzing HAB as to the Pope quote), HAB Papers, Box 116/5.

CHAPTER TWENTY-TWO: CODE PINK

189 **the book was derived from a series of lectures the chief justice annually gave at a summer seminar in Salzburg:** WHR letter to Robert Lantz, April 6, 1979, WHR Papers, Box 193. Rehnquist explained that "a good deal of the basic material will be delivered in lecture form at the American Studies Seminar in Salzburg, Austria." Rehnquist assured Lantz that there would be no copyright problems, saying the foundation was supportive of his turning the lectures into a book. Rehnquist suggested to Lantz in 1998 that he could revise *The Supreme Court* easily "because of the series of lectures which I give annually on this subject," WHR letter to Robert Lantz, August 24, 1998, WHR Papers, Box 185.

189 **Rehnquist appreciated the summer lecture circuit (fn):** The two quoted passages are from WHR letters to Jim Rehnquist, October 9, 1985 and January 25, 1991, WHR Papers, Box 172/4.

190 **Janet Rehnquist later ran into ethical problems of her own (fn):** "Review of the Management of Inspector General Operations [of the] Department of Health and Human Services," Report to Congressional Committees, US General Accounting Office, June 2003, found at http://gao.gov/products/GAO-03-685. See also "Inquiries on Gun and Ousters Focus on Health Dept. Official, by Robert Pear," *New York Times,* November 13, 2002; and "Report Calls Health Department Inspector General a Poor Manager," by Robert Pear, *New York Times,* June 6, 2003.

191 **Rehnquist was friendly during the 1970s with Howard Simons:** WHR letter to Simons suggesting lunch, September 20, 1979,WHR Papers, Box 113.

192 **"We are always interested in clear, logical reasoning . . . no matter how unlikely the source":** "The Rehnquist Court," by David G. Savage, *Los Angeles Times,* September 29, 1991.

192 **Douglas warned them not to have anything to do with Nina Totenberg:** Memo from WOD, June 12, 1972, found in WHR Papers, Box 5. See also "Nina Totenberg: Queen of the Leaks," *Vanity Fair,* January 1992.

192 **Rehnquist just tersely replied, "I intend to spend my time learning about my new job," not giving interviews:** July 22, 1986 letter, WHR papers, Box 10.

193 **Rehnquist penned a note back to Ginsburg in a barely legible scrawl: "Ruth, I think participating even as a moderator would be a mistake":** WHR to Ginsburg, December 15, 2004, WHR Papers, Box 171.

194 **permit Forman's crew to film inside the Supreme Court:** Forman letter to WHR, September 9, 1995, WHR Papers, Box 144.

195 **Forman sent word through Lantz that he would set up a special screening in Washington:** Lantz letter to WHR, August 12, 1996, WHR Papers, Box 144.

195 **Bill Douglas and his wife Cathy had hosted a reception for Henry Fonda and Jane Alexander . . . Thurgood Marshall and some of the other justices and staff had also been the guests at a screening:** Toni House (Supreme Court Public Information Officer) memo, August 26, 1996, WHR Papers, Box 144.

195 **Rehnquist was blunt, to make sure that Lantz got his point:** WHR letter to Lantz, September 4, 1996, WHR Papers, Box 144.

195 **Lantz evidently got the message:** Lantz letter to WHR, January 6, 1997, WHR Papers, Box 184.

195 **Rehnquist decided he didn't need an agent:** Lantz's "glitter world approach to historical writing did not fully mesh with Bill," wrote Rehnquist's friend, Herman Obermayer. See Obermayer, *Rehnquist: A Personal Portrait,* pp. 189–190.

CHAPTER TWENTY-THREE: A BETTING MAN

197 **Rehnquist was an inveterate bettor, but he liked to say that he was *not* a gambler:** Obermayer, *Rehnquist: A Personal Portrait,* p. 155.

197 **"He hated to lose":** Obermayer, *Rehnquist: A Personal Portrait,* p. 155. Also, the comments of Justice John Paul Stevens are illustrative of Rehnquist's competitiveness: "We always bet on the [Washington] Redskins [football] games, and I tend to like the Redskins so I would always bet on the Redskins. He always wanted to make sure he was on the winning side, that's all." "Interview Transcript: Justice John Paul Stevens," by Jeffrey Rosen, *New York Times Magazine* website, posted April 12, 2010. Note: The interview was conducted on June 22, 2007, by Rosen for his September 23, 2007, *Times Magazine* article about Stevens.

197 **If Rehnquist became bored, he would hector Blackmun with a jotted note, challenging his seatmate to a test of wits:** See various notes passed between HAB and WHR, HAB Papers, Box 116/5.

198 **After Rehnquist managed to get a Ping-Pong table installed for the clerks in the Court's gym, he made bets with the other justices on the games between clerks:** Author interview with Ron Blunt, January 7, 1985.

198 **So extensive were Rehnquist's betting matrixes that the leading scholarly journal for political scientists, *PS,* even reproduced one:** "Supreme Court Justices Really Do Follow the Election Returns," by Forrest Maltzman, Lee Sigelman, and Paul J. Wahlbeck, *PS*, October 2004, found at www.apsanet.org.

198 **Rehnquist bet on at least twenty elections:** Obermayer, *Rehnquist: A Personal Portrait,* p. 166.

198 **Rehnquist was never one to let someone else off the hook. That became clear during an otherwise routine oral argument . . . "Oh, Cuyler, yes," Rehnquist said knowingly. "He played center field for the Chicago Cubs in 1933" . . . He didn't want to admit Stevens had gotten the best of him:** This episode is based on the following sources: author interview with Ron Blunt, January 7, 1985; author interview with David Jaffe, January 7, 1985; HAB handwritten bench note to WHR, December 1, 1982, HAB Papers, Box 116/5; "Order in the Court—Cinnamon Toast," unbylined Associated Press story, *Hartford Courant,* February 7, 1983; and transcript and audio recording of the Court's oral argument in *Morris v. Slappy,* found at http://www.oyez.org/cases/1980–1989/1982/1982_81_1095. Note: The Oyez site contains separate links for the audio recording and the transcript of the oral argument in *Morris v. Slappy.* The exchange concerning Kiki Cuyler occurs at the 49:20 mark.

200 **Stevens professed a hope that someday all those Rehnquist opinions he loathed would be overturned:** See, generally, Stevens, *Five Chiefs,* pp. 173–200.

200 **Stevens wrote in an accompanying note, "May I impose on you to sign these two volumes so that they can be used as holiday gifts?" . . . "I don't sign books" . . . He had the books sent right back to Rehnquist:** Stevens note to WHR, December 11, 1992; WHR handwritten notation replying to memo

(addressed to "Sir") from his secretary ("J."), December 14, 1992; Stevens note to WHR, December 14, 1992, WHR Papers, Box 139.

CHAPTER TWENTY-FOUR: "BIZARRE IDEAS AND OUTRAGEOUS THOUGHTS"

203 **Rehnquist had calculated his earliest possible retirement date:** Author interview with WHR, December 13, 1984.

203 **Potter Stewart had done exactly that, and it had worked out well for him:** Garrow, "Mental Decrepitude on the U.S. Supreme Court," p. 1066.

203 **Chafing under the Court's isolation, Rehnquist thought this sounded good:** Author interview with WHR, December 13, 1984. Also see Greenhouse, "The Apprenticeship of William H. Rehnquist," p. 1370.

203 **Rehnquist was in ill health:** Rehnquist's various hospitalizations and surgeries are documented in FBI investigative files, comprising more than 1,500 pages, which were compiled for his 1971 and 1986 confirmation hearings. The FBI released its files on Rehnquist, with some redactions, under the Freedom of Information Act after his death. The FBI files were posted on the Web for a time. Amanda Rogers downloaded the files in their entirety from http://william-rehnquist.com/main.php, a site that has since been taken down. A hard copy of the entire FBI record is in my possession. Rehnquist described various other hospitalizations, including a visit to the emergency room at Bethesda Naval Hospital, in a letter to Powell dated July 2, 1981, LP Papers, Series 10.2.2. A useful contemporaneous article on the state of Rehnquist's health is "Justice Rehnquist Back at Work After Treatment for Drug Reaction," by Lawrence K. Altman, *New York Times,* January 12, 1982. Rehnquist's care in not bending over to pick up anything but the lightest of objects was witnessed by the author, author interview with WHR, December 13, 1984.

203 **couldn't sit or stand for long periods, and he couldn't exercise. Surgery hadn't helped. In almost constant pain and suffering from insomnia:** FBI investigative summary of WHR hospitalization records from George Washington University Hospital (hereinafter, *FBI investigative summary*), pp. 94–97. Note: This report was prepared by the FBI in 1986, during its investigation of Rehnquist prior to his confirmation hearings to become chief justice. The FBI file number is WFO 77B-86748.

204 **he was taking over seven times that amount—1,500 milligrams daily, three times the normal dosage. When he got a three-month prescription, it lasted only a month:** FBI investigative summary (see above), p. 93.

204 **exhibited an addict's behavior:** "Rehnquist's Drug Habit," by Jack Shafer, *Slate,* January 5, 2007.

204 **slowly lowering his dosage . . . finally was able to quit:** "Sedative Withdrawal Made Rehnquist Delusional in '81," by Alan Cooperman, *Washington Post,* January 5, 2007.

205 **When Rehnquist returned to the bench on January 11, still on the lowered dosage, he seemed to be fine . . . Court upheld the constitutionality of a forty-year prison sentence imposed on a Virginia man for possession and distribution of nine ounces of marijuana:** "Justice Rehnquist Back at Work," *New York*

Times, January 12, 1982, and "40-Year Drug Term Held Legislative Prerogative," *New York Times,* January 12, 1982.

206 **He was, in other words, incapacitated for at least three months:** The timing is deduced from forensic audio analysis performed by Pat Ward of the Oyez Project, referenced in e-mail from Oyez's Jerry Goldman (Professor, Chicago-Kent College of Law) to author, September 30, 2010, in author's files. Note: The Oyez Project headed by Goldman is a multimedia relational database devoted to archiving and analyzing Supreme Court oral arguments and decisions. It was created with funding from the National Science Foundation and utilizes experts in linguistics, psychology, computer science, and political science.

206 **Garrow made a strong case in the *University of Chicago Law Review* for a constitutional amendment imposing mandatory retirement for Supreme Court justices:** See Garrow, "Mental Decrepitude on the U.S. Supreme Court."

CHAPTER TWENTY-FIVE: BICENTENNIAL BOMBSHELL

209 **Burger arrived at White House:** Biskupic, *Scalia,* p. 104.

209 **meeting with President Ronald Reagan near the end of the Court's term ostensibly to discuss the coming 1987 celebration of the 200th anniversary of the Constitution . . . The palace guard around Reagan had doubts about scheduling the meeting . . . Burger dropped a bombshell:** "Reagan's Mr. Right," *Time,* June 30, 1986.

210 **Meese was a trusted conservative:** See "Mr. Power" (Edwin Meese), by John A. Jenkins, *New York Times Magazine,* October 12, 1986; and Biskupic, *Scalia,* p. 102.

210 **Meese himself was out of the running . . . Regan, a former Wall Street CEO, wanted to keep Burger's resignation a complete secret:** "Reagan's Mr. Right," *Time,* June 30, 1986.

211 **Reagan pulled Regan, his counsel Peter Wallison, and Meese into the Oval Office . . . institutional rivalry among senior aides . . . Wallison, aligned more closely to Regan than to Meese, didn't think much of the research:** Wallison, *Ronald Reagan,* p. 151.

211 **Regan, Wallison, and Meese—decided they would cull down the resultant list themselves:** Biskupic, *Scalia,* p. 105.

211 **memo praised his "sheer cleverness" and listed case after case where Rehnquist had turned back the judicial clock to pre-Warren times:** Undated, unattributed memo titled "Justice William Rehnquist," Reagan Library, Peter Wallison Files, OA 14287.

212 **if Rehnquist turned it down, Reagan would have no problem with Scalia:** Wallison, *Ronald Reagan,* p. 152.

212 **Rehnquist and Scalia had gotten through the White House gates without waking the "sleeping watchdogs":** Wallison, *Ronald Reagan,* p. 153.

212 **Reagan was aware of Rehnquist's hospitalization a few years earlier for prescription drug addiction:** "Reagan's Mr. Right," *Time,* June 30, 1986.

212 **Rehnquist decided to tackle the issue head on . . . the president offered Rehnquist the chief's job on the spot:** Biskupic, *Scalia,* p. 105.

212 **"It would be an honor":** "Reagan's Mr. Right," *Time,* June 30, 1986.

212 **Reagan then mentioned that he was thinking of either Bork or Scalia to succeed him. What did Rehnquist think of them? . . . he didn't try to make a case for either:** Biskupic, *Scalia,* p. 105.

213 **Scalia was jittery all weekend. He badly wanted the job . . . "the president had no idea whether he would get another appointment":** Biskupic, *Scalia,* p. 108.

213 **"tidiness of the selection process pleased the president's advisers":** "Reagan's Mr. Right," *Time,* June 30, 1986.

213 **Burger had messengers deliver a copy of his resignation letter:** Biskupic, *Scalia,* p. 109.

213 **Wallison was ecstatic:** Wallison, *Ronald Reagan,* p. 154.

CHAPTER TWENTY-SIX: A SCORE TO SETTLE

Details of the confirmation hearings and votes on the nominations of Rehnquist and Scalia come from the *CQ Almanac.* Rehnquist's testimony and Kennedy's comments about Rehnquist are from the official transcript of the hearings. Direct link: http://gpo.gov/fdsys/pkg/GPO-CHRG-REHNQUIST/content-detail.html. Kennedy's remarks: http://gpo.gov/fdsys/pkg/GPO-CHRG-REHNQUIST/pdf/GPO-CHRG-REHNQUIST-2-10.pdf. Kennedy's views on Rehnquist's record (disqualifying on its face), and his belief that the odds nonetheless favored Rehnquist's confirmation, are described in his memoir, *True Compass,* at pp. 323 and 404. Background on Walter Sheridan comes from his obituary, "Walter Sheridan Dies; Helped to Investigate Hoffa," by Martin Weil, *Washington Post,* January 14, 1995, as well as from numerous *New York Times* accounts of Sheridan's involvement both in the Senate rackets committee hearings and in later events involving the Kennedy brothers. (Illustratively, see "Kennedy Enlisting a Diversified Staff; Raising $1 Million," by R. W. Apple, *New York Times,* September 18, 1964.) Note: Sheridan's unique relationship with the Kennedys is further demonstrated in Laurence Leamer's *The Kennedy Men:* Robert Kennedy called Sheridan immediately after learning of the assassination of his brother in 1963, asking Sheridan to "check out" whether Hoffa was responsible. See Leamer, *The Kennedy Men,* p. 740. The NAACP's lobbying efforts are extensively documented in the NAACP records at the Library of Congress.

Sources other than the above follow:

217 **Ted Kennedy put the family's personal private investigator on the case and told him to start digging:** Sheridan telephoned the author before the confirmation hearings began and explained that he was conducting an investigation for Kennedy. Kennedy's antipathy toward Rehnquist was clear during the 1986 confirmation hearing, but the extent of Kennedy's feelings even in 1971 are quite apparent in an excellent "Talk of the Town" piece written by James Stevenson in *The New Yorker,* "Kennedy on Fifth Avenue," December 4, 1971.

219 **including an ex-FBI agent who testified he'd been called to the scene of an election-day fracas and identified Rehnquist as the instigator:** The FBI agent was James J. Brosnahan, who later became a San Francisco trial lawyer. Brosnahan told the author in an e-mail dated March 28, 2012 (in author's files), that he was contacted by a Senate Judiciary Committee staff member and asked to testify. He reluctantly agreed to do so because he believed it was important to set the record

straight. Brosnahan didn't recall who contacted him, but he did not think it was Walter Sheridan. "I am unable to give you the names, which indicates it probably wasn't Walter Sheridan because that name I know." Almost twenty-six years after his testimony, Brosnahan was still adamant that Rehnquist lied at his 1971 and 1986 confirmation hearings in denying involvement in minority voter challenges: "Justice Rehnquist was in charge of that Phoenix [voter-challenge] program for several years covering several elections based on what I know." Brosnahan also recalled rough questioning by Senator Orrin Hatch (R-UT) as Hatch tried to cast doubt on Brosnahan's recollection. He "was trying to cross-examine me that maybe I didn't really know Rehnquist." But Brosnahan was resolute, for what he considered a very good reason. Brosnahan knew Rehnquist personally. "I think I testified, and it was correct, that the firm of [Powers & Rehnquist], composed of two lawyers, had offered me a job to head up their litigation."

219 **Elsie Douglas, repeated her 1971 assertion that Rehnquist was lying:** "Rehnquist's View on Memos Disputed by Aide to Jackson," unbylined UPI story, *New York Times,* August 11, 1986.

219 **The NAACP remained one of Rehnquist's most persistent critics (fn):** See "Corps of Clerks Lacking in Diversity," by Tony Mauro, *USA Today,* March 13, 1998. Mauro's investigative report was an unprecedented piercing of the veil of secrecy around the Court's hiring practices. To compile a comprehensive hiring history for each sitting justice, Mauro conducted interviews with clerks themselves and consulted public sources such as employee directories. Each justice then was sent a list of the racial and gender breakdown of his or her clerks for verification. Mauro's reporting showed that Rehnquist was not the only justice who never hired a black law clerk. Justices Anthony Kennedy, Antonin Scalia, and David Souter also had never done so. Of the seventy-nine clerks Rehnquist had hired through 1998, eleven were female. Using the same methodology as Mauro, the author's researcher Chelsey D. Goff compiled law-clerk hiring data through the remainder of Rehnquist's tenure. The updated hiring statistics revealed that Rehnquist changed the gender diversity of his clerk pool after the NAACP protests (doubling the proportion of females hired after 1998, to 25 percent), but not its racial makeup. Supreme Court Public Information Officer Kathleen Arberg declined to provide, or verify, law-clerk demographics. For additional context on Mauro's reporting, and why few members of the Supreme Court press corps took note of it, see "May It Please the Court," by Steven Brill, *Brill's Content,* February 2001. Brill's reporting provides perspective on how Mauro's article "touched a nerve both inside and outside the walls of the High Court." It describes Justice Antonin Scalia being confronted by a CBS News crew whose producer wanted to know why Scalia had never hired a black law clerk, Rehnquist's rebuffing a group of minority lawyers who wanted to meet with him to discuss the Court's hiring practices, the fireworks at the appropriations hearing, and Justice Clarence Thomas's comments that he was frustrated about the lack of minority clerks. Perhaps most significantly, Brill raises questions about what he sees as a too-deferential relationship between the Court's regular reporters and the justices they cover. Also see "Protest Outside High Court," unbylined AP story, *New York Times,* October 6, 1998, and "Needed: More Minority Clerks at the Court," editorial, *New York Times,* March 18, 1999.

219 **Rehnquist had arranged that he would not be questioned about his prescription drug addiction . . . "I do not think I have any obligation to give the press a health briefing":** Garrow, "Mental Decrepitude on the U.S. Supreme Court," p. 1069.

220 **finally gave the committee access to twenty-five documents . . . no smoking guns:** "Rehnquist Memos from Nixon Years Studied by Panel," by Linda Greenhouse, *New York Times,* August 7, 1986.

220 **Wallison's handwritten notes in the White House files indicate that he counseled a more forthright approach than Rehnquist eventually took:** Undated notes of Peter Wallison, Reagan Library, Peter Wallison Files, OA 14287.

220 **Wallison turned to Cutler . . . Korologos, a legendary Washington fixer whose roots went back to the Nixon years, did spin-doctoring for the nominee:** Reagan Library, Peter Wallison Files, OA 14287.

221 **boasted of the help he gave Rehnquist:** Details can be found at http://www.hellenext.org/master-classes/featured-master-classes/tom-korologos/.

221 **It was a remark that Biden would grow to regret as the full extent of Scalia's unbridled conservatism became clear:** Quoted in Biskupic, *Scalia,* p. 121.

221 **He felt that the Judiciary Committee, in particular, had treated him badly:** Garrow, "The Rehnquist Years," *New York Times Magazine,* October 6, 1996, p. 67.

222 **"somewhat downcast because we have just finished our vacation . . . pleased to have all of the hassle in connection with the confirmation over":** WHR letter to Mother, September 24, 1986, WHR Papers, Box 172/6.

222 **White House aides wrote his boss a memo urging that all of the other justices should attend . . . Favored senators would be invited, but those who engaged in "reprehensible" attacks on Rehnquist were snubbed:** Reagan Library, Peter Wallison Files, OA 14287.

222 **talking points for the president to use in phone calls:** Talking points for various thank-you telephone calls by President Reagan, prepared by William L. Ball (Assistant to the President for Legislative Affairs), September 18, 1986, Reagan Library, Case Files 406399–406401.

222 **"It was almost like a wedding":** WHR letter to Mother, September 29, 1986, WHR Papers, Box 172/6.

CHAPTER TWENTY-SEVEN: HIGH EXPECTATIONS

223 **invited by the Reagans to a state dinner at the White House honoring German Chancellor and Mrs. Helmut Kohl:** WHR letter to Nancy and Tim (Spears, daughter and son-in-law), October 27, 1986, WHR Papers, Box 172/11.

223 **Nan, fifty-seven years old, had been diagnosed with ovarian cancer:** Contemporaneous reports of agent interviews in FBI investigative files indicate that Nan received this diagnosis before July 1, 1986. Also see *Stanford Magazine,* July/August 2005, "Head of the Class," by Charles Lane.

223 **Rehnquist, normally a stoic, described her travail as "a tough time":** WHR letter to Jean Laurin, November 25, 1988, WHR Papers, Box 172/3.

224 **put on headphones and listened to his Walkman before falling asleep, so as not to disturb Nan:** WHR letter to Jean (Laurin), February 26, 1990, WHR Papers, Box 172/3.

224 **illness dragged on for years:** WHR letter to Jean (Laurin), November 2, 1990, WHR Papers, Box 172/3. Also see various WHR letters in Blackmun Papers, including WHR letter to HAB, July 16, 1987.

224 **Rehnquist was aghast at the mess they came back to, and said so in a letter to Jim that described the carnage in detail:** WHR letter to Jim, October 17, 1975, WHR Papers, Box 172/4.

224 **Rehnquist then sent his son a letter asking for the accrued interest—$289 in all:** WHR letter to Jim, June 19, 1989, WHR Papers, Box 172/4.

224 **All three children were expected to earn money for college:** WHR letter to Nancy (daughter), February 19, 1980, WHR Papers, Box 172/11.

224 **"More of his carelessness":** WHR letter to Nancy, October 2, 1975, WHR Papers, Box 172/5.

225 **"not really first rate, law schools":** WHR letter to Jean, April 19, 1984, WHR Papers, Box 172/3.

225 **"somewhat more diligent than my son":** WHR letter to William Greenhalgh, February 4, 1981, WHR Papers, Box 172/1.

225 **Rehnquist took to calling Jim "Weakfish":** WHR letter to Jim, April 1, 2002, WHR Papers, Box 172/4.

225 **"a very nice, stable guy with good expectations":** WHR letter to Nancy, December 10, 1981, WHR Papers, Box 172/11.

226 **"surgeon's report is encouraging":** WHR note to Conference, September 20, 1990, HAB Papers, Box 1407/13.

226 **a death sentence for sure:** WHR letter to Jean, November 2, 1990, WHR Papers, Box 172/3.

CHAPTER TWENTY-EIGHT: THE BRENNAN COURT

229 **the "Brennan Court," with Rehnquist dissenting each time, mandated:** The various cases in which Justice William J. Brennan, rather than Rehnquist, controlled the majority and thus dictated the opinion writing are comprehensively described in Congressional Quarterly's *Congress and the Nation,* Supreme Court Overview, 1985–1988. The same *Congress and the Nation* overview was also the basis for footnotes 1 through 9. The overview is Document Number catn85-0012178499 in the CQ Press Electronic Library. Direct url: http://library.cqpress.com/congress/document.php?id=catn85-0012178499&type=query&num=catn85–0012178499+&.

230 **"the most significant defeats for the policy objectives of a chief executive [Reagan] in a half a century":** *Congress and the Nation,* Supreme Court Overview, 1985–1988, see url above.

231 **the average age of the justices was almost sixty-nine:** *Congress and the Nation,* Supreme Court Overview, 1985–1988.

231 **Powell had sent a kind note to Rehnquist when his confirmation twin became the chief:** Handwritten note from LP to WHR, June 18, 1986, LP Papers Series 10.2.2. The letter is signed "with affection."

231 **Powell was a critical swing vote:** *Congress and the Nation,* Supreme Court Overview, 1985–1988.

232 **Ted Kennedy was on the Senate floor inveighing against him:** The quote from Kennedy can be found in the CQ Press Electronic Library, *Congress and the Nation Online Edition.* Direct url: http://library.cqpress.com/catn/document.php?id=catn85-0000126321 3&type=query&num=Bork+confirmation+hearings&.

232 **Within days, Ginsburg, too, was in trouble amid allegations of ethics breaches:** *Congress and the Nation,* Supreme Court Overview, 1985–1988.

233 **Reagan finally found his man in Anthony Kennedy, fifty-one, a Meese crony:** *Oxford Companion to the Supreme Court,* p. 556.

233 **Conservatives did not doubt he would vote to overturn *Roe:*** *Congress and the Nation,* Supreme Court Overview, 1985–1988.

233 **he could not corral the increasingly restive O'Connor or the staunchly conservative Scalia to agree with everything he had written. Nor did he try:** "The Mysterious Mr. Rehnquist: Where Is the Chief Justice Going and Who Will Follow?" by Joan Biskupic, *Washington Post,* September 25, 1994.

233 **Scalia tried to muscle the conservative fence-sitters back into line, to no avail:** Biskupic, "The Mysterious Mr. Rehnquist."

234 **Rehnquist wrote to his sister, Jean, a few weeks after Souter arrived (fn 1):** WHR letter to Jean Laurin (sister), November 2, 1990, WHR Papers, Box 172/3.

CHAPTER TWENTY-NINE: FEDERALISM, OCCASIONALLY

237 **When O'Connor, Kennedy, and Souter voted together on any case that term, they were never in the minority:** *Congress and the Nation Online Edition,* Supreme Court Overview, 1989–1992. This overview is Document Number catn89-0001359448 in the CQ Press Electronic Library. Direct url: http://library.cqpress.com/catn/document.php?id=catn89-0001359448&type=query&num=catn89–0001359448&.

238 **It was the first time since the New Deal that the Court had struck down a federal law on the grounds that it exceeded Congress's commerce power:** "High Court Kills Law Banning Guns in a School Zone," by Linda Greenhouse, *New York Times,* April 27, 1995.

238 **federal statutes were invalidated in whole or in part on federalism grounds in nine cases:** Lori A. Ringhand, in an excellent analysis in the *University of Pennsylvania Journal of Constitutional Law,* notes (at p. 1036) that thirty federal statutes were invalidated in thirty-four decisions by the Rehnquist Court during its nineteen terms. Apart from the nine federalism decisions, which are notable conservative outcomes, the majority of the remaining invalidations occurred in 1st Amendment cases and are thus considered by Ringhand to be liberal outcomes. While acknowledging the strain of federalism that marked the Rehnquist Court from 1995 to 2001, Ringhand actually calls the Rehnquist Court's record "ideologically mixed" and concludes that the record of the Rehnquist Court is more similar to the Warren and Burger Courts than is generally acknowledged. The appendices in her article are comprehensive and definitive. Direct url for Ringhand's article: http://media.nj.com/njv_tom_moran/other/Rehnquist-court-by-the-numbers.pdf.

238 **By then, among other things, the Rehnquist Court also had overruled:** "The Revolution Next Time?" by Linda Greenhouse, Opinionator, *New York Times* website, December 16, 2010.

239 **No major federal programs got the ax:** Greenhouse, Opinionator, December 16, 2010.

239 **"The Rehnquist Court has revived the doctrine of federalism . . . It hasn't gone after Social Security":** "Rehnquist's Legacy: A Balanced Court," by Jane Roh, FoxNews.com, June 14, 2005. Direct url: http://www.foxnews.com/story/0,2933,159308,00.html.

239 **it was clear that the federalism boomlet was over:** "The Year Rehnquist May Have Lost His Court," by Linda Greenhouse, *New York Times,* July 5, 2004.

239 **A huge data set—of cases and votes—made it possible to rate how the nine teammates played together over time:** I analyzed Supreme Court voting trends using the database tools that are available online in the CQ Press Supreme Court Collection. The Collection constitutes a definitive body of work, and it has the advantage of being quite easy to use. To utilize the CQ Press Supreme Court toolbox, follow this link: http://library.cqpress.com/scc/blocanalysis.php. (The Voting Bloc Analysis tool was most frequently used in my analysis, followed by the Justice Role Finder. The toolbox explains each in more detail.) For cases through the Court's 2000 term, the CQ Press Supreme Court Collection relies on coding from the Supreme Court Database of Professor Harold J. Spaeth of Michigan State University. Spaeth's data set, created with National Science Foundation funding, is in the public domain. Follow this link to Spaeth's database: http://scdb.wustl.edu/about.php. Spaeth's coding methodology is explained here: http://scdb.wustl.edu/_brickFiles/2011_01/SCDB_2011_01_codebook.pdf.

For cases beginning with the 2001 term, CQ Press editors have independently captured and coded Supreme Court data, making the CQ Press Supreme Court Collection a hybrid of Spaeth's excellent work and that of CQ Press's own experts. The CQ Press data set contains numerous enhancements to the Spaeth data set in order to facilitate analysis. Because case coding often requires making a judgment call—even whether a case has been "decided" is sometimes debated among experts—the tallies of voting alignments yielded by the CQ Press data may not always match those of other generally accepted sources. Coding variances, however, do not alter the broad trends described in this chapter. Note: Voting alignments and other statistical tabulations are based upon Court actions through the end of calendar 2011.

241 **Robert Pinsky wrote of mules:** "Sayings of the Old," *The New Yorker,* September 12, 2011, at p. 68.

241 **Rehnquist, the commentary said, had a "willingness to accept majority opinion and to compromise [that] has set him apart from Scalia and Thomas":** "Rehnquist's Legacy: A Balanced Court," by Jane Roh, FoxNews.com, June 14, 2005.

243 **the Roberts Court is even more ideologically partisan and conservative than Rehnquist's:** Professors Andrew D. Martin (Washington University School of Law) and Kevin M. Quinn (UC Berkeley School of Law) have created a statistical model—which they call the "Martin-Quinn Measure of Judicial Ideology"—that

plots the relative location of Supreme Court justices on an ideological continuum. With funding from a National Science Foundation grant, the two professors assigned "Martin-Quinn Scores" to all justices since 1937, enabling ideological shifts in the Court to be plotted over time. Martin and Quinn rate the Roberts Court (based on data through late 2010) as the most conservative in their database. The previous high came in the early 1950s. Direct url to the Martin-Quinn database, an excellent site and a definitive resource: http://mqscores.wustl.edu/. The authors' seminal article on Martin-Quinn scores is cited in the bibliography and is available at this url: http://mqscores.wustl.edu/media/pa02.pdf. For an article explaining the Martin-Quinn scores in a relatively jargon-free way, see "Why Newer Appointees Offer Fewer Surprises From Bench," by Adam Liptak, *New York Times,* April 18, 2010. Another helpful Martin-Quinn article is "Supreme Court May Be Most Conservative in Modern History," by Nate Silver, *New York Times,* March 29, 2012.

CHAPTER THIRTY: A FRAGILE MAJORITY

245 **Bender saw Rehnquist for what he really was—"the first true conservative justice":** Author interview with Paul Bender, January 12, 2011.

245 **"*Lopez* really was the beginning of the revolution":** Author interview with Paul Bender, January 12, 2011.

245 **"Roberts and Alito are more conservative than Rehnquist ever was":** Author interview with Paul Bender, January 12, 2011.

246 **Some declared that *Hibbs* was the end of the federalism revolution—and scholars who made it a sport to study such things puzzled over how Rehnquist could so cavalierly have brought it about:** "The Revolution Next Time?" by Linda Greenhouse, Opinionator, *New York Times* website, December 16, 2010.

247 ***Miranda* warnings, Rehnquist said, were only "procedural safeguards [that] were not themselves rights protected by the Constitution":** This statement is found at 417 U.S. 444 (1974).

247 **given the chance to further cut back on *Miranda* safeguards a decade later in two other cases, the Court each time used Rehnquist's opinion in *Tucker* as a touchstone:** See Kamisar's chapter in *The Rehnquist Legacy* (Bradley, Craig, ed.), pp. 115–117, for background on *Tucker* and its progeny.

247 **By 2000, the police and public were so accustomed to the strict procedures of *Miranda* that overruling it would only have led to chaos:** This point is made by Kamisar, one of many who have voiced such an opinion, in *The Rehnquist Legacy* at p. 123.

247 **"For the Court to suddenly say, after years of the public hearing 'You have the right to remain silent' on *Dragnet* and *Law and Order* and all the courtroom procedural shows, that the *Miranda* warning isn't required?":** Author interview with Dennis Hutchinson, January 3, 2011.

248 **Rehnquist never tried to hide his distaste for *stare decisis:*** Rehnquist wrote to his son Jim ("Dear Weakfish") on December 17, 1986: "Stare decisis in constitutional law is pretty much of a sham." WHR Papers, Box 172/4. Also,

Rehnquist wryly explained to me his own views on legal precedent: "Well, it turns out that any time five people decide that we're not stuck with the footnote, we're not stuck with the footnote! And things have a way of evolving on much more of a common sense reaction to things than a strictly doctrinal approach, where you, you know, A follows from B follows from C." Author interview with WHR, December 13, 1984.

248 **"I doubt that any justice in Supreme Court history has dismissed his own majority opinions more summarily or nonchalantly":** See Kamisar's chapter in *The Rehnquist Legacy,* pp. 120 and 124.

250 **Alan Dershowitz called the majority's "limited-to-the-present-circumstances" clause the "one telltale line that revealed [*Bush v. Gore's*] true purpose":** Dershowitz, *Supreme Injustice,* pp. 81–82.

250 **When Rehnquist privately wrote, shortly after becoming chief justice, that "*stare decisis* in constitutional law is pretty much of a sham":** Letter to Weakfish (Jim Rehnquist), December 17, 1986, WHR Papers, Box 172/4.

251 **Rehnquist disciplined himself to become an efficient master of the short game:** See Greenburg, *Supreme Conflict,* p. 14: "A new day brought a new case. No grudges, just move on."

251 **The sheer volume of work he cranked out was mind-numbing: 440 opinions, 330 dissents:** These and other enumerations of Rehnquist's opinions, dissents, and participation in cases come from the Supreme Court Collection in the CQ Press Electronic Library.

251 **"They're all kind of a long, grey line," he had said in 1985. "I can't remember back for the whole thirteen years":** Author interview with WHR, December 13, 1984.

CHAPTER THIRTY-ONE: SPLENDOR OF STRIPES

253 **the pompous Burger wore a reproduction of Jay's first robe:** Burger obituary, *New York Times,* June 26, 1995.

253 **until Rehnquist decided it was time for a change:** "Behind the Gavel, a Sense of Style," by John Eligon, *New York Times,* September 6, 2008. Note: Harry Blackmun kept many clippings about Rehnquist and his stripes. See HAB Papers, Box 1407/14.

254 **"We had immediately and uniformly given him a negative response to that suggestion. Nevertheless, with regard to his own robes, he went right ahead":** Stevens, *Five Chiefs,* p. 173.

254 **he moved the Christmas festivities to a conference room and kept right on singing:** Author interview with Paul Bender, January 12, 2011.

254 **Rehnquist "could get things done with a glare":** The quote is from "U.S. Supreme Court Justice Clarence Thomas Visits UA [University of Alabama]," by Stephanie Taylor, *Tuscaloosa News,* October 23, 2009.

254 **John Paul Stevens didn't understand the petulance:** The entire quote is from Stevens, *Five Chiefs,* p. 173.

254 **complaining about "inappropriate" dress . . . The women should wear black, navy, or charcoal grey:** Author interview with Paul Bender, January 12, 2011.

255 **Burger, Rehnquist's supposed opposite, had once chastised the solicitor general's office about the color of a vest:** Burger obituary, *New York Times,* June 26, 1995.

255 **Rehnquist's intolerance particularly bothered Blackmun:** Various contemporaneous notes that Blackmun made to himself about Rehnquist's demeanor are in HAB Papers, Box 116/5.

255 **"Invoking the wrath of Rehnquist":** Found in HAB Papers, Box 1407/14. The article Blackmun clipped was from *Legal Times,* March 13, 1995.

255 **"I shall abide by your judgment on this. I do not wish to embarrass you in any way. I can take the subway":** HAB memo to WHR, December 16, 1986, HAB Papers, Box 1407/12.

CHAPTER THIRTY-TWO: CLINTON'S TRIAL

Background on the Clinton impeachment proceeding and Rehnquist's role in it, and the basic chronology of impeachment events, comes from "President Clinton Survives Impeachment Trial; His Reputation Does Not," in *CQ Almanac 1999.* Direct url: http://library.cqpress.com/cqalmanac/cqal99-18-24510-1085981.

Sources other than the above follow:

258 **All three, the Rehnquist Court said, were infringements either on the prerogatives of the states or on those of the Court itself:** "The 1996–1997 Term Analyzed," *Supreme Court Yearbook,* in CQ Press Electronic Library. Direct url: http://library.cqpress.com/scc/scyb96-0000064491.

258 **Rehnquist doubted the will of the House of Representatives to actually move ahead:** WHR letter to Robert Lantz, August 24, 1998, WHR Papers, Box 185.

258 **He ruled, for example, that the senators were not merely "jurors":** *CQ Almanac 1999.*

259 **"might even acquire intrinsic value by the second half of this century":** WHR letter to Jim and Anna (Rehnquist), January 18, 2001, WHR Papers, Box 172/4.

259 **made light of his own participation in the proceedings:** WHR interview with Charlie Rose, PBS, March 11, 2004, transcript found at www.sedhe.net/blog/archives/000307.html.

259 **value the donation for tax purposes at $30,000, courtesy of an appraisal by Sotheby's:** "Rehnquist's Scandalous Shmatte," by Mickey Kaus, *Slate,* June 29, 2000. Direct url: http://www.slate.com/articles/news_and_politics/kausfiles_special/2000/06/rehnquists_scandalous_shmatte.html.

CHAPTER THIRTY-THREE: "NEVER LET THE WAR END UNTIL YOU'VE WON IT"

261 **Rehnquist's longtime friend Cynthia Holcomb Hall . . . became closer to him after Nan's death (fn):** "Rehnquist and Hall," unbylined article, *Legal Times,* June 6, 1994. The article, found in HAB Papers, Box 1407/14, quotes an Associated Press dispatch, confirming "what *Newsweek* had hinted at several weeks ago," that the two were dating. Both Rehnquist and Hall had declined comment at the time. Also see various letters from, to, or regarding Cynthia

Holcomb Hall, including a typewritten note from "J." (WHR secretary), September 20, 1993, regarding birthday party planning and Rehnquist's dodging a dinner invitation from Hall ("I did not tell her you were playing poker, just that you were busy"), WHR Papers, Box 140; Hall letter to WHR, September 14, 1994, inviting Rehnquist for a visit ("I can make your trip interesting for sure"), WHR Papers, Box 142; and Hall letter to WHR, July 15, 2004, regarding the *New York Times*'s Linda Greenhouse ("I dislike her not only for her left leaning reporting, but also because she tried to hook us up romantically and made my life miserable for a week or two"), WHR Papers, Box 170. Note: Hall incorrectly blamed Greenhouse for the gossip item. Hall died in 2011 at age eighty-two: "Cynthia Holcomb Hall Dies at 82," by Carol J. Williams, *Los Angeles Times,* March 2, 2011.

262 **"I wouldn't want to hold it forever":** "The Rehnquist Years," by David J. Garrow, *New York Times Magazine,* October 6, 1996, quoting a June 1992 interview with Brian Lamb of C-SPAN, at p. 85.

262 **Even Bush expected this:** Greenburg, *Supreme Conflict,* p. 21. White House counsel Harriet Miers had been vetting possible replacements. Note: Miers later was nominated by Bush for the second vacancy on the Court, but soon withdrew her nomination amid vocal conservative opposition. See "A Troubled Nomination Implodes," by John Cochran, CQ Press Public Affairs Collection, October 31, 2005. Direct url: http://library.cqpress.com/cqpac/document.php?id=weeklyreport109-000001938774&type=query&num=Miers&.

262 **He thought retired justices just went on to die:** Toobin, *The Nine,* p. 278.

262 **he was bothered by a persistent sore throat:** Toobin, *The Nine,* p. 278.

262 **The chief was also having trouble singing hymns:** Barrett, "A Rehnquist Ode on the Vinson Court," p. 293.

262 **The eighty-year-old chief justice, a lifelong smoker, had anaplastic thyroid cancer:** Toobin, *The Nine,* p. 278.

262 **a type that was aggressive and usually rapidly fatal:** "Rehnquist Treated for Thyroid Cancer, Supreme Court Says," by Linda Greenhouse and Katharine Q. Seelye, *New York Times,* October 26, 2004.

262 **They performed a tracheotomy, cutting a hole in his throat through which Rehnquist breathed and spoke:** Rehnquist obituary, "Supreme Court Chief Justice William Rehnquist Dies," by Linda Greenhouse, *New York Times,* September 3, 2005.

262 **Rehnquist came out of the hospital on October 29:** This can be inferred from an e-mail dated October 29, 2004, from Sally Rider to Ed Turner in the Supreme Court Public Information Office, WHR Papers, Box 171.

262 **The justices rallied around their chief:** The various messages from other justices are in WHR Papers, Box 171.

262 **Too weak to climb stairs . . . Unable to eat:** Obermayer, *Rehnquist: A Personal Portrait,* pp. 217–218.

262 **Chemotherapy only made him more frail:** Toobin, *The Nine,* p. 282.

262 **Friends brought him lollipops so that he could have the sensation of taste, but he began refusing them:** Obermayer, *Rehnquist: A Personal Portrait,* pp. 217–218.

263 **Doctors who heard about his plight e-mailed and phoned his office with hopes to involve him in clinical trials:** E-mails and notations of telephone messages from the doctors are in WHR Papers, Box 171.

263 **Rehnquist relied on two trusted, elderly Stanford classmates—one a doctor, the other a lawyer:** Notes regarding conference call with Mark Kasanin (1929–2007) and Dr. Laurence Serrurier (1930–2011), January 14, 2005, in WHR Papers, Box 171.

263 **"May I tell you how happy I am that you are going to be at the next Conference":** Stevens letter to WHR, January 4, 2005, WHR Papers, Box 171.

264 **Rehnquist's secretary typed up the press-office query and gave it to him. Ever at odds with the media, Rehnquist scrawled a reply: "I have no further comment":** Unsigned typewritten memo to Rehnquist dated January 7, 2005, posing questions, with Rehnquist's handwritten reply, WHR Papers, Box 171.

264 **O'Connor sought him out for a heart-to-heart talk about retirement:** Greenburg, *Supreme Conflict,* p. 10. Note: During fact checking to verify Greenburg's account of the Rehnquist-O'Connor conversations, Supreme Court Public Information Officer Kathleen Arberg stated (on O'Connor's behalf) in an April 26, 2012, e-mail to the author that O'Connor refused to comment on her discussions with Rehnquist.

264 **"That's for me to know, and you to find out":** Greenburg, *Supreme Conflict,* p. 202.

264 **O'Connor went to see Rehnquist again. His illness had placed an extra burden on the others:** Greenburg, *Supreme Conflict,* pp. 17–18.

264 **Confident of that, O'Connor had already hired her law clerks for the coming year**: Greenburg, *Supreme Conflict,* p. 18.

265 **The chief was emphatic: "I want to stay another year" . . . "I don't think we need two vacancies":** Greenburg, *Supreme Conflict,* p. 18.

265 **"Well, okay, I'll retire then":** Greenburg, *Supreme Conflict,* p. 20.

265 **Rumors were rampant:** Greenburg, *Supreme Conflict,* p. 21.

265 **wondering what it would be like if he were unfortunate enough to live as long as his ninety-one-year-old mother:** WHR letter to Jean (sister), March 21, 1998, in WHR Papers, Box 172/3.

265 **"Leave the party while you're still having fun":** Letter to Jim (Rehnquist), October 20, 1981, in WHR Papers, Box 172/4.

266 **"Never let the war end until you've won it":** Letter to Weakfish (Jim), March 20, 1979, in WHR Papers, Box 172/4.

266 **Out went a surprise message to his family from his new address: felix @sc-us.gov. Henceforth, Rehnquist typed, that was how to reach him:** The entire thread containing Rehnquist's e-mail to his family ("This will serve as my new email address"), the response from Jim ("Dad, is this really you?"), and Rehnquist's reply ("Yes, it is really me") is in WHR Papers, Box 353/12. The thread spans June 22, 2005, through June 27, 2005.

SELECTED BIBLIOGRAPHY

ARCHIVES

Harry A. Blackmun Papers, Library of Congress, Washington, DC
William O. Douglas Papers, Library of Congress, Washington, DC
Robert Jackson Papers, Library of Congress, Washington, DC
Thurgood Marshall Papers, Library of Congress, Washington, DC
NAACP Records, Library of Congress, Washington, DC
Nixon Presidential Library, Yorba Linda, California
Lewis Powell Papers, Washington and Lee University, Lexington, Virginia
Reagan Presidential Library, Simi Valley, California
Rehnquist Papers, Hoover Institution Archives, Palo Alto, California

NEWSPAPERS, MAGAZINES, JOURNALS, PRESS AGENCIES, AND DATABASES

ABA Journal, Albuquerque Journal, Albuquerque Tribune, Arizona Republic, BBC, *Boston Globe, Brill's Content, CBS Evening News, CQ Almanac Online Edition, CQ Press Electronic Library Supreme Court Collection, Hartford Courant, Harvard Crimson, Huffington Post, Lakeland (Florida) Ledger, Legal Times (Washington, DC), Los Angeles Times, New York Times, PS, Scotusblog, Slate, Stanford Daily, Stanford Magazine, The New Yorker, Tuscaloosa (Alabama) News, USA Today, Variety, Washington Post*

LAW REVIEW ARTICLES

Aynes, Richard L. "Charles Fairman, Felix Frankfurter, and the Fourteenth Amendment," 70 *Chicago-Kent Law Review* 1197 (1995).

Ball, Howard, and Phillip Cooper. "Fighting Justices: Hugo L. Black and William O. Douglas and Supreme Court Conflict," 38 *American Journal of Legal History* 1 (1994).

Barrett, John Q. "A Rehnquist Ode on the Vinson Court (circa Summer 1953)," 11 *Green Bag 2d* 289 (Spring 2008).

Chemerinsky, Erwin. "Politics, Not History, Explains the Rehnquist Court," 13 *Temple Political & Civil Rights Law Review* 647 (2004).

Fairman, Charles. "Does the Fourteenth Amendment Incorporate the Bill of Rights? An Original Understanding," 2 *Stanford Law Review* 5 (1949).

Garrow, David J. "Mental Decrepitude on the U.S. Supreme Court: The Historical Case for a 28th Amendment," 67 *University of Chicago Law Review* 995 (2000).

Greenhouse, Linda. "The Apprenticeship of William H. Rehnquist," 154 *University of Pennsylvania Law Review* 1365 (June 2006).

Kamisar, Yale. "On the Fortieth Anniversary of the *Miranda* Case: Why We Needed It, How We Got It—and What Happened to It," 5 *Ohio State Journal of Criminal Law* 163 (2007).

Kmiec, Douglas W. "Young Mr. Rehnquist's Theory of Moral Rights—Mostly Observed," 58 *Stanford Law Review* 1827 (2006).

Martin, Andrew D., and Kevin M. Quinn. "Dynamic Ideal Point Estimation via Markov Chain Monte Carlo for the U.S. Supreme Court, 1953–1999," 10 *Journal of Political Analysis* 134 (2002).

Peppers, Todd C., and Christopher Zorn. "Law Clerk Influence on Supreme Court Decision Making," Version 5.2, June 14, 2007. Available at Social Science Research Network: ssrn.com/abstract=925705.

Ray, Laura Krugman. "Judicial Fictions: Images of Supreme Court Justices in the Novel, Drama, and Film." 39 *Arizona Law Review* 151 (1997).

Rehnquist, William H. "Contemporary Theories of Rights," 58 *Stanford Law Review* 1997 (2006).

___. "Oral Advocacy: A Disappearing Art," 35 *Mercer Law Review* 1015 (1984).

Ringhand, Lori A. "The Rehnquist Court: A By the Numbers Retrospective," 9 *University of Pennsylvania Journal of Constitutional Law* 1033 (2007).

Roberts, Jr., John G., "William H. Rehnquist: A Remembrance," 31 *Vermont Law Review* 431 (2007).

Snyder, Brad. "The Judicial Genealogy (and Mythology) of John Roberts: Clerkships from Gray to Brandeis to Friendly to Roberts," 71 *Ohio State Law Journal* 1149 (December 8, 2010). Available at Social Science Research Network: ssrn.com/abstract=1722362.

Snyder, Brad, and John Q. Barrett. "Rehnquist's Missing Letter: A Former Law Clerk's 1955 Thoughts on Justice Jackson and *Brown*," 53 *Boston College Law Review* 631 (2012).

Stras, David R. "The Supreme Court's Declining Plenary Docket: A Membership-Based Explanation," Minnesota Legal Studies Research Paper No. 09-39. Available at Social Science Research Network: ssrn.com/abstract=1476537.

Wildenthal, Bryan H. "Nationalizing the Bill of Rights: Revisiting the Original Understanding of the Fourteenth Amendment in 1866–67," 68 *Ohio State Law Journal* 1509 (2007).

Williamson, Richard A. "A Question of Judgment: The Fortas Case and the Struggle for the Supreme Court—By Robert Shogun," 14 *William and Mary Law Review* 762 (1973).

BOOKS

Biskupic, Joan. 2009. *American Original: The Life and Constitution of Supreme Court Justice Antonin Scalia.* New York: Sarah Crichton Books.

_____. 2005. *Sandra Day O'Connor: How the First Woman on the Supreme Court Became Its Most Influential Justice.* New York: HarperCollins Publishers.

Bradley, Craig, ed. 2006. *The Rehnquist Legacy.* New York: Cambridge University Press.

Dean, John W. 2001. *The Rehnquist Choice.* New York: Touchstone.

Dershowitz, Alan M. 2001. *Supreme Injustice: How the High Court Hijacked Election 2000.* New York: Oxford University Press.

Gentry, Curt. 1991. *J. Edgar Hoover: The Man and the Secrets.* New York: W. W. Norton.

Greenburg, Jan Crawford. 2007. *Supreme Conflict: The Inside Story of the Struggle for Control of the United States Supreme Court.* New York: Penguin Press.

Greenhouse, Linda. 2005. *Becoming Justice Blackman: Harry Blackman's Supreme Court Journey.* New York: Henry Holt and Company.

Hall, Kermit L., ed. 2005. *The Oxford Companion to the Supreme Court of the United States.* New York: Oxford University Press.

Holroyd, Michael. 1968. *Lytton Strachey: A Critical Biography: The Years of Achievement 1910–1932.* New York: Holt, Rinehart and Winston.

Hutchinson, Dennis J. 1998. *The Man Who Once Was Whizzer White: A Portrait of Justice Byron R. White.* New York: The Free Press.

Irons, Peter. 1994. *Brennan Vs. Rehnquist: The Battle for the Constitution.* New York: Alfred A. Knopf.

Jeffries, Jr., John C. 1994. *Justice Lewis F. Powell, Jr.* New York: Scribner.

Kennedy, Edward M. 2009. *True Compass: A Memoir.* New York: Hachette Book Group.

Kleindienst, Richard G. 1985. *Justice: The Memoirs of Attorney General Richard G. Kleindienst.* Ottawa: Jameson Books.

Kluger, Richard. 1975. *Simple Justice: The History of Brown v. Board of Education, the Epochal Supreme Court Decision That Outlawed Segregation, and of Black America's Century-Long Struggle for Equality Under Law.* New York: Random House.

Leamer, Laurence. 2001. *The Kennedy Men.* New York: William Morrow.

Marshall, Thomas. 2008. *Public Opinion and the Rehnquist Court.* Albany: State University of New York Press.

Mayer, Jane, and Jill Abramson. 1994. *Strange Justice: The Selling of Clarence Thomas.* New York: Houghton Mifflin.

Obermayer, Herman J. 2009. *Rehnquist: A Personal Portrait of the Distinguished Chief Justice of the United States.* New York: Threshold Editions.

O'Connor, Sandra Day, and H. Alan Day. 2002. *Lazy B: Growing Up on a Cattle Ranch in the American Southwest.* New York: Random House.

Rehnquist, William H. 2004. *The Centennial Crisis: The Disputed Election of 1876.* New York: Knopf Publishing Group.

_____. 1998. *All the Laws But One: Civil Liberties in Wartime.* New York: William Morrow & Co.

_____. 1992. *Grand Inquests: The Historic Impeachments of Justice Samuel Chase and President Andrew Johnson.* New York: Knopf Publishing Group.

_____. 1987. *The Supreme Court: How It Was, How It Is.* New York: William Morrow & Co.

Savage, David G. 1992. *Turning Right: The Making of the Rehnquist Supreme Court.* New York: John Wiley & Sons.

Schwartz, Bernard. 1993. *A History of the Supreme Court.* New York: Oxford University Press.

Simon, James F. 1995. *The Center Holds: The Power Struggle Inside the Rehnquist Court.* New York: Simon & Schuster.

Stern, Seth, and Stephen Wermiel. 2010. *Justice Brennan: Liberal Champion.* Boston: Houghton Mifflin Harcourt.

Stevens, John Paul. 2011. *Five Chiefs: A Supreme Court Memoir.* New York: Little, Brown and Company.

Toobin, Jeffrey. 2007. *The Nine: Inside the Secret World of the Supreme Court.* New York: Anchor Books.

Tushnet, Mark V. 2005. *A Court Divided: The Rehnquist Court and the Future of Constitutional Law.* New York: W. W. Norton.

Wallison, Peter J. 2004. *Ronald Reagan: The Power of Conviction and the Success of His Presidency.* Boulder: Westview Press.

White, G. Edward. 2007. *The American Judicial Tradition.* New York: Oxford University Press.

Woodward, Bob, and Scott Armstrong. 2005. *The Brethren: Inside the Supreme Court.* New York: Simon & Schuster.

Yalof, David Alistair. 1999. *Pursuit of Justices.* Chicago: University of Chicago Press.

INDEX

James Kim, www.jameskimphotography.com

JOHN A. JENKINS has been writing from Washington, DC, about the law and lawyers since 1971, when, shortly before his graduation from the University of Maryland College of Journalism, he went to work as a reporter covering the Justice Department for the prominent legal publisher BNA (now Bloomberg BNA). Four years later, his magazine writing career began with a series of investigative articles about the legal profession for the *Washington Monthly.* His work has appeared in the *New York Times Magazine*, *GQ*, and many other newspapers and national magazines in the United States and abroad. As a longtime Washington publishing executive, he built the textbook and reference-publishing enterprise of Congressional Quarterly and created *First Street*, a revolutionary political intelligence tool for tracking money and influence in politics. He is the recipient of four Certificates of Merit from the American Bar Association Gavel Awards, one of the highest honors in legal journalism. He lives with his wife and children in Washington.

PublicAffairs is a publishing house founded in 1997. It is a tribute to the standards, values, and flair of three persons who have served as mentors to countless reporters, writers, editors, and book people of all kinds, including me.

I. F. STONE, proprietor of *I. F. Stone's Weekly*, combined a commitment to the First Amendment with entrepreneurial zeal and reporting skill and became one of the great independent journalists in American history. At the age of eighty, Izzy published *The Trial of Socrates*, which was a national bestseller. He wrote the book after he taught himself ancient Greek.

BENJAMIN C. BRADLEE was for nearly thirty years the charismatic editorial leader of *The Washington Post*. It was Ben who gave the *Post* the range and courage to pursue such historic issues as Watergate. He supported his reporters with a tenacity that made them fearless and it is no accident that so many became authors of influential, best-selling books.

ROBERT L. BERNSTEIN, the chief executive of Random House for more than a quarter century, guided one of the nation's premier publishing houses. Bob was personally responsible for many books of political dissent and argument that challenged tyranny around the globe. He is also the founder and longtime chair of Human Rights Watch, one of the most respected human rights organizations in the world.

• • •

For fifty years, the banner of Public Affairs Press was carried by its owner Morris B. Schnapper, who published Gandhi, Nasser, Toynbee, Truman, and about 1,500 other authors. In 1983, Schnapper was described by *The Washington Post* as "a redoubtable gadfly." His legacy will endure in the books to come.

Peter Osnos, *Founder and Editor-at-Large*